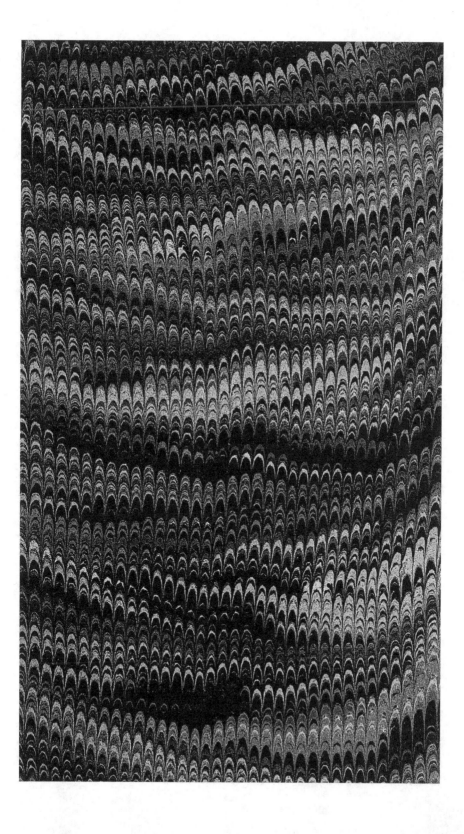

DAVID LIVINGSTONE, M.D.

MISSIONARY TRAVELS

AND

RESEARCHES IN SOUTH AFRICA

LONDON
JOHN MURRAY, ALBEMARLE STREET

MISSIONARY TRAVELS

AND

RESEARCHES IN SOUTH AFRICA;

INCLUDING A SKETCH OF

SIXTEEN YEARS' RESIDENCE IN THE INTERIOR OF AFRICA,

AND A JOURNEY FROM THE CAPE OF GOOD HOPE TO LOANDA ON THE WEST
COAST; THENCE ACROSS THE CONTINENT, DOWN THE RIVER
ZAMBESI, TO THE EASTERN OCEAN.

BY DAVID LIVINGSTONE, LL.D., D.C.L.,

FELLOW OF THE FACULTY OF PHYSICIANS AND SURGEONS, GLASGOW; CORRESPONDING MEMBER OF THE
GEOGRAPHICAL AND STATISTICAL SOCIETY OF NEW YORK; GOLD MEDALLIST AND CORRESPONDING
MEMBER OF THE ROYAL GEOGRAPHICAL SOCIETIES OF LONDON AND PARIS;
F.S.A., ETC. ETC.

*Tsetse Fly.—Magnified.—*See page 571.

WITH PORTRAIT, MAPS BY ARROWSMITH, AND NUMEROUS ILLUSTRATIONS.

LONDON:
JOHN MURRAY, ALBEMARLE STREET.
1857.

LONDON ; PRINTED BY W. CLOWES AND SONS, STAMFORD STREET,
AND CHARING CROSS.

CHAPTER XIX.

24th.—IONGA PANZA'S sons agreed to act as guides into the
territory of the Portuguese if I would give them the shell given
by Shinte. I was strongly averse to this, and especially to give
it beforehand; but yielded to the entreaty of my people to
appear as if showing confidence in these hopeful youths. They
urged that they wished to leave the shell with their wives, as a
sort of payment to them for enduring their husbands' absence
so long. Having delivered the precious shell, we went west-
by-north to the river Chikápa, which here (lat. 10° 22' S.) is
forty or fifty yards wide, and at present was deep; it was seen
flowing over a rocky broken cataract with great noise about
half a mile above our ford. We were ferried over in a canoe,
made out of a single piece of bark sewed together at the ends,
and having sticks placed in it at different parts to act as ribs.
The word Chikapa means bark or skin; and as this is the only
river in which we saw this kind of canoe used, and we heard

2 A 2

that this stream is so low during most of the year as to be easily fordable, it probably derives its name from the use made of the bark canoes when it is in flood. We now felt the loss of our pontoon, for the people to whom the canoe belonged, made us pay once when we began to cross, then a second time when half of us were over, and a third time when all were over but my principal man Pitsane and myself. Loyánke took off his cloth and paid my passage with it. The Makololo always ferried their visitors over rivers without pay, and now began to remark that they must in future fleece the Mambari as these Chiboque had done to us; they had all been loud in condemnation of the meanness, and when I asked if they could descend to be equally mean, I was answered that they would only do it in revenge. They like to have a plausible excuse for meanness.

Next morning our guides went only about a mile, and then told us they would return home. I expected this when paying them beforehand, in accordance with the entreaties of the Makololo, who are rather ignorant of the world. Very energetic remonstrances were addressed to the guides, but they slipped off one by one in the thick forest through which we were passing, and I was glad to hear my companions coming to the conclusion, that, as we were now in parts visited by traders, we did not require the guides, whose chief use had been to prevent misapprehension of our objects in the minds of the villagers. The country was somewhat more undulating now than it had been, and several fine small streams flowed in deep woody dells. The trees are very tall and straight, and the forests gloomy and damp; the ground in these solitudes is quite covered with yellow and brown mosses, and light-coloured lichens clothe all the trees. The soil is extremely fertile, being generally a black loam covered with a thick crop of tall grasses. We passed several villages too. The headman of a large one scolded us well for passing, when he intended to give us food. Where slave-traders have been in the habit of coming, they present food, then demand three or four times its value as a custom. We were now rather glad to get past villages without intercourse with the inhabitants.

We were travelling W.N.W., and all the rivulets we here crossed had a northerly course, and were reported to fall into the Kasai or Loke; most of them had the peculiar boggy banks of the country. As we were now in the alleged latitude of the Coanza, I was much astonished at the entire absence of any knowledge of that river among the natives of this quarter. But I was then ignorant of the fact that the Coanza rises considerably to the west of this, and has a comparatively short course from its source to the sea.

The famous Dr. Lacerda seems to have laboured under the same mistake as myself, for he recommended the government of Angola to establish a chain of forts along the banks of that river, with a view to communication with the opposite coast. As a chain of forts along its course would lead southwards instead of eastwards, we may infer that the geographical data within reach of that eminent man, were no better than those according to which I had directed my course to the Coanza where it does not exist.

26th.—We spent Sunday on the banks of the Quilo, or Kweelo; here a stream of about ten yards wide. It runs in a deep glen, the sides of which are almost five hundred yards of slope, and rocky, the rocks being hardened calcareous tufa lying on clay shale and sandstone below, with a capping of ferruginous conglomerate. The scenery would have been very pleasing, but fever took away much of the joy of life, and severe daily intermittents rendered me very weak and always glad to recline.

As we were now in the slave-market, it struck me that the sense of insecurity felt by the natives, might account for the circumstance that those who have been sold as slaves, and freed again, when questioned, profess to like the new state better than their primitive one. They lived on rich fertile plains, which seldom inspire that love of country which the mountains do. If they had been mountaineers they would have pined for home. To one who has observed the hard toil of the poor in old civilized countries, the state in which the inhabitants here live is one of glorious ease. The country is full of little villages. Food abounds, and very little labour is required for its cultivation; the soil is so rich that no manure is required; when a garden becomes too poor for good crops of maize, millet, &c., the owner removes a little farther into the forest, applies fire round the roots of the larger trees to kill them, cuts down the smaller, and a new rich garden is ready for the seed. The gardens usually present

the appearance of a great number of tall dead trees standing
without bark, and maize growing between them. The old
gardens continue to yield manioc for years, after the owners have
removed to other spots, for the sake of millet and maize. But
while vegetable aliment is abundant, there is a want of salt and
animal food, so that numberless traps are seen, set for mice, in all
the forests of Londa. The vegetable diet leaves great craving
for flesh, and I have no doubt, but that, when an ordinary quantity of mixed food is supplied to freed slaves, they actually do
feel more comfortable than they did at home. Their assertions,
however, mean but little, for they always try to give an answer to
please, and if one showed them a nugget of gold, they would
generally say that these abounded in their country.

One could detect, in passing, the variety of character found
among the owners of gardens and villages. Some villages were
the pictures of neatness. We entered others enveloped in a
wilderness of weeds, so high that, when sitting on ox-back in the
middle of the village, we could only see the tops of the huts.
If we entered at midday, the owners would come lazily forth, pipe
in hand, and leisurely puff away in dreamy indifference. In
some villages weeds are not allowed to grow; cotton, tobacco,
and different plants used as relishes, are planted round the huts;
fowls are kept in cages, and the gardens present the pleasant
spectacle of different kinds of grain and pulse at various periods
of their growth. I sometimes admired the one class, and at times
wished I could have taken the world easy for a time, like the
other. Every village swarms with children, who turn out to see
the white man pass, and run along with strange cries and antics;
some run up trees to get a good view: all are agile climbers
throughout Londa. At friendly villages they have scampered
alongside our party for miles at a time. We usually made a
little hedge around our sheds; crowds of women came to the
entrance of it, with children on their backs, and long pipes in
their mouths, gazing at us for hours. The men, rather than
disturb them, crawled through a hole in the hedge, and it was
common to hear a man in running off say to them, "I am going
to tell my mama to come and see the white man's oxen."

In continuing our W.N.W. course, we met many parties of
native traders, each carrying some pieces of cloth and salt, with

a few beads to barter for bees'-wax. They are all armed with Portuguese guns, and have cartridges with iron balls. When we meet, we usually stand a few minutes. They present a little salt, and we give a bit of ox-hide, or some other trifle, and then part with mutual good wishes. The hide of the oxen we slaughtered had been a valuable addition to our resources, for we found it in so great repute for girdles all through Londa, that we cut up every skin into strips about two inches broad, and sold them for meal and manioc as we went along. As we came nearer Angola we found them of less value, as the people there possess cattle themselves.

The village on the Kweelo, at which we spent Sunday, was that of a civil, lively old man, called Sakandála, who offered no objections to our progress. We found we should soon enter on the territory of the Bashinjé (Chinge of the Portuguese), who are mixed with another tribe, named Bangala, which have been at war with the Babindéle or Portuguese. Rains and fever, as usual, helped to impede our progress until we were put on the path, which leads from Cassange and Bihe to Matiamvo, by a headman named Kamboéla. This was a well-beaten footpath, and, soon after entering upon it, we met a party of half-caste traders from Bihe, who confirmed the information we had already got of this path leading straight to Cassange, through which they had come on their way from Bihe to Cabángo. They kindly presented my men with some tobacco, and marvelled greatly when they found that I had never been able to teach myself to smoke. On parting with them we came to a trader's grave. This was marked by a huge cone of sticks placed in the form of the roof of a hut, with a palisade around it. At an opening on the western side an ugly idol was placed: several strings of beads and bits of cloth were hung around. We learned that he had been a half-caste, who had died on his way back from Matiamvo.

As we were now alone, and sure of being on the way to the abodes of civilisation, we went on briskly.

On the 30th we came to a sudden descent from the high land, indented by deep, narrow valleys, over which we had lately been travelling. It is generally so steep, that it can only be descended at particular points, and even there I was obliged to dismount,

though so weak that I had to be led by my companions to prevent my toppling over in walking down. It was annoying to feel
myself so helpless, for I never liked to see a man, either sick or
well, giving in effeminately. Below us lay the valley of the
Quángo. If you sit on the spot where Mary Queen of Scots
viewed the battle of Langside, and look down on the vale of
Clyde, you may see in miniature the glorious sight which a much
greater and richer valley presented to our view. It is about a
hundred miles broad, clothed with dark forest, except where
the light-green grass covers meadow-lands on the Quango, which
here and there glances out in the sun as it wends its way to
the north. The opposite side of this great valley appears like
a range of lofty mountains, and the descent into it about a mile,
which, measured perpendicularly, may be from a thousand to
twelve hundred feet. Emerging from the gloomy forests of Londa,
this magnificent prospect made us all feel as if a weight had
been lifted off our eyelids. A cloud was passing across the
middle of the valley, from which rolling thunder pealed, while
above all was glorious sunlight; and when we went down to the
part where we saw it passing, we found that a very heavy
thunder-shower had fallen under the path of the cloud: and the
bottom of the valley, which from above seemed quite smooth, we
discovered to be intersected and furrowed by great numbers of
deep-cut streams. Looking back from below, the descent appears
as the edge of a table-land, with numerous indented dells and
spurs jutting out all along, giving it a serrated appearance. Both
the top and sides of the sierra are covered with trees, but large
patches of the more perpendicular parts are bare, and exhibit the
red soil, which is general over the region we have now entered.

The hollow affords a section of this part of the country; and
we find that the uppermost stratum is the ferruginous conglomerate already mentioned. The matrix is rust of iron (or
hydrous peroxide of iron and hæmatite), and in it are embedded
water-worn pebbles of sandstone and quartz. As this is the rock
underlying the soil of a large part of Londa, its formation must
have preceded the work of denudation by an arm of the sea,
which washed away the enormous mass of matter required, before
the valley of Cassange could assume its present form. The strata
under the conglomerate are all of red clay shale of different

degrees of hardness, the most indurated being at the bottom.
This red clay shale is named " keele " in Scotland, and has always
been considered as an indication of gold; but the only thing we
discovered was, that it had given rise to a very slippery clay soil,
so different from that which we had just left, that Mashauana,
who always prided himself on being an adept at balancing himself
in the canoe on water, and so sure of foot on land that he could
afford to express contempt for any one less gifted, came down
in a very sudden and undignified manner, to the delight of all
whom he had previously scolded for falling.

Here we met with the bamboo as thick as a man's arm, and
many new trees. Others, which we had lost sight of since
leaving Shinte, now re-appeared; but nothing struck us more
than the comparative scragginess of the trees in this hollow.
Those on the high lands we had left were tall and straight; here
they were stunted, and not by any means so closely planted
together. The only way I could account for this was by supposing, as the trees were of different species, that the greater
altitude suited the nature of those above, better than the lower
altitude did the other species below.

Sunday, 2nd April.—We rested beside a small stream, and
our hunger being now very severe, from having lived on manioc
alone since leaving Ionga Panza's, we slaughtered one of our
four remaining oxen. The people of this district seem to feel the
craving for animal food as much as we did, for they spend much
energy in digging large white larvæ out of the damp soil adjacent
to their streams, and use them as a relish for their vegetable diet.
The Bashinje refused to sell any food for the poor old ornaments
my men had now to offer. We could get neither meal nor manioc ;
but should have been comfortable, had not the Bashinje chief
Sansáwé pestered us for the customary present. The native
traders informed us, that a display of force was often necessary
before they could pass this man.

Sansawe, the chief of a portion of the Bashinje, having sent the
usual formal demand for a man, an ox, or a tusk, spoke very
contemptuously of the poor things we offered him instead. We
told his messengers, that the tusks were Sekeletu's: everything
was gone, except my instruments, which could be of no use to
them whatever. One of them begged some meat, and, when it

was refused, said to my men, "You may as well give it, for we shall take all after we have killed you to-morrow." The more humbly we spoke, the more insolent the Bashinje became, till at last we were all feeling savage and sulky, but continued to speak as civilly as we could. They are fond of argument, and when I denied their right to demand tribute from a white man, who did not trade in slaves, an old white-headed negro put rather a posing question: "You know that God has placed chiefs among us whom we ought to support. How is it that you, who have a book that tells you about him, do not come forward at once to pay this chief tribute, like every one else?" I replied by asking, "How could I know that this was a chief, who had allowed me to remain a day and a half near him without giving me anything to eat?" This, which to the uninitiated may seem sophistry, was, to the central Africans, quite a rational question, for he at once admitted that food ought to have been sent, and added, that probably his chief was only making it ready for me, and that it would come soon.

After being wearied by talking all day to different parties sent by Sansawe, we were honoured by a visit from himself: he is quite a young man, and of rather a pleasing countenance. There cannot have been much intercourse between real Portuguese and these people even here, so close to the Quango, for Sansawe asked me to show him my hair, on the ground that, though he had heard of it, and some white men had even passed through his country, he had never seen straight hair before. This is quite possible, as most of the slave-traders are not Portuguese, but half-castes. The difference between their wool and our hair, caused him to burst into a laugh, and the contrast between the exposed and unexposed parts of my skin, when exhibited in evidence of our all being made of one stock originally, and the children of one Maker, seemed to strike him with wonder. I then showed him my watch, and wished to win my way into his confidence by conversation; but when about to exhibit my pocket compass he desired me to desist, as he was afraid of my wonderful things. I told him, if he knew my aims, as the tribes in the interior did, and as I hoped he would yet know them and me, he would be glad to stay, and see also the pictures of the magic lantern; but as it was now getting dark he had evidently got enough of my witchery, and began to use some charms to dispel any kindly feelings he might have found stealing round his heart. He asked leave to go, and when his party moved off a little way, he sent for my spokesman, and told him that, " if we did not add a red jacket and a man, to our gift of a few copper rings and a few pounds of meat, we must return by the way we had come." I said in reply, " that we should certainly go forward next day, and if he commenced hostilities, the blame before God would be that of Sansawe;" and my man added of his own accord, "How many white men have you killed in this path?" which might be interpreted into, " You have never killed any white man, and you will find ours more difficult to manage than you imagine." It expressed a determination, which we had often repeated to each other, to die rather than yield one of our party to be a slave.

Hunger has a powerful effect on the temper. When we had got a good meal of meat, we could all bear the petty annoyances of these borderers on the more civilized region in front, with equanimity; but having suffered considerably of late, we were all rather soured in our feelings, and not unfrequently I overheard my companions remark in their own tongue, in answer to threats of attack, "That's what we want—only begin then;" or with clenched teeth they would exclaim to each other, "These things have never travelled, and do not know what men are." The worrying, of which I give only a slight sketch, had considerable influence on my own mind, and more especially, as it was impossible to make any allowance for the Bashinje, such as I was willing to award to the Chiboque. They saw that we had nothing to give, nor would they be benefited in the least, by enforcing the impudent order to return whence we had come. They were adding insult to injury, and this put us all into a fighting spirit, and, as nearly as we could judge, we expected to be obliged to cut our way through the Bashinje next morning.

3rd April.—As soon as day dawned we were astir, and, setting off in a drizzling rain, passed close to the village. This rain probably damped the ardour of the robbers. We, however, expected to be fired upon from every clump of trees, or from some of the rocky hillocks among which we were passing; and it was only after two hours' march that we began to breathe freely, and my men remarked, in thankfulness, " We are children of Jesus." We continued our course, notwithstanding the rain, across the bottom of the Quango valley, which we found broken by clay shale rocks jutting out, though lying nearly horizontally. The grass in all the hollows, at this time quite green, was about two feet higher than my head while sitting on ox-back. This grass, wetted by the rain, acted as a shower-bath on one side of our bodies; and some deep gullies, full of *discoloured* water, completed the cooling process. We passed many villages during this drenching, one of which possessed a flock of sheep; and after six hours we came to a stand near the river Quango (lat. 9° 53′ S., long. 18° 37′ E.), which may be called the boundary of the Portuguese claims to territory on the west. As I had now no change of clothing, I was glad to cower under the shelter of my blanket, thankful to God for his goodness in bringing us so far, without losing one of the party.

4th April.—We were now on the banks of the Quango, a river one hundred and fifty yards wide, and very deep. The water was discoloured—a circumstance which we had observed in no river in Londa or in the Makololo country. This fine river flows among extensive meadows clothed with gigantic grass and reeds, and in a direction nearly north.

The Quango is said by the natives to contain many venomous water-snakes, which congregate near the carcase of any hippopotamus that may be killed in it. If this is true, it may account for all the villages we saw, being situated far from its banks. We were advised not to sleep near it; but, as we were anxious to cross to the western side, we tried to induce some of the Bashinje to lend us canoes for the purpose. This brought out the chief of these parts, who informed us that all the canoe-men were his children, and nothing could be done without his authority. He then made the usual demand for a man, an ox, or a gun, adding that otherwise, we must return to the country from which we had come. As I did not believe that this man had any power over the canoes of the other side, and suspected that if I gave him my blanket—the only thing I now had in reserve—he might leave us in the lurch after all, I tried to persuade my men to go at once to the bank, about two miles off, and obtain possession of the canoes before we gave up the blanket; but they thought that this chief might attack us in the act of crossing, should we do so. The chief came himself to our encampment and made his demand again. My men stripped off the last of their copper rings and gave them; but he was still intent on a man. He thought, as others did, that my men were slaves. He was a young man, with his woolly hair elaborately dressed: that behind was made up into a cone, about eight inches in diameter at the base, carefully swathed round with red and black thread. As I resisted

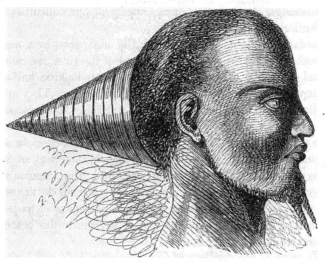

Bashinje chief's mode of wearing the hair.

the proposal to deliver up my blanket until they had placed us on the western bank, this chief continued to worry us with his demands till I was tired. My little tent was now in tatters, and having a wider hole behind than the door in front, I tried in vain to lie down out of sight of our persecutors. We were on a reedy flat, and could not follow our usual plan of a small stockade, in which we had time to think over and concoct our plans. As I was trying to persuade my men to move on to the bank in spite of these people, a young half-caste Portuguese sergeant of militia, Cypriano di Abreu, made his appearance, and gave the same advice. He had come across the Quango in search of bees'-wax. When we moved off from the chief who had been plaguing us, his people opened a fire from our sheds, and continued to blaze away some time in the direction we were going, but none of the bullets reached us. It is probable that they expected a demonstration of the abundance of ammunition they possessed, would make us run; but when we continued to move quietly to the ford, they proceeded no farther than our sleeping-place. Cypriano assisted us in making a more satisfactory arrangement with the ferrymen than parting with my blanket; and as soon as we reached the opposite bank, we were in the territory of the Bangala, who are subjects of the Portuguese, and often spoken of as the Cassanges or Cassantse; and happily all our difficulties with the border tribes were at an end.

Passing with light hearts through the high grass by a narrow footpath for about three miles to the west of the river, we came to several neat square houses with many cleanly-looking half-caste Portuguese standing in front of them to salute us. They are all enrolled in the militia, and our friend Cypriano is the commander of a division established here. The Bangala were very troublesome to the Portuguese traders, and at last proceeded so far as to kill one of them; the government of Angola then sent an expedition against them, which being successful, the Bangala were dispersed, and are now returning to their former abodes as vassals. The militia are quartered amongst them, and engage in trade and agriculture for their support, as no pay is given to this branch of the service by the government.

We came to the dwelling of Cypriano after dark, and I pitched my little tent in front of it for the night. We had the company of mosquitoes here. We never found them troublesome on the banks of the pure streams of Londa. On the morning of the 5th Cypriano generously supplied my men with pumpkins and maize, and then invited me to breakfast, which consisted of ground-nuts and roasted maize, then boiled manioc-roots and ground-nuts, with guavas and honey as a dessert. I felt sincerely grateful for this magnificent breakfast.

At dinner Cypriano was equally bountiful, and several of his friends joined us in doing justice to his hospitality. Before eating, all had water poured on the hands by a female slave to wash them. One of the guests cut up a fowl with a knife and fork. Neither forks nor spoons were used in eating. The repast was partaken of with decency and good manners, and concluded by washing the hands as at first.

All of them could read and write with ease. I examined the

books they possessed, and found a small work on medicine, a small cyclopædia, and a Portuguese dictionary, in which the definition of a "priest" seemed strange to a Protestant, namely, "one who takes care of the conscience." They had also a few tracts containing the Lives of the Saints, and Cypriano had three small wax images of saints in his room. One of these was St. Anthony, who, had he endured the privations he did in his cell in looking after these lost sheep, would have lived to better purpose. Neither Cypriano nor his companions knew what the Bible was, but they had relics in German-silver cases hung round their necks, to act as charms and save them from danger by land or by water, in the same way as the heathen have medicines. It is a pity that the church to which they belong, when unable to attend to the wants of her children, does not give them the sacred writings in their own tongue; it would surely be better to see them good Protestants, if these would lead them to be so, than entirely ignorant of God's message to man. For my part, I would much prefer to see the Africans good Roman Catholics, than idolatrous heathen.·

Much of the civility shown to us here was, no doubt, owing to the flattering letters of recommendation I carried from the Chevalier Du Prat, of Cape Town; but I am inclined to believe, that my friend Cypriano was influenced too by feelings of genuine kindness, for he quite bared his garden in feeding us during the few days which I remained, anxiously expecting the clouds to disperse, so far as to allow of my taking observations for the determination of the position of the Quango. He slaughtered an ox for us, and furnished his mother and her maids with maniocroots, to prepare farina for the four or five days of our journey to Cassange, and never even hinted at payment. My wretched appearance must have excited his compassion. The farina is prepared by washing the roots well, then rasping them down to a pulp. Next, this is roasted slightly on a metal plate over a fire, and is then used with meat as a vegetable. It closely resembles wood sawings, and on that account is named "wood-meal." It is insipid, and employed to lick up any gravy remaining on one's plate. Those who have become accustomed to it, relish it even after they have returned to Europe.

·. The manioc cultivated here is of the sweet variety: the bitter,

to which we were accustomed in Londa, is not to be found very
extensively in this fertile valley. May is the beginning of winter,
yet many of the inhabitants were busy planting maize; that
which we were now eating was planted in the beginning of
February. The soil is exceedingly fertile, of a dark red colour,
and covered with such a dense heavy crop of coarse grass, that
when a marauding party of Ambonda once came for plunder
while it was in a dried state, the Bangala encircled the common
enemy with a fire which completely destroyed them. This, which
is related on the authority of Portuguese who were then in the
country, I can easily believe to be true, for the stalks of the
grass are generally as thick as goose-quills, and no flight could be
made through the mass of grass in any direction where a footpath does not exist. Probably, in the case mentioned, the direction of the wind was such, as to drive the flames across the paths,
and prevent escape along them. On one occasion I nearly lost
my waggon by fire, in a valley where the grass was only about
three feet high. We were roused by the roar, as of a torrent,
made by the fire coming from the windward. I immediately set
fire to that on our leeward, and had just time to drag the
waggon on to the bare space there, before the windward flames
reached the place where it had stood.

We were detained by rains, and a desire to ascertain our
geographical position, till Monday the 10th, and only got the
latitude 9° 50' S.; and after three days' pretty hard travelling
through the long grass, reached Cassange, the farthest inland
station of the Portuguese in Western Africa. We crossed several
fine little streams running into the Quango; and as the grass
continued to tower about two feet over our heads, it generally
obstructed our view of the adjacent country, and sometimes
hung over the path, making one side of the body wet with the
dew every morning, or when it rained kept me wet during the
whole day. I made my entrance, in a somewhat forlorn state as
to clothing, among our Portuguese allies. The first gentleman I
met in the village asked if I had a passport, and said, it was
necessary to take me before the authorities. As I was in the same
state of mind, in which individuals are, who commit a petty de-
predation, in order to obtain the shelter and food of a prison,
I gladly accompanied him to the house of the Commandant or

Chefe, Senhor de Silva Rego. Having shown my passport to this gentleman, he politely asked me to supper, and as we had eaten nothing except the farina of Cypriano from the Quango to this, I suspect I appeared particularly ravenous to the other gentlemen around the table. They seemed, however, to understand my position pretty well, from having all travelled extensively themselves; had they not been present, I might have put some in my pocket to eat by night, for, after fever, the appetite is excessively keen, and manioc is one of the most unsatisfying kinds of food. Captain Antonio Rodrigues Neves then kindly invited me to take up my abode in his house. Next morning this generous man arrayed me in decent clothing, and continued during the whole period of my stay to treat me as if I had been his brother. I feel deeply grateful to him for his disinterested kindness; he not only attended to my wants, but also furnished food for my famishing party free of charge.

The village of Cassange (pronounced Kassanjé) is composed of thirty or forty traders' houses, scattered about without any regularity, on an elevated flat spot in the great Quango or Cassange valley. They are built of wattle and daub, and surrounded by plantations of manioc, maize, &c. Behind them, there are usually kitchen gardens, in which the common European vegetables, as potatoes, peas, cabbages, onions, tomatoes, &c. &c., grow. Guavas and bananas appear, from the size and abundance of the trees, to have been introduced many years ago, while the land was still in the possession of the natives, but pine-apples, orange, fig, and cashew-trees have but lately been tried. There are about forty Portuguese traders in this district, all of whom are officers in the militia, and many of them have become rich from adopting the plan of sending out Pombeiros, or native traders, with large quantities of goods, to trade in the more remote parts of the country. Some of the governors of Loanda, the capital of this, the kingdom of Angola, have insisted on the observance of a law which, from motives of humanity, forbids the Portuguese themselves from passing beyond the boundary. They seem to have taken it for granted, that, in cases where the white trader was killed, the aggression had been made by him, and they wished to avoid the necessity of punishing those who had been provoked to shed Portuguese blood. This indicates a much greater impartiality than has obtained in our own dealings with the Caffres, for we have engaged in most expensive wars with them without once inquiring whether any of the fault lay with our frontier colonists. The Cassange traders seem inclined to spread along the Quango, in spite of the desire of their government to keep them on one spot, for mutual protection in case of war. If I might judge from the week of feasting I passed among them, they are generally prosperous.

As I always preferred to appear in my own proper character, I was an object of curiosity to these hospitable Portuguese. They evidently looked upon me as an agent of the English Government, engaged in some new movement for the suppression of slavery. They could not divine what a " missionario " had to do with the latitudes and longitudes, which I was intent on observing. When we became a little familiar, the questions put were rather amusing, " Is it common for missionaries to be doctors ?" " Are you a doctor of medicine and a ' doutor mathematico' too ? You must be more than a missionary to know how to calculate the longitude! Come ; tell us at once what rank you hold in the English army." They may have given credit to my reason for wearing the moustache, as that explains why men have beards and women have none ; but that which puzzled many besides my Cassange friends was the anomaly of my being a " sacerdote," with a wife and four children! I usually got rid of the last question by putting another, " Is it not better to have children with a wife, than to have children without a wife ? " But all were most kind and hospitable, and as one of their festivals was near, they invited me to partake of the feast.

The anniversary of the Resurrection of our Saviour was observed on the 16th April as a day of rejoicing, though the Portuguese have no priests at Cassange. The coloured population dressed up a figure intended to represent Judas Iscariot, and paraded him on a riding-ox about the village ; sneers and maledictions were freely bestowed on the poor wretch thus represented. The slaves and free coloured population, dressed in their gayest clothing, made visits to all the principal merchants, and wishing them " a good feast," expected a present in return. This, though frequently granted in the shape of pieces of calico to make new dresses, was occasionally refused, but the rebuff did not much affect the petitioner.

At ten A.M. we went to the residence of the Commandant, and on a signal being given, two of the four brass guns belonging to the Government, commenced firing, and continued some time, to the great admiration of my men, whose ideas of the power of a cannon are very exalted. The Portuguese flag was hoisted and trumpets sounded, as an expression of joy at the resurrection of our Lord. Captain Neves invited all the principal inhabitants of the place, and did what he could to feast them in a princely style. All manner of foreign preserved fruits and wine from Portugal, biscuits from America, butter from Cork, and beer from England, were displayed, and no expense spared in rendering the entertainment joyous. After the feast was over they sat down to the common amusement of card-playing, which continued till eleven o'clock at night. As far as a mere traveller could judge, they seemed to be polite and willing to aid each other. They live in a febrile district, and many of them had enlarged spleens. They have neither doctor, apothecary, school, nor priest, and, when taken ill, trust to each other and to Providence. As men left in such circumstances must think for themselves, they have all a good idea of what ought to be done in the common diseases of the country, and what they have of either medicine or skill, they freely impart to each other.

None of these gentlemen had Portuguese wives. They usually come to Africa, in order to make a little money, and return to Lisbon. Hence they seldom bring their wives with them, and never can be successful colonists in consequence. It is common for them to have families by native women. It was particularly gratifying to me, who had been familiar with the stupid prejudice against colour, entertained only by those who are themselves becoming tawny, to view the liberality with which people of colour were treated by the Portuguese. Instances, so common in the south, in which half-caste children are abandoned, are here extremely rare. They are acknowledged at table, and provided for by their fathers, as if European. The coloured clerks of the merchants sit at the same table with their employers, without any embarrassment. The civil manners of superiors to inferiors is probably the result of the position they occupy—a few whites among thousands of blacks; but nowhere else in Africa is there so much goodwill between Europeans and natives as here. If some border colonists had the absolute certainty of our Government declining to bear them out in their arrogance, we should probably hear less of Caffre insolence. It is insolence which begets insolence.

From the village of Cassange we have a good view of the surrounding country: it is a gently undulating plain, covered with grass and patches of forest. The western edge of the Quango valley appears about twenty miles off as if it were a range of lofty mountains, and passes by the name of Tala Mungongo, "Behold the range." In the old Portuguese map, to which I had been trusting in planning my route, it is indicated as Talla Mugongo, or "*Castle of rocks!*" and the Coanza is put down as rising therefrom; but here I was assured that the Coanza had its source near Bihe, far to the south-west of this, and we should not see that river till we came near Pungo Andongo. It is somewhat remarkable, that more accurate information about this country has not been published. Captain Neves and others had a correct idea of the courses of the rivers, and communicated their knowledge freely; yet about this time, maps were sent to Europe from Angola representing the Quango and Coanza as the same river, and Cassange placed about one hundred miles from its true position. The frequent recurrence of the same name, has probably helped to increase the confusion. I have crossed several Quangos, but all insignificant, except that which drains this valley. The repetition of the favourite names of chiefs, as Catendé, is also perplexing, as one Catende may be mistaken for another. To avoid this confusion as much as possible, I have refrained from introducing many names. Numerous villages are studded all over the valley; but these possess no permanence, and many more existed previous to the Portuguese expedition of 1850 to punish the Bangala.

This valley, as I have before remarked, is all fertile in the extreme. My men could never cease admiring its capability for raising their corn (*Holcus sorghum*), and despising the comparatively limited cultivation of the inhabitants. The Portuguese informed me that no manure is ever needed, but that the more the ground is tilled, the better it yields. Virgin soil does not give such a heavy crop as an old garden, and, judging from the size of the maize and manioc in the latter, I can readily believe the statement. Cattle do well, too. Viewing the valley as a whole, it may be said that its agricultural and pastoral riches are lying waste. Both the Portuguese and their descendants turn their attention almost exclusively to trade in wax and ivory, and though the country would yield any amount of corn and dairy produce, the native Portuguese live chiefly on manioc, and the Europeans purchase their flour, bread, butter, and cheese from the Americans.

As the traders of Cassange were the first white men we had come to, we sold the tusks belonging to Sekeletu, which had been brought to test the difference of prices in the Makololo and white men's country. The result was highly satisfactory to my companions, as the Portuguese give much larger prices for ivory than traders from the Cape can possibly give, who labour under the disadvantage of considerable overland expenses and ruinous restrictions. Two muskets, three small barrels of gunpowder, and English calico and baize sufficient to clothe my whole party, with large bunches of beads, all for one tusk, were quite delightful for those who had been accustomed to give two tusks for one gun. With another tusk we procured calico, which here is the chief currency, to pay our way down to the coast. The remaining two were sold for money to purchase a horse for Sekeletu at Loanda.

The superiority of this new market was quite astounding to the Makololo, and they began to abuse the traders by whom they had, while in their own country, been visited, and, as they now declared, "cheated." They had no idea of the value of time and carriage, and it was somewhat difficult for me to convince them, that the reason of the difference of prices lay entirely in what they themselves had done in coming here, and that, if the Portuguese should carry goods to their country, they would by no means be so liberal in their prices. They imagined that, if the Cassange traders came to Linyanti, they would continue to vend their goods at Cassange prices. I believe I gave them at last a clear idea of the manner in which prices were regulated by the expences incurred; and when we went to Loanda, and saw goods delivered at a still cheaper rate, they concluded that it would be better for them to come to that city, than to turn homewards at Cassange.

It was interesting for me to observe the effects of the restrictive policy, pursued by the Cape government towards the Bechuanas. Like all other restrictions on trade, the law of preventing friendly tribes from purchasing arms and ammunition, only injures the men who enforce it. The Cape Government, as already observed, in order to gratify a company of independent Boers, whose well-known predilection for the practice of slavery caused them to stipulate, that a number of peaceable honest tribes should be kept defenceless, agreed to allow free trade in arms and ammunition to the Boers, and prevent the same trade to the Bechuanas. The Cape Government thereby unintentionally aided, and continues to aid, the Boers to enslave the natives. But arms and ammunition flow in on all sides by new channels, and where formerly the price of a large tusk procured but one musket, one tusk of the same size now brings ten. The profits are reaped by other nations, and the only persons really the losers, in the long run, are our own Cape merchants, and a few defenceless tribes of Bechuanas on our immediate frontier.

Mr. Rego, the Commandant, very handsomely offered me a soldier as a guard to Ambaca. My men told me that they had been thinking it would be better to turn back here, as they had been informed by the people of colour at Cassange that I was leading them down to the sea-coast only to sell them, and they would be taken on board ship, fattened, and eaten, as the white men were cannibals. I asked if they had ever heard of an Englishman buying or selling people; if I had not refused to take a slave when she was offered to me by Shinte; but as I had always behaved as an English teacher, if they now doubted my intentions, they had better not go to the coast: I, however, who expected to meet some of my countrymen there, was determined to go on. They replied that they only thought it right to tell me what had been told to them, but they did not intend to leave me, and would follow wherever I should lead the way. This affair being disposed of for the time, the Commandant gave them an ox, and me a friendly dinner before parting. All the merchants of Cassange accompanied us, in their hammocks carried by slaves, to the edge of the plateau on which their village stands, and we parted with the feeling in my mind that I should never forget their disinterested kindness. They not only did everything

From a Sketch by Captain Henry Need, H.M. Brig Linnet.

SCENE IN ANGOLA.—THE MASHEELA, OR ANGOLESE PALANQUIN, COMING TO REST UNDER A BAOBAB AND EUPHORBIAS.

they could to make my men and me comfortable during our stay, but, there being no hotels in Loanda, they furnished me with letters of recommendation to their friends in that city, requesting them to receive me into their houses, for without these, a stranger might find himself a lodger in the streets. May God remember them in their day of need!

The latitude and longitude of Cassange, the most easterly station of the Portuguese in Western Africa, is lat. 9° 37′ 30″ S., and long. 17° 49′ E.; consequently we had still about 300 miles to traverse before we could reach the coast. We had a black militia corporal as a guide. He was a native of Ambaca, and, like nearly all the inhabitants of that district, known by the name of Ambakistas, could both read and write. He had three slaves with him, and was carried by them in a "tipoia," or hammock slung to a pole. His slaves were young, and unable to convey him far at a time, but he was considerate enough to walk except when we came near to a village. He then mounted his tipoia and entered the village in state; his departure was made in the same manner, and he continued in the hammock till the village was out of sight. It was interesting to observe the manners of our soldier-guide. Two slaves were always employed in carrying his tipoia, and the third carried a wooden box, about three feet long, containing his writing materials, dishes, and clothing. He was cleanly in all his ways, and, though quite black himself, when he scolded any one of his own colour, abused him as a "negro." When he wanted to purchase any article from a village, he would sit down, mix a little gunpowder as ink, and write a note in a neat hand to ask the price, addressing it to the shopkeeper with the rather pompous title, "Illustrissimo Senhor" (Most Illustrious Sir). This is the invariable mode of address throughout Angola. The answer returned would be in the same style, and, if satisfactory, another note followed to conclude the bargain. There is so much of this note correspondence carried on in Angola, that a very large quantity of paper is annually consumed. Some other peculiarities of our guide were not so pleasing. A land of slaves is a bad school for even the free; and I was sorry to find less truthfulness and honesty in him, than in my own people. We were often cheated through his connivance with the sellers of food, and could perceive that he got a share of the plunder from them. The food is very cheap, but it was generally made dear enough, until I refused to allow him to come near the place where we were bargaining. But he took us safely down to Ambaca, and I was glad to see, on my return to Cassange, that he was promoted to be sergeant-major of a company of militia.

Having left Cassange on the 21st, we passed across the remaining portion of this excessively fertile valley to the foot of Tala Mungongo. We crossed a fine little stream called the Lui on the 22nd, and another named the Luare on the 24th, then slept at the bottom of the height, which is from a thousand to fifteen hundred feet. The clouds came floating along the valley, and broke against the sides of the ascent, and the dripping rain on the tall grass, made the slaps in the face it gave, when the hand or a stick was not held up before it, anything but agreeable. This edge of the valley is exactly like the other; jutting spurs and defiles give the red ascent the same serrated appearance as that which we descended from the highlands of Londa. The whole of this vast valley has been removed by denudation, for pieces of the plateau which once filled the now vacant space stand in it, and present the same structure of red horizontal strata of equal altitudes with those of the acclivity which we are now about to ascend. One of these insulated masses, named Kasala, bore E.S.E. from the place where we made our exit from the valley, and about ten miles W.S.W. from the village of Cassange. It is remarkable for its perpendicular sides; even the natives find it extremely difficult, almost impossible, to reach its summit, though there is the temptation of marabou-nests and feathers, which are highly prized. There is a small lake reported to exist on its southern end, and, during the rainy season, a sort of natural moat is formed around the bottom. What an acquisition this would have been in feudal times in England! There is land sufficient for considerable cultivation on the top, with almost perpendicular sides more than a thousand feet in height.

We had not yet got a clear idea of the nature of Tala Mungongo. A gentleman at Cassange described it as a range of very high mountains, which it would take four hours to climb; so, though the rain and grass had wetted us miserably, and I was suffering from an attack of fever got while observing by night for the position of Cassange, I eagerly commenced the ascent. The path was steep and slippery ; deep gorges appear on each side of it, leaving but a narrow path along certain spurs of the sierra for the traveller; but we accomplished the ascent in an hour, and when there, found we had just got on to a table-land similar to that we had left, before we entered the great Quango valley. We had come among lofty trees again. One of these, bearing a fruit about the size of a thirty-two pounder, is named Mononga-zambi.

.We took a glance back to this valley, which equals that of the Mississippi in fertility, and thought of the vast mass of material which had been scooped out and carried away in its formation. This naturally led to reflection on the countless ages required for the previous formation and deposition of the same material (clay shale) ; then of the rocks, whose abrasion formed *that*, until the mind grew giddy in attempting to ascend the steps, which lead up through a portion of the eternity before man. The different epochs of geology are like landmarks in that otherwise shoreless sea. Our own epoch, or creation, is but another added to the number of that wonderful series which presents a grand display of the mighty power of God : every stage of progress in the earth and its habitants, is such a display. So far from this science having any tendency to make men undervalue the power or love of God, it leads to the probability that the exhibition of mercy we have in the gift of his Son, may possibly not be the only manifestation of grace which has taken place in the countless ages, during which, works of creation have been going on.

Situated a few miles from the edge of the descent, we found the village of Tala Mungongo, and were kindly accommodated with a house to sleep in, which was very welcome, as we were all both wet and cold. We found that the greater altitude, and the approach of winter, lowered the temperature so much, that many of my men suffered severely from colds. At this, as at several other Portuguese stations, they have been provident enough to erect travellers' houses on the same principle as khans or caravanserais of the East. They are built of the usual wattle and daub, and have benches of rods for the wayfarer to make his bed on ; also chairs and a table, and a large jar of water. These benches, though far from luxurious couches, were better than the ground under the rotten fragments of my gipsy-tent, for we had still showers occasionally, and the dews were very heavy. I continued to use them for the sake of the shelter they afforded, until I found that they were lodgings also, for certain inconvenient bedfellows.

27th.—Five hours' ride through a pleasant country of forest and meadow like those of Londa, brought us to a village of Basongo, a tribe living in subjection to the Portuguese. We crossed several little streams, which were flowing in the westerly direction in which we were marching, and unite to form the Quize, a feeder of the Coanza. The Basongo were very civil, as indeed all the tribes were who had been conquered by the Portuguese. The Basongo and Bangala are yet only partially subdued. The farther west we go from this, the less independent we find the black population until we reach the vicinity of Loanda, where the free natives are nearly identical in their feelings towards the government with the slaves. But the governors of Angola wisely accept the limited allegiance and tribute rendered by the more distant tribes, as better than none.

All the inhabitants of this region, as well as those of Londa, may be called true negroes, if the limitations formerly made be borne in mind. The dark colour, thick lips, heads elongated backwards and upwards and covered with wool, flat noses, with other negro peculiarities, are general; but while these characteristics place them in the true negro family, the reader would imbibe a wrong idea, if he supposed that all these features combined are often met with in one individual. All have a certain thickness and prominence of lip, but many are met with in every village in whom thickness and projection are not more marked than in Europeans. All are dark, but the colour is shaded off in different individuals from deep black to light yellow. As we go westward, we observe the light colour predominating over the dark, and then again, when we come within the influence of damp from the sea air, we find the shade deepen into the general blackness of the coast population. The shape of the head, with its woolly crop, though general, is not universal. The tribes on the eastern side of the continent, as the Caffres, have heads finely developed and strongly European. Instances of this kind are frequently seen, and after I became so familiar with the dark colour as to forget it in viewing the countenance, I was struck by the strong resemblance some natives bore to certain of our own notabilities. The Bushmen and Hottentots are exceptions to these remarks, for both the shape of their heads and growth of wool are peculiar—the latter, for instance, springs from the scalp in tufts with bare spaces between, and when the crop is short, resembles a number of black peppercorns stuck on the skin, and very unlike the thick frizzly masses which cover the heads of the Balonda and Maravi. With every disposition to pay due deference to the opinions of those who have made ethnology their special study, I have felt myself unable to believe that the exaggerated features usually put forth as those of the typical negro, characterize the majority of any nation of south central Africa. The monuments of the ancient Egyptians seem to me to embody the ideal of the inhabitants of Londa, better than the figures of any work of ethnology I have met with.

. Passing through a fine fertile and well-peopled country to Sanza, we found the Quize river again touching our path, and here we had the pleasure of seeing a field of wheat growing luxuriantly without irrigation. The ears were upwards of four inches long, an object of great curiosity to my companions, because they had tasted my bread at Linyanti, but had never before seen wheat growing. This small field was cultivated by Mr. Miland, an agreeable Portuguese merchant. His garden was interesting, as showing what the land at this elevation is capable of yielding, for, besides wheat, we saw European vegetables in a flourishing condition, and we afterwards discovered that the coffee-plant has propagated itself on certain spots of this same district. It may be seen on the heights of Tala Mungongo, or nearly 300 miles from the west coast, where it was first introduced by the Jesuit missionaries.

We spent Sunday the 30th of April at Ngio, close to the ford of the Quize as it crosses our path to fall into the Coanza. The country becomes more open, but is still abundantly fertile, with a thick crop of grass between two and three feet high. It is also well wooded and watered. Villages of Basongo are dotted over the landscape, and frequently a square house of wattle and daub, belonging to native Portuguese, is placed beside them for the purposes of trade. The people here possess both cattle and pigs. The different sleeping-places on our path, from eight to ten miles apart, are marked by a cluster of sheds made of sticks and grass. There is a constant stream of people going and returning to and from the coast. The goods are carried on the head, or on one shoulder, in a sort of basket attached to the extremities of two poles between five and six feet long, and called Motete. When the basket is placed on the head, the poles project forwards horizontally, and when the carrier wishes to rest himself, he plants them on the ground and the burden against a tree, so he is not obliged to lift it up from the ground to the level of the head. It stands against the tree propped up by the poles at that level. The carrier frequently plants the poles on the ground, and stands holding the burden until he has taken breath, thus avoiding the trouble of placing the burden on the ground and lifting it up again.

When a company of these carriers, or our own party, arrives at one of these sleeping-places, immediate possession is taken of the sheds. Those who come late and find all occupied, must then erect others for themselves; but this is not difficult, for there is no lack of long grass. No sooner do any strangers appear at the spot, than the women may be seen emerging from their villages bearing baskets of manioc-meal, roots, ground-nuts, yams, bird's-eye pepper, and garlic for sale. Calico, of which we had brought some from Cassange, is the chief medium of exchange. We found them all civil, and it was evident, from the amount of talking and laughing in bargaining, that the ladies enjoyed their occupation. They must cultivate largely, in order to be able to supply the constant succession of strangers. Those, however, near to the great line of road, purchase also much of the food from the more distant villages for the sake of gain.

Pitsane and another of the men had violent attacks of fever, and it was no wonder, for the dampness and evaporation from the ground was excessive. When at any time I attempted to get an observation of a star, if the trough of mercury were placed on the ground, so much moisture was condensed on the inside of the glass roof over it, that it was with difficulty the reflection of the star could be seen. When the trough was placed on a box to prevent the moisture entering from below, so much dew was deposited on the outside of the roof, that it was soon necessary, for the sake of distinct vision, to wipe the glass. This would not have been of great consequence, but a short exposure to this dew was so sure to bring on a fresh fever, that I was obliged

From Sketches by Capt. H. Need, R.N.

SCENE AT A SLEEPING-PLACE IN ANGOLA.—MEAT DRYING IN THE SUN.   TREE EUPHORBIAS AND PALM-OIL TREE.

to give up observations by night altogether. The inside of the only covering I now had was not much better, but under the blanket, one is not so liable to the chill which the dew produces.

It would have afforded me pleasure to have cultivated a more intimate acquaintance with the inhabitants of this part of the country, but the vertigo produced by frequent fevers made it as much as I could do to stick on the ox and crawl along in misery. In crossing the Lombe, my ox Sinbad, in the indulgence of his propensity to strike out a new path for himself, plunged overhead into a deep hole, and so soused me, that I was obliged to move on to dry my clothing, without calling on the Europeans who live on the bank. This I regretted, for all the Portuguese were very kind, and like the Boers placed in similar circumstances, feel it a slight to be passed without a word of salutation. But we went on to a spot where orange-trees had been planted by the natives themselves, and where abundance of that refreshing fruit was exposed for sale.

On entering the district of Ambaca, we found the landscape enlivened by the appearance of lofty mountains in the distance, the grass comparatively short, and the whole country at this time looking gay and verdant. On our left we saw certain rocks of the same nature with those of Pungo Andongo, and which closely resemble the Stonehenge group on Salisbury Plain, only the stone pillars here are of gigantic size. This region is all wonderfully fertile, famed for raising cattle, and all kinds of agricultural produce, at a cheap rate. The soil contains sufficient ferruginous matter, to impart a red tinge to nearly the whole of it. It is supplied with a great number of little flowing streams which unite in the Lucalla. This river drains Ambaca, then falls into the Coanza to the south-west at Massangano. We crossed the Lucalla by means of a large canoe kept there by a man who farms the ferry from the government, and charges about a penny per head. A few miles beyond the Lucalla, we came to the village of Ambaca, an important place in former times, but now a mere paltry village, beautifully situated on a little elevation in a plain surrounded on all hands by lofty mountains. It has a gaol, and a good house for the Commandant, but neither fort nor church, though the ruins of a place of worship are still standing.

We were most kindly received by the Commandant of Ambaca,

Arsenio de Carpo, who spoke a little English.   He recommended
wine for my debility, and here I took the first glass of that
beverage I had taken in Africa. I felt much refreshed, and could
then realize and meditate on the weakening effects of the fever.
They were curious even to myself, for, though I had tried several
times since we left Ngio to take lunar observations, I could not
avoid confusion of time and distance, neither could I hold the
instrument steady, nor perform a simple calculation; hence many
of the positions of this part of the route were left till my return
from Loanda.   Often, on getting up in the mornings, I found my
clothing as wet from perspiration as if it had been dipped in
water.   In vain had I tried to learn or collect words of the
Bunda, or dialect spoken in Angola.   I forgot the days of the
week and the names of my companions, and, had I been asked,
I probably could not have told my own.   The complaint itself
occupied many of my thoughts.   One day I supposed that I had
got the true theory of it, and would certainly cure the next
attack whether in myself or companions, but some new symptoms
would appear, and scatter all the fine speculations which had
sprung up, with extraordinary fertility, in one department of my
brain.

This district is said to contain upwards of 40,000 souls.   Some
ten or twelve miles to the north of the village of Ambaca, there
once stood the missionary station of Cahenda, and it is now quite
astonishing to observe the great numbers who can read and write
in this district.   This is the fruit of the labours of the Jesuit and
Capuchin missionaries, for they taught the people of Ambaca;
and ever since the expulsion of the teachers by the Marquis of
Pombal, the natives have continued to teach each other.   These
devoted men are still held in high estimation throughout the
country to this day. All speak well of them (os padres Jesuitas),
and now that they are gone from this lower sphere, I could not
help wishing that these our Roman Catholic fellow-Christians had
felt it to be their duty to give the people the Bible, to be a light
to their feet when the good men themselves were gone.

When sleeping in the house of the Commandant an insect, well
known in the southern country by the name Tampan, bit my foot.
It is a kind of tick, and chooses by preference the parts between
the fingers or toes for inflicting its bite.   It is seen from the size

of a pin's head to that of a pea, and is common in all the native huts in this country. It sucks the blood until quite full, and is then of a dark-blue colour, and its skin so tough and yielding, that it is impossible to burst it by any amount of squeezing with the fingers. I had felt the effects of its bite in former years, and eschewed all native huts ever after, but as I was here again assailed in a European house, I shall detail the effects of the bite. These are, a tingling sensation of mingled pain and itching, which commences ascending the limb until the poison imbibed reaches the abdomen, where it soon causes violent vomiting and purging. Where these effects do not follow, as we found afterwards at Tete, fever sets in; and I was assured by intelligent Portuguese there, that death has sometimes been the result of this fever. The anxiety my friends at Tete manifested to keep my men out of the reach of the tampans of the village, made it evident that they had seen cause to dread this insignificant insect. The only inconvenience I afterwards suffered from this bite, was the continuance of the tingling sensation in the point bitten, for about a week.

May 12th.—As we were about to start this morning, the Commandant, Senhor Arsenio, provided bread and meat most bountifully for my use on the way to the next station, and sent two militia soldiers as guides, instead of our Cassange corporal, who left us here. About mid-day we asked for shelter from the sun in the house of Senhor Mellot, at Zangu, and though I was unable to sit and engage in conversation, I found on rising from his couch that he had at once proceeded to cook a fowl for my use; and at parting he gave me a glass of wine, which prevented the violent fit of shivering I expected that afternoon. The universal hospitality of the Portuguese was most gratifying, as it was quite unexpected. And even now, as I copy my journal, I remember it all with a glow of gratitude.

We spent Sunday, the 14th of May, at Cabinda, which is one of the stations of the sub-commandants, who are placed at different points in each district of Angola, as assistants of the head-commandant, or chefe. It is situated in a beautiful glen, and surrounded by plantations of bananas and manioc. The country was gradually becoming more picturesque, the farther we proceeded west. The ranges of lofty blue mountains of Libollo,

which in coming towards Ambaca we had seen thirty or forty
miles to our south, were now shut from our view by others nearer
at hand, and the grey ranges of Cahenda and Kiwe, which, while
we were in Ambaca, stood clearly defined eight or ten miles off to
the north, were now close upon our right. As we looked back
towards the open pastoral country of Ambaca, the broad green
gently undulating plains seemed in a hollow surrounded on all
sides by rugged mountains, and as we went westward we were
entering upon quite a wild-looking mountainous district called
Golungo Alto.

  We met numbers of Mambari on their way back to Bihe.
Some of them had belonged to the parties which had penetrated
as far as Linyanti, and foolishly showed their displeasure at the
prospect of the Makololo preferring to go to the coast markets
themselves, to intrusting them with their ivory. The Mambari
repeated the tale of the mode in which the white men are said
to trade. "The ivory is left on the shore in the evening, and
next morning the seller finds a quantity of goods placed there
in its stead by the white men who live in the sea." "Now,"
added they to my men, " how can you Makololo trade with
these ' Mermen ' ? Can you enter into the sea, and tell them to
come ashore ? " It was remarkable to hear this idea repeated
so near the sea as we now were. My men replied that they
only wanted to see for themselves ; and as they were now getting
some light on the nature of the trade carried on by the Mambari,
they were highly amused on perceiving the reasons why the
Mambari would rather have met them on the Zambesi, than so
near the sea-coast.

  There is something so exhilarating to one of Highland blood in
being near or on high mountains, that I forgot my fever as we
wended our way among the lofty tree-covered masses of mica
schist, which form the highlands around the romantic residence
of the Chefe of Golungo Alto. (Lat. 9° 8' 30" S., long. 15°
2' E.) The whole district is extremely beautiful. The hills are
all bedecked with trees of various hues of foliage, and among
them towers the graceful palm, which yields the oil of commerce
for making our soaps, and the intoxicating toddy. Some clusters
of hills look like the waves of the sea driven into a narrow
open bay, and have assumed the same form as if, when all

were chopping up perpendicularly, they had suddenly been congealed. The cottages of the natives, perched on the tops of many of the hillocks, looked as if the owners possessed an eye for the romantic, but they were probably influenced more by the desire to overlook their gardens, and keep their families out of the reach of the malaria, which is supposed to prevail most on the banks of the numerous little streams which run among the hills.

We were most kindly received by the Commandant, Lieutenant Antonio Canto e Castro, a young gentleman whose whole subsequent conduct will ever make me regard him with great affection. Like every other person of intelligence whom I had met, he lamented deeply the neglect with which this fine country has been treated. This district contained, by the last census, 26,000 hearths, or fires; and if to each hearth we reckon four souls, we have a population of 104,000. The number of carregadores (carriers) who may be ordered out at the pleasure of Government to convey merchandise to the coast is in this district alone about 6000, yet there is no good road in existence. This system of compulsory carriage of merchandise, was adopted in consequence of the increase in numbers and activity of our cruisers, which took place in 1845. Each trader who went, previous to that year, into the interior, in the pursuit of his calling, proceeded on the plan of purchasing ivory and bees'-wax, and a sufficient number of slaves to carry these commodities. The whole were intended for exportation as soon as the trader reached the coast. But when the more stringent measures of 1845 came into operation, and rendered the exportation of slaves almost impossible, there being no roads proper for the employment of wheel conveyances, this new system of compulsory carriage of ivory and bees'-wax to the coast was resorted to by the Government of Loanda. A trader who requires two or three hundred carriers to convey his merchandise to the coast, now applies to the General Government for aid. An order is sent to the Commandant of a district to furnish the number required. Each head-man of the villages to whom the order is transmitted, must furnish from five to twenty or thirty men, according to the proportion that his people bear to the entire population of the district. For this accommodation the trader must pay a tax to the Government of 1000 reis, or about three shillings per load carried. The trader is obliged to pay the carrier also the sum of 50 reis, or about twopence a day, for his sustenance. And as a day's journey is never more than from eight to ten miles, the expense which must be incurred for this compulsory labour is felt to be heavy by those who were accustomed to employ slave labour alone. Yet no effort has been made to form a great line of road for wheel carriages. The first great want of a country has not been attended to, and no development of its vast resources has taken place. The fact, however, of a change from one system of carriage to another, taken in connection with the great depreciation in the prices of slaves near this coast, proves the effectiveness of our efforts at repressing the slave-trade on the ocean.

The latitude of Golungo Alto, as observed at the residence of the Commandant, was 9° 8′ 30″ S., longitude 15° 2′ E. A few days' rest with this excellent young man, enabled me to regain much of my strength, and I could look with pleasure on the luxuriant scenery before his door. We were quite shut in among green hills, many of which were cultivated up to their tops with manioc, coffee, cotton, ground-nuts, bananas, pine-apples, guavas, papaws, custard-apples, pitangas, and jambos, fruits brought from South America by the former missionaries. The high hills all around, with towering palms on many points, made this spot appear more like the Bay of Rio de Janeiro in miniature than any scene I ever saw; and all who have seen that, confess it to be unequalled in the world beside. The fertility evident in every spot of this district was quite marvellous to behold, but I shall reserve further notices of this region till our return from Loanda.

We left Golungo Alto on the 24th of May, the winter in these parts. Every evening, clouds come rolling in great masses over the mountains in the west, and pealing thunder accompanies the fall of rain during the night or early in the morning. The clouds generally remain on the hills till the morning is well spent, so that we become familiar with morning mists, a thing we never once saw at Kolobeng. The thermometer stands at 80° by day, but sinks as low as 76° by night.

In going westward we crossed several fine little gushing streams which never dry. They unite in the Luinha (pronounced Lu-eenya) and Lucalla. As they flow over many little cascades, they might easily be turned to good account, but they are all allowed to run on idly to the ocean. We passed through forests of gigantic timber, and at an open space named Cambondo, about eight miles from Golungo Alto, found numbers of carpenters converting these lofty trees into planks, in exactly the same manner as was followed by the illustrious Robinson Crusoe. A tree of three or four feet in diameter, and forty or fifty feet up to the nearest branches, was felled. It was then cut into lengths of a few feet, and split into thick junks, which again were reduced to planks an inch thick by persevering labour with the axe. The object of the carpenters was to make little chests, and they drive a constant trade in them at Cambondo. When finished with hinges, lock, and key, all of their own manufacture, one costs only a shilling and eightpence. My men were so delighted with them that they carried several of them on their heads all the way to Linyanti.

At Trombeta, we were pleased to observe a great deal of taste displayed by the Sub-Commandant, in the laying out of his ground, and adornment of his house with flowers. This trifling incident was the more pleasing, as it was the first attempt at neatness I had seen since leaving the establishment of Mozinkwa in Londa. Rows of trees had been planted along each side of the road, with pine-apples and flowers between. This arrange-ment I had an opportunity of seeing in several other districts of this country, for there is no difficulty in raising any plant or tree, if it is only kept from being choked by weeds.

This gentleman had now a fine estate which but a few years ago was a forest, and cost him only 16l. He had planted about 900 coffee-trees upon it, and as these begin to yield in three years from being planted, and in six attain their maximum, I have no doubt but that ere now his 16l. yields him sixty fold. All sorts of fruit-trees and grape-vines yield their fruit twice in each year, without any labour or irrigation being bestowed on them. All grains and vegetables if only sown do the same, and if advantage is taken of the mists of winter, even three crops of pulse may be raised. Cotton was now standing in the pods in his fields, and he did not seem to care about it. I understood him to say

2 c 2

that this last plant flourishes, but the wet of one of the two rainy seasons with which this country is favoured, sometimes proves troublesome to the grower. I am not aware whether wheat has ever been tried, but I saw both figs and grapes bearing well. The great complaint of all cultivators is the want of a good road to carry their produce to market. Here all kinds of food are remarkably cheap.

Farther on we left the mountainous country, and, as we descended towards the west coast, saw the lands assuming a more sterile uninviting aspect. On our right ran the river Senza, which nearer the sea takes the name of Bengo. It is about fifty yards broad, and navigable for canoes. The low plains adjacent to its banks are protected from inundation by embankments, and the population is entirely occupied in raising food and fruits for exportation to Loanda by means of canoes. The banks are infested by myriads of the most ferocious mosquitoes I ever met. Not one of our party could get a snatch of sleep. I was taken into the house of a Portuguese, but was soon glad to make my escape and lie across the path on the lee side of the fire, where the smoke blew over my body. My host wondered at my want of taste, and I at his want of feeling, for, to our astonishment, he, and the other inhabitants, had actually become used to what was at least equal to a nail through the heel of one's boot, or the tooth-ache.

As we were now drawing near to the sea, my companions were looking at everything in a serious light. One of them asked me if we should all have an opportunity of watching each other at Loanda. "Suppose one went for water, would the others see if he were kidnapped?" I replied, "I see what you are driving at; and if you suspect me, you may return, for I am as ignorant of Loanda as you are: but nothing will happen to you but what happens to myself. We have stood by each other hitherto, and will do so to the last." The plains adjacent to Loanda are somewhat elevated and comparatively sterile. On coming across these we first beheld the sea: my companions looked upon the boundless ocean with awe. On describing their feelings afterwards, they remarked that "we marched along with our father, believing that what the ancients had always told us was true, that the world has no end; but all at once the world said to us, 'I am finished;

there is no more of me!'" They had always imagined that the world was one extended plain without limit.

They were now somewhat apprehensive of suffering want, and I was unable to allay their fears with any promise of supply, for my own mind was depressed by disease and care. The fever had induced a state of chronic dysentery, so troublesome that I could not remain on the ox more than ten minutes at a time; and as we came down the declivity above the city of Loanda on the 31st of May, I was labouring under great depression of spirits, as I understood that, in a population of twelve thousand souls, there was but one genuine English gentleman. I naturally felt anxious to know whether he were possessed of good nature, or was one of those crusty mortals, one would rather not meet at all.

This gentleman, Mr. Gabriel, our commissioner for the suppression of the slave-trade, had kindly forwarded an invitation, to meet me on the way from Cassange, but unfortunately it crossed me on the road. When we entered his porch, I was delighted to see a number of flowers cultivated carefully, and inferred from this circumstance that he was, what I soon discovered him to be, a real whole-hearted Englishman.

Seeing me ill, he benevolently offered me his bed. Never shall I forget the luxuriant pleasure I enjoyed in feeling myself again on a good English couch, after six months' sleeping on the ground. I was soon asleep; and Mr. Gabriel, coming in almost immediately, rejoiced at the soundness of my repose.

CHAPTER XX.

Continued sickness — Kindness of the Bishop of Angola and her Majesty's officers — Mr. Gabriel's unwearied hospitality — Serious deportment of the Makololo — They visit ships of war — Politeness of the officers and men — The Makololo attend mass in the cathedral — Their remarks — Find employment in collecting firewood and unloading coal — Their superior judgment respecting goods — Beneficial influence of the Bishop of Angola — The city of St. Paul de Loanda — The harbour — Custom-house — No English merchants — Sincerity of the Portuguese government in suppressing the slave-trade — Convict soldiers — Presents from bishop and merchants for Sekeletu — Outfit — Leave Loanda 20th September, 1854 — Accompanied by Mr. Gabriel as far as Icollo i Bengo — Sugar manufactory — Geology of this part of the country — Women spinning cotton — Its price — Native weavers — Market-places — Cazengo; its coffee-plantations — South American trees — Ruins of iron-foundry — Native miners — The banks of the Lucalla — Cottages with stages — Tobacco-plants — Town of Massangano — Sugar and rice — Superior district for cotton — Portuguese merchants and foreign enterprise — Ruins — The fort and its ancient guns — Former importance of Massangano — Fires — The tribe Kisama — Peculiar variety of domestic fowl — Coffee-plantations — Return to Golungo Alto — Self-complacency of the Makololo — Fever — Jaundice — Insanity.

In the hope that a short enjoyment of Mr. Gabriel's generous hospitality would restore me to my wonted vigour, I continued under his roof; but my complaint having been caused by long exposure to malarious influences, I became much more reduced than ever, even while enjoying rest. Several Portuguese gentlemen called on me shortly after my arrival; and the Bishop of Angola, the Right Reverend Joaquim Moreira Reis, then the acting governor of the province, sent his secretary to do the same, and likewise to offer the services of the government physician.

Some of her Majesty's cruisers soon came into the port, and, seeing the emaciated condition to which I was reduced, offered to convey me to St. Helena or homewards; but though I had reached the coast, I had found that, in consequence of the great amount of forest, rivers, and marsh, there was no possibility of a highway for waggons, and I had brought a party of Sekeletu's people with me, and found the tribes near the Portuguese settlement so very unfriendly, that it would be altogether impossible for my men to return alone. I therefore resolved to decline the tempting offers of my naval friends, and take back my Makololo companions to their chief, with a view of trying to make a path from his country to the east coast by means of the great river Zambesi or Leeambye.

I however gladly availed myself of the medical assistance of Mr. Cockin, the surgeon of the "Polyphemus," at the suggestion of his commander, Captain Phillips. Mr. Cockin's treatment, aided by the exhilarating presence of the warm-hearted naval officers, and Mr. Gabriel's unwearied hospitality and care, soon brought me round again. On the 14th I was so far well as to call on the bishop, in company with my party, who were arrayed in new robes of striped cotton cloth and red caps, all presented to them by Mr. Gabriel. He received us, as head of the provisional government, in the grand hall of the palace. He put many intelligent questions respecting the Makololo; and then gave them free permission to come to Loanda as often as they pleased. This interview pleased the Makololo extremely.

Every one remarked the serious deportment of the Makololo. They viewed the large stone houses and churches in the vicinity of the great ocean with awe. A house with two stories was, until now, beyond their comprehension. In explanation of this strange thing, I had always been obliged to use the word for hut; and as huts are constructed by the poles being let into the earth, they never could comprehend how the poles of one hut could be founded upon the roof of another, or how men could live in the upper story, with the conical roof of the lower one in the middle. Some Makololo, who had visited my little house at Kolobeng, in trying to describe it to their countrymen at Linyanti, said, "It is not a hut; it is a mountain with several caves in it."

Commander Bedingfeld and Captain Skene invited them to visit their vessels, the "Pluto" and "Philomel." Knowing their fears, I told them that no one need go if he entertained the least suspicion of foul play. Nearly the whole party went; and when on deck, I pointed to the sailors, and said, "Now these are all my countrymen, sent by our Queen for the purpose of putting down the trade of those that buy and sell black men." They replied, "Truly! they are just like you!" and all their fears seemed to vanish at once, for they went forward amongst the men, and the jolly tars, acting much as the Makololo would have done in similar circumstances, handed them a share of the bread and beef which they had for dinner. The commander allowed them to fire off a cannon; and having the most exalted ideas of its power, they were greatly pleased when I told them, "That is what they put down the slave-trade with." The size of the brig-of-war amazed them. "It is not a canoe at all: it is a town!" The sailors' deck they named "the Kotla;" and then, as a climax to their description of this great ark, added, " and what sort of a town is it that you must climb up into with a rope?"

The effect of the politeness of the officers and men on their minds was most beneficial. They had behaved with the greatest kindness to me all the way from Linyanti; and I now rose rapidly in their estimation, for, whatever they may have surmised before, they now saw that I was respected among my own countrymen, and always afterwards treated me with the greatest deference.

On the 15th there was a procession and service of the mass in the cathedral; and wishing to show my men a place of worship, I took them to the church, which now serves as the chief one of the See of Angola and Congo. There is an impression on some minds, that a gorgeous ritual is better calculated to inspire devotional feelings, than the simple forms of the Protestant worship. But here the frequent genuflexions, changing of positions, burning of incense, with the priests' backs turned to the people, the laughing, talking, and manifest irreverence of the singers, with firing of guns, &c., did not convey to the minds of my men the idea of adoration. I overheard them, in talking to each other, remark that "they had seen the white men charming their demons;" a phrase identical with one they had used when seeing the Balonda beating drums before their idols.

In the beginning of August I suffered a severe relapse, which reduced me to a mere skeleton. I was then unable to attend to my men for a considerable time; but when in convalescence from this last attack, I was thankful to find that I was free from that lassitude, which, in my first recovery, showed the continuance of the malaria in the system. I found that my men, without prompting, had established a brisk trade in firewood. They sallied forth at cock-crowing in the mornings, and by daylight reached the uncultivated parts of the adjacent country, collected a bundle of firewood, and returned to the city. It was then divided into smaller fagots, and sold to the inhabitants; and as they gave larger quantities than the regular wood-carriers, they found no difficulty in selling. A ship freighted with coal for the cruisers having arrived from England, Mr. Gabriel procured them employment in unloading her at sixpence a-day. They continued at this work for upwards of a month, and nothing could exceed their astonishment at the vast amount of cargo one ship contained. As they themselves always afterwards expressed it, they had laboured every day from sunrise to sunset for a moon and a half, unloading, as quickly as they could, "stones that burn," and were tired out, still leaving plenty in her. With the money so obtained they purchased clothing, beads, and other articles to take back to their own country. Their ideas of the value of different kinds of goods, rather astonished those who had dealt only with natives on the coast. Hearing it stated with confidence that the Africans preferred the thinnest fabrics, provided they had gaudy colours and a large extent of surface, the idea was so new to my experience in the interior, that I dissented, and, in order to show the superior good sense of the Makololo, took them to the shop of Mr. Schut. When he showed them the amount of general goods which they might procure at Loanda for a single tusk, I requested them, without assigning any reason, to point out the fabrics they prized most. They all, at once selected the strongest pieces of English calico and other cloths, showing that they had regard to strength without reference to colour. I believe that most of the Bechuana nation would have done the same. But I was assured that the people near the coast, with whom the Portuguese have to deal, have not so much regard to durability. This probably arises from calico being the chief circulating medium; quantity being then of more importance than quality.

During the period of my indisposition, the bishop sent frequently to make inquiries, and as soon as I was able to walk, I went to thank him for his civilities. His whole conversation and conduct showed him to be a man of great benevolence and kindness of heart. Alluding to my being a Protestant, he stated that he was a Catholic from conviction; and though sorry to see others, like myself, following another path, he entertained no uncharitable feelings, nor would he ever sanction persecuting measures. He compared the various sects of Christians, in their way to heaven, to a number of individuals choosing to pass down the different streets of Loanda to one of the churches,—all would arrive at the same point at last. His good influence both in the city and the country is universally acknowledged: he was promoting the establishment of schools, which, though formed more on the monastic principle than Protestants might approve, will no doubt be a blessing. He was likewise successfully attempting to abolish the non-marriage custom of the country; and several marriages had taken place in Loanda among those who but for his teaching would have been content with concubinage.

St. Paul de Loanda has been a very considerable city, but is now in a state of decay. It contains about twelve thousand inhabitants, most of whom are people of colour.* There are various evidences of its former magnificence, especially two cathedrals, one of which, once a Jesuit college, is now converted into a workshop; and in passing the other we saw with sorrow a number of oxen feeding within its stately walls. Three forts continue in a good state of repair. Many large stone houses are to be found. The palace of the governor and government offices are commodious structures; but nearly all the houses of the native inhabitants are of wattle and daub. Trees are planted all over the town for the sake of shade; and the city presents an imposing appearance from the sea. It is provided with an effective police; and the custom-house department is extremely well managed. All parties agree in representing the Portuguese authorities as both polite and obliging; and if ever any inconvenience is felt by strangers visiting the port, it must be considered the fault of the system, and not of the men.

The harbour is formed by the low sandy island of Loanda, which is inhabited by about 1300 souls, upwards of 600 of whom are industrious native fishermen, who supply the city with abun-

* From the census of 1850-51 we find the population of this city arranged thus:—830 whites, only 160 of whom are females. This is the largest collection of whites in the country, for Angola itself contains only about 1000 whites. There are 2400 half-castes in Loanda, and only 120 of them slaves; and there are 9000 blacks, more than 5000 of whom are slaves.

From a Sketch by Captain Henry Need, H. M. Brig Linnet.

ST. PAUL DE LOANDA—THE FORT OF SAN MIGUEL ON THE RIGHT.

dance of good fish daily. The spac between it and the mainland, on which the city is built, is the station for ships.   When a
high south-west wind blows, the waves of the ocean dash over
part of the island, and, driving large quantities of sand before
them, gradually fill up the harbour.   Great quantities of soil are
also washed in the rainy season from the heights above the city,
so that the port, which once contained water sufficient to float the
largest ships close to the custom-house, is now at low water dry.
The ships are compelled to anchor about a mile north of their old
station.   Nearly all the water consumed in Loanda is brought from
the river Bengo by means of launches, the only supply that the
city affords being from some deep wells of slightly brackish water ;
unsuccessful attempts have been made by different governors to
finish a canal, which the Dutch, while in possession of Loanda
during the seven years preceding 1648, had begun, to bring
water from the river Coanza to the city.   There is not a single
English merchant at Loanda, and only two American.   This is
the more remarkable, as nearly all the commerce is carried on
by means of English calico brought hither viâ Lisbon.   Several
English houses attempted to establish a trade about 1845, and
accepted bills on Rio de Janeiro in payment for their goods, but
the increased activity of our cruisers had such an effect upon the
mercantile houses of that city, that most of them failed.   The
English merchants lost all, and Loanda got a bad name in the
commercial world in consequence.

One of the arrangements of the custom-house may have had
some influence in preventing English trade. Ships coming here
must be consigned to some one on the spot; the consignee receives one hundred dollars per mast, and he generally makes a
great deal more for himself, by putting a percentage on boats and
men hired for loading and unloading, and on every item that
passes through his hands. The port charges are also rendered
heavy by twenty dollars being charged as a perquisite of the Secretary of Government, with a fee for the chief physician, something
for the hospital, custom-house officers, guards, &c. &c.   But with
all these drawbacks, the Americans carry on a brisk and profitable
trade in calico, biscuit, flour, butter, &c. &c.

The Portuguese home Government has not generally received
the credit for sincerity in suppressing the slave-trade, which I

conceive to be its due. In 1839 my friend Mr. Gabriel saw 37 slave-ships lying in this harbour, waiting for their cargoes, under the protection of the guns of the forts. At that time slavers had to wait many months at a time for a human freight, and a certain sum per head was paid to the Government for all that were exported. The duties derived from the exportation of slaves far exceeded those from other commerce, and by agreeing to the suppression of this profitable traffic, the Government actually sacrificed the chief part of the export revenue. Since that period, however, the revenue from lawful commerce has very much exceeded that on slaves. The intentions of the home Portuguese Government, however good, cannot be fully carried out under the present system. The pay of the officers is so very small, that they are nearly all obliged to engage in trade ; and owing to the lucrative nature of the slave-trade, the temptation to engage in it is so powerful, that the philanthropic statesmen of Lisbon need hardly expect to have their humane and enlightened views carried out. The law, for instance, lately promulgated for the abolition of the carrier system (carregadores) is but one of several equally humane enactments against this mode of compulsory labour, but there is very little probability of the benevolent intentions of the legislature being carried into effect.

Loanda is regarded somewhat as a penal settlement, and those who leave their native land for this country do so with the hope of getting rich in a few years, and then returning home. They have thus no motive for seeking the permanent welfare of the country. The Portuguese law preventing the subjects of any other nation from holding landed property unless they become naturalized, the country has neither the advantage of native nor foreign enterprise, and remains very much in the same state as our allies found it in 1575. Nearly all the European soldiers sent out are convicts, and, contrary to what might be expected from men in their position, behave remarkably well. A few riots have occurred, but nothing at all so serious as have taken place in our own penal settlements. It is a remarkable fact that the whole of the arms of Loanda are every night in the hands of those who have been convicts. Various reasons for this mild behaviour are assigned by the officers, but none of these, when viewed in connection with our own experience in Australia, appear to be valid. Religion seems to have no connexion with the change. Perhaps the climate may have some influence in subduing their turbulent disposition, for the inhabitants generally are a timid race; they are not at all so brave as our Caffres. The people of Ambriz ran away like a flock of sheep, and allowed the Portuguese to take possession of their copper-mines and country, without striking a blow. If we must have convict settlements, attention to the climate might be of advantage in the selection. Here even bulls are much tamer than with us. I never met with a ferocious one in this country, and the Portuguese use them generally for riding; an ox is seldom seen.

The objects which I had in view in opening up the country, as stated in a few notes of my journey, published in the newspapers of Angola, so commended themselves to the general government and merchants of Loanda, that, at the instance of his Excellency the Bishop, a handsome present for Sekeletu was granted by the Board of Public Works (Junta da Fazenda Publica). It consisted of a colonel's complete uniform and a horse for the chief, and suits of clothing for all the men who accompanied me. The merchants also made a present, by public subscription, of handsome specimens of all their articles of trade, and two donkeys, for the purpose of introducing the breed into his country, as tsetse cannot kill this beast of burden. These presents were accompanied by letters from the Bishop and merchants; and I was kindly favoured with letters of recommendation to the Portuguese authorities in Eastern Africa.

I took with me a good stock of cotton-cloth, fresh supplies of ammunition and beads, and gave each of my men a musket. As my companions had amassed considerable quantities of goods, they were unable to carry mine, but the bishop furnished me with twenty carriers, and sent forward orders to all the commandants of the districts through which we were to pass, to render me every assistance in their power. Being now supplied with a good new tent made by my friends on board the Philomel, we left Loanda on the 20th September, 1854, and passed round by sea to the mouth of the river Bengo. Ascending this river, we went through the district in which stand the ruins of the convent of St. Antonio; thence into Icollo i Bengo, which contains a population of 6530 blacks, 172 mulattoes, and 11 whites,

and is so named from having been the residence of a former
native king. The proportion of slaves is only 3·38 per cent. of
the inhabitants. The commandant of this place, Laurence José
Marquis, is a frank old soldier and a most hospitable man; he is
one of the few who secure the universal approbation of their fellow-
men for stern unflinching honesty, and has risen from the ranks to
be a major in the army. We were accompanied thus far by our
generous host, Edmund Gabriel, Esq., who, by his unwearied
attentions to myself, and liberality in supporting my men, had
become endeared to all our hearts. My men were strongly impressed with a sense of his goodness, and often spoke of him in
terms of admiration all the way to Linyanti.

While here we visited a large sugar manufactory belonging to
a lady, Donna Anna da Sousa. The flat alluvial lands on the
banks of the Senza or Bengo are well adapted for raising sugar-
cane, and this lady had a surprising number of slaves, but somehow the establishment was far from being in a flourishing condition. It presented such a contrast to the free-labour establishments of the Mauritius which I have since seen, where, with not
one tenth of the number of hands, or such good soil, a man of
colour had, in one year, cleared 5000*l.* by a single crop, that I
quote the fact in hopes it may meet the eye of Donna Anna.

The water of the river is muddy, and it is observed that such
rivers have many more mosquitoes than those which have clear
water. It was remarked to us here that these insects are much
more numerous at the period of new moon than at other times;
at any rate we were all thankful to get away from the Senza and
its insect plagues.

The whole of this part of the country is composed of marly
tufa, containing the same kind of shells as those at present alive
in the seas. As we advanced eastward and ascended the higher
lands, we found eruptive trap, which had tilted up immense
masses of mica and sandstone schists. The mica schist almost
always dipped towards the interior of the country, forming those
mountain-ranges of which we have already spoken as giving a
highland character to the district of Golungo Alto. The trap
has frequently run through the gorges made in the upheaved
rocks, and at the points of junction between the igneous and
older rocks, there are large quantities of strongly magnetic iron-

ore. The clayey soil formed by the disintegration of the mica schist and trap, is the favourite soil for the coffee, and it is on these mountain sides, and others possessing a similar red clay soil, that this plant has propagated itself so widely. The meadow-lands adjacent to the Senza and Coanza being underlaid by that marly tufa which abounds towards the coast, and containing the same shells, show that previous to the elevation of that side of the country, this region possessed some deeply indented bays.

28th September, Kalungwembo.—We were still on the same path by which we had come, and, there being no mosquitoes, we could now better enjoy the scenery. Ranges of hills occupy both sides of our path, and the fine level road is adorned with a beau-tiful red flower named Bolcamaria. The markets or sleeping-places are well supplied with provisions by great numbers of women, every one of whom is seen spinning cotton with a spindle and distaff, exactly like those which were in use amongst the ancient Egyptians. A woman is scarcely ever seen going to the fields, though with a pot on her head, a child on her back, and the hoe over her shoulder, but she is employed in this way. The cotton was brought to the market for sale, and I bought a pound for a penny. This was the price demanded, and probably double what they ask from each other. We saw the cotton growing luxuriantly all around the market-places from seeds dropped accidentally. It is seen also about the native huts, and, so far as I could learn, it was the American cotton so influenced by climate as to be perennial. We met in the road natives passing with bundles of cops, or spindles full of cotton thread, and these they were carrying to other parts to be woven into cloth. The women are the spinners, and the men perform the weaving. Each web is about 5 feet long, and 15 or 18 inches wide. The loom is of the simplest construction, being nothing but two beams placed one over the other, the web standing perpendicularly. The threads of the web are separated by means of a thin wooden lath, and the woof passed through, by means of the spindle on which it has been wound in spinning.

The mode of spinning and weaving in Angola, and indeed throughout South Central Africa, is so very like the same occu-pations in the hands of the ancient Egyptians, that I introduce a woodcut from the interesting work of Sir Gardner Wilkinson.

The lower figures are engaged in spinning in the real African method, and the weavers in the left-hand corner have their web in the Angolese fashion.

Ancient Spinning and Weaving, perpetuated in Africa at the present day.
From Wilkinson's 'Ancient Egyptians,' pp. 85, 86.

Numbers of other articles are brought for sale to these sleeping-places. The native smiths there carry on their trade. I bought ten very good table-knives made of country iron for two pence each.

Labour is extremely cheap, for I was assured that even carpenters, masons, smiths, &c., might be hired for fourpence a day, and agriculturists would gladly work for half that sum.*

* In order that the reader may understand the social position of the people of this country, I here give the census of the district of Golungo Alto for the year 1854, though the numbers are evidently not all furnished :—

238	householders or yeomen.	300	shoemakers.
4224	patrons, or head-men of several hamlets.	181	potters.
23	native chiefs or sovas.	25	tailors.
292	macotas or councillors.	12	barbers.
5838	carriers.	206	iron-founders.
126	carpenters.	486	bellows-blowers.
72	masons.	586	coke-makers.
		173	iron-miners.

184 soldiers

Being anxious to obtain some more knowledge of this interesting country, and its ancient missionary establishments, than the
line of route by which we had come afforded, I resolved to visit
the town of Massangano, which is situated to the south of Golungo
Alto, and at the confluence of the rivers Lucalla and Coanza.
This led me to pass through the district of Cazengo, which is
rather famous for the abundance and excellence of its coffee.
Extensive coffee plantations were found to exist on the sides of
the several lofty mountains that compose this district. They
were not planted by the Portuguese. The Jesuit and other missionaries are known to have brought some of the fine old Mocha
seed, and these have propagated themselves far and wide; hence
the excellence of the Angola coffee. Some have asserted that, as
new plantations were constantly discovered even during the period
of our visit, the coffee-tree was indigenous; but the fact that
pine-apples, bananas, yams, orange-trees, custard apple-trees,
pitangas, guavas, and other South American trees, were found by
me in the same localities with the recently-discovered coffee,
would seem to indicate that all foreign trees must have been

184 soldiers of militia.	9578 free women.
3603 privileged gentlemen, *i.e.* who may wear boots.	393 possessors of land.
18 vagabonds.	300 female gardeners.
717 old men.	139 hunters of wild animals.
54 blind men and women.	980 smiths.
81 lame men and women.	314 mat-makers.
770 slave men.	4065 males under 7 years of age.
807 slave women.	6012 females under 7 years of age.

These people possess 300 idol-houses, 600 sheep, 5000 goats, 500 oxen, 398
gardens, 25,120 hearths. The authorities find great difficulty in getting the
people to furnish a correct account of their numbers. This census is quoted
merely for the purpose of giving a general idea of the employments of the
inhabitants.

The following is taken from the census of Icollo i Bengo, and is added for
a similar reason :—

3232 living without the marriage tie. (All those who have not been married by a priest are so distinguished.)	11 tailors.
	2 shoemakers.
	3 barbers.
4 orphans—2 black and 2 white.	5 mat-makers.
9 native chiefs.	12 sack-makers.
2 carpenters.	21 basket-makers.
21 potters.	

The cattle in the district are : 10 asses, 401 oxen, 492 cows, 3933 sheep,
1699 goats, 909 swine; and as an annual tax is levied of sixpence per head on
all stock, it is probable that the returns are less than the reality.

2 D

introduced by the same agency. It is known that the Jesuits also introduced many other trees for the sake of their timber alone. Numbers of these have spread over the country, some have probably died out, and others failed to spread, like a lonely specimen which stands in what was the Botanic Garden of Loanda, and, though most useful in yielding a substitute for frankincense, is the only one of the kind in Africa.

A circumstance which would facilitate the extensive propagation of the coffee on the proper clay soil, is this. The seed, when buried beneath the soil, generally dies, while that which is sown broadcast, with no covering except the shade of the trees, vegetates readily. The agent in sowing in this case is a bird, which eats the outer rind, and throws the kernel on the ground. This plant cannot bear the direct rays of the sun, consequently, when a number of the trees are discovered in a forest, all that is necessary is to clear away the brushwood, and leave as many of the tall forest-trees as will afford good shade to the coffee-plants below. The fortunate discoverer has then a flourishing coffee plantation.

This district, small though it be, having only a population of 13,822, of whom ten only are white, nevertheless yields an annual tribute to the Government of thirteen hundred cotton cloths, each 5 feet by 18 or 20 inches, of their own growth and manufacture.

Accompanied by the Commandant of Cazengo, who was well acquainted with this part of the country, I proceeded in a canoe down the river Lucalla to Massangano. This river is about 85 yards wide, and navigable for canoes from its confluence with the Coanza, to about six miles above the point where it receives the Luinha. Near this latter point stand the strong massive ruins of an iron-foundry, erected in the times (1768), and by the order, of the famous Marquis of Pombal. The whole of the buildings were constructed of stone, cemented with oil and lime. The dam for water-power was made of the same materials, and 27 feet high. This had been broken through by a flood, and solid blocks, many yards in length, were carried down the stream, affording an instructive example of the transporting power of water. There was nothing in the appearance of the place to indicate unhealthiness; but eight Spanish and Swedish workmen, being brought hither for the purpose of instructing the natives in the art of smelting iron, soon fell victims to disease and " irregularities." The effort of the Marquis to improve the mode of manufacturing iron was thus rendered abortive. Labour and subsistence are, however, so very cheap that almost any amount of work can be executed, at a cost that renders expensive establishments unnecessary.

A party of native miners and smiths is still kept in the employment of the Government, who, working the rich black magnetic iron-ore, produce for the Government, from 480 to 500 bars of good malleable iron every month. They are supported by the appropriation of a few thousands of a small fresh-water fish, called " cacusu," a portion of the tax levied upon the fishermen of the Coanza. This fish is so much relished in the country, that those who do not wish to eat them can easily convert them into money. The Commandant of the district of Massangano, for instance, has a right to a dish of three hundred every morning, as part of his salary. Shell-fish are also found in the Coanza, and the " Peixemulher," or woman-fish, of the Portuguese, which is probably a Manatee.

The banks of the Lucalla are very pretty, well planted with orange-trees, bananas, and the palm (*Elois Guineensis*) which yields the oil of commerce. Large plantations of maize, manioc, and tobacco, are seen along both banks, which are enlivened by the frequent appearance of native houses embosomed in dense shady groves, with little boys and girls playing about them. The banks are steep, the water having cut out its bed in dark red alluvial soil. Before every cottage a small stage is erected, to which the inhabitants may descend to draw water without danger from the alligators. Some have a little palisade made in the water for safety from these reptiles, and others use the shell of the fruit of the baobab-tree attached to a pole about ten feet long, with which, while standing on the high bank, they may draw water without fear of accident.

Many climbing plants run up the lofty silk, cotton, and baobab trees, and hang their beautiful flowers in gay festoons on the branches. As we approach Massangano, the land on both banks of the Lucalla becomes very level, and large portions are left marshy after the annual floods; but all is very fertile. As an illustration of the strength of the soil, I may state, that we saw tobacco-plants in gardens near the confluence eight feet high, and each plant had thirty-six leaves, which were eighteen inches long by six or eight inches broad. But it is not a pastoral district. In our descent we observed the tsetse, and consequently the people had no domestic animals, save goats.

We found the town of Massangano on a tongue of rather high land, formed by the left bank of the Lucalla, and right bank of the Coanza, and received true Portuguese hospitality from Senhor Lubata. The town has more than a thousand inhabitants; the district has 28,063, with only 315 slaves. It stands on a mound of calcareous tufa, containing great numbers of fossil shells, the most recent of which, resemble those found in the marly tufa close to the coast. The fort stands on the south side of the town, on a high perpendicular bank overhanging the Coanza. This river is here a noble stream, about a hundred and fifty yards wide, admitting navigation in large canoes from the bar at its mouth to Cambambe, some thirty miles above this town. There, a fine waterfall hinders farther ascent. Ten or twelve large canoes laden with country produce pass Massangano every day. Four galleons were constructed here as long ago as 1650, which must have been of good size, for they crossed the ocean to Rio Janeiro.

Massangano district is well adapted for sugar and rice, while Cambambe is a very superior field for cotton; but the bar at the mouth of the Coanza would prevent the approach of a steamer into this desirable region, though a small one could ply on it with ease when once in. It is probable that the objects of those who attempted to make a canal from Calumbo to Loanda, were not merely to supply that city with fresh water, but to afford facilities for transportation. The remains of the canal show it to have been made on a scale suited for the Coanza canoes. The Portuguese began another on a smaller scale in 1811, and, after three years' labour, had finished only 6000 yards. Nothing great or useful will ever be effected here, so long as men come merely to get rich, and then return to Portugal.

The latitude of the town and fort of Massangano, is 9° 37′ 46″ S., being nearly the same as that of Cassange. The country between Loanda and this point being comparatively flat, a railroad might be constructed at small expense. The level country is prolonged along the north bank of the Coanza, to the edge of the Cassange basin, and a railway carried thither would be convenient for the transport of the products of the rich districts of Cassange, Pungo Andongo, Ambaca, Cambambe, Golungo Alto, Cazengo, Muchima, and Calumbo; in a word, the whole of Angola and independent tribes adjacent to this kingdom.

The Portuguese merchants generally look to foreign enterprise; and to their own Government, for the means by which this amelioration might be effected; but, as I always stated to them when conversing on the subject, foreign capitalists would never run the risk, unless they saw the Angolese doing something for themselves, and the laws so altered that the subjects of other nations should enjoy the same privileges in the country with themselves. The Government of Portugal has indeed shown a wise and liberal policy by its permission for the alienation of the crown lands in Angola; but the law giving it effect is so fenced round with limitations, and so deluged with verbiage, that to plain people it seems anything but a straightforward licence to foreigners to become *bona fide* landholders and cultivators of the soil. At present the tolls paid on the different lines of road for ferries and bridges, are equal to the interest of large sums of money, though but a small amount has been expended in making available roads.

There are two churches and a hospital in ruins at Massangano; and the remains of two convents are pointed out, one of which is said to have been an establishment of black Benedictines, which, if successful, considering the materials the brethren had to work on, must have been a laborious undertaking. There is neither priest nor schoolmaster in the town, but I was pleased to observe a number of children taught by one of the inhabitants. The cultivated lands attached to all these conventual establishments in Angola, are now rented by the Government of Loanda, and thither the bishop lately removed all the gold and silver vessels belonging to them.

The fort of Massangano is small, but in good repair: it contains some very ancient guns, which were loaded from the breech, and must have been formidable weapons in their time. The natives of this country entertain a remarkable dread of great guns, and this tends much to the permanence of the Portuguese authority. They dread a cannon greatly, though the carriage be so rotten that it would fall to pieces at the first shot; the fort of Pungo Andongo is kept securely by cannon perched on cross sticks alone!

Massangano was a very important town at the time the Dutch held forcible possession of Loanda and part of Angola; but when, in the year 1648, the Dutch were expelled from this country by a small body of Portuguese, under the Governor Salvador Correa de Sá Benevides, Massangano was left to sink into its present decay. Since it was partially abandoned by the Portuguese, several baobab-trees have sprung up and attained a diameter of eighteen or twenty inches, and are about twenty feet high. No certain conclusion can be drawn from these instances, as it is not known at what time after 1648 they began to grow; but their present size shows that their growth is not unusually slow.

Several fires occurred during our stay, by the thatch having, through long exposure to a torrid sun, become like tinder. The roofs became ignited without any visible cause except the intense solar rays, and excited terror in the minds of the inhabitants, as the slightest spark carried by the wind would have set the whole town in a blaze. There is not a single inscription on stone visible in Massangano. If destroyed to-morrow, no one could tell where it, and most Portuguese interior villages, stood, any more than we can do those of the Balonda.

During the occupation of this town, the Coanza was used for the purpose of navigation, but their vessels were so frequently plundered by their Dutch neighbours, that, when they regained the good port of Loanda, they no longer made use of the river. We remained here four days, in hopes of obtaining an observation for the longitude, but at this season of the year the sky is almost constantly overcast by a thick canopy of clouds of a milk-and-water hue; this continues until the rainy season (which was now close at hand) commences.

The lands on the north side of the Coanza belong to the Quisamas (Kisamas), an independent tribe, which the Portuguese have not been able to subdue. The few who came under my observation possessed much of the Bushman or Hottentot feature, and were dressed in strips of soft bark hanging from the waist to the knee. They deal largely in salt, which their country produces in great abundance. It is brought in crystals of about 12 inches long and 1½ in diameter. This is hawked about everywhere in Angola, and, next to calico, is the most common medium of barter. The Kisama are brave; and when the Portuguese army followed them into their forests, they reduced the invaders to extremity by tapping all the reservoirs of water, which were no other than the enormous baobabs of the country, hollowed into cisterns. As the Kisama country is ill supplied with water otherwise, the Portuguese were soon obliged to retreat. Their country lying near to Massangano is low and marshy, but becomes more elevated in the distance, and beyond them lie the lofty dark mountain-ranges of the Libollo, another powerful and independent people. Near Massangano I observed what seemed to be an effort of nature to furnish a variety of domestic fowls, more capable than the common kind, of bearing the heat of the sun. This was a hen and chickens, with all their feathers curled upwards; thus giving shade to the body without increasing the heat. They are here named " kisafu " by the native population, who pay a high price for them when they wish to offer them as a sacrifice, and by the Portuguese they are termed " arripiada," or shivering. There seems to be a tendency in nature to afford varieties adapted to the convenience of man. A kind of very short-legged fowl among the Boers was obtained, in consequence of observing that such were more easily caught for transportation, in their frequent removals in search of pasture. A similar instance of securing a variety, occurred with the short-limbed sheep in America.

Returning by ascending the Lucalla into Cazengo, we had an opportunity of visiting several flourishing coffee plantations, and observed that several men, who had begun with no capital but honest industry, had in the course of a few years acquired a comfortable subsistence. One of these, Mr. Pinto, generously furnished me with a good supply of his excellent coffee, and my men with a breed of rabbits to carry to their own country. Their lands, granted by Government, yielded, without much labour, coffee sufficient for all the necessaries of life.

The fact of other avenues of wealth opening up so readily, seems like a providential invitation to forsake the slave-trade and engage

Double-handled Angola hoe.

in lawful commerce.   We saw the female population occupied, as usual, in the spinning of cotton and cultivation of their lands. Their only instrument for culture is a double-handled hoe, which is worked with a sort of dragging motion.   Many of the men were employed in weaving.   The latter appear to be less indus- trious than the former, for they require a month to finish a single web.   There is, however, not much inducement to industry, for, notwithstanding the time consumed in its manufacture, each web is sold for only two shillings.

On returning to Golungo Alto, I found several of my men laid up with fever.   One of the reasons for my leaving them there was, that they might recover from the fatigue of the journey from Loanda, which had much more effect upon their feet than hun- dreds of miles had on our way westwards.   They had always been accustomed to moisture in their own well-watered land, and we certainly had a superabundance of that in Loanda.   The roads, however, from Loanda to Golungo Alto were both hard and dry, and they suffered severely in consequence; yet they were com- posing songs to be sung when they should reach home.   The Argonauts were nothing to them; and they remarked very im- pressively to me, "It was well you came with Makololo, for no tribe could have done what we have accomplished in coming to the white man's country: we are the true ancients who can tell wonderful things."   Two of them now had fever in the continued form, and became jaundiced, the whites or conjunctival membrane

of their eyes becoming as yellow as saffron ; and a third suffered
from an attack of mania.   He came to his companions one day,
·and said, "Remain well.   I am called away by the gods!" and
set off at the top of his speed.   The young men caught him before he had gone a mile, and bound him.   By gentle treatment
and watching for a few days he recovered.   I have observed
several instances of this kind in the country, but very few cases
of idiocy, and I believe that continued insanity is rare.

CHAPTER XXI.

WHILE waiting for the recovery of my men, I visited, in company with my friend Mr. Canto, the deserted convent of St.
Hilarion, at Bango, a few miles north-west of Golungo Alto. It
is situated in a magnificent valley, containing a population num-
bering 4000 hearths. This is the abode of the Sova, or Chief
Bango, who still holds a place of authority under the Portuguese.
The garden of the convent, the church, and dormitories of the
brethren, are still kept in a good state of repair. I looked at the
furniture, couches, and large chests for holding the provisions of
the brotherhood with interest, and would fain have learned something of the former occupants; but all the books and sacred
vessels had lately been removed to Loanda, and even the graves of
the good men stand without any record: their resting-places are,
however, carefully tended. All speak well of the Jesuits and
other missionaries, as the Capuchins, &c., for having attended
diligently to the instruction of the children. They were supposed to have a tendency to take the part of the people against
the Government, and were supplanted by priests, concerning whom
no regret is expressed that they were allowed to die out. In

viewing the present fruits of former missions, it is impossible not to feel assured that, if the Jesuit teaching has been so permanent, that of Protestants, who leave the Bible in the hands of their converts, will not be less abiding. The chief Bango has built a large two-story house close by the convent, but superstitious fears prevent him from sleeping in it. The Portuguese take advantage of all the gradations into which native society has divided itself. This man, for instance, is still a sova or chief, has his councillors, and maintains the same state, as when the country was independent. When any of his people are guilty of theft, he pays down the amount of goods stolen at once, and reimburses himself out or the property of the thief so effectually, as to be benefited by the transaction. The people under him are divided into a number of classes. There are his councillors, as the highest, who are generally head-men of several villages, and the carriers, the lowest free men. One class above the last, obtains the privilege of wearing shoes from the chief, by paying for it; another, the soldiers or militia, pay for the privilege of serving, the advantage being, that they are not afterwards liable to be made carriers. They are also divided into gentlemen and little gentlemen, and, though quite black, speak of themselves as white men, and of the others, who may not wear shoes, as "blacks." The men of all these classes trust to their wives for food, and spend most of their time in drinking the palm-toddy. This toddy is the juice of the palm-oil tree (*Elois Guineensis*), which, when tapped, yields a sweet clear liquid, not at all intoxicating while fresh, but, when allowed to stand till the afternoon, causes inebriation and many crimes. This toddy, called malova, is the bane of the country. Culprits are continually brought before the commandants for assaults, committed through its influence. Men come up with deep gashes on their heads, and one, who had burned his father's house, I saw making a profound bow to Mr. Canto, and volunteering to explain why he did the deed.

There is also a sort of fraternity of freemasons, named Empacasseiros, into which no one is admitted unless he is an expert hunter, and can shoot well with the gun. They are distinguished by a fillet of buffalo-hide around their heads, and are employed as messengers in all cases requiring express. They are very trustworthy, and, when on active service, form the best native troops the Portuguese possess. The militia are of no value as soldiers, but cost the country nothing, being supported by their wives. Their duties are chiefly to guard the residences of commandants, and to act as police.

The chief recreations of the natives of Angola are marriages and funerals. When a young woman is about to be married, she is placed in a hut alone and anointed with various unguents, and many incantations are employed, in order to secure good fortune and fruitfulness. Here, as almost everywhere in the south, the height of good fortune is to bear sons. They often leave a husband altogether, if they have daughters only. In their dances, when any one may wish to deride another, in the accompanying song a line is introduced, "So and so has no children, and never will get any." She feels the insult so keenly, that it is not uncommon for her to rush away and commit suicide. After some days, the bride elect is taken to another hut, and adorned with all the richest clothing and ornaments that the relatives can either lend or borrow. She is then placed in a public situation, saluted as a lady, and presents made by all her acquaintances are placed around her. After this she is taken to the residence of her husband, where she has a hut for herself, and becomes one of several wives, for polygamy is general. Dancing, feasting, and drinking on such occasions are prolonged for several days. In case of separation, the woman returns to her father's family, and the husband receives back what he gave for her. In nearly all cases a man gives a price for the wife, and, in cases of mulattoes, as much as 60l. is often given to the parents of the bride. This is one of the evils the Bishop was trying to remedy.

In cases of death the body is kept several days, and there is a grand concourse of both sexes, with beating of drums, dances, and debauchery, kept up with feasting, &c., according to the means of the relatives. The great ambition of many of the blacks of Angola is to give their friends an expensive funeral. Often when one is asked to sell a pig, he replies, "I am keeping it in case of the death of any of my friends." A pig is usually slaughtered and eaten on the last day of the ceremonies, and its head thrown into the nearest stream or river. A native will sometimes appear intoxicated on these occasions, and, if blamed for his intemperance, will reply, "Why! my mother is dead!" as if he

From a Sketch by Captain Henry Need. H.M. Brig Linnet.

GROUP OF NATIVE WOMEN UNDER THE MOKOLANE PALMS.

thought it a sufficient justification. The expenses of funerals are so heavy, that often years elapse before they can defray them.

These people are said to be very litigious and obstinate: constant disputes are taking place respecting their lands. A case came before the weekly court of the Commandant, involving property in a palm-tree worth two pence. The judge advised the pursuer to withdraw the case, as the mere expenses of entering it would be much more than the cost of the tree. "O no," said he; "I have a piece of calico with me for the clerk, and money for yourself. It's my right, I will not forego it." The calico itself cost three or four shillings. They rejoice if they can say of an enemy, "I took him before the court."

My friend Mr. Canto, the Commandant, being seized with fever in a severe form, it afforded me much pleasure to attend *him* in his sickness, who had been so kind to *me* in mine. He was for some time in a state of insensibility, and I, having the charge of his establishment, had thus an opportunity of observing the workings of slavery. When a master is ill, the slaves run riot among the eatables. I did not know this, until I observed that every time the sugar-basin came to the table it was empty. On visiting my patient by night, I passed along a corridor, and unexpectedly came upon the washerwoman, eating pine-apples and sugar. All the sweetmeats were devoured, and it was difficult for me to get even bread and butter, until I took the precaution of locking the pantry door. Probably the slaves thought, that, as both they and the luxuries were the master's property, there was no good reason why they should be kept apart.

Debarred by my precaution from these sources of enjoyment, they took to killing the fowls and goats, and, when the animal was dead, brought it to me saying, "We found this thing lying out there." They then enjoyed a feast of flesh. A feeling of insecurity prevails throughout this country. It is quite common to furnish visitors with the keys of their rooms. When called on to come to breakfast or dinner, each locks his door and puts the key in his pocket. At Kolobeng we never locked our doors by night or by day for months together; but there slavery is unknown. The Portuguese do not seem at all bigoted in their attachment to slavery, nor yet in their prejudices against colour. Mr. Canto gave an entertainment in order to draw all classes together and promote general good will.   Two sovas or native chiefs were present, and took ·their places without the 'least appearance of embarrassment.   The sova of Kilombo appeared in the dress of a general, and the sova of Bango was gaily attired in a red coat, profusely ornamented with tinsel.   The latter had a band of musicians with him consisting of six trumpeters and four drummers, who performed very well.   These men are fond of titles, and the Portuguese Government humours them by conferring honorary captaincies, &c.: the sova of Bango was at present anxious to obtain the title of "Major of all the Sovas."   At the tables of other gentlemen I observed the same thing constantly occurring. At this meeting Mr. Canto communicated some ideas which I had written out on the dignity of labour, and the superiority of. free over slave labour.   The Portuguese gentlemen present were anxiously expecting an arrival of American cotton-seed from Mr. Gabriel.   They are now in the transition state from unlawful to lawful trade, and turn eagerly to cotton, coffee, and sugar, as new sources of wealth.   Mr. Canto had been commissioned by them to purchase three sugar-mills.   Our cruisers have been the principal agents in compelling them to abandon the slave-trade; and our Government, in furnishing them with a supply of cotton-seed, showed a generous intention to aid them in commencing a more honourable course.   It can scarcely be believed, however, that after Lord Clarendon had been at the trouble of procuring fresh cotton-seed through our minister at Washington, and had sent it out to the care of H. M. Commissioner at Loanda, probably from having fallen into the hands of a few incorrigible slave-traders, it never reached its destination.   It was most likely cast into the sea off Ambriz, and my friends at Golungo Alto were left without the means of commencing a new enterprise.

Mr. Canto mentioned that there is now much more cotton in the country than can be consumed; and if he had possession of a few hundred pounds, he would buy up all the oil and cotton at a fair price, and thereby bring about a revolution in the agriculture of the country.   These commodities are not produced in greater quantity, because the people have no market for those, which now spring up almost spontaneously around them.   The above was put down in my journal, when I had no idea that enlarged supplies of cotton from new sources were so much needed at home.

It is common to cut down cotton-trees as a nuisance, and cultivate beans, potatoes, and manioc, sufficient only for their own consumption. I have the impression that cotton, which is deciduous in America, is perennial here; for the plants I saw in winter were not dead, though going by the name Algodão Americana, or American cotton. The rents paid for gardens belonging to the old convents are merely nominal, varying from one shilling to three pounds per annum. The higher rents being realized from those in the immediate vicinity of Loanda, none but Portuguese or half-castes can pay them.

When about to start, the horse which the Governor had kindly presented for Sekeletu was seized with inflammation, which delayed us some time longer, and we ultimately lost it. We had been careful to watch it when coming through the district of Matamba, where we had discovered the tsetse, that no insect might light upon it. The change of diet here, may have had some influence in producing the disease; for I was informed by Dr. Welweitsch, an able German naturalist, whom we found pursuing his arduous labours here, and whose life we hope may be spared to give his researches to the world, that, of fifty-eight kinds of grasses found at Loanda, only three or four species exist here, and these of the most diminutive kinds. The twenty-four different species of grass of Golungo Alto are nearly all gigantic. Indeed, gigantic grasses, climbers, shrubs, and trees, with but few plants, constitute the vegetation of this region.

November 20th.—An eclipse of the sun, which I had anxiously hoped to observe with a view of determining the longitude, happened this morning, and, as often took place in this cloudy climate, the sun was covered four minutes before it began. When it shone forth, the eclipse was in progress, and a few minutes before it should (according to my calculations) have ended, the sun was again completely obscured. The greatest patience and perseverance are required, if one wishes to ascertain his position when it is the rainy season.

Before leaving, I had an opportunity of observing a curious insect, which inhabits trees of the fig family (*Ficus*), upwards of twenty species of which are found here. Seven or eight of them cluster round a spot on one of the smaller branches, and there keep up a constant distillation of a clear fluid, which, dropping to the ground, forms a little puddle below. If a vessel is placed under them in the evening, it contains three or four pints of fluid in the morning. The natives say that, if a drop falls into the eyes, it causes inflammation of these organs. To the question whence is this fluid derived, the people reply that the insects suck it out of the tree, and our own naturalists give the same answer. I have never seen an orifice, and it is scarcely possible that the tree can yield so much. A similar but much smaller homopterous insect, of the family *Cercopidæ*, is known in England as the frog-hopper (*Aphrophora spumaria*), when full grown and furnished with wings; but while still in the pupa state it is called "*cuckoo-spit*," from the mass of froth in which it envelops itself. The circulation of sap in plants in our climate, especially of the graminaceæ, is not quick enough to yield much moisture. The African species is five or six times the size of the English. In the case of branches of the fig-tree, the point the insects congregate on is soon marked by a number of incipient roots, such as are thrown out when a cutting is inserted in the ground, for the purpose of starting another tree. I believe that both the English and African insects belong to the same family, and differ only in size, and that the chief part of the moisture is derived from the atmosphere. I leave it for naturalists to explain how these little creatures distil both by night and day as much water as they please, and are more independent than her Majesty's steam-ships, with their apparatus for condensing steam, for, without coal, their abundant supplies of sea-water are of no avail. I tried the following experiment:—Finding a colony of these insects busily distilling on a branch of the *Ricinus communis*, or castor-oil plant, I denuded about 20 inches of the bark on the tree side of the insects, and scraped away the inner bark, so as to destroy all the ascending vessels. I also cut a hole in the side of the branch, reaching to the middle, and then cut out the pith and internal vessels. The distillation was then going on at the rate of one drop each 67 seconds, or about 2 ounces 5½ drams in 24 hours. Next morning the distillation, so far from being affected by the attempt to stop the supplies, supposing they had come up through the branch from the tree, was increased to a drop every 5 seconds, or 12 drops per minute, making 1 pint (16 ounces) in every 24 hours. I then cut the branch so much, that during the day it broke; but they still went on at the rate of a drop every 5 seconds, while another colony on a branch of the same tree gave a drop every 17 seconds only, or at the rate of about 10 ounces 4½ drams in 24 hours. I finally cut off the branch; but this was too much for their patience, for they immediately decamped, as insects will do from either a dead branch or a dead animal, which Indian hunters soon know, when they sit down on a recently killed bear. The presence of greater moisture in the air increased the power of these distillers: the period of greatest activity was in the morning, when the air and everything else was charged with dew.

Having but one day left for experiment, I found again that another colony on a branch, denuded in the same way, yielded a drop every 2 seconds, or 4 pints 10 ounces in 24 hours, while a colony on a branch untouched, yielded a drop every 11 seconds, or 16 ounces 2⅟₈ drams in 24 hours. I regretted somewhat the want of time to institute another experiment, namely, to cut a branch and place it in water, so as to keep it in life, and then observe if there was any diminution of the quantity of water in the vessel. This alone was wanting to make it certain that they draw water from the atmosphere. I imagine that they have some power of which we are not aware, besides that nervous influence which causes constant motion to our own involuntary muscles, the power of life-long action without fatigue. The reader will remember, in connection with this insect, the case of the ants already mentioned.

December 14th.—Both myself and men having recovered from severe attacks of fever, we left the hospitable residence of Mr. Canto with a deep sense of his kindness to us all, and proceeded on our way to Ambaca. (Lat. 9° 16′ 35″ S., long. 15° 23′ E.)

Frequent rains had fallen in October and November, which were nearly always accompanied with thunder. Occasionally the quantity of moisture in the atmosphere is greatly increased without any visible cause: this imparts a sensation of considerable cold, though the thermometer exhibits no fall of the mercury. The greater humidity in the air, affording a better conducting medium for the radiation of heat from the body, is as dangerous as a sudden fall of the thermometer: it causes considerable disease among the natives, and this season is denominated "carneirado," as if by the disease they were slaughtered like sheep. The season of these changes, which is the most favourable for Europeans, is the most unhealthy for the native population; and this is by no means a climate, in which either natives or Europeans can indulge in irregularities with impunity.

Owing to the weakness of the men who had been sick, we were able to march but short distances. Three hours and a half brought us to the banks of the Caloi, a small stream which flows into the Senza. This is one of the parts of the country reputed to yield petroleum, but the geological formation, being mica schist dipping towards the eastward, did not promise much for our finding it. Our hospitable friend Mr. Mellot accompanied us to another little river, called the Quango, where I saw two fine boys, the sons of the sub-commandant, Mr. Feltao, who, though only from six to eight years old, were subject to fever. We then passed on in the bright sunlight, the whole country looking so fresh and green after the rains, and everything so cheering, one could not but wonder to find it so feverish.

We found on reaching Ambaca that the gallant, old soldier Laurence José Marquis, had, since our passing Icollo i Bengo, been promoted, on account of his stern integrity, to the government of this important district. The office of commandant is much coveted by the officers of the line who come to Angola, not so much for the salary as for the perquisites, which, when managed skilfully, in the course of a few years make one rich. An idea may be formed of the conduct of some of these officials from the following extract from the Boletim of Loanda of the 28th of October, 1854.

" The acting governor-general of the province of Angola and its dependencies determines as follows.

" Having instituted an investigation (Syndecancia) against the commandant of the fort of ——, a captain of the army of Portugal in commisssion in this province, ——, on account of numerous complaints, which have come before this Government, of violences and extortions practised by the said commandant, and those complaints appearing by the result of the investigation to be well founded, it will be convenient to exonerate the captain referred to, from the command of the fort of ——, to which he had been nominated by the Portfolio of this general Government, No. 41, of 27th December of the past year; and if not otherwise determined, the same official shall be judged by a council of war for the criminal acts, which are to him attributed."

Even this public mention of his crimes, attaches no stigma to the man's character. The council of war, by which these delinquents always prefer to be judged, is composed of men who eagerly expect to occupy the post of commandant themselves, and anticipate their own trial for similar acts at some future time. The severest sentence a council of war awards, is a few weeks' suspension from office in his regiment.

This want of official integrity, which is not at all attributable to the Home Government of Portugal, would prove a serious impediment in the way of foreign enterprise developing the resources of this rich province. And to this cause indeed, may be ascribed the failure of the Portuguese laws for the entire suppression of the slave-trade. The officers ought to receive higher pay, if integrity is expected from them. At present, a captain's pay for a year, will only keep him in good uniform. The high pay our own officers receive, has manifest advantages.

Before leaving Ambaca, we received a present of ten head of cattle from Mr. Schut of Loanda, and, as it shows the cheapness of provisions here, I may mention that the cost was only about a guinea per head.

On crossing the Lucalla, we made a détour to the south, in order to visit the famous rocks of Pungo Andongo. As soon as we crossed the rivulet Lotete, a change in the vegetation of the country was apparent. We found trees identical with those to be seen south of the Chobe. The grass too stands in tufts, and is of that kind which the natives consider to be best adapted for cattle. Two species of grape-bearing vines abound everywhere in this district, and the influence of the good pasturage is seen in the plump condition of the cattle. In all my previous inquiries respecting the vegetable products of Angola I was invariably directed to Pungo Andongo. Do you grow wheat? " O yes, in Pungo Andongo."—Grapes, figs, or peaches? " O yes, in Pungo Andongo."—Do you make butter, cheese, &c. ? The uniform answer was, " O yes, there is abundance of all these in Pungo Andongo." But when we arrived here, we found that the

2 E 2

A few of the Rocks of Pungo Andongo, as seen from Col. Pires' house at Cahuey, with the Makololo party passing.

answers all referred to the activity of one man, Colonel Manuel
Antonio Pires. The presence of the wild grape shows that
vineyards might be cultivated with success; the wheat grows
well without irrigation; and any one who tasted the butter and
cheese at the table of Colonel Pires would prefer them to the
stale produce of the Irish dairy, in general use throughout that
province. The cattle in this country are seldom milked, on
account of the strong prejudice which the Portuguese entertain
against the use of milk. They believe that it may be used with
safety in the morning; but if taken after midday, that it will
cause fever. It seemed to me that there was not much reason
for carefully avoiding a few drops in their coffee, after having
devoured ten times the amount in the shape of cheese at dinner.

The fort of Pungo Andongo (lat. 9° 42' 14" S., long. 15° 30' E.)
is situated in the midst of a group of curious columnar-shaped
rocks, each of which is upwards of three hundred feet in
height. They are composed of conglomerate, made up of a
great variety of rounded pieces in a matrix of dark red sandstone. They rest on a thick stratum of this last rock, with
very few of the pebbles in its substance. On this a fossil
palm has been found, and if of the same age as those on the
eastern side of the continent, on which similar palms now lie,
there may be coal underneath this, as well as under that at Tete.
The asserted existence of petroleum-springs at Dande, and near
Cambambe, would seem to indicate the presence of this useful
mineral, though I am not aware of any one having actually seen
a seam of coal tilted up to the surface in Angola, as we have at
Tete. The gigantic pillars of Pungo Andongo, have been formed
by a current of the sea coming from the S.S.E., for, seen from the
top, they appear arranged in that direction, and must have with-
stood the surges of the ocean at a period of our world's history,
when the relations of land and sea were totally different from what
they are now, and long before "the morning stars sang together,
and all the sons of God shouted for joy, to see the abodes prepared
which man was soon to fill." The embedded pieces in the conglomerate are of gneiss, clay shale, mica and sandstone schists, trap,
and porphyry, most of which are large enough to give the whole the
appearance of being the only remaining vestiges of vast primæval
banks of shingle. Several little streams run amongst these rocks,

and in the central part of the pillars stands the village, completely environed by well-nigh inaccessible rocks. The pathways into the village, might be defended by a small body of troops against an army; and this place was long the stronghold of the tribe called Jinga, the original possessors of the country.

We were shown a foot-print carved on one of these rocks. It is spoken of as that of a famous queen, who reigned over all this region. In looking at these rude attempts at commemoration, one feels the value of letters. In the history of Angola, we find that the famous Queen Donna Anna de Souza came from the vicinity, as Ambassadress from her brother Gola Bandy, king of the Jinga, to Loanda, in 1621, to sue for peace, and astonished the governor by the readiness of her answers. The governor proposed, as a condition of peace, the payment by the Jinga of an annual tribute. "People talk of tribute after they have conquered, and not before it : we come to talk of peace, not of subjection," was the ready answer. The governor was as much nonplussed as our Cape governors often are, when they tell the Caffres "to put it all down in writing, and they will then be able to answer them." She remained some time in Loanda, gained all she sought, and, after being taught by the missionaries, was baptized, and returned to her own country with honour. She succeeded to the kingdom on the death of her brother, whom it was supposed she poisoned, but in a subsequent war with the Portuguese, she lost nearly all her army in a great battle fought in 1627. She returned to the church after a long period of apostacy, and died in extreme old age; and the Jinga still live as an independent people to the north of this their ancient country. No African tribe has ever been destroyed.

In former times the Portuguese imagined that this place was particularly unhealthy, and banishment to the black rocks of Pungo Andongo, was thought by their judges to be a much severer sentence than transportation to any part of the coast; but this district is now well known to be the most healthy part of Angola. The water is remarkably pure, the soil is light, and the country open and undulating, with a general slope down towards the river Coanza, a few miles distant. That river is the southern boundary of the Portuguese, and beyond, to the S. and S.W., we see the high mountains of the Libollo. On the S.E. we have also a mountainous country, inhabited by the Kimbonda or Ambonda, who are said by Colonel Pires to be a very brave and independent people, but hospitable and fair in their dealings. They are rich in cattle, and their country produces much bees'-wax, which is carefully collected, and brought to the Portuguese, with whom they have always been on good terms.

The Ako (Haco), a branch of this family, inhabit the left bank of the Coanza above this village, who, instead of bringing slaves for sale, as formerly, now occasionally bring wax for the purchase of a slave from the Portuguese. I saw a boy sold for twelve shillings: he said that he belonged to the country of Matiamvo. Here I bought a pair of well-made boots of good tanned leather, which reached above the knee, for five shillings and eight pence, and that was just the price given for one pound of ivory by Mr. Pires; consequently the boy was worth two pairs of boots, or two pounds of ivory. The Libollo on the S. have not so good a character, but the Coanza is always deep enough to form a line of defence. Colonel Pires is a good example of what an honest industrious man in this country may become. He came as a servant in a ship, and by a long course of persevering labour, has raised himself to be the richest merchant in Angola. He possesses some thousands of cattle; and, on any emergency, can appear in the field with several hundred armed slaves.

While enjoying the hospitality of this merchant prince in his commodious residence, which is outside the rocks, and commands a beautiful view of all the adjacent country, I learned that all my despatches, maps, and journal, had gone to the bottom of the sea in the mail packet, "Forerunner." I felt so glad that my friend Lieutenant Bedingfeld, to whose care I had committed them, though in the most imminent danger, had not shared a similar fate, that I was at once reconciled to the labour of rewriting. I availed myself of the kindness of Colonel Pires, and remained till the end of the year, reproducing my lost papers.

Colonel Pires having another establishment on the banks of the Coanza, about six miles distant, I visited it with him about once a week for the purpose of recreation. The difference of temperature caused by the lower altitude, was seen in the cashew-trees, for while, near the rocks, these trees were but coming into flower, those at the lower station were ripening their fruit.

Cocoa-nut trees and bananas bear well at the lower station, but yield little or no fruit at the upper. The difference indicated by the thermometer was 7°. The general range near the rocks was 67° at 7 A.M., 74° at midday, and 72° in the evening.

A slave-boy belonging to Colonel Pires, having stolen and eaten some lemons in the evening, went to the river to wash his mouth, so as not to be detected by the flavour. An alligator seized him and carried him to an island in the middle of the stream; there the boy grasped hold of the reeds, and baffled all the efforts of the reptile to dislodge him, till his companions, attracted by his cries, came in a canoe to his assistance. The alligator at once let go his hold, for when out of his own element he is cowardly. The boy had many marks of the teeth in his abdomen and thigh, and those of the claws on his legs and arms.

The slaves in Colonel Pires' establishments, appeared more like free servants than any I had elsewhere seen. Everything was neat and clean, while generally, where slaves are the only domestics, there is an aspect of slovenliness, as if they went on the principle of always doing as little for their masters as possible.

In the country near to this station were a large number of the ancient burial-places of the Jinga. These are simply large mounds of stones, with drinking and cooking vessels of rude pottery on them. Some are arranged in a circular form, two or three yards in diameter, and shaped like a haycock. There is not a single vestige of any inscription. The natives of Angola generally have a strange predilection for bringing their dead to the sides of the most frequented paths. They have a particular anxiety to secure the point where cross roads meet. On and around the graves, are planted tree euphorbias and other species of that family. On the grave itself, they also place water-bottles, broken pipes, cooking vessels, and sometimes a little bow and arrow.

The Portuguese Government, wishing to prevent this custom, affixed a penalty on any one burying in the roads, and appointed places of public sepulture in every district in the country. The people persist, however, in spite of the most stringent enforcement of the law, to follow their ancient custom.

The country between the Coanza and Pungo Andongo is

covered with low trees, bushes, and fine pasturage. In the latter, we were pleased to see our old acquaintances the gaudy gladiolus, Amaryllis toxicaria, hymanthus, and other bulbs in as flourishing a condition as at the Cape.

It is surprising that so little has been done in the way of agriculture in Angola. Raising wheat by means of irrigation has never been tried; no plough is ever used; and the only instrument is the native hoe, in the hands of slaves. The chief object of agriculture is the manioc, which does not contain nutriment sufficient to give proper stamina to the people. The half-caste Portuguese have not so much energy as their fathers. They subsist chiefly on the manioc, and, as that can be eaten either raw, roasted, or boiled, as it comes from the ground; or fermented in water, and then roasted or dried after fermentation, and baked or pounded into fine meal; or rasped into meal and cooked as farina; or made into confectionery with butter and sugar, it does not so soon pall upon the palate as one might imagine, when told that it constitutes their principal food. The leaves boiled make an excellent vegetable for the table; and, when eaten by goats, their milk is much increased. The wood is a good fuel, and yields a large quantity of potash. If planted in a dry soil, it takes two years to come to perfection, requiring, during that time, one weeding only. It bears drought well, and never shrivels up, like other plants, when deprived of rain. When planted in low alluvial soils, and either well supplied with rain or annually flooded, twelve, or even ten months, are sufficient to bring it to maturity. The root rasped while raw, placed upon a cloth, and rubbed with the hands while water is poured upon it, parts with its starchy glutinous matter, and this, when it settles at the bottom of the vessel, and the water poured off, is placed in the sun till nearly dry, to form tapioca. The process of drying is completed on an iron plate over a slow fire, the mass being stirred meanwhile with a stick, and when quite dry it appears agglutinated into little globules, and is in the form we see the tapioca of commerce. This is never eaten by weevils, and so little labour is required in its cultivation, that on the spot it is extremely cheap. Throughout the interior parts of Angola, fine manioc-meal, which could with ease have been converted either into superior starch or tapioca, is commonly sold at the rate of about ten pounds for a

penny. All this region, however, has no means of transport to
Loanda, other than the shoulders of the carriers and slaves,
over a footpath.

Cambambe, to which the navigation of the Coanza reaches, is
reported to be thirty leagues below Pungo Andongo. A large
waterfall is the limit on that side; and another exists higher up,
at the confluence of the Lombe (lat. 9° 41' 26" S., and about
long. 16° E.), over which hippopotami and elephants are sometimes drawn and killed. The river between is rapid, and generally
rushes over a rocky bottom. Its source is pointed out as S.E. or
S.S.E. of its confluence with the Lombe, and near Bihe. The
situation of Bihe is not well known. When at Sanza, we were
assured that it lies nearly south of that point, and eight days
distant. This statement seemed to be corroborated by our
meeting many people going to Matiamvo and to Loanda from
Bihe. Both parties had come to Sanza, and then branched off,
one to the east, the other to the west. The source of the
Coanza is thus probably not far from Sanza.

I had the happiness of doing a little good in the way of administering to the sick, for there are no doctors in the interior of
Angola. Notwithstanding the general healthiness of this fine district, and its pleasant temperature, I was attacked by fever myself.
While confined to my room, a gentleman of colour, a canon of the
church, kindly paid me a visit. He was on a tour of visitation in
the different interior districts, for the purpose of baptizing and
marrying. He had lately been on a visit to Lisbon, in company
with the Prince of Congo, and had been invested with an order
of honour by the King of Portugal as an acknowledgment of
his services. He had all the appearance of a true negro, but
commanded the respect of the people, and Colonel P., who had
known him for thirty years, pronounced him to be a good man.
There are only three or four priests in Loanda, all men of
colour, but educated for the office. About the time of my
journey in Angola, an offer was made to any young men of
ability who might wish to devote themselves to the service of
the Church, to afford them the requisite education at the University of Coimbra in Portugal. I was informed, on what seemed
good authority, that the Prince of Congo is professedly a Christian, and that there are no fewer than twelve churches in that

kingdom, the fruits of the mission established in former times at San Salvador, the capital. These churches are kept in partial repair by the people, who also keep up the ceremonies of the Church, pronouncing some gibberish over the dead, in imitation of the Latin prayers which they had formerly heard. Many of them can read and write. When a King of Congo dies, the body is wrapped up in a great many folds of cloth, until a priest can come from Loanda to consecrate his successor. The King of Congo still retains the title of Lord of Angola, which he had when the Jinga, the original possessors of the soil, owed him allegiance; and, when he writes to the Governor of Angola, he places his own name first, as if addressing his vassal. The Jinga paid him tribute annually in cowries, which were found on the island that shelters Loanda harbour, and, on refusing to continue payment, the King of Congo gave over the island to the Portuguese, and thus their dominion commenced in this quarter.

There is not much knowledge of the Christian religion in either Congo or Angola, yet it is looked upon with a certain degree of favour. The prevalence of fever, is probably the reason why no priest occupies a post in any part of the interior. They come on tours of visitation like that mentioned, and it is said that no expense is incurred, for all the people are ready not only to pay for their services, but also to furnish every article in their power, gratuitously. In view of the desolate condition of this fine missionary field, it is more than probable that the presence of a few Protestants would soon provoke the priests, if not to love, to good works.

CHAPTER XXII.

January 1, 1855.—HAVING, through the kindness of Colonel
Pires, reproduced some of my lost papers, I left Pungo Andongo
the first day of this year; and at Candumba, slept in one of the
dairy establishments of my friend, who had sent forward orders
for an ample supply of butter, cheese, and milk. Our path lay
along the right bank of the Coanza. This is composed of the
same sandstone rock, with pebbles, which forms the flooring of the
country. The land is level, has much open forest, and is well
adapted for pasturage.

On reaching the confluence of the Lombe, we left the river, and
proceeded in a north-easterly direction, through a fine open green
country, to the village of Malange, where we struck into our
former path. A few miles to the west of this, a path branches off
to a new district named the Duke Braganza. This path crosses
the Lucalla, and several of its feeders. The whole of the country
drained by these, is described as extremely fertile. The territory

west of Braganza is reported to be mountainous, well wooded and
watered; wild coffee is abundant, and the people even make their
huts of coffee-trees. The rivers Dande, Senza, and Lucalla, are
said to rise in one mountain-range. Numerous tribes inhabit the
country to the north, who are all independent. The Portuguese
power extends chiefly over the tribes through whose lands we
have passed. It may be said to be firmly seated only between
the rivers Dande and Coanza. It extends inland about three
hundred miles to the river Quango; and the population, according
to the imperfect data afforded by the census, given annually by
the commandants of the fifteen or sixteen districts into which it is
divided, cannot be under 600,000 souls.

Leaving Malange, we passed quickly, without deviation, along
the path by which we had come. At Sanza (lat. 9° 37′ 46″ S.,
long. 16° 59′ E.) we expected to get a little seed-wheat, but this
was not now to be found in Angola. The underlying rock of
the whole of this section, is that same sandstone which we have
before noticed, but it gradually becomes finer in the grain, with
the addition of a little mica, the further we go eastward; we enter
upon clay-shale at Tala Mungongo (lat. 9° 42′ 37″ S., long. 17°
27′ E.), and find it dipping a little to the west. The general
geological structure, is a broad fringe of mica and sandstone schist
(about 15° E.), dipping in towards the centre of the country,
beneath these horizontal and sedimentary rocks of more recent
date, which form an inland basin. The fringe is not, however, the
highest in altitude, though the oldest in age.

While at this latter place, we met a native of Bihe who has
visited the country of Shinte three times, for the purposes of trade.
He gave us some of the news of that distant part, but not a word
of the Makololo, who have always been represented in the countries to the north as a desperately savage race, whom no trader
could visit with safety. The half-caste traders whom we met at
Shinte's, had returned to Angola with sixty-six slaves and upwards
of fifty tusks of ivory. As we came along the path, we daily met
long lines of carriers bearing large square masses of bees'-wax,
each about a hundred pounds weight, and numbers of elephants'
tusks, the property of Angolese merchants. Many natives were
proceeding to the coast also on their own account, carrying bees'-
wax, ivory, and sweet oil. They appeared to travel in perfect

security; and at different parts of the road, we purchased fowls
from them at a penny each. My men took care to celebrate their
own daring in having actually entered ships, while the natives of
these parts, who had endeavoured to frighten them on their way
down, had only seen them at a distance. Poor fellows! they were
more than ever attentive to me; and, as they were not obliged
to erect sheds for themselves, in consequence of finding them
already built at the different sleeping-places, all their care was
bestowed in making me comfortable. Mashauana, as usual, made
his bed with his head close to my feet, and never during the
entire journey did I have to call him twice, for anything I needed.

During our stay at Tala Mungongo, our attention was attracted
to a species of red ant, which infests different parts of this country.
It is remarkably fond of animal food. The commandant of the
village having slaughtered a cow, slaves were obliged to sit up
the whole night, burning fires of straw around the meat, to
prevent them from devouring most of it. These ants are frequently met with in numbers, like a small army. At a little
distance, they appear as a brownish-red band, two or three inches
wide, stretched across the path, all eagerly pressing on in one
direction. If a person happens to tread upon them, they rush
up his legs and bite with surprising vigour. The first time I
encountered this, by no means contemptible enemy, was near
Cassange. My attention being taken up in viewing the distant
landscape, I accidentally stepped upon one of their nests. Not
an instant seemed to elapse, before a simultaneous attack was
made on various unprotected parts, up the trousers from below,
and on my neck and breast above. The bites of these furies were
like sparks of fire, and there was no retreat. I jumped about for
a second or two, then in desperation tore off all my clothing, and
rubbed and picked them off seriatim as quickly as possible. Ugh!
they would make the most lethargic mortal look alive. Fortunately no one observed this rencontre, or word might have
been taken back to the village that I had become mad. I was
once assaulted in a similar way, when sound asleep at night in my
tent, and it was only by holding my blanket over the fire that I
could get rid of them. It is really astonishing, how such small
bodies can contain so large an amount of ill-nature. They not
only bite, but twist themselves round after the mandibles are

inserted, to produce laceration and pain, more than would be effected by the single wound. Frequently while sitting on the ox, as he happened to tread near a band, they would rush up his legs to the rider, and soon let him know that he had disturbed their march. They possess no fear, attacking with equal ferocity the largest as well as the smallest animals. When any person has leaped over the band, numbers of them leave the ranks and rush along the path, seemingly anxious for a fight. They are very useful in ridding the country of dead animal matter, and, when they visit a human habitation, clear it entirely of the destructive white ants and other vermin. They destroy many noxious insects and reptiles. The severity of their attack is greatly increased by their vast numbers, and rats, mice, lizards, and even the *python natalensis*, when in a state of surfeit from recent feeding, fall victims to their fierce onslaught. These ants never make hills like the white ant. Their nests are but a short distance beneath the soil, which has the soft appearance of the abodes of ants in England. Occasionally they construct galleries over their path to the cells of the white ant, in order to secure themselves from the heat of the sun during their marauding expeditions.

January 15th, 1855.—We descended, in one hour, from the heights of Tala Mungongo. I counted the number of paces made on the slope downward, and found them to be sixteen hundred, which may give a perpendicular height of from twelve to fifteen hundred feet. Water boiled at 206° at Tala Mungongo above, and at 208° at the bottom of the declivity, the air being as 72° in the shade in the former case, and 94° in the latter. The temperature generally throughout the day was from 94° to 97° in the coolest shade we could find.

The rivulets which cut up the valley of Cassange were now dry; but the Lui and Luare contained abundance of rather brackish water. The banks are lined with palm, wild date-trees, and many guavas, the fruit of which was now becoming ripe. A tree much like the mango abounds, but it does not yield fruit. In these rivers a kind of edible muscle is plentiful, the shells of which exist in all the alluvial beds of the ancient rivers, as far as the Kuruman. The brackish nature of the water, probably enables it to exist here. On the open grassy lawns, great numbers of a species of lark are seen. They are black, with yellow shoulders. Another black bird, with a long tail (*Centropus Senegalensis*), floats awkwardly, with its tail in a perpendicular position, over the long grass. It always chooses the highest points, and is caught on them with bird-lime, the long black tail-feathers being highly esteemed by the natives for plumes. We saw here also the "Lehututu" (*Tragopan Leadbeaterii*), a large bird strongly resembling a turkey; it is black on the ground, but when it flies, the outer half of the wings are white. It kills serpents, striking them dexterously behind the head. It derives its native name from the noise it makes, and it is found as far as Kolobeng. Another species like it, is called the Abyssinian hornbill.

Before we reached Cassange, we were overtaken by the Commandant, Senhor Carvalho, who was returning, with a detachment of fifty men and a field-piece, from an unsuccessful search after some rebels. The rebels had fled, and all he could do was to burn their huts. He kindly invited me to take up my residence with him, but, not wishing to pass by the gentleman, (Captain Neves) who had so kindly received me on my first arrival in the Portuguese possessions, I declined. Senhor Rego had been superseded in his command, because the Governor Amaral, who had come into office since my departure from Loanda, had determined that the law which requires the office of commandant to be exclusively occupied by military officers of the line, should once more come into operation. I was again most kindly welcomed by my friend Captain Neves, whom I found labouring under a violent inflammation and abscess of the hand. There is nothing in the situation of this village to indicate unhealthiness, except perhaps the rank luxuriance of the vegetation. Nearly all the Portuguese inhabitants suffer from enlargement of the spleen, the effects of frequent intermittents, and have generally a sickly appearance. Thinking that this affection of the hand, was simply an effort of nature to get rid of malarious matter from the system, I recommended the use of quinine. He himself applied the leaf of a plant called cathory, famed among the natives as an excellent remedy for ulcers. The cathory-leaves, when boiled, exude a gummy juice, which effectually shuts out the external air. Each remedy of course claimed the merit of the cure.

Many of the children are cut off by fever. A fine boy of

Captain Neves' had since my passage westward shared a similar fate. Another child died during the period of my visit. During his sickness, his mother, a woman of colour, sent for a diviner in order to ascertain what ought to be done. The diviner, after throwing his dice, worked himself into the state of ecstacy in which they pretend to be in communication with the Barimo. He then gave the oracular response, that the child was being killed by the spirit of a Portuguese trader, who once lived at Cassange. The case was this:—On the death of the trader, the other Portuguese merchants in the village came together, and sold the goods of the departed to each other, each man accounting for the portion received, to the creditors of the deceased at Loanda. The natives, looking on, and not understanding the nature of written mercantile transactions, concluded that the merchants of Cassange had simply stolen the dead man's goods, and that now the spirit was killing the child of Captain Neves for the part he had taken in the affair. The diviner in his response revealed the impression made on his own mind by the sale, and likewise the native ideas of departed souls. As they give the whites credit for greater stupidity than themselves in all these matters, the mother of the child came, and told the father that he ought to give a slave to the diviner, as a fee to make a sacrifice to appease the spirit and save the life of the child. The father quietly sent for a neighbour, and, though the diviner pretended to remain in his state of ecstacy, the brisk application of two sticks to his back suddenly reduced him to his senses, and a most undignified flight.

The mother of this child seemed to have no confidence in European wisdom; and though I desired her to keep the child out of currents of wind, she preferred to follow her own custom, and even got it cupped on the cheeks. The consequence was that the child was soon in a dying state, and the father, wishing it to be baptized, I commended its soul to the care and compassion of Him who said, "Of such is the kingdom of heaven." The mother at once rushed away, and commenced that doleful wail which is so affecting, as it indicates sorrow without hope. She continued it without intermission until the child was buried. In the evening her female companions used a small musical instrument, which produced a kind of screeching sound, as an accompaniment of the death wail.

2 F

In the construction of this instrument they make use of caoutchouc, which, with a variety of other gums, is found in different parts of this country.

The intercourse which the natives have had with white men, does not seem to have much ameliorated their condition. A great number of persons are reported to lose their lives annually in different districts of Angola, by the cruel superstitions to which they are addicted, and the Portuguese authorities either know nothing of them, or are unable to prevent their occurrence. The natives are bound to secrecy by those who administer the ordeal, which generally causes the death of the victim. A person, when accused of witchcraft, will often travel from distant districts in order to assert her innocency and brave the test. They come to a river on the Cassange called Dua, drink the infusion of a poisonous tree, and perish unknown.

A woman was accused by a brother-in-law of being the cause of his sickness while we were at Cassange. She offered to take the ordeal, as she had the idea that it would but prove her conscious innocence. Captain Neves refused his consent to her going, and thus saved her life, which would have been sacrificed, for the poison is very virulent. When a strong stomach rejects it, the accuser reiterates his charge; the dose is repeated, and the person dies. Hundreds perish thus every year in the valley of Cassange.

The same superstitious ideas being prevalent through the whole of the country north of the Zambesi, seems to indicate that the people must originally have been one. All believe that the souls of the departed still mingle among the living, and partake in some way of the food they consume. In sickness, sacrifices of fowls and goats are made to appease the spirits. It is imagined that they wish to take the living away from earth and all its enjoyments. When one man has killed another, a sacrifice is made, as if to lay the spirit of the victim. A sect is reported to exist, who kill men in order to take their hearts and offer them to the Barimo.

The chieftainship is elective from certain families. Among the Bangalas of the Cassange valley, the chief is chosen from three families in rotation. A chief's brother inherits in preference to his son. The sons of a sister belong to her brother; and he often sells his nephews to pay his debts. By this and other unnatural customs, more than by war, is the slave-market supplied.

The prejudices in favour of these practices are very deeply rooted in the native mind. Even at Loanda they retire out of the city in order to perform their heathenish rites without the cognizance of the authorities. Their religion, if such it may be called, is one of dread. Numbers of charms are employed to avert the evils with which they feel themselves to be encompassed. Occasionally you meet a man, more cautious or more timid than the rest, with twenty or thirty charms hung round his neck. He seems to act upon the principle of Proclus, in his prayer to all the gods and goddesses. Among so many he surely must have the right one. The disrespect which Europeans pay to the objects of their fear, is to their minds only an evidence of great folly.

While here, I reproduced the last of my lost papers and maps; and as there is a post twice a-month from Loanda, I had the happiness to receive a packet of the 'Times,' and, among other news, an account of the Russian war up to the terrible charge of the light cavalry. The intense anxiety I felt to hear more, may be imagined by every true patriot; but I was forced to brood on in silent thought, and utter my poor prayers for friends who perchance were now no more, until I reached the other side of the continent.

A considerable trade is carried on by the Cassange merchants with all the surrounding territory by means of native traders, whom they term "Pombeiros." Two of these, called in the history of Angola "the trading blacks" (os feirantes pretos), Pedro João Baptista and Antonio José, having been sent by the first Portuguese trader that lived at Cassange, actually returned from some of the Portuguese possessions in the East with letters from the governor of Mozambique in the year 1815, proving, as is remarked, "the possibility of so important a communication between Mozambique and Loanda." This is the only instance of native Portuguese subjects crossing the continent. No European ever accomplished it, though this fact has lately been quoted as if the men had been "*Portuguese.*"

Captain Neves was now actively engaged in preparing a present, worth about fifty pounds, to be sent by Pombeiros to Matiamvo. It consisted of great quantities of cotton cloth, a large carpet, an arm-chair with a canopy and curtains of crimson calico, an iron bedstead, mosquito curtains, beads, &c., and a number of pictures rudely painted in oil by an embryo black painter at Cassange.

Matiamvo, like most of the natives in the interior of the country, has a strong desire to possess a cannon, and had sent ten large tusks to purchase one; but being government property, it could not be sold: he was now furnished with a blunderbuss, mounted as a cannon, which would probably please him as well.

Senhor Graça and some other Portuguese have visited this chief at different times; but no European resides beyond the Quango; indeed, it is contrary to the policy of the government of Angola, to allow their subjects to penetrate further into the interior. The present would have been a good opportunity for me to have visited that chief, and I felt strongly inclined to do so, as he had expressed dissatisfaction respecting my treatment by the Chiboque, and even threatened to punish them. As it would be improper to force my men to go thither, I resolved to wait and see whether the proposition might not emanate from themselves. When I can get the natives to agree in the propriety of any step, they go to the end of the affair without a murmur. I speak to them and treat them as rational beings, and generally get on well with them in consequence.

I have already remarked on the unhealthiness of Cassange; and Captain Neves, who possesses an observing turn of mind, had noticed that always when the west wind blows, much fever immediately follows. As long as easterly winds prevail, all enjoy good health; but in January, February, March, and April, the winds are variable, and sickness is general. The unhealthiness of the westerly winds probably results from malaria, appearing to be heavier than common air, and sweeping down into the valley of Cassange from the western plateau, somewhat in the same way as the carbonic acid gas from bean-fields is supposed by colliers to do into coalpits. In the west of Scotland, strong objections are made, by that body of men, to farmers planting beans in their vicinity, from the belief that they render the mines unhealthy. The gravitation of the malaria from the more elevated land of Tala Mungongo towards Cassange, is the only way the unhealthiness of this spot on the prevalence of the westerly winds can be accounted for. The banks of the Quango, though much more marshy, and covered with ranker vegetation, are comparatively healthy; but thither the westerly wind does not seem to convey the noxious agent.

Feb. 20th.—On the day of starting from Cassange, the westerly wind blew strongly, and on the day following we were brought to a stand, by several of our party being laid up with fever. This complaint is the only serious drawback Angola possesses. It is in every other respect an agreeable land, and admirably adapted for yielding a rich abundance of tropical produce for the rest of the world. Indeed I have no hesitation in asserting, that, had it been in the possession of England, it would now have been yielding as much or more of the raw material for her manufactures, as an equal extent of territory in the cotton-growing States of America. A railway from Loanda to this valley, would secure the trade of most of the interior of South Central Africa.*

* The following statistics may be of interest to mercantile men. They show that since the repression of the slave-trade in Angola the value of the exports in lawful commerce has steadily augmented. We have no returns since 1850, but the prosperity of legitimate trade has suffered no check. The duties are noted in Portuguese money, "milreis," each of which is about three shillings in value.

RETURN of the Quantities and Value of the Staple Articles, the produce of the Province of ANGOLA, exported from ST. PAUL DE LOANDA between July 1, 1848, and June 30, 1849, specifying the quantities and value of those exported in Portuguese ships and in ships of other nations.

ARTICLES.			IN PORTUGUESE SHIPS.		IN SHIPS OF OTHER NATIONS.	
			Amount.	Value.	Amount.	Value.
				£. s. d.		£. s. d.
Ivory ..	.. ..	Cwt.	1454	35,350 0 0	515	12,875 0 0
Palm oil	.. ..	„	1440	2,160 0 0	6,671 1 qr.	10,036 17 6
Coffee ..	.. ..	„	152	304 0 0	684	1,368 0 0
Hides ..	.. ..	No.	1837	633 17 6	849	318 17 6
Gum ..	.. ..	Cwt.	147	205 16 0	4,763	6,668 4 0
Beeswax	.. ..	„	1109	6,654 0 0	544	3,264 0 0
Orchella	.. ..	Tons	630	23,940 0 0	..	.. .. ..
				69,247 13 6		34,530 19 0

TOTAL Quantity and Value of Exports from LOANDA.

							£. s. d.
Ivory	.. ..	.. ..	Cwt.	1,969	..	..	48,225 0 0
Palm oil	.. ..	.. ..	„	8,111 1 qr.	..	..	12,196 17 6
Coffee	.. ..	.. ..	„	836	..	..	1,672 0 0
Hides	.. ..	.. ..	No.	2,686	..	..	952 15 0
Gum	.. ..	.. ..	Cwt.	4,910	..	..	6,874 0 0
Beeswax..	.. ..	.. ..	„	1,653	..	..	9,918 0 0
Orchella..	.. ..	.. ..	Tons.	630	—	..	23,940 0 0
							£103,778 12 6

ABSTRACT

. As soon as we could move towards the Quango we did so, meeting in our course several trading parties, both native and Portuguese. We met two of the latter carrying a tusk weighing 126 lbs. The owner afterwards informed us that its fellow on the left side of the same elephant was 130 lbs. It was 8 feet 6½ inches long, and 21 inches in circumference at the part on which the lip of the animal rests. The elephant was rather a

ABSTRACT VIEW of the Net Revenue of the Customs at St. Paul de Loanda in quinquennial periods from 1818–19 to 1843–44, both included; and thence in each year to 1848–49.

	Duties on Importation.		Duties on Exportation.		Duties on Re-exportation.		Duties on Slaves.		Tonnage dues, Store rents, and other incidental receipts.	
	Mil.	reis.	Mil.	reis.	Mil.	reis.	Mil.	reis.	Mil.	reis.
1818–19	573	876	..		..		137,320	800	148,608	661
1823–24	3,490	752	460	420	..		120,843	000	133,446	892
1828–29	4,700	684	800	280	..		125,330	000	139,981	364
1833–34	7,490	000	1,590	000	..		139,280	000	158,978	640
1838–39	25,800	590	2,720	000	..		135,470	320	173,710	910
1843–44	53,240	000	4,320	000	..		72,195	230	138,255	230
1844–45	99,380	264	6,995	095	..		17,676	000	134,941	359
1845–46	150,233	789	9,610	735	..		5,116	500	181,423	550
1846–47	122,501	186	8,605	821	..		549	000	114,599	235
1847–48	119,246	826	9,718	676	4,097	868	1,231	200	146,321	476
1848–49	131,105	453	9,969	960	2,164	309	1,183	500	157,152	400
	718,763	420	54,790	987			756,195	550		
	=£102,680		=£7,827				=£108,028			

	Net Revenue of Customs.			Revenue from other sources.			Total Net Revenue.			Total Amount of Charges.		
	£.	s.	d.	£.	s.	d.	£.	s.	d.	£.	s.	d.
1844–45	26,988	5	5	9,701	10	8	36,689	16	1	53,542	5	4
1845–46	36,284	14	2	24,580	4	10	60,864	19	0	56,695	9	7
1846–47	28,919	16	11	23,327	9	11	52,247	6	10	52,180	9	7
1847–48	29,264	5	10	24,490	11	8	53,754	17	6	53,440	8	8
1848–49	31,430	9	7	18,868	3	10	51,298	13	5	50,686	3	3

The above account exhibits the total revenue and charges of the government of St. Paul de Loanda in each year, from 1844–45 to 1848–49, both included. The above three tables are copied from the appendix to a despatch-sent by Mr. Gabriel to Viscount Palmerston, dated 5th August, 1850, and, among other facts of interest, show a very satisfactory diminution in the duties upon slaves.

The returns from 1818 to 1844 have been obtained from different sources as the average revenue; those from 1844 to 1849 are from the Custom-house records.

small one, as is common in this hot central region. Some idea may be formed of the strength of his neck, when it is recollected that he bore a weight of 256 lbs. The ivory which comes from the east and north-east of Cassange, is very much larger than any to be found further south. Captain Neves had one weighing 120 lbs.; and this weight is by no means uncommon. They have been found weighing even 158 lbs.

Before reaching the Quango we were again brought to a stand by fever in two of my companions, close to the residence of a Portuguese who rejoiced in the name of William Tell, and who lived here, in spite of the prohibition of the government. We were using the water of a pond, and this gentleman having come to invite me to dinner, drank a little of it, and caught fever in consequence. If malarious matter existed in water, it would have been a wonder had we escaped; for, travelling in the sun, with the thermometer from 96°. to 98° in the shade, the evaporation from our bodies causing much thirst, we generally partook of every water we came to. We had probably thus more disease than others might suffer who had better shelter.

Mr. Tell remarked that his garden was rather barren, being still, as he said, wild; but when more worked it would become better, though no manure be applied. My men were busy collecting a better breed of fowls and pigeons than those in their own country. Mr. Tell presented them with some large specimens from Rio Janeiro. Of these they were wonderfully proud, and bore the cock in triumph through the country of the Balonda, as evidence of having been to the sea. But when at the village of Shinte, a hyæna came into our midst when we were all sound asleep, and picked out the giant in his basket from eighty-four others, and he was lost, to the great grief of my men. The anxiety these people have always shown to improve the breed of their domestic animals, is, I think, a favourable point in their character. On looking at the common breeds in the possession of the Portuguese, which are merely native cattle, and seeing them slaughter both heifer-calves and cows, which they themselves never do, and likewise making no use of the milk, they concluded that the Portuguese must be an inferior race of white men. They never ceased remarking on the fine ground for gardens over which we were passing; and when I happened to mention that most of the flour which the Portuguese consumed, came from another country, they exclaimed, " Are they ignorant of tillage?" "They know nothing but buying and selling: they are not men!" I hope it may reach the ears of my Angolese friends, and that they may be stirred up to develop the resources of their fine country.

On coming back to Cypriano's village on the 28th, we found that his step-father had died after we had passed, and, according to the custom of the country, he had spent more than his patrimony in funeral orgies. He acted with his wonted kindness, though, unfortunately, drinking has got him so deeply into debt, that he now keeps out of the way of his creditors. He informed us that the source of the Quango is eight days, or one hundred miles, to the south of this, and in a range called Mosamba, in the country of the Basongo. We can see from this, a sort of break in the high land which stretches away round to Tala Mongongo, through which the river comes.

A death had occurred in a village about a mile off, and the people were busy beating drums and firing guns. The funeral rites are half festive, half mourning, partaking somewhat of the character of an Irish wake. There is nothing more heartrending than their death wails. When the natives turn their eyes to the future world, they have a view cheerless enough of their own utter helplessness and hopelessness. They fancy themselves completely in the power of the disembodied spirits, and look upon the prospect of following them, as the greatest of misfortunes. Hence they are constantly deprecating the wrath of departed souls, believing that, if they are appeased, there is no other cause of death but witchcraft, which may be averted by charms. The whole of the coloured population of Angola are sunk in these gross superstitions, but have the opinion, notwithstanding, that they are wiser in these matters than their white neighbours. Each tribe has a consciousness of following its own best interests in the best way. They are by no means destitute of that self-esteem which is so common in other nations; yet they fear all manner of phantoms, and have half-developed ideas and traditions of something or other, they know not what. The pleasures of animal life are ever present to their minds as the supreme good; and, but for the innumerable invisibilities, they might enjoy their luxurious climate as much as it is possible for man to do. I have often thought, in travelling through their land, that it presents pictures of beauty which angels might enjoy. How often have I beheld, in still mornings, scenes the very essence of beauty, and all bathed in a quiet air of delicious warmth! yet the occasional soft motion imparted a pleasing sensation of coolness as of a fan. Green grassy meadows, the cattle feeding, the goats browsing, the kids skipping, the groups of herdboys with miniature bows, arrows, and spears; the women wending their way to the river with watering-pots poised jauntily on their heads; men sewing under the shady banians; and old grey-headed fathers sitting on the ground, with staff in hand, listening to the morning gossip, while others carry trees or branches to repair their hedges; and all this, flooded with the bright African sunshine, and the birds singing among the branches before the heat of the day has become intense, form pictures which can never be forgotten.

We were informed that a chief named Gando, living on the other side of the river, having been accused of witchcraft, was killed by the ordeal, and his body thrown into the Quango.

The ferrymen demanded thirty yards of calico, but received six thankfully. The canoes were wretched, carrying only two persons at a time; but my men being well acquainted with the water, we all got over in about two hours and a half. They excited the admiration of the inhabitants by the manner in which they managed the cattle and donkeys in crossing. The most stubborn of beasts found himself powerless in their hands. Five or six, seizing hold on one, bundled him at once into the stream, and, in this predicament, he always thought it best policy to give in and swim. The men sometimes swam along with the cattle, and forced them to go on by dashing water at their heads. The difference between my men and those of the native traders who accompanied us, was never more apparent than now; for while my men felt an interest in everything we possessed in common, theirs were rather glad when the oxen refused to cross, for, being obliged to slaughter them on such occasions, the loss to their masters was a welcome feast to themselves.

On the eastern side of the Quango we passed on, without visiting our friend of the conical head-dress, to the residence of some Ambakistas who had crossed the river in order to secure the first

chances of trade in wax. I have before remarked on the knowledge of reading and writing that these Ambakistas possess; they
are famed for their love of all sorts of learning within their reach,
a knowledge of the history of Portugal, Portuguese law, &c. &c.
They are remarkably keen in trade, and are sometimes called the
Jews of Angola. They are employed as clerks and writers, their
feminine delicacy of constitution enabling them to write a fine
lady's hand, a kind of writing much esteemed amongst the Portuguese. They are not physically equal to the European Portuguese,
but possess considerable ability; and it is said that half-castes, in
the course of a few generations, return to the black colour of the
maternal ancestor. The black population of Angola has become
much deteriorated. They are not so strongly formed as the independent tribes. A large quantity of aguardente, an inferior kind
of spirit, is imported into the country, which is most injurious in
its effects. We saw many parties carrying casks of this baneful
liquor to the independent chiefs beyond; and were informed that
it is difficult for any trader to convey it far, carriers being in the
habit of helping themselves by means of a straw, and then inject-
ing an equal amount of water, when near the point of delivery.
To prevent this, it is common to see large demijohns with padlocks
on the corks. These are frequently stolen. In fact, the carriers
are much addicted to both lying and thieving, as might be expected from the lowest class of a people, on whom the debasing
slave system has acted for two centuries.

The Bashinje, in whose country we now are, seem to possess
more of the low negro character and physiognomy, than either
the Balonda or Basongo; their colour is generally dirty black,
foreheads low and compressed, noses flat and much expanded
laterally, though this is partly owing to the alæ spreading over
the cheeks, by the custom of inserting bits of sticks or reeds in
the septum; their teeth are deformed by being filed to points;
their lips are large. They make a nearer approach to a general
negro appearance than any tribes I met; but I did not notice
this on my way down. They cultivate pretty largely, and rely
upon their agricultural products for their supplies of salt, flesh,
tobacco, &c., from Bangalas. Their clothing consists of pieces of
skin, hung loosely from the girdle in front and behind. They
plait their hair fantastically. We saw some women coming with

their hair woven into the form of a European hat, and it was only by a closer inspection that its nature was detected. Others had it arranged in tufts, with a threefold cord along the ridge of each tuft; while others, again, follow the ancient Egyptian fashion, having the whole mass of wool plaited into cords, all hanging down as far as the shoulders. This mode, with the somewhat Egyptian cast of countenance in other parts of Londa, reminded me strongly of the paintings of that nation in the British Museum.

We had now rain every day, and the sky seldom presented that cloudless aspect and clear blue, so common in the dry lands of the south. The heavens are often overcast by large white motionless masses, which stand for hours in the same position, and the intervening spaces are filled with a milk-and-water-looking haze. Notwithstanding these unfavourable circumstances, I obtained good observations for the longitude of this important point on both sides of the Quango, and found the river running in 9° 50′ S. lat., 18° 33′ E. long.

On proceeding to our former station near Sansawe's village, he ran to meet us with wonderful urbanity, asking if we had seen Moene Put, king of the white men (or Portuguese); and added, on parting, that he would come to receive his dues in the evening. I replied that, as he had treated us so scurvily, even forbidding his people to sell us any food, if he did not bring a fowl and some eggs, as part of his duty as a chief, he should receive no present from me. When he came, it was in the usual Londa way of showing the exalted position he occupies, mounted on the shoulders of his spokesman, as schoolboys sometimes do in England, and as was represented to have been the case in the southern islands when Captain Cook visited them. My companions, amused at his idea of dignity, greeted him with a hearty laugh. He visited the native traders first, and then came to me with two cocks as a present. I spoke to him about the impolicy of the treatment we had received at his hands, and quoted the example of the Bangalas, who had been conquered by the Portuguese, for their extortionate demands of payment for firewood, grass, water, &c.; and concluded by denying his right to any payment for simply passing through uncultivated land. To all this he agreed; and then I gave him, as a token of friendship, a pannikin of coarse powder, two iron spoons, and two yards of coarse printed calico. He looked rather saucily at these articles, for he had just received a barrel containing 18 lbs. of powder, 24 yards of calico, and two bottles of brandy, from Senhor Pascoal the Pombeiro. Other presents were added the next day, but we gave nothing more; and the Pombeiros informed me that it was necessary to give largely, because they are accompanied by slaves and carriers who are no great friends to their masters; and if they did not secure the friendship of these petty chiefs, many slaves and their loads might be stolen while passing through the forests. It is thus a sort of black-mail that these insignificant chiefs levy; and the native traders, in paying, do so simply as a bribe to keep them honest. This chief was a man of no power; but in our former ignorance of this, he plagued us a whole day in passing.

Finding the progress of Senhor Pascoal and the other Pombeiros excessively slow, I resolved to forego his company to Cabango, after I had delivered to him some letters to be sent back to Cassange. I went forward with the intention of finishing my writing, and leaving a packet for him at some village. We ascended the eastern acclivity that bounds the Cassange valley, which has rather a gradual ascent up from the Quango, and we found that the last ascent, though apparently not quite so high as that at Tala Mungongo, is actually much higher. The top is about 5000 feet above the level of the sea, and the bottom 3500 feet; water boiling on the heights at 202°, the thermometer in the air showing 96°; and at the bottom at 205°, the air being 75°. We had now gained the summit of the western subtending ridge, and began to descend towards the centre of the country, hoping soon to get out of the Chiboque territory, which, when we ascended from the Cassange valley, we had entered, but on the 19th of April the intermittent, which had begun on the 16th of March, was changed into an extremely severe attack of rheumatic fever. This was brought on by being obliged to sleep on an extensive plain covered with water. The rain poured down incessantly, but we formed our beds by dragging up the earth into oblong mounds, somewhat like graves in a country churchyard, and then placing grass upon them. The rain continuing to deluge us, we were unable to leave for two days, but as soon as it became fair we continued our march. The heavy dew upon the high grass was so cold, as to cause shivering, and I was forced to lie by for eight days, tossing and groaning with violent pain in the head. This was the most severe attack I had endured. It made me quite unfit to move, or even know what was passing outside my little tent. Senhor Pascoal, who had been detained by the severe rain at a better spot, at last came up, and, knowing that leeches abounded in the rivulets, procured a number, and applied some dozens to the nape of the neck and the loins. This partially relieved the pain. He was then obliged to move forward, in order to purchase food for his large party. After many days I began to recover, and wished to move on, but my men objected to the attempt on account of my weakness. When Senhor Pascoal had been some time at the village in front, as he had received instructions from his employer Captain Neves to aid me as much as possible, and being himself a kindly-disposed person, he sent back two messengers to invite me to come on, if practicable.

It happened that the head-man of the village where I had lain twenty-two days, while bargaining and quarrelling in my camp for a piece of meat, had been struck on the mouth by one of my men. My principal men paid five pieces of cloth and a gun as an atonement; but the more they yielded, the more exorbitant he became, and he sent word to all the surrounding villages to aid him in avenging the affront of a blow on the beard. As their courage usually rises with success, I resolved to yield no more, and departed. In passing through a forest in the country beyond, we were startled by a body of men rushing after us. They began by knocking down the burdens of the hindermost of my men, and several shots were fired, each party spreading out on both sides of the path. I fortunately had a six-barrelled revolver, which my friend Captain Henry Need, of her Majesty's brig "Linnet," had considerately sent to Golungo Alto after my departure from Loanda. Taking this in my hand, and forgetting fever, I staggered quickly along the path with two or three of my men, and fortunately encountered the chief. The sight of the six barrels gaping into his stomach, with my own ghastly visage looking daggers at his face, seemed to produce an instant revolution in his martial feelings, for he cried out, "Oh! I have only come to speak to you, and wish peace only." Mashauana had hold of him by the hand, and found him shaking. We examined his gun, and found that it had been discharged. Both parties crowded up to their chiefs. One of the opposite party coming too near, one of mine drove him back with a battle-axe. The enemy protested their amicable intentions, and my men asserted the fact of having the goods knocked down as evidence of the contrary. Without waiting long, I requested all to sit down, and Pitsane, placing his hand upon the revolver, somewhat allayed their fears. I then said to the chief, "If you have come with peaceable intentions, we have no other; go away home to your village." He replied, "I am afraid lest you shoot me in the back." I rejoined, "If I wanted to kill you, I could shoot you in the face as well." Mosantu called out to me, "That's only a Makalaka trick; don't give him your back." But I said, "Tell him to observe that I am not afraid of him;" and, turning, mounted my ox. There was not much danger in the fire that was opened at first, there being so many trees. The enemy probably expected that the sudden attack would make us forsake our goods, and allow them to plunder with ease. The villagers were no doubt pleased with being allowed to retire unscathed, and we were also glad to get away without having shed a drop of blood, or having compromised ourselves for any future visit. My men were delighted with their own bravery, and made the woods ring with telling each other how "brilliant their conduct before the enemy" would have been, had hostilities not been brought to a sudden close.

I do not mention this little skirmish as a very frightful affair. The negro character in these parts, and in Angola, is essentially cowardly, except when influenced by success. A partial triumph over any body of men would induce the whole country to rise in arms, and this is the chief danger to be feared. These petty chiefs have individually but little power, and with my men, now armed with guns, I could have easily beaten them off singly; but, being of the same family, they would readily unite in vast numbers, if incited by prospects of successful plunder. They are by no means equal to the Cape Caffres in any respect whatever.

In the evening we came to Moena Kikanje, and found him a sensible man. He is the last of the Chiboque chiefs in this direction, and is in alliance with Matiamvo, whose territory commences a short distance beyond. His village is placed on the east bank of the Quilo, which is here twenty yards wide, and breast deep.

The country was generally covered with forest, and we slept every night at some village. I was so weak, and had become so deaf from the effects of the fever, that I was glad to avail myself of the company of Senhor Pascoal and the other native traders. Our rate of travelling was only two geographical miles per hour, and the average number of hours three and a half per day, or seven miles. Two-thirds of the month was spent in stoppages, there being only ten travelling days in each month. The stoppages were caused by sickness, and the necessity of remaining in different parts to purchase food; and also because, when one carrier was sick, the rest refused to carry his load.

One of the Pombeiros had eight good-looking women in a chain, whom he was taking to the country of Matiamvo to sell for ivory. They always looked ashamed when I happened to come near them, and must have felt keenly their forlorn and degraded position. I believe they were captives taken from the rebel Cassanges. The way in which slaves are spoken of in Angola and eastern Africa, must sound strangely even to the owners, when they first come from Europe. In Angola the common appellation is "o diabo," or "brutu;" and it is quite usual to hear gentlemen call out "O diabo! bring fire." In eastern Africa, on the contrary, they apply the term "bicho" (an animal), and you hear the phrase, "Call the *animal* to do this or that." In fact, slave-owners come to regard their slaves as not human, and will curse them as the "race of a dog." Most of the carriers of my travelling companions were hired Basongo, and required constant vigilance to prevent them stealing the goods they carried. Salt, which is one of the chief articles conveyed into the country, became considerably lighter as we went along, but the carriers shielded themselves, by saying that it had been melted by the rain. Their burdens were taken from them every evening, and placed in security under the guardianship of Senhor Pascoal's own slaves. It was pitiable to observe the worrying life he led. There was the greatest contrast possible between the conduct of his people, and that of my faithful Makololo.

We crossed the Loange, a deep but narrow stream, by a bridge. It becomes much larger, and contains hippopotami, lower down. It is the boundary of Londa on the west. We slept also on the banks of the Pezo, now flooded, and could not but admire their capabilities for easy irrigation. On reaching the river Chikapa (lat. 10° 10′ S., long. 19° 42′ E.), the 25th of March, we found it fifty or sixty yards wide, and flowing E.N.E. into the Kasai. The adjacent country is of the same level nature as that part of Londa formerly described; but, having come further to the eastward than our previous course, we found that all the rivers had worn for themselves much deeper valleys than at the points we had formerly crossed them.

Surrounded on all sides by large gloomy forests, the people of these parts have a much more indistinct idea of the geography of their country, than those who live in hilly regions. It was only after long and patient inquiry, that I became fully persuaded that the Quilo runs into the Chikapa. As we now crossed them both considerably further down, and were greatly to the eastward of our first route, there can be no doubt that these rivers take the same course as the others, into the Kasai, and that I had been led into a mistake in saying that any of them flowed to the westward. Indeed it was only at this time, that I began to perceive that all the western feeders of the Kasai, except the Quango, flow first from the western side towards the centre of the country, then gradually turn, with the Kasai itself, to the north; and, after the confluence of the Kasai with the Quango, an immense body of water, collected from all these branches, finds its way out of the country by means of the river Congo or Zaire on the west coast.

The people living along the path we are now following were quite accustomed to the visits of native traders, and did not feel in any way bound to make presents of food, except for the purpose of cheating: thus, a man gave me a fowl and some meal, and, after a short time, returned. I offered him a handsome present of beads; but these he declined, and demanded a cloth instead, which was far more than the value of his gift. They did the same with my men, until we had to refuse presents altogether. Others made high demands because I slept in a "house of cloth," and must be rich. They seemed to think that they had a perfect right to payment, for simply passing through the country.

Beyond the Chikapa, we crossed the Kamáue, a small deep stream, proceeding from the S.S.W., and flowing into the Chikapa.

On the 30th of April we reached the Loajima, where we had to form a bridge to effect our passage. This was not so difficult an operation as some might imagine; for a tree was growing in a horizontal position across part of the stream, and, there being no want of the tough climbing plants which admit of being knitted like ropes, Senhor P. soon constructed a bridge. The Loajima was here about twenty-five yards wide, but very much deeper than where I had crossed before on the shoulders of Mashauana. The last rain of this season had fallen on the 28th, and had suddenly been followed by a great decrease of the temperature. The people in these parts seemed more slender in form, and their colour a lighter olive, than any we had hitherto met. The mode of dressing the great masses of woolly hair, which lay upon their

No. 1.   A Londa lady's mode of wearing the hair.

shoulders, together with their general features, again reminded me of the ancient Egyptians. Several were seen with the upward inclination of the outer angles of the eyes, but this was not general. A few of the ladies adopt a curious custom of attaching the hair to a hoop which encircles the head, giving it somewhat the appearance of the glory round the head of the Virgin (woodcut No. 1). Some have a small hoop behind that represented in the woodcut. Others wear an ornament of woven hair and hide adorned with beads. The hair of the tails of buffaloes, which are to be found further east, is sometimes added. This is

2 G

represented in No. 2. While others, as in No. 3, weave their own hair on pieces of hide into the form of buffalo-horns, or,

No. 2.

as in No. 4, make a single horn in front. The features given are frequently met with, but they are by no means universal. Many tattoo their bodies by inserting some black substance

No. 3.

beneath the skin, which leaves an elevated cicatrix about half
an inch long: these are made in the form of stars, and other
figures, of no particular beauty.

No. 4. A young man's fashion.

CHAPTER XXIII.

WE made a little détour to the southward, in order to get provisions in a cheaper market. This led us along the rivulet called
Tamba, where we found the people, who had not been visited so
frequently by the slave-traders as the rest, rather timid and very
civil. It was agreeable to get again among the uncontaminated,
and to see the natives look at us without that air of supercilious-
ness, which is so unpleasant and common in the beaten track.
The same olive colour prevailed. They file their teeth to a point,
which makes the smile of the women frightful, as it reminds one
of the grin of an alligator. The inhabitants throughout this
country, exhibit as great a variety of taste, as appears on the
surface of society amongst ourselves. Many of the men are
dandies; their shoulders are always wet with the oil dropping
from their lubricated hair, and everything about them is ornamented in one way or another. Some thrum a musical instrument
the livelong day, and, when they wake at night, proceed at once
to their musical performance. Many of these musicians are too
poor to have iron keys to their instrument, but make them of

bamboo, and persevere, though no one hears the music but themselves.   Others try to appear warlike by never going out of their huts, except with a load of bows and arrows, or a gun ornamented with a strip of hide for every animal they have shot; and others never go anywhere without a canary in a cage.   Ladies may be seen carefully tending little lapdogs, which are intended to be eaten.   Their villages are generally in forests, and composed of groups of irregularly planted brown huts, with banana and cotton trees, and tobacco growing around.   There is also at every hut a high stage erected for drying manioc roots and meal, and elevated cages to hold domestic fowls.   Round baskets are laid on the thatch of the huts, for the hens to lay in, and on the arrival of strangers, men, women, and children ply their calling as hucksters, with a great deal of noisy haggling; all their transactions are conducted with civil banter and good temper.

My men, having the meat of the oxen which we slaughtered from time to time for sale, were entreated to exchange it for meal; no matter how small the pieces offered were, it gave them pleasure to deal.

The landscape around is green, with a tint of yellow, the grass long, the paths about a foot wide, and generally worn deeply in the middle.   The tall overhanging grass, when brushed against by the feet and legs, disturbed the lizards and mice, and occasionally a serpent, causing a rustling amongst the herbage.   There are not many birds; every animal is entrapped and eaten.   Gins are seen on both sides of the path every ten or fifteen yards, for miles together.   The time and labour required to dig up moles and mice from their burrows, would, if applied to cultivation, afford food for any amount of fowls or swine, but the latter are seldom met with.

We passed on through forests abounding in climbing-plants, many of which are so extremely tough, that a man is required to go in front with a hatchet; and when the burdens of the carriers are caught, they are obliged to cut the climbers with their teeth, for no amount of tugging will make them break.   The paths in all these forests are so zigzag, that a person may imagine he has travelled a distance of thirty miles, which, when reckoned as the crow flies, may not be fifteen.

We reached the river Moamba (lat. 9° 38′ S., long. 20° 13′ 34″

E.) on the 7th May. This is a stream of thirty yards wide, and, like the Quilo, Loange, Chikapa, and Loajima, contains both alligators and hippopotami. We crossed it by means of canoes. Here, as on the slopes down to the Quilo and Chikapa, we had an opportunity of viewing the geological structure of the country,— a capping of ferruginous conglomerate, which in many parts looks as if it had been melted, for the rounded nodules resemble masses of slag, and they have a smooth scale on the surface; but in all probability it is an aqueous deposit, for it contains water-worn pebbles of all sorts, and generally small. Below this mass, lies a pale-red hardened sandstone, and beneath that, a trap-like whinstone. Lowest of all lies a coarse-grained sandstone containing a few pebbles, and in connection with it, a white calcareous rock is occasionally met with, and so are banks of loose round quartz pebbles. The slopes are longer from the level country above, the further we go eastward, and everywhere we meet with circumscribed bogs on them, surrounded by clumps of straight, lofty, evergreen trees, which look extremely graceful on a ground of yellowish grass. Several of these bogs pour forth a solution of iron, which exhibits on its surface the prismatic colours. The level plateaus between the rivers, both east and west of the Moamba, across which we travelled, were less woody than the river glens. The trees on them are scraggy and wide apart. There are also large open grass-covered spaces, with scarcely even a bush. On these rather dreary intervals between the rivers, it was impossible not to be painfully struck with the absence of all animal life. Not a bird was to be seen, except occasionally a tomtit, some of the *Sylviadæ* and *Drymoica*, also a black bird (*Dicrurus Ludwigii*, Smith), common throughout the country. We were gladdened by the voice of birds only near the rivers, and there they are neither numerous nor varied. The Senegal longclaw, however, maintains its place, and is the largest bird seen. We saw a butcher-bird in a trap as we passed. There are remarkably few small animals, they having been hunted almost to extermination, and few insects except ants, which abound in considerable number and variety. There are scarcely any common flies to be seen, nor are we ever troubled by mosquitoes.

The air is still, hot, and oppressive; the intensely bright sunlight glances peacefully on the evergreen forest leaves, and all feel glad when the path comes into the shade. The want of life in the scenery made me long to tread again the banks of the Zambesi, and see the graceful antelopes feeding beside the dark buffaloes and sleek elands. Here hippopotami are known to exist only by their footprints on the banks. Not one is ever seen to blow or put his head up at all; they have learned to breathe in silence, and keep out of sight. We never heard one uttering the snorting sound so common on the Zambesi.

We crossed two small streams, the Kanesi and Fombeji, before reaching Cabango, a village situated on the banks of the Chihombo. The country was becoming more densely peopled as we proceeded, but it bears no population compared to what it might easily sustain. Provisions were to be had in great abundance; a fowl and basket of meal weighing 20 lbs. were sold for a yard and a half of very inferior cotton-cloth, worth not more than three pence. An idea of the cheapness of food may be formed from the fact, that Captain Neves purchased 380 lbs. of tobacco from the Bangalas, for about two pounds sterling. This, when carried into central Londa, might purchase seven thousand five hundred fowls, or feed with meal and fowls seven thousand persons for one day, giving each a fowl and 5 lbs. of meal. When food is purchased here with either salt or coarse calico, four persons can be well fed with animal and vegetable food at the rate of one penny a day. The chief vegetable food is the manioc and lotsa meal. These contain a very large proportion of starch, and when eaten alone for any length of time, produce most distressing heartburn. As we ourselves experienced in coming north, they also cause a weakness of vision, which occurs in the case of animals fed on pure gluten or amyllaceous matter only. I now discovered that when these starchy substances are eaten along with a proportion of ground-nuts, which contain a considerable quantity of oil, no injurious effects follow.

While on the way to Cabango, we saw fresh tracks of elands, the first we had observed in this country. A poor little slave-girl, being ill, turned aside in the path, and, though we waited all the next day making search for her, she was lost. She was tall and slender for her age, as if of too quick growth, and probably, unable to bear the fatigue of the march, lay down and slept in the forest, then, waking in the dark, went farther and farther astray. The treatment of the slaves witnessed by my men, certainly did not raise slaveholders in their estimation. Their usual exclamation was, " Ga ba na pelu " (They have no heart) ; and they added, with reference to the slaves, " Why do they let them ?" as if they thought that the slaves had the natural right to rid the world of such heartless creatures, and ought to do it. The uneasiness of the trader was continually showing itself, and, upon the whole, he had reason to be on the alert both day and night. The carriers perpetually stole the goods intrusted to their care, and he could not openly accuse them, lest they should plunder him of all, and leave him quite in the lurch. He could only hope to manage them after getting all the remaining goods safely into a house in Cabango ; he might then deduct something from their pay, for what they had purloined on the way.

Cabango (lat. 9° 31' S., long. 20° 31' or 32' E.) is the dwelling-place of Muanzánza, one of Matiamvo's subordinate chiefs. His village consists of about two hundred huts, and ten or twelve square houses, constructed of poles with grass interwoven. The latter are occupied by half-caste Portuguese from Ambaca, agents for the Cassange traders. The cold in the mornings was now severe to the feelings, the thermometer ranging from 58° to 60°, though, when protected, sometimes standing as high as 64° at six A.M. When the sun is well up, the thermometer in the shade rises to 80°, and in the evenings it is about 78°.

A person having died in this village, we could transact no business with the chief, until the funeral obsequies were finished. These occupy about four days, during which there is a constant succession of dancing, wailing, and feasting. Guns are fired by day, and drums beaten by night, and all the relatives, dressed in fantastic caps, keep up the ceremonies with spirit proportionate to the amount of beer and beef expended. When there is a large expenditure, the remark is often made afterwards, " What a fine funeral that was ! " A figure, consisting chiefly of feathers and beads, is paraded on these occasions, and seems to be regarded as an idol.

Having met with an accident to one of my eyes, by a blow from a branch in passing through a forest, I remained some days here, endeavouring, though with much pain, to draw a sketch of the country thus far, to be sent back to Mr. Gabriel at Loanda.

I was always anxious to transmit an account of my discoveries on every possible occasion, lest, anything happening in the country to which I was going, they should be entirely lost. I also fondly expected a packet of letters and papers which my good angel at Loanda would be sure to send, if they came to hand, but I afterwards found that, though he had offered a large sum to any one who would return with an assurance of having delivered the last packet he sent, no one followed me with it to Cabango. The unwearied attentions of this good Englishman, from his first welcome to me when, a weary, dejected, and worn-down stranger, I arrived at his residence, and his whole subsequent conduct, will be held in lively remembrance by me to my dying day.

Several of the native traders here having visited the country of Luba, lying far to the north of this, and there being some visitors also from the town of Mai, which is situated far down the Kasai, I picked up some information respecting those distant parts. In going to the town of Mai the traders crossed only two large rivers, the Loajima and Chihombo. The Kasai flows a little to the east of the town of Mai, and near it there is a large waterfall. They describe the Kasai as being there of very great size, and that it thence bends round to the west. On asking an old man, who was about to return to his chief Mai, to imagine himself standing at his home, and point to the confluence of the Quango and Kasai, he immediately turned, and, pointing to the westward, said, " When we travel five days (thirty-five or forty miles) in that direction, we come to it." He stated also that the Kasai received another river, named the Lubilash. There is but one opinion among the Balonda respecting the Kasai and Quango. They invariably describe the Kasai as receiving the Quango, and, beyond the confluence, assuming the name of Zairé or Zerézeré. And the Kasai, even previous to the junction, is much larger than the Quango, from the numerous branches it receives. Besides those we have already crossed, there is the Chihombo at Cabango ; and, forty-two miles beyond this, eastward, runs the Kasai itself ; fourteen miles beyond that the Kaunguesi ; then, forty-two miles further east, flows the Lolua ; besides numbers of little streams, all of which contribute to swell the Kasai.

About thirty-four miles east of the Lolua, or a hundred and thirty-two miles E.N.E. of Cabango, stands the town of Matiamvo, the paramount chief of all the Balonda. The town of Mai is pointed out as to the N.N.W. of Cabango, and thirty-two days or two hundred and twenty-four miles distant, or about lat. S. 5° 45'. The chief town of Luba, another independent chief, is eight days farther in the same direction, or lat. S. 4° 50'. Judging from the appearance of the people who had come for the purposes of trade from Mai, those in the north are in quite as uncivilised a condition as the Balonda. They are clad in a kind of cloth made of the inner bark of a tree. Neither guns nor native traders are admitted into the country, the chief of Luba entertaining a dread of innovation. If a native trader goes thither, he must dress like the common people in Angola, in a loose robe resembling a kilt. The chief trades in shells and beads only. His people kill the elephants by means of spears, poisoned arrows, and traps. All assert that elephants' tusks from that country, are heavier, and of greater length, than any others.

It is evident, from all the information I could collect both here and elsewhere, that the drainage of Londa falls to the north and then runs westward. The countries of Luba and Mai are evidently lower than this, and yet this is of no great altitude—probably not much more than 3500 feet above the level of the sea. Having here received pretty certain information on a point in which I felt much interest, namely, that the Kasai is not navigable from the coast, owing to the large waterfall near the town of Mai, and that no great kingdom exists in the region beyond, between this and the equator, I would fain have visited Matiamvo. This seemed a very desirable step, as it is good policy as well as right, to acknowledge the sovereign of a country; and I was assured, both by Balonda and native traders, that a considerable branch of the Zambesi rises in the country east of his town, and flows away to the south. The whole of this branch, extending down even to where it turns westward to Masiko, is probably placed too far eastwards on the map. It was put down when I believed Matiamvo and Cazembe to be further east than I have since seen reason to believe them. All, being derived from native testimony, is offered to the reader with diffidence, as needing verification by actual explorers. The people of that part, named Kanyika and Kanyoka, living on its banks, are represented as both numerous and friendly, but Matiamvo will on no account

permit any white person to visit them, as his principal supplies of
ivory are drawn from them. Thinking that we might descend this
branch of the Zambesi to Masiko, and thence to the Barotse, I felt
a strong inclination to make the attempt. The goods, however, we
had brought with us to pay our way, had, by the long detention
from fever and weakness in both myself and men, dwindled to a
mere fragment; and, being but slightly acquainted with the
Balonda dialect, I felt that I could neither use persuasion nor
presents to effect my object. From all I could hear of Matiamvo,
there was no chance of my being allowed to proceed through his
country to the southward. If I had gone merely to visit him, all
the goods would have been expended by the time I returned to
Cabango; and we had not found mendicity so pleasant on our
way to the north, as to induce us to desire to return to it.

The country of Matiamvo is said to be well peopled, but they
have little or no trade. They receive calico, salt, gunpowder,
coarse earthenware, and beads, and give in return ivory and
slaves. They possess no cattle, Matiamvo alone having a single
herd, which he keeps entirely for the sake of the flesh. The
present chief is said to be mild in his government, and will depose
an under-chief for unjust conduct. He occasionally sends the
distance of a hundred miles or more, to behead an offending
officer. But though I was informed by the Portuguese that he
possesses absolute power, his name had less influence over his
subjects with whom I came in contact, than that of Sekeletu has,
over his people living at a much greater distance from the capital.

As we thought it best to strike away to the S.E. from Cabango
to our old friend Katema, I asked a guide from Muanzanza as
soon as the funeral proceedings were over. He agreed to furnish
one, and also accepted a smaller present from me than usual,
when it was represented to him by Pascoal and Faria that I was
not a trader. He seemed to regard these presents as his proper
dues; and as a cargo of goods had come by Senhor Pascoal, he
entered the house for the purpose of receiving his share, when
Senhor Faria gravely presented him with the commonest earthenware vessel, of which great numbers are brought for this trade.
The chief received it with expressions of abundant gratitude, as
these vessels are highly valued because from their depth they can
hold so much food or beer. The association of ideas is some-

times so very ludicrous, that it is difficult to maintain one's gravity.

Several of the children of the late Matiamvo came to beg from me, but never to offer any food. Having spoken to one young man named Liula (Heavens) about their stinginess, he soon brought bananas and manioc. I liked his appearance and conversation; and believe that the Balonda would not be difficult to teach, but their mode of life would be a drawback. The Balonda in this quarter are much more agreeable-looking than any of the inhabitants nearer the coast. The women allow their teeth to remain in their beautifully white state, and would be comely, but for the custom of inserting pieces of reed into the cartilage of the nose. They seem generally to be in good spirits, and spend their time in everlasting talk, funeral ceremonies, and marriages. This flow of animal spirits must be one reason why they are such an indestructible race. The habitual influence on their minds of the agency of unseen spirits, may have a tendency in the same direction, by preserving the mental quietude of a kind of fatalism.

We were forced to prepay our guide and his father too, and he went but one day, although he promised to go with us to Katema. He was not in the least ashamed at breaking his engagements, and probably no disgrace will be attached to the deed by Muanzanza. Among the Bakwains he would have been punished. My men would have stripped him of the wages which he wore on his person, but thought that, as we had always acted on the mildest principles, they would let him move off with his unearned gains.

They frequently lamented the want of knowledge in these people, saying in their own tongue, "Ah! they don't know that we are men as well as they, and that we are only bearing with their insolence with patience because we are men." Then would follow a hearty curse, showing that the patience was nearly expended; but they seldom quarrelled in the language of the Balonda. The only one who ever lost his temper, was the man who struck a head-man of one of the villages on the mouth, and he was the most abject individual in our company.

The reason why we needed a guide at all, was, to secure the convenience of a path, which, though generally no better than a sheep-walk, is much easier than going straight in one direction, through tangled forests and tropical vegetation. We knew the general direction we ought to follow, and also if any deviation occurred from our proper route; but to avoid impassable forests and untreadable bogs, and to get to the proper fords of the rivers, we always tried to procure a guide, and he always followed the common path from one village to another when that lay in the direction we were going.

After leaving Cabango on the 21st, we crossed several little streams running into the Chihombo on our left, and in one of them I saw tree ferns (*Cyathea dregei*) for the first time in Africa. The trunk was about four feet high and ten inches in diameter. We saw also grass trees of two varieties, which in damp localities had attained a height of forty feet. On crossing the Chihombo, which we did about twelve miles above Cabango, we found it waist-deep and rapid. We were delighted to see the evidences of buffalo and hippopotami on its banks. As soon as we got away from the track of the slave-traders, the more kindly spirit of the southern Balonda appeared, for an old man brought a large present of food from one of the villages, and volunteered to go as guide himself. The people, however, of the numerous villages which we passed, always made efforts to detain us, that they might have a little trade in the way of furnishing our suppers. At one village, indeed, they would not show us the path at all, unless we remained at least a day with them. Having refused, we took a path in the direction we ought to go, but it led us into an inextricable thicket. Returning to the village again, we tried another footpath in a similar direction; but this led us into an equally impassable and trackless forest. We were thus forced to come back and remain. In the following morning they put us in the proper path, which in a few hours led us through a forest, that would otherwise have taken us days to penetrate.

Beyond this forest we found the village of Nyakalonga, a sister of the late Matiamvo, who treated us handsomely. She wished her people to guide us to the next village, but this they declined unless we engaged in trade. She then requested us to wait an hour or two till she could get ready a present of meal, manioc-roots, ground-nuts, and a fowl. It was truly pleasant to meet with people possessing some civility, after the hauteur we had experienced on the slave-path. She sent her son to the next village without requiring payment. The stream which ran past

her village was quite impassable there, and for a distance of about
a mile on either side, the bog being soft and shaky, and, when the
crust was broken through, about six feet deep.

On the 28th we reached the village of the chief Bango (lat.
12° 22′ 53″ S., long. 20° 58′ E.), who brought us a handsome
present of meal, and the meat of an entire pallah. We here
slaughtered the last of the cows presented to us by Mr. Schut,
which I had kept milked, until it gave only a teaspoonful at a
time. My men enjoyed a hearty laugh when they found that I
had given up all hope of more, for they had been talking among
themselves about my perseverance. We offered a leg of the cow
to Bango; but he informed us that neither he nor his people ever
partook of beef, as they looked upon cattle as human, and living
at home like men. None of his people purchased any of the
meat, which was always eagerly done everywhere else. There
are several other tribes who refuse to keep cattle, though not to
eat them when offered by others, because, say they, oxen bring
enemies and war; but this is the first instance I have met with in
which they have been refused as food. The fact of killing the
pallahs for food, shows that the objection does not extend to
meat in general.

The little streams in this part of the country did not flow in
deep dells, nor were we troubled with the gigantic grasses, which
annoyed our eyes on the slopes of the streams before we came to
Cabango. The country was quite flat, and the people cultivated
manioc very extensively. There is no large collection of the
inhabitants in any one spot. The ambition of each seems to be
to have his own little village; and we see many coming from
distant parts with the flesh of buffaloes and antelopes as the tribute claimed by Bango. We have now entered again the country
of the game; but they are so exceedingly shy that we have not
yet seen a single animal. The arrangement into many villages,
pleases the Africans vastly, for every one who has a few huts under
him, feels himself in some measure to be a chief. The country at
this time is covered with yellowish grass quite dry. Some of the
bushes and trees are green; others are shedding their leaves, the
young buds pushing off the old foliage. Trees, which in the south
stand bare during the winter months, have here but a short period
of leaflessness. Occasionally, however, a cold north wind comes

up even as far as Cabango, and spreads a wintry aspect on all the exposed vegetation. The tender shoots of the evergreen trees on the south side become as if scorched; the leaves of manioc, pumpkins, and other tender plants, are killed; while the same kinds, in spots sheltered by forests, continue green through the whole year. All the interior of South Africa has a distinct winter of cold, varying in intensity with the latitudes. In the central parts of the Cape colony, the cold in the winter is often severe, and the ground is covered with snow. At Kuruman snow seldom falls, but the frost is keen. There is frost even as far as the Chobe, and a partial winter in the Barotse valley; but beyond the Orange River we never have cold and damp combined. Indeed a shower of rain seldom or never falls during winter, and hence the healthiness of the Bechuana climate. From the Barotse valley northwards, it is questionable if it ever freezes; but during the prevalence of the south wind, the thermometer sinks as low as 42°, and conveys the impression of bitter cold.

Nothing can exceed the beauty of the change from the wintry appearance to that of spring, at Kolobeng. Previous to the commencement of the rains, an easterly wind blows strongly by day, but dies away at night. The clouds collect in increasing masses, and relieve in some measure the bright glare of the southern sun. The wind dries up everything; and when at its greatest strength is hot, and raises clouds of dust. The general temperature during the day rises above 96°: then showers begin to fall; and if the ground is but once well soaked with a good day's rain, the change produced is marvellous. In a day or two a tinge of green is apparent all over the landscape; and in five or six days, the fresh leaves sprouting forth, and the young grass shooting up, give an appearance of spring which it requires weeks of a colder climate to produce. The birds, which in the hot dry windy season had been silent, now burst forth into merry twittering songs, and are busy building their nests. Some of them, indeed, hatch several times a-year. The lowering of the temperature, by rains or other causes, has much the same effect as the increasing mildness of our own spring. The earth teems with myriads of young insects; in some parts of the country hundreds of centipedes, myriapedes, and beetles, emerge from their hiding-places, somewhat as our snails at home do; and in the evenings the white ants swarm by thousands. A stream of them is seen to rush out of a hole, and, after flying one or two hundred yards, they descend; and if they light upon a piece of soil proper for the commencement of a new colony, they bend up their tails, unhook their wings, and, leaving them on the surface, quickly begin their mining operations. If an attempt is made to separate the wings from the body by drawing them away backwards, they seem as if hooked into the body, and tear away large portions of the insect; but if turned forward, as the ant itself does, they snap off with the greatest ease. Indeed they seem formed only to serve the insect in its short flight to a new habitation, and then to be thrown aside. Nothing can exceed the eagerness with which at the proper time they rush out from their birthplace. Occasionally this occurs in a house, and then, in order to prevent every corner from being filled with them, I have seen a fire placed over the orifice; but they hesitate not even to pass through the fire. While swarming they appear like snow-flakes floating about in the air, and dogs, cats, hawks, and almost every bird, may be seen busily devouring them. The natives, too, profit by the occasion, and actively collect them for food, they being about half an inch long, as thick as a crowquill, and very fat. When roasted they are said to be good, and some-what resemble grains of boiled rice. An idea may be formed of this dish by what once occurred on the banks of the Zouga. The Bayeiye chief Palani visiting us while eating, I gave him a piece of bread and preserved apricots; and as he seemed to relish it much, I asked him if he had any food equal to that in his country. "Ah," said he, "did you ever taste white ants?" As I never had, he replied, "Well, if you had, you never could have desired to eat anything better." The general way of catching them is to dig into the ant-hill, and wait till all the builders come forth to repair the damage; then brush them off quickly into a vessel, as the ant-eater does into his mouth.

The fall of the rain makes all the cattle look fresh and clean, and both men and women proceed cheerily to their already hoed gardens, and sow the seed. The large animals in the country leave the spots where they had been compelled to congregate for the sake of water, and become much wilder. Occasionally a herd of buffaloes or antelopes smell rain from afar, and set off in a straight line towards the place. Sometimes they make mistakes, and are obliged to return to the water they had left.

Very large tracts of country are denuded of old grass during the winter, by means of fire, in order to attract the game to that which there springs up unmixed with the older crop. This new herbage has a renovating tendency, for as long as they feed on the dry grass of the former season they continue in good condition; but no sooner are they able to indulge their appetites on the fresh herbage, than even the marrow in their bones becomes dissolved, and a red soft uneatable mass is left behind. After this, commences the work of regaining their former plumpness.

May 30*th.*—We left Bango, and proceeded to the river Loembwe, which flows to the N.N.E., and abounds in hippopotami. It is about sixty yards wide and four feet deep, but usually contains much less water than this, for there are fishing-weirs placed right across it. Like all the African rivers in this quarter, it has morasses on each bank, yet the valley in which it winds, when seen from the high lands above, is extremely beautiful. This valley is about the fourth of a mile wide, and it was easy to fancy the similarity of many spots on it to the goodly manors in our own country, and feel assured that there was still ample territory left for an indefinite increase of the world's population. The villages are widely apart, and difficult of access, from the paths being so covered with tall grass, that even an ox can scarcely follow the track. The grass cuts the feet of the men; yet we met a woman with a little child, and a girl, wending their way home with loads of manioc. The sight of a white man always infuses a tremor into their dark bosoms, and in every case of the kind, they appeared immensely relieved when I had fairly passed, without having sprung upon them. In the villages, the dogs run away with their tails between their legs, as if they had seen a lion. The women peer from behind the walls till he comes near them, and then hastily dash into the house. When a little child, unconscious of danger, meets you in the street, he sets up a scream at the apparition, and conveys the impression that he is not far from going into fits. Among the Bechuanas, I have been obliged to reprove the women for making a hobgoblin of the white man, and telling their children that they would send for him to bite them.

2 H

Having passed the Loembwe, we were in a more open country, with every few hours a small valley, through which ran a little rill in the middle of a bog. These were always difficult to pass, and being numerous, kept the lower part of the person constantly wet. At different points in our course we came upon votive offerings to the Barimo. These usually consisted of food; and every deserted village still contained the idols and little sheds with pots of medicine in them. One afternoon we passed a small frame house, with the head of an ox in it as an object of worship. The dreary uniformity of gloomy forests and open flats, must have a depressing influence on the minds of the people. Some villages appear more superstitious than others, if we may judge from the greater number of idols they contain.

Only on one occasion did we witness a specimen of quarrelling. An old woman, standing by our camp, continued to belabour a good-looking young man for hours with her tongue. Irritated at last, he uttered some words of impatience, when another man sprang at him, exclaiming, "How dare you curse my 'Mama'?". They caught each other, and a sort of pushing, dragging, wrestling-match ensued. The old woman who had been the cause of the affray, wished us to interfere, and the combatants themselves hoped as much, but we, preferring to remain neutral, allowed them to fight it out. It ended by one falling under the other, both, from their scuffling, being in a state of nudity. They picked up their clothing, and ran off in different directions, each threatening to bring his gun and settle the dispute in mortal combat. Only one, however, returned, and the old woman continued her scolding till my men, fairly tired of her tongue, ordered her to be gone. This trifling incident was one of interest to me, for, during the whole period of my residence in the Bechuana country, I never saw unarmed men strike each other. Their disputes are usually conducted with great volubility and noisy swearing, but they generally terminate by both parties bursting into a laugh.

At every village attempts were made to induce us to remain a night. Sometimes large pots of beer were offered to us as a temptation. Occasionally the head-man would peremptorily order us to halt under a tree which he pointed out. At other times young men volunteered to guide us to the impassable part of the next bog, in the hope of bringing us to a stand, for all are excessively eager to trade; but food was so very cheap that we sometimes preferred paying them to keep it, and let us part in good humour. A good-sized fowl could be had for a single charge of gunpowder. Each native who owns a gun, carries about with him a measure capable of holding but one charge, in which he receives his powder.   Throughout this region the women are almost entirely naked, their gowns being a patch of cloth frightfully narrow, with no flounces; and nothing could exceed the eagerness with which they offered to purchase strips of calico of an inferior description.   They were delighted with the larger pieces we gave, though only about two feet long, for a fowl, and a basket of upwards of 20 lbs. of meal.   As we had now only a small remnant of our stock, we were obliged to withstand their importunity, and then many of the women, with true maternal feelings, held up their little naked babies, entreating us to sell only a little rag for them.   The fire, they say, is their only clothing by night, and the little ones derive heat by clinging closely to their parents. Instead of a skin or cloth to carry their babies in, the women plait a belt about four inches broad, of the inner bark of a tree, and this, hung from the one shoulder to the opposite side, like a soldier's belt, enables them to support the child by placing it on their side in a sitting position.   Their land is very fertile, and they can raise ground-nuts and manioc in abundance.   Here I observed no cotton, nor any domestic animals except fowls and little dogs.   The chief possessed a few goats, and I never could get any satisfactory reason, why the people also did not rear them.

On the evening of the 2nd of June we reached the village of Kawawa, rather an important personage in these parts.   This village consists of forty or fifty huts, and is surrounded by forest. Drums were beating over the body of a man who had died the preceding day, and some women were making a clamorous wail at the door of his hut, and addressing the deceased as if alive. The drums continued beating the whole night, with as much regularity as a steam-engine thumps, on board ship.   We observed that a person dressed fantastically with a great number of feathers, left the people at the dance and wailing, and went away into the deep forest in the morning, to return again to the obsequies in the evening; he is intended to represent one of the Barimo.

2 H 2

In the morning we had agreeable intercourse with Kawawa; he visited us, and we sat and talked nearly the whole day with him and his people. When we visited him in return, we found him in his large court-house, which, though of a beehive shape, was remarkably well built. As I had shown him a number of curiosities, he now produced a jug, of English ware, shaped like an old man holding a can of beer in his hand, as the greatest curiosity he had to exhibit.

We had now an opportunity of hearing a case brought before him for judgment. A poor man and his wife were accused of having bewitched the man, whose wake was now held in the village. Before Kawawa even heard the defence, he said, "You have killed one of my children. Bring all yours before me, that I may choose which of them shall be mine instead." The wife eloquently defended herself, but this availed little, for these accusations are the means resorted to by some chiefs, to secure subjects for the slave-market. He probably thought that I had come to purchase slaves, though I had already given a pretty full explanation of my pursuits both to himself and his people. We exhibited the pictures of the magic-lantern in the evening, and all were delighted except Kawawa himself. He showed symptoms of dread, and several times started up as if to run away, but was prevented by the crowd behind. Some of the more intelligent understood the explanations well, and expatiated eloquently on them to the more obtuse. Nothing could exceed the civilities which had passed between us during this day; but Kawawa had heard that the Chiboque had forced us to pay an ox, and now thought he might do the same. When therefore I sent next morning to let him know that we were ready to start, he replied in his figurative way, "If an ox came in the way of a man, ought he not to eat it? I had given one to the Chiboque, and must give him the same, together with a gun, gunpowder, and a black robe, like that he had seen spread out to dry the day before; that, if I refused an ox, I must give one of my men, and a book by which he might see the state of Matiamvo's heart towards him, and which would forewarn him, should Matiamvo ever resolve to cut off his head." Kawawa came in the coolest manner possible to our encampment after sending this message, and told me he had seen all our goods, and must have all he asked, as he had command of the Kasai in our front, and would prevent us from passing it, unless we paid this tribute. I replied that the goods were my property and not his; that I would never have it said that a white man had paid tribute to a black; and that I should cross the Kasai in spite of him. He ordered his people to arm themselves, and when some of my men saw them rushing for their bows, arrows, and spears, they became somewhat panic-stricken. I ordered them to move away, and not to fire unless Kawawa's people struck the first blow. I took the lead, and expected them all to follow, as they usually had done, but many of my men remained behind. When I knew this, I jumped off the ox, and made a rush to them with the revolver in my hand. Kawawa ran away amongst his people, and they turned their backs too. I shouted to my men to take up their luggage and march; some did so with alacrity, feeling that they had disobeyed orders by remaining, but one of them refused, and was preparing to fire at Kawawa, until I gave him a punch on the head with the pistol, and made him go too. I felt here, as else-where, that subordination must be maintained at all risks. We all moved into the forest, the people of Kawawa standing about a hundred yards off, gazing, but not firing a shot or an arrow. It is extremely unpleasant to part with these chieftains thus, after spending a day or two in the most amicable intercourse, and in a part where the people are generally civil. This Kawawa, however, is not a good specimen of the Balonda chiefs, and is rather notorious in the neighbourhood for his folly. We were told, that he has good reason to believe that Matiamvo will some day cut off his head, for his disregard of the rights of strangers.

Kawawa was not to be balked of his supposed rights by the unceremonious way in which we had left him, for, when we had reached the ford of the Kasai, about ten miles distant, we found that he had sent four of his men, with orders to the ferrymen to refuse us passage. We were here duly informed that we must deliver up all the articles mentioned, and one of our men besides. This demand for one of our number always nettled every heart. The canoes were taken away before our eyes, and we were sup-posed to be quite helpless without them, at a river a good hundred yards broad, and very deep. Pitsane stood on the bank, gazing with apparent indifference on the stream, and made an accurate observation of where the canoes were hidden among the reeds. The ferrymen casually asked one of my Batoka if they had rivers in his country, and he answered with truth, "No, we have none." Kawawa's people then felt sure we could not cross. I thought of swimming when they were gone; but after it was dark, by the unasked loan of one of the hidden canoes, we soon were snug in our bivouac on the southern bank of the Kasai. I left some beads, as payment for some meal, which had been presented by the ferrymen; and, the canoe having been left on their own side of the river, Pitsane and his companions laughed uproariously at the disgust our enemies would feel, and their perplexity as to who had been our paddler across. They were quite sure that Kawawa would imagine that we had been ferried over by his own people, and would be divining to find out who had done the deed. When ready to depart in the morning, Kawawa's people appeared on the opposite heights, and could scarcely believe their eyes when they saw us prepared to start away to the south. At last one of them called out, "Ah! ye are bad." To which Pitsane and his companions retorted, "Ah! ye are good; and we thank you for the loan of your canoe." We were careful to explain the whole of the circumstances to Katema and the other chiefs, and they all agreed that we were perfectly justifiable under the circumstances, and that Matiamvo would approve our conduct. When anything that might bear an unfavourable construction happens among themselves, they send explanations to each other. The mere fact of doing so, prevents them from losing their character, for there is public opinion even amongst them.

CHAPTER XXIV.

AFTER leaving the Kasai, we entered upon the extensive level plains which we had formerly found in a flooded condition. The water on them was not yet dried up, as it still remained in certain hollow spots. Vultures were seen floating in the air, showing that carrion was to be found; and, indeed, we saw several of the large game, but so exceedingly wild as to be unapproachable. Numbers of caterpillars mounted the stalks of grass, and many dragonflies and butterflies appeared, though this was winter. The caprimulgus or goat-sucker, swifts, and different kinds of swallows, with a fiery-red bee-eater in flocks, showed that the lowest temperature here, does not destroy the insects on which they feed. Jet-black larks, with yellow shoulders, enliven the mornings with their songs, but they do not continue so long on the wing as ours, nor soar so high. We saw many of the pretty white ardea, and other water-birds, flying over the spots not yet dried up; and occasionally wild ducks, but these only in numbers sufficient to remind us that we were approaching the Zambesi, where every water-fowl has a home.

While passing across these interminable-looking plains, the eye rests with pleasure on a small flower, which exists in such numbers as to give its own hue to the ground. One broad band of yellow stretches across our path. On looking at the flowers which formed this golden carpet, we saw every variety of that colour, from the palest lemon to the richest orange. Crossing a hundred yards of this, we came upon another broad band of the same flower, but blue, and this colour is varied from the lightest tint, to dark blue and even purple. I had before observed the same flower possessing different colours in different parts of the country, and once, a great number of liver-coloured flowers, which elsewhere were yellow. Even the colour of the birds changed with the district we passed through; but never before did I see such a marked change, as from yellow to blue, repeated again and again on the same plain. Another beautiful plant attracted my attention so strongly on these plains, that I dismounted to examine it; to my great delight I found it to be an old home acquaintance, a species of Drosera, closely resembling our own sundew (*Drosera Anglica*); the flower-stalk never attains a height of more than two or three inches, and the leaves are covered with reddish hairs, each of which has a drop of clammy fluid at its tip, making the whole appear as if spangled over with small diamonds. I noticed it first in the morning, and imagined the appearance was caused by the sun shining on drops of dew, but, as it continued to maintain its brilliancy during the heat of the day, I proceeded to investigate the cause of its beauty, and found that the points of the hairs exuded pure liquid, in, apparently, capsules of clear glutinous matter. They were thus like dewdrops preserved from evaporation. The clammy fluid is intended to entrap insects, which, dying on the leaf, probably yield nutriment to the plant.

During our second day on this extensive plain, I suffered from my twenty-seventh attack of fever, at a part where no surface-water was to be found. We never thought it necessary to carry water with us in this region; and now, when I was quite unable to move on, my men soon found water to allay my burning thirst by digging with sticks a few feet beneath the surface. We had thus an opportunity of observing the state of these remarkable plains at different seasons of the year. Next day we pursued our way, and on the 8th of June, we forded the Lotembwa to the N.W. of Dilolo, and regained our former path.

The Lotembwa here is about a mile wide, about three feet deep, and full of the lotus, papyrus, arum, mat-rushes, and other aquatic plants. I did not observe the course in which the water flowed, while crossing; but, having noticed before that the Lotembwa on the other side of the lake Dilolo flowed in a southerly direction, I supposed that this was simply a prolongation of the same river beyond Dilolo, and that it rose in this large marsh, which we had not seen in our progress to the N.W. But when we came to the Southern Lotembwa, we were informed by Shakatwala that the river we had crossed flowed in an opposite direction,—not into Dilolo, but into the Kasai. This phenomenon of a river running in opposite directions struck even his mind as strange; and, though I did not observe the current, simply from taking it for granted that it was towards the lake, I have no doubt that his assertion, corroborated as it was by others, is correct, and that the Dilolo is actually the watershed between the river systems that flow to the east and west.

I would have returned, in order to examine more carefully this most interesting point, but, having had my lower extremities chilled in crossing the Northern Lotembwa, I was seized with vomiting of blood, and, besides, saw no reason to doubt the native testimony. The distance between Dilolo and the valleys leading to that of the Kasai is not more than fifteen miles, and the plains between are perfectly level; and, had I returned, I should only have found that this little lake Dilolo, by giving a portion to the Kasai and another to the Zambesi, distributes its waters to the Atlantic and Indian Oceans. I state the fact exactly as it opened to my own mind; for it was only now, that I apprehended the true form of the river systems and continent. I had seen the various rivers of this country on the western side flowing from the subtending ridges into the centre, and had received information from natives and Arabs, that most of the rivers on the eastern side of the same great region, took a somewhat similar course from an elevated ridge there, and that all united in two main drains, the one flowing to the N. and the other to the S., and that the northern drain found its way out by the Congo to the W., and the southern by the Zambesi to the E. I was thus on the watershed, or highest point, of these two great systems, but still not more than 4000 feet above the level of the sea, and 1000 feet lower than the top of the western ridge we had already crossed; yet, instead of lofty snow-clad mountains appearing to verify the conjectures of the speculative, we had extensive plains, over which one may travel a month without seeing anything higher than an ant-hill or a tree. I was not then aware that any one else had discovered the elevated trough form of the centre of Africa.

I had observed that the old schistose rocks on the sides, dipped in towards the centre of the country, and their strike nearly corresponded with the major axis of the continent; and also that where the later erupted trap-rocks had been spread out in tabular masses over the central plateau, they had borne angular fragments of the older rocks in their substance; but the partial generalization which the observations led to, was, that great volcanic action had taken place in ancient times, somewhat in the same way it does now, at distances of not more than three hundred miles from the sea, and that this igneous action, extending along both sides of the continent, had tilted up the lateral rocks in the manner they are now seen to lie. The greater energy, and more extended range of igneous action, in those very remote periods when Africa was formed, embracing all the flanks, imparted to it its present very simple literal outline. This was the length to which I had come.

The trap-rocks, which now constitute the "filling-up" of the great valley, were always a puzzle to me, till favoured with Sir Roderick Murchison's explanation of the original form of the continent, for then I could see clearly why these trap-rocks, which still lie in a perfectly horizontal position on extensive areas, held in their substance angular fragments, containing algæ of the old schists, which form the bottom of the original lacustrine basin: the traps, in bursting through, had broken them off and preserved them. There are, besides, ranges of hills in the central parts, composed of clay and sandstone schists, with the ripple mark distinct, in which no fossils appear; but as they are usually tilted away from the masses of horizontal trap, it is probable that they too were a portion of the original bottom, and fossils may yet be found in them.*

The characteristics of the rainy season in this wonderfully humid region, may account in some measure for the periodical floods of the Zambesi, and perhaps the Nile. The rains seem to follow the course of the sun, for they fall in October and November, when the sun passes over this zone on his way south. On reaching the tropic of Capricorn in December, it is dry; and December and January are the months in which injurious droughts are most dreaded near that tropic (from Kolobeng to Linyanti). As he returns again to the north, in February, March, and April, we have the great rains of the year; and the plains, which in October and November were well moistened, and imbibed rain like sponges, now become supersaturated, and pour forth those floods of clear water which inundate the banks of the Zambesi. Somewhat the same phenomenon probably, causes the periodical inundations of the Nile. The two rivers rise in the same region; but there is a difference in the period of flood, possibly from their

---

* After dwelling upon the geological structure of the Cape Colony as developed by Mr. A. Bain, and the existence in very remote periods of lacustrine conditions in the central part of South Africa, as proved by freshwater and terrestrial fossils, Sir Roderick Murchison thus writes :—

" Such as South Africa is now, such have been her main features during countless past-ages, anterior to the creation of the human race. For the old rocks which form her outer fringe, unquestionably circled round an interior marshy or lacustrine country, in which the Dicynodon flourished, at a time when not a single animal was similar to any living thing which now inhabits the surface of our globe. The present central and meridian zone of waters, whether lakes or marshes, extending from Lake Tchad to Lake 'Ngami, with hippopotami on their banks, are therefore but the great modern residual geographical phenomena of those of a mesozoic age. The differences, however, between the geological past of Africa and her present state, are enormous. Since that primeval time, the lands have been much elevated above the sea-level—eruptive rocks piercing in parts through them; deep rents and defiles have been suddenly formed in the subtending ridges through which some rivers escape outwards.

" Travellers will eventually ascertain whether the basin-shaped structure, which is here announced as having been the great feature of the most ancient, as it is of the actual geography of South Africa (i.e. from primeval times to the present day), does, or does not, extend into Northern Africa. Looking at that much broader portion of the continent, we have some reason to surmise that the higher mountains also form, in a general sense, its flanks only."— p. cxxiii. *President's Address, Royal Geographical Society*, 1852.

being on opposite sides of the equator. The waters of the Nile are said to become turbid in June; and the flood attains its greatest height in August, or the period when we may suppose the supersaturation to occur. The subject is worthy the investigation of those who may examine the region between the equator and 10° S.; for the Nile does not show much increase when the sun is at its furthest point north, or tropic of Cancer, but at the time of its returning to the equator, exactly as in the other case when he is on Capricorn, and the Zambesi is affected.*

From information derived from Arabs of Zanzibar, whom I met at Naliele in the middle of the country, the region to the east of the parts of Londa over which we have travelled, resembles them in its conformation. They report swampy steppes, some of which have no trees, where the inhabitants use grass, and stalks of native corn, for fuel. A large shallow lake is also pointed out in that direction, named Tanganyénka, which requires three days for crossing in canoes. It is connected with another named Kalagwe (Garague?), farther north, and may be the Nyanja of the Maravim. From this lake is derived, by numerous small streams, the river Loapula, the eastern branch of the Zambesi, which, coming from the N.E., flows past the town of Cazembe.

The southern end of this lake is ten days north-east of the town of Cazembe; and as that is probably more than five days from Shinte, we cannot have been nearer to it than 150 miles. Probably this lake is the watershed between the Zambesi and the Nile, as Lake Dilolo is that between the Leeba and Kasai. But however

* The above is from my own observation, together with information derived from the Portuguese in the interior of Angola; and I may add that the result of many years' observation by Messrs. Gabriel and Brand at Loanda, on the west coast, is in accordance therewith. It rains there between the 1st and 30th of November, but January and December are usually both warm and dry. The heavier rains commence about the 1st of February, and last until the 15th of May. Then no rain falls between the 20th of May and the 1st of November. The rain averages from 12 to 15 inches per annum. In 1852 it was 12,034 inches; in 1853, 15,473 inches. Although I had no means of measuring the amount of rain which fell in Londa, I feel certain that the annual quantity exceeds very much that which falls on the coast, because for a long time we noticed that every dawn was marked by a deluging shower, which began without warning-drops or thunder. I observed that the rain ceased suddenly on the 28th of April, and the lesser rains commenced about a fortnight before the beginning of November.

this may be, the phenomena of the rainy season show that it is not necessary to assume the existence of high snowy mountains, until we get reliable information. This, it is to be hoped, will be one of the results of the researches of Captain Burton in his present journey.

The original valley formation of the continent, determined the northern and southern course of the Zambesi in the centre, and also of that ancient river which once flowed from the Linyanti basin to the Orange river. It also gave direction to the southern and northern flow of the Kasai and the Nile. We find that between the latitudes, say 6° and 12° S., from which, in all probability, the head waters of these rivers diverge, there is a sort of elevated partition in the great longitudinal valley. Presuming on the correctness of the native information, which places the humid region to which the Nile and Zambesi probably owe their origin, within the latitudes indicated, why does so much more rain fall there than in the same latitudes north of the equator? Why does Darfur not give rise to great rivers, like Londa and the country east of it? The prevailing winds in the ocean opposite the territory pointed out are said to be from the N.-E. and S.-E. during a great part of the year; they extend their currents on one side at least of the equator, quite beyond the middle of the continent, and even until in Angola they meet the sea-breeze from the Atlantic. If the reader remembers the explanation, given at page 95,* that the comparative want of

---

* Since the explanation in page 95 was printed I have been pleased to see the same explanation given by the popular astronomer and natural philosopher M. Babinet, in reference to the climate of France. It is quoted from a letter of a correspondent of the *Times* in Paris :—

"In the normal meteorological state of France and Europe, the west wind, which is the counter-current of the trade-winds that constantly blow from the east under the tropics—the west wind, I say, after having touched France and Europe by the western shores, re-descends by Marseilles and the Mediterranean, Constantinople and the Archipelago, Astrakan and the Caspian Sea, in order to merge again into the great circuit of the general winds, and be thus carried again into the equatorial current. Whenever these masses of air, impregnated with humidity during their passage over the ocean, meet with an obstacle, such as a chain of mountains, for example, they slide up the acclivity, and, when they reach the crest, find themselves relieved from a portion of the column of air which pressed upon them. Thus, dilating by reason of their elas-

rain on the Kalahari Desert is caused by the mass of air losing
its humidity as it passes up, and glides over the subtending
ridge, and will turn to the map, he may perceive that the
same cause is in operation in an intense degree by the mountains of Abyssinia to render the region about Darfur still
more arid; and that the flanking ranges mentioned, lie much
nearer the equator than those which rob the Kalahari of humidity. The Nile, even while running through a part of that
region, receives remarkably few branches. Observing also that
there is no known abrupt lateral mountain-range between 6°
and 12° S., but that there is an elevated partition there, and
that the southing and northing of the south-easters and north-
easters probably cause a confluence of the two great atmospheric
currents, he will perceive an accumulation of humidity on
the flanks and crown of the partition, instead of, as elsewhere,
opposite the Kalahari and Darfur, a deposition of the atmospheric moisture on the eastern slopes of the subtending ridges.
This explanation is offered with all deference to those who have
made meteorology their special study, and as a hint to travellers
who may have opportunity to examine the subject more fully.

ticity, they cause a considerable degree of cold, and a precipitation of
humidity in the form of fogs, clouds, rain, or snow. A similar effect
occurs whatever be the obstacle they find in their way. Now, this is
what had gradually taken place before 1856. By some cause or other
connected with the currents of the atmosphere, the warm current from
the west had annually ascended northward, so that, instead of passing
through France, it came from the Baltic and the north of Germany, thus
momentarily disturbing the ordinary law of the temperatures of Europe.
But in 1856 a sudden change occurred. The western current again passed,
as before, through the centre of France. It met with an obstacle in the
air which had not yet found its usual outlet towards the west and south.
Hence a stoppage, a rising, a consequent dilation and fall of temperature,
extraordinary rains and inundations. But now that the natural state of
things is restored, nothing appears to prognosticate the return of similar
disasters. Were the western current found annually to move further
north, we might again experience meteorological effects similar to those
of 1856. Hence the regular seasons may be considered re-established in
France for several years to come. The important meteorological com-
munications which the Imperial Observatory is daily establishing with the
other countries of Europe, and the introduction of apparatus for measuring
the velocity of the aërial currents and prevailing winds, will soon afford
prognostics sufficiently certain to enable an enlightened Government to
provide in time against future evils."

I often observed, while on a portion of the partition, that the air by night was generally quite still, but as soon as the sun's rays began to shoot across the upper strata of the atmosphere in the early morning, a copious discharge came suddenly down from the accumulated clouds. It always reminded me of the experiment of putting a rod into a saturated solution of a certain salt, causing instant crystallization. This, too, was the period when I often observed the greatest amount of cold.

After crossing the Northern Lotembwa, we met a party of the people of Kangenke, who had treated us kindly on our way to the north, and sent him a robe of striped calico, with an explanation of the reason for not returning through his village. We then went on to the Lake Dilolo. It is a fine sheet of water, six or eight miles long, and one or two broad, and somewhat of a triangular shape. A branch proceeds from one of the angles, and flows into the Southern Lotembwa. Though labouring under fever, the sight of the blue waters, and the waves lashing the shore, had a most soothing influence on the mind, after so much of lifeless, flat, and gloomy forest. The heart yearned for the vivid impressions, which are always created by the sight of the broad expanse of the grand old ocean. That has life in it; but the flat uniformities over which we had roamed, made me feel as if buried alive. We found Moene Dilolo (Lord of the Lake) a fat jolly fellow, who lamented that when they had no strangers they had plenty of beer, and always none when they came. He gave us a handsome present of meal and putrid buffalo's flesh. Meat cannot be too far gone for them, as it is used only in small quantities as a sauce to their tasteless manioc. They were at this time hunting antelopes, in order to send the skins as a tribute to Matiamvo. Great quantities of fish are caught in the lake; and numbers of young water-fowl are now found in the nests among the reeds.

Our progress had always been slow, and I found that our rate of travelling could only be five hours a-day for five successive days. On the sixth, both men and oxen showed symptoms of knocking up. We never exceeded two and a half, or three miles an hour in a straight line, though all were anxious to get home. The difference in the rate of travelling between ourselves and the slave-traders, was our having a rather quicker step, a longer day's journey, and twenty travelling days a-month instead of their ten. When one of my men became ill, but still could walk, others parted his luggage among them; yet we had often to stop one day a-week, besides Sundays, simply for the sake of rest. The latitude of Lake Dilolo is 11° 32′ 1″ S., long. 22° 27′ E.

June 14th.—We reached the collection of straggling villages over which Katema rules, and were thankful to see old familiar faces again. Shakatwala performed the part of a chief, by bringing forth abundant supplies of food in his master's name. He informed us that Katema too, was out, hunting skins for Matiamvo.

In different parts of this country, we remarked that when old friends were inquired for, the reply was, "Ba hola—they are getting better;" or if the people of a village were inquired for, the answer was, "They are recovering," as if sickness was quite a common thing. Indeed, many with whom we had made acquaintance in going north, we now found were in their graves. On the 15th, Katema came home from his hunting, having heard of our arrival. He desired me to rest myself and eat abundantly, for, being a great man, I must feel tired; and he took good care to give the means of doing so. All the people in these parts are extremely kind and liberal with their food, and Katema was not behindhand. When he visited our encampment, I presented him with a cloak of red baize, ornamented with gold tinsel, which cost thirty shillings, according to the promise I had made in going to Loanda; also a cotton robe, both large and small beads, an iron spoon, and a tin pannikin containing a quarter of a pound of powder. He seemed greatly pleased with the liberality shown, and assured me that the way was mine, and that no one should molest me in it, if he could help it. We were informed by Shakatwala that the chief never used any part of a present, before making an offer of it to his mother, or the departed spirit to whom he prayed. Katema asked if I could not make a dress for him like the one I wore, so that he might appear as a white man when any stranger visited him. One of the councillors, imagining that he ought to second this by begging, Katema checked him by saying, "Whatever strangers give, be it little or much, I always receive it with thankfulness, and never trouble them for more." On departing, he mounted on the shoulders of his spokesman, as the most dignified mode of retiring. The spokesman being a slender man, and the chief six feet high, and stout in proportion, there would have been a breakdown, had he not been accustomed to it. We were very much pleased with Katema; and next day he presented us with a cow, that we might enjoy the abundant supplies of meal he had given with good animal food. He then departed for the hunting-ground, after assuring me that the town and everything in it were mine, and that his factotum, Shakatwala, would remain and attend to every want, and also conduct us to the Leeba.

On attempting to slaughter the cow Katema had given, we found the herd as wild as buffaloes; and one of my men having only wounded it, they fled many miles into the forest, and were with great difficulty brought back. Even the herdsman was afraid to go near them. The majority of them were white, and they were all beautiful animals. After hunting it for two days, it was despatched at last by another ball. Here we saw a flock of jackdaws, a rare sight in Londa, busy with the grubs in the valley, which are eaten by the people too.

Leaving Katema's town on the 19th, and proceeding four miles to the eastward, we forded the southern branch of Lake Dilolo. We found it a mile and a quarter broad; and as it flows into the Lotembwa, the lake would seem to be a drain of the surrounding flats, and to partake of the character of a fountain.   The ford was waist-deep, and very difficult, from the masses of arum and rushes through which we waded.   Going to the eastward about three miles, we came to the Southern Lotembwa itself, running in a valley two miles broad.   It is here eighty or ninety yards wide, and contains numerous islands covered with dense sylvan vegetation.   In the rainy season the valley is flooded, and as the waters dry up, great multitudes of fish are caught.   This happens very extensively over the country, and fishing-weirs are met with everywhere.   A species of small fish, about the size of the minnow, is caught in bagfuls, and dried in the sun.   The taste is a pungent aromatic bitter, and it was partaken of freely by my people, although they had never met with it before.   On many of the paths which had been flooded, a nasty sort of slime of decayed vegetable matter is left behind, and much sickness prevails during the drying up of the water.   We did not find our friend Mozinkwa at his pleasant home on the Lokaloeje; his wife was dead, and he had removed elsewhere.   He followed us some distance, but our reappearance seemed to stir up his sorrows.   We found the pontoon at the village in which we left it.   It had been carefully preserved; but a mouse had eaten a hole in it, and rendered it useless.

We traversed the extended plain on the north bank of the Leeba, and crossed this river a little farther on at Kanyonke's village, which is about twenty miles west of the Peri hills, our former ford.   The first stage beyond the Leeba, was at the rivulet Loambo, by the village of Chebende, nephew of Shinte; and next day, we met Chebende himself, returning from the funeral of Samoana, his father.   He was thin and haggard-looking, compared to what he had been before, the probable effect of the orgies in which he had been engaged.   Pitsane and Mohorisi, having concocted the project of a Makololo village on the banks of the Leeba, as an approach to the white man's market, spoke to Chebende, as an influential man, on the subject, but he cautiously avoided expressing an opinion.   The idea which had sprung up in their own minds of an establishment somewhere near the confluence of

placed in the shade of my tent, which was pitched under the thickest tree we could find. The sensation of cold, after the heat of the day, was very keen. The Balonda at this season never leave their fires till nine or ten in the morning. As the cold was so great here, it was probably frosty at Linyanti; I therefore feared to expose my young trees there. The latitude of Shinte's town is 12° 37' 35" S., longitude 22° 47' E.

We remained with Shinte till the 6th of July, he being unwilling to allow us to depart before hearing in a formal manner, in the presence of his greatest councillor Chebende, a message from Limbōa, the brother of Masiko. When Masiko fled from the Makololo country, in consequence of a dislike of being in a state of subjection to Sebituane, he came into the territory of Shinte, who received him kindly, and sent orders to all the villages in his vicinity to supply him with food. Limboa fled in a westerly direction with a number of people, and also became a chief. His country was sometimes called Nyenko, but by the Mambari and native Portuguese traders "Mboela"—the place where they "turned again," or back. As one of the fruits of polygamy, the children of different mothers are always in a state of variance. Each son endeavours to gain the ascendancy, by enticing away the followers of the others. The mother of Limboa, being of a high family, he felt aggrieved, because the situation chosen by Masiko was better than his. Masiko lived at a convenient distance from the Saloisho hills, where there is abundance of iron-ore, with which the inhabitants manufacture hoes, knives, &c. They are also skilful in making wooden vessels. Limboa felt annoyed because he was obliged to apply for these articles through his brother, whom he regarded as his inferior, and accordingly resolved to come into the same district. As this was looked upon as an assertion of superiority, which Masiko would resist, it was virtually a declaration of war. Both Masiko and Shinte pleaded my injunction to live in peace and friendship, but Limboa, confident of success, now sent the message which I was about to hear—"That he, too, highly approved of the 'word' I had given, but would only for once transgress a little, and live at peace for ever afterwards." He now desired the aid of Shinte to subdue his brother. Messengers came from Masiko at the same time, desiring assistance to repel him. Shinte felt inclined to aid

Limboa, but, as he had advised them both to wait till I came, I now urged him to let the quarrel alone, and he took my advice.

We parted on the best possible terms with our friend Shinte; and proceeded by our former path to the village of his sister Nyamoana, who is now a widow. She received us with much apparent feeling, and said, "We had removed from our former abode to the place where you found us, and had no idea then that it was the spot where my husband was to die." She had come to the river Lofujé, as they never remain in a place where death has once visited them. We received the loan of five small canoes from her, and also one of those we had left here before, to proceed down the Leeba. After viewing the Coanza at Massangano, I thought the Leeba at least a third larger, and upwards of two hundred yards wide. We saw evidence of its rise during its last flood having been upwards of forty feet in perpendicular height; but this is probably more than usual, as the amount of rain was above the average. My companions purchased also a number of canoes from the Balonda. These are very small, and can carry only two persons. They are made quite thin and light, and as sharp as racing-skiffs, because they are used in hunting animals in the water. The price paid, was a string of beads equal to the length of the canoe. We advised them to bring canoes for sale to the Makololo, as they would gladly give them cows in exchange.

In descending the Leeba we saw many herds of wild animals, especially the tahetsi (*Aigoceros equina*), one magnificent antelope, the putokuane (*Antilope niger*), and two fine lions. The Balobale, however, are getting well supplied with guns, and will soon thin out the large game. At one of the villages we were entreated to attack some buffaloes, which grazed in the gardens every night, and destroyed the manioc. As we had had no success in shooting at the game we had seen, and we all longed to have a meal of meat, we followed the footprints of a number of old bulls. They showed a great amount of cunning, by selecting the densest parts of very closely-planted forests, to stand or recline in during the day. We came within six yards of them several times before we knew that they were so near. We only heard them rush away among the crashing branches, catching only a glimpse of them. It was somewhat exciting to feel, as we trod on the dry leaves with stealthy steps, that, for anything we knew, we might next moment be charged by one of the most dangerous beasts of the forest. We threaded out their doublings for hours, drawn on by a keen craving for animal food, as we had been entirely without salt for upwards of two months, but never could get a shot.

In passing along the side of water everywhere, except in Londa, green frogs spring out at your feet, and light in the water, as if taking a "header;" and on the Leeambye and Chobe we have great numbers of small green frogs (*Rana fasciata*, Boié), which light on blades of grass with remarkable precision; but on coming along the Leeba, I was struck by the sight of a light green toad about an inch long. The leaf might be nearly perpendicular, but it stuck to it like a fly. It was of the same size as the *Brachymerus bi-fasciatus* (Smith),* which I saw only once in the Bakwain country. Though small, it was hideous, being coloured jet-black, with vermilion spots.

Before reaching the Makondo rivulet, latitude 13° 23' 12" S., we came upon the tsetse in such numbers, that many bites were inflicted on my poor ox, in spite of a man with a branch warding them off. The bite of this insect does not affect the donkey as it

* The discovery of this last species is thus mentioned by that accomplished naturalist, Dr. Smith: "On the banks of the Limpopo river, close to the tropic of Capricorn, a massive tree was cut down to obtain wood to repair a waggon. The workman, while sawing the trunk longitudinally nearly along its centre, remarked, on reaching a certain point, 'It is hollow, and will not answer the purpose for which it is wanted.' He persevered, however, and when a division into equal halves was effected, it was discovered that the saw in its course had crossed a large hole in which were five specimens of the species just described, each about an inch in length. Every exertion was made to discover a means of communication between the external air and the cavity, but without success. Every part of the latter was probed with the utmost care, and water was kept in each half for a considerable time, without any passing into the wood. The inner surface of the cavity was black, as if charred, and so was likewise the adjoining wood for half an inch from the cavity. The tree, at the part where the latter existed, was 19 inches in diameter, the length of the trunk was 18 feet. The age, which was observed at the time, I regret to say does not appear to be noted. When the Batrachia above mentioned were discovered, they appeared inanimate, but the influence of a warm sun to which they were subjected, soon imparted to them a moderate degree of vigour. In a few hours from the time they were liberated, they were tolerably active, and able to move from place to place apparently with great ease."

does cattle. The next morning, the spots on which my ox had been bitten, were marked by patches of hair, about half an inch broad, being wetted by exudation. Poor Sinbad had carried me all the way from the Leeba to Golungo Alto, and all the way back again, without losing any of his peculiarities, or ever becoming reconciled to our perversity, in forcing him away each morning from the pleasant pasturage on which he had fed. I wished to give the climax to his usefulness, and allay our craving for animal food at the same time, but, my men having some compunction, we carried him to end his days in peace at Naliele.

Having despatched a message to our old friend Manenko, we waited a day opposite her village, which was about fifteen miles from the river. Her husband was instantly despatched to meet us, with liberal presents of food, she being unable to travel in consequence of a burn on the foot. Sambanza gave us a detailed account of the political affairs of the country, and of Kolimbota's evil doings, and next morning performed the ceremony called "Kasendi," for cementing our friendship. It is accomplished thus:—The hands of the parties are joined (in this case Pitsane and Sambanza were the parties engaged); small incisions are made on the clasped hands; on the pits of the stomach of each; and on the right cheeks and foreheads. A small quantity of blood is taken off from these points in both parties by means of a stalk of grass. The blood from one person is put into one pot of beer, and that of the second into another; each then drinks the other's blood, and they are supposed to become perpetual friends or relations. During the drinking of the beer, some of the party continue beating the ground with short clubs, and utter sentences by way of ratifying the treaty. The men belonging to each, then finish the beer. The principals in the performance of "Kasendi" are henceforth considered blood-relations, and are bound to disclose to each other any impending evil. If Sekeletu should resolve to attack the Balonda, Pitsane would be under obligation to give Sambanza warning to escape, and so on the other side. They now presented each other with the most valuable presents they had to bestow. Sambanza walked off with Pitsane's suit of green-baize faced with red, which had been made in Loanda; and Pitsane, besides abundant supplies of food, obtained two shells similar to that I had received from Shinte.

On one occasion I became blood-relation to a young woman by accident. She had a large cartilaginous tumour between the bones of the fore-arm, which, as it gradually enlarged, so distended the muscles as to render her unable to work. She applied to me to excise it. I requested her to bring her husband, if he were willing to have the operation performed, and, while removing the tumour, one of the small arteries squirted some blood into my eye. She remarked, when I was wiping the blood out of it, "You were a friend before, now you are a blood-relation; and when you pass this way, always send me word, that I may cook food for you." In creating these friendships, my men had the full intention of returning; each one had his *Molekane* (*friend*) in every village of the friendly Balonda. Mohorisi even married a wife in the town of Katema, and Pitsane took another in the town of Shinte. These alliances were looked upon with great favour by the Balonda chiefs, as securing the goodwill of the Makololo.

In order that the social condition of the tribes may be understood by the reader, I shall mention that, while waiting for Sambanza, a party of Barotse came from Nyenko, the former residence of Limboa, who had lately crossed the Leeba on his way towards Masiko. The head-man of this party had brought Limboa's son to his father, because the Barotse at Nyenko had, since the departure of Limboa, elected Nananko, another son of Santuru, in his stead; and our visitor, to whom the boy had been intrusted as a guardian, thinking him to be in danger, fled with him to his father. The Barotse, whom Limboa had left behind at Nyenko, on proceeding to elect Nananko, said, "No, it is quite too much for Limboa to rule over two places." I would have gone to visit Limboa and Masiko too, in order to prevent hostilities, but the state of my ox would not allow it. I therefore sent a message to Limboa by some of his men, protesting against war with his brother, and giving him formal notice that the path up the Leeba had been given to us by the Balonda, the owners of the country, and that no attempt must ever be made to obstruct free intercourse.

On leaving this place we were deserted by one of our party, Mboenga, an Ambonda man, who had accompanied us all the way to Loanda and back. His father was living with Masiko, and it was natural for him to wish to join his own family again.

He went off honestly, with the exception of taking a fine "tari" skin given me by Nyamoana, but he left a parcel of gun-flints which he had carried for me all the way from Loanda. I regretted parting with him thus, and sent notice to him that he need not have run away, and if he wished to come to Sekeletu again, he would be welcome. We subsequently met a large party of Barotse fleeing in the same direction, but when I represented to them that there was a probability of their being sold as slaves in Londa, and none in the country of Sekeletu, they concluded to return. The grievance which the Barotse most feel, is being obliged to live with Sekeletu at Linyanti, where there is neither fish nor fowl, nor any other kind of food, equal in quantity to what they enjoy in their own fat valley.

A short distance below the confluence of the Leeba and Leeambye, we met a number of hunters belonging to the tribe called Mambowe, who live under Masiko. They had dried flesh of hippopotami, buffaloes, and alligators. They stalk the animals by using the stratagem of a cap made of the skin of a leche's or poku's head, having the horns still attached, and another made so as to represent the upper white part of the crane called jabiru (*Mycteru Senegalensis*), with its long neck and beak above. With these on, they crawl through the grass; they can easily put up their heads so far as to see their prey without being recognised until they are within bowshot. They presented me with three fine water-turtles,* one of which, when cooked, had upwards of forty eggs in its body. The shell of the egg is flexible, and it is of the same size at both ends, like those of the alligator. The flesh, and especially the liver, is excellent. The hunters informed us, that when the message inculcating peace among the tribes came to Masiko, the common people were so glad at the prospect of "binding up the spears," that they ran to the river, and bathed and plunged in it for joy. This party had been sent by Masiko to the Makololo for aid to repel their enemy, but, afraid to go thither, had spent the time in hunting. They have a dread of the Makololo, and hence the joy they expressed when peace was

---

* It is probably a species allied to the *Sternotherus sinuatus* of Dr. Smith, as it has no disagreeable smell. This variety annually leaves the water with so much regularity for the deposit of its eggs, that the natives decide on the time of sowing their seed by its appearance.

proclaimed. The Mambowe hunters were much alarmed until my name was mentioned. They then joined our party, and on the following day discovered a hippopotamus dead, which they had previously wounded. This was the first feast of flesh my men had enjoyed, for, though the game was wonderfully abundant, I had quite got out of the way of shooting, and missed perpetually. Once I went with the determination of getting so close that I should not miss a zebra. We went along one of the branches that stretch out from the river, in a small canoe, and two men, stooping down as low as they could, paddled it slowly along to an open space near to a herd of zebras and pokus. Peering over the edge of the canoe, the open space seemed like a patch of wet ground, such as is often seen on the banks of a river, made smooth as the resting-place of alligators. When we came within a few yards of it, we found by the precipitate plunging of the reptile, that this was a large alligator itself. Although I had been most careful to approach near enough, I unfortunately only broke the hind leg of a zebra. My two men pursued it, but the loss of a hind leg does not prevent this animal from a gallop. As I walked slowly after the men on an extensive plain covered with a great crop of grass, which was *laid* by its own weight, I observed that a solitary buffalo, disturbed by others of my own party, was coming to me at a gallop. I glanced around, but the only tree on the plain was a hundred yards off, and there was no escape elsewhere. I therefore cocked my rifle, with the intention of giving him a steady shot in the forehead, when he should come within three or four yards of me. The thought flashed across my mind, " What if your gun misses fire ?" I placed it to my shoulder as he came on at full speed, and that is tremendous, though generally he is a lumbering-looking animal in his paces. A small bush, and bunch of grass fifteen yards off, made him swerve a little, and exposed his shoulder. I just heard the ball crack there, as I fell flat on my face. The pain must have made him renounce his purpose, for he bounded close past me on to the water, where he was found dead. In expressing my thankfulness to God among my men, they were much offended with themselves for not being present to shield me from this danger. The tree near me was a camel-thorn, and reminded me that we had come back to the land of thorns again, for the country we had left is one of evergreens.

July 27th.—We reached the town of Libonta, and were received with demonstrations of joy such as I had never witnessed before. The women came forth to meet us, making their curious dancing gestures, and loud lulliloos. Some carried a mat and stick, in imitation of a spear and shield. Others rushed forward and kissed the hands and cheeks of the different persons of their acquaintance among us, raising such a dust that it was quite a relief to get to the men assembled and sitting with proper African decorum in the kotla. We were looked upon as men risen from the dead, for the most skilful of their diviners had pronounced us to have perished long ago. After many expressions of joy at meeting, I arose, and, thanking them, explained the causes of our long delay, but left the report to be made by their own countrymen. Formerly I had been the chief speaker, now I would leave the task of speaking to them. Pitsane then delivered a speech of upwards of an hour in length, giving a highly flattering picture of the whole journey, of the kindness of the white men in general, and of Mr. Gabriel in particular. He concluded by saying that I had done more for them than they expected; that I had not only opened up a path for them to the other white men, but conciliated all the chiefs along the route. The oldest man present, rose and answered this speech, and, among other things, alluded to the disgust I felt at the Makololo for engaging in marauding expeditions against Lechulatebe and Sebolamak-waia, of which we had heard from the first persons we met, and which my companions most energetically denounced as "mashue hela," entirely bad. He entreated me not to lose heart, but to reprove Sekeletu as my child. Another old man followed with the same entreaties. The following day we observed as our thanksgiving to God for his goodness in bringing us all back in safety to our friends. My men decked themselves out in their best, and I found that, although their goods were finished, they had managed to save suits of European clothing, which, being white, with their red caps, gave them rather a dashing appearance. They tried to walk like the soldiers they had seen in Loanda, and called themselves my "braves" (batla-bani). During the service they all sat with their guns over their shoulders, and excited the unbounded admiration of the women and children. I addressed them all on the goodness of God in preserving us from all the dangers of strange tribes and disease. We had a similar service in the afternoon. The men gave us two fine oxen for slaughter, and the women supplied us abundantly with milk, meal, and butter. It was all quite gratuitous, and I felt ashamed that I could make no return. My men explained the total expenditure of our means, and the Libontese answered gracefully, "It does not matter; you have opened a path for us, and we shall have sleep." Strangers came flocking from a distance, and seldom empty-handed. Their presents I distributed amongst my men.

Our progress down the Barotse valley was just like this. Every village gave us an ox, and sometimes two. The people were wonderfully kind. I felt, and still feel, most deeply grateful, and tried to benefit them in the only way I could, by imparting the knowledge of that Saviour, who can comfort and supply them in the time of need, and my prayer is, that he may send his good Spirit to instruct them and lead them into his kingdom. Even now, I earnestly long to return, and make some recompense to them for their kindness. In passing them on our way to the north, their liberality might have been supposed to be influenced by the hope of repayment on our return, for the white man's land is imagined to be the source of every ornament they prize most. But though we set out from Loanda with a considerable quantity of goods, hoping both to pay our way through the stingy Chiboque, and to make presents to the kind Balonda, and still more generous Makololo, the many delays caused by sickness made us expend all my stock, and all the goods my men procured by their own labour at Loanda, and we returned to the Makololo as poor as when we set out. Yet no distrust was shown, and my poverty did not lessen my influence. They saw that I had been exerting myself for their benefit alone, and even my men remarked, "Though we return as poor as we went, we have not gone in vain." They began immediately to collect tusks of hippopotami and other ivory for a second journey.

CHAPTER XXV.

On the 31st of July we parted with our kind Libonta friends.
We planted some of our palm-tree seeds in different villages of
this valley. They began to sprout even while we were there, but,
unfortunately, they were always destroyed by the mice which
swarm in every hut.

At Chitlane's village, we collected the young of a colony of
the linkololo (*Anastomus lamalligerus*), a black, long-legged bird,
somewhat larger than a crow, which lives on shellfish (*Ampullaria*),
and breeds in society at certain localities among the reeds. These
places are well known, as they continue there from year to year, and
belong to the chiefs, who at particular times of the year gather most
of the young. The produce of this " harvest," as they call it, which

was presented to me, was a hundred and seventy-five unfledged birds. They had been rather late in collecting them, in consequence of waiting for the arrival of Mpololo, who acts the part of chief, but gave them to me, knowing that this would be pleasing to him, otherwise this colony would have yielded double the amount. The old ones appear along the Leeambye in vast flocks, and look lean and scraggy. The young are very fat, and when roasted are esteemed one of the dainties of the Barotse valley. In presents of this kind, as well as of oxen, it is a sort of feast of joy, the person to whom they are presented having the honour of distributing the materials of the feast. We generally slaughtered every ox at the village where it was presented, and then our friends and we rejoiced together.

The village of Chitlane is situated, like all others in the Barotse valley, on an eminence, over which floods do not rise; but this last year, the water approached nearer to an entire submergence of the whole valley, than has been known in the memory of man. Great numbers of people were now suffering from sickness, which always prevails when the waters are drying up; and I found much demand for the medicines I had brought from Loanda. The great variation of the temperature each day, must have a trying effect upon the health. At this village there is a real Indian banian-tree, which has spread itself over a considerable space by means of roots from its branches; it has been termed in consequence "the tree with legs" (more oa maotu). It is curious that trees of this family are looked upon with veneration, and all the way from the Barotse to Loanda, are thought to be preservatives from evil.

On reaching Naliele on the 1st of August, we found Mpololo in great affliction on account of the death of his daughter and her child. She had been lately confined; and her father naturally remembered her when an ox was slaughtered, or when the tribute of other food, which he receives in lieu of Sekeletu, came in his way, and sent frequent presents to her. This moved the envy of one of the Makololo who hated Mpololo, and, wishing to vex him, he entered the daughter's hut by night, and strangled both her and her child. He then tried to make fire in the hut and burn it, so that the murder might not be known; but the squeaking noise of rubbing the sticks awakened a servant, and the murderer was detected. Both he and his wife were thrown into the river; the latter having "known of her husband's intentions, and not revealing them." She declared she had dissuaded him from the crime, and, had any one interposed a word, she might have been spared.

Mpololo exerted himself in every way to supply us with other canoes, and we left Shinte's with him. The Mambowe were well received, and departed with friendly messages to their chief Masiko. My men were exceedingly delighted with the cordial reception we met with everywhere; but a source of annoyance was found where it was not expected. Many of their wives had married other men during our two years' absence. Mashauana's wife, who had borne him two children, was among the number. He wished to appear not to feel it much, saying, "Why, wives are as plentiful as grass, and I can get another: she may go;" but he would add, "If I had that fellow, I would open his ears for him." As most of them had more wives than one, I tried to console them by saying that they had still more than I had, and that they had enough yet; but they felt the reflection to be galling, that while they were toiling, another had been devouring their corn. Some of their wives came with very young infants in their arms. This excited no discontent; and for some, I had to speak to the chief, to order the men, who had married the only wives some of my companions ever had, to restore them.

Sunday, August 5th.—A large audience listened most attentively to my morning address. Surely some will remember the ideas conveyed, and pray to our merciful Father, who would never have thought of Him but for this visit. The invariably kind and respectful treatment I have received from these, and many other heathen tribes in this central country, together with the attentive observations of many years, have led me to the belief that, if one exerts himself for their good, he will never be ill treated. There may be opposition to his doctrine, but none to the man himself.

While still at Naliele, a party which had been sent after me by Masiko arrived. He was much disappointed, because I had not visited him. They brought an elephant's tusk, two calabashes of honey, two baskets of maize, and one of ground-nuts, as a present. Masiko wished to say that he had followed the injunction which I had given, as the will of God, and lived in peace until his brother Limboa came, captured his women as they went to their gardens, and then appeared before his stockade. Masiko offered to lead his men out; but they objected, saying, "Let us servants be killed; you must not be slain." Those who said this were young Barotse, who had been drilled to fighting by Sebituane, and used shields of ox-hide. They beat off the party of Limboa, ten being wounded, and ten slain in the engagement. Limboa subsequently sent three slaves, as a self-imposed fine to Masiko for attacking him. I succeeded in getting the Makololo to treat the messengers of Masiko well, though, as they regarded them as rebels, it was somewhat against the grain at first to speak civilly to them.

Mpololo, attempting to justify an opposite line of conduct, told me how they had fled from Sebituane, even though he had given them numbers of cattle after their subjection by his arms, and was rather surprised to find that I was disposed to think more highly of them for having asserted their independence, even at the loss of milk. For this food, all who have been accustomed to it from infancy in Africa, have an excessive longing. I pointed out how they might be mutually beneficial to each other by the exchange of canoes and cattle.

There are some very old Barotse living here, who were the companions of the old chief Santuru. These men, protected by their age, were very free in their comments on the "upstart" Makololo. One of them, for instance, interrupted my conversation one day with some Makololo gentlemen, with the advice "not to believe them, for they were only a set of thieves;" and it was taken in quite a good-natured way. It is remarkable that none of the ancients here had any tradition of an earthquake having occurred in this region. Their quick perception of events recognisable by the senses, and retentiveness of memory, render it probable, that no perceptible movement of the earth has taken place between 7° and 27° S. in the centre of the continent, during the last two centuries at least. There is no appearance of recent fracture or disturbance of rocks to be seen in the central country, except the falls of Gonye. Nor is there any evidence, or tradition of hurricanes.

I left Naliele on the 13th of August, and when proceeding along the shore at mid-day, a hippopotamus struck the canoe with her forehead, lifting one half of it quite out of the water, so as nearly to overturn it. The force of the butt she gave, tilted

2 K

Mashauana out into the river : the rest of us sprang to the shore, which was only about ten yards off. Glancing back, I saw her come to the surface a short way off, and look to the canoe, as if to see if she had done much mischief. It was a female, whose young one had been speared the day before. No damage was done, except wetting person and goods. This is so unusual an occurrence, when the precaution is taken to coast along the shore, that my men exclaimed, "Is the beast mad?" There were eight of us in the canoe at the time, and the shake it received, shows the immense power of this animal in the water.

On reaching Gonye, Mokwala the head-man having presented me with a tusk, I gave it to Pitsane, as he was eagerly collecting ivory for the Loanda market. The rocks of Gonye are reddish grey sandstone, nearly horizontal, and perforated by madrepores, the holes showing the course of the insect in different directions. The rock itself has been impregnated with iron, and that hardened, forms a glaze on the surface—an appearance common to many of the rocks of this country.

August 22nd.—This is the end of winter. The trees which line the banks begin to bud and blossom; and there is some show of the influence of the new sap, which will soon end in buds that push off the old foliage by assuming a very bright orange colour. This orange is so bright that I mistook it for masses of yellow blossom. There is every variety of shade in the leaves, yellow, purple, copper, liver-colour, and even inky black.

Having got the loan of other canoes from Mpololo, and three oxen as provision for the way, which made the number we had been presented with in the Barotse valley amount to thirteen, we proceeded down the river towards Sesheke, and were as much struck as formerly with the noble river. The whole scenery is lovely, though the atmosphere is murky in consequence of the continuance of the smoky tinge of winter.

This peculiar tinge of the atmosphere was observed every winter at Kolobeng, but it was not so observable in Londa as in the south, though I had always considered that it was owing to the extensive burnings of the grass, in which hundreds of miles of pasturage are annually consumed. As the quantity burnt in the north is very much greater than in the south, and the smoky tinge of winter was not observed, some other explanation than

BOAT CAPSIZED BY AN HIPPOPOTAMUS ROBBED OF HER YOUNG.

these burnings must be sought for. I have sometimes imagined that the lowering of the temperature in the winter, rendered the vapour in the upper current of air visible, and imparted this hazy appearance.

The amount of organic life is surprising. At the time the river begins to rise, the *Ibis religiosa* comes down in flocks of fifties, with prodigious numbers of other water-fowl. Some of the sandbanks appear whitened during the day with flocks of pelicans—I once counted three hundred ; others are brown with ducks (*Anas histrionica*)—I got fourteen of these by one shot (*Querquedula Hottentota*, Smith), and other kinds. Great numbers of gulls (*Procellaria turtur*, Smith), and several others, float over the surface. The vast quantity of small birds, which feed on insects, show that the river teems also with specimens of minute organic life. In walking among bushes on the banks, we are occasionally stung by a hornet which makes its nest in form like that of our own wasp, and hangs it on the branches of trees. The breeding στοργη is so strong in this insect, that it pursues any one twenty or thirty yards who happens to brush too closely past its nest. The sting, which it tries to inflict near the eye, is more like a discharge of electricity from a powerful machine, or a violent blow, than aught else. It produces momentary insensibility, and is followed by the most pungent pain. Yet this insect is quite timid when away from its nest. It is named Murotuani by the Bechuanas.

We have tsetse between Nameta and Sekhosi. An insect of prey, about an inch in length, long-legged and gaunt-looking, may be observed flying about and lighting upon the bare ground. It is a tiger in its way, for it springs upon tsetse and other flies, and, sucking out their blood, throws the bodies aside.

Long before reaching Sesheke, we had been informed that a party of Matebele, the people of Mosilekatse, had brought some packages of goods for me to the south bank of the river, near the Victoria Falls, and though they declared that they had been sent by Mr. Moffat, the Makololo had refused to credit the statement of their sworn enemies. They imagined that the parcels were directed to me as a mere trick, whereby to place witch-craft-medicine into the hands of the Makololo. When the Matebele on the south bank called to the Makololo on the north to

come over in canoes, and receive the goods sent by Moffat to
"Nake," the Makololo replied, "Go along with you, we know
better than that; how could he tell Moffat to send his things
here, he having gone away to the north?" The Matebele
answered, "Here are the goods; we place them now before you,
and if you leave them to perish, the guilt will be yours." When
they had departed, the Makololo thought better of it, and, after
much divination, went over with fear and trembling, and carried
the packages carefully to an island in the middle of the stream;
then, building a hut over them to protect them from the weather,
they left them; and there I found they had remained from
September, 1854, till September, 1855, in perfect safety. Here,
as I had often experienced before, I found the news was very
old, and had lost much of its interest by keeping, but there
were some good eatables from Mrs. Moffat. Amongst other
things, I discovered that my friend, Sir Roderick Murchison,
while in his study in London, had arrived at the same conclusion
respecting the form of the African continent as I had lately come
to, on the spot (see note p. 475); and that, from the attentive
study of the geological map of Mr. Bain and other materials,
some of which were furnished by the discoveries of Mr. Oswell
and myself, he had not only clearly enunciated the peculiar
configuration as an hypothesis in his discourse before the
Geographical Society in 1852, but had even the assurance to
send me out a copy for my information! There was not much
use in nursing my chagrin at being thus fairly "cut out," by the
man who had foretold the existence of the Australian gold before
its discovery, for here it was, in black and white. In his easy-
chair he had forestalled me by three years, though I had been
working hard through jungle, marsh, and fever, and, since the
light dawned on my mind at Dilolo, had been cherishing the
pleasing delusion that I should be the first to suggest the idea,
that the interior of Africa was a watery plateau of less elevation
than flanking hilly ranges.

Having waited a few days at Sesheke till the horses which we
had left at Linyanti should arrive, we proceeded to that town,
and found the waggon and everything we had left in November,
1853, perfectly safe. A grand meeting of all the people was
called to receive our report, and the articles which had been sent

by the governor and merchants of Loanda.   I explained that
none of these were my property, but that they were sent to show
the friendly feelings of the white men, and their eagerness to
enter into commercial relations with the Makololo.   I then
requested my companions to give a true account of what they
had seen.   The wonderful things lost nothing in the telling, the
climax always being that they had finished the whole world, and
had turned only when there was no more land.   One glib old
gentleman asked—"Then you reached Ma Robert (Mrs. L.)?"
They were obliged to confess that she lived a little beyond the
world!   The presents were received with expressions of great
satisfaction and delight; and on Sunday, when Sekeletu made
his appearance at church in his uniform, it attracted more attention than the sermon; and the kind expressions they made use
of respecting myself were so very flattering, that I felt inclined
to shut my eyes.   Their private opinion must have tallied with
their public report, for I very soon received offers from volun-
teers to accompany me to the east coast.   They said they wished
to be able to return and relate strange things like my recent
companions; and Sekeletu immediately made arrangements with
the Arab Ben-Habib to conduct a fresh party with a load of
ivory to Loanda.   These, he said, must go with him and learn to
trade: they were not to have anything to do in the disposal of
the ivory, but simply look and learn.   My companions were to
remain and rest themselves, and then return to Loanda when the
others had come home.   Sekeletu consulted me as to sending
presents back to the governor and merchants of Loanda, but, not
possessing much confidence in this Arab, I advised him to send
a present by Pitsane, as he knew who ought to receive it.

Since my arrival in England, information has been received
from Mr. Gabriel that this party had arrived on the west coast,
but that the ivory had been disposed of to some Portuguese merchants in the interior, and the men had been obliged to carry it
down to Loanda.   They had not been introduced to Mr. Gabriel,
but that gentleman, having learnt that they were in the city,
went to them, and pronounced the names Pitsane, Mashauana,
when all started up and crowded round him.   When Mr. G.
obtained an interpreter, he learned that they had been ordered
by Sekeletu to be sure and go to my brother, as he termed him.

Mr. G. behaved in the same liberal manner as he had done to my companions, and they departed for their distant home, after bidding him a formal and affectionate adieu.

It was to be expected that they would be imposed upon in their first attempt at trading, but I believe that this could not be so easily repeated. It is, however, unfortunate that in dealing with the natives in the interior, there is no attempt made at the establishment of fair prices. The trader shows a quantity of goods, the native asks for more, and more is given. The native, being ignorant of the value of the goods or of his ivory, tries what another demand will bring. After some haggling, an addition is made, and that bargain is concluded to the satisfaction of both parties. Another trader comes, and perhaps offers more than the first; the customary demand for an addition is made, and he yields. The natives by this time are beginning to believe that the more they ask, the more they will get: they continue to urge, the trader bursts into a rage, and the trade is stopped, to be renewed next day by a higher offer. The natives naturally conclude that they were right the day before, and a most disagreeable commercial intercourse is established. A great amount of time is spent in concluding these bargains. In other parts, it is quite common to see the natives going from one trader to another, till they have finished the whole village; and some give presents of brandy to tempt their custom. Much of this unpleasant state of feeling between natives and Europeans, results from the commencements made by those who were ignorant of the language, and from the want of education being given at the same time.

During the time of our absence at Loanda, the Makololo had made two forays, and captured large herds of cattle. One, to the lake, was in order to punish Lechulatebe for the insolence he had manifested after procuring some fire-arms; and the other to Sebola Makwaia, a chief living far to the N.E. This was most unjustifiable, and had been condemned by all the influential Makololo. Ben-Habib, however, had, in coming from Zanzibar, visited Sebola Makwaia, and found that the chief town was governed by an old woman of that name. She received him kindly, and gave him a large quantity of magnificent ivory, sufficient to set him up as a trader, at a very small cost; but, his party having discharged their guns, Ben-Habib observed that the female chief and her people were extremely alarmed, and would have fled and left their cattle in a panic, had he not calmed their fears. Ben-Habib informed the uncle of Sekeletu that he could easily guide him thither, and he might get a large number of cattle without any difficulty. This uncle advised Sekeletu to go; and, as the only greatness he knew, was imitation of his father's deeds, he went, but was not so successful as was anticipated. Sebola Makwaia had fled on hearing of the approach of the Makololo; and, as the country is marshy and intersected in every direction by rivers, they could not easily pursue her. They captured canoes, and, pursuing up different streams, came to a small lake called "Shuia." Having entered the Loangwa, flowing to the eastward, they found it advisable to return, as the natives in those parts became more warlike the further they went in that direction. Before turning, the Arab pointed out an elevated ridge in the distance, and said to the Makololo, "When we see that, we always know that we are only ten or fifteen days from the sea." On seeing him afterwards, he informed me that on the same ridge, but much further to the north, the Banyassa lived, and that the rivers flowed from it towards the S.W. He also confirmed the other Arab's account that the Loapula, which he had crossed at the town of Cazembe, flowed in the same direction, and into the Leeambye.

Several of the influential Makololo who had engaged in these marauding expeditions, had died before our arrival, and Nokwane had succumbed to his strange disease. Ramosantane had perished through vomiting blood from over-fatigue in the march, and Lerimo was affected by a leprosy peculiar to the Barotse valley. In accordance with the advice of my Libonta friends, I did not fail to reprove "my child Sekeletu" for his marauding. This was not done in an angry manner, for no good is ever achieved by fierce denunciations. Motibe, his father-in-law, said to me, "Scold him much, but don't let others hear you."

The Makololo expressed great satisfaction with the route we had opened up to the west, and soon after our arrival a "picho" was called, in order to discuss the question of removal to the Barotse valley, so that they might be nearer the market. Some of the older men objected to abandoning the line of defence afforded by the rivers Chobe and Zambesi, against their southern enemies the Matebele. The Makololo generally have an aversion to the Barotse valley, on account of the fevers which are annually engendered in it as the waters dry up. They prefer it only as a cattle station, for, though the herds are frequently thinned by an epidemic disease (*peripneumonia*), they breed so fast, that the losses are soon made good. Wherever else the Makololo go, they always leave a portion of their stock in the charge of herdsmen in that prolific valley. Some of the younger men objected to removal, because the rankness of the grass at the Barotse did not allow of their running fast, and because there "it never becomes cool."

Sekeletu at last stood up, and, addressing me, said, "I am perfectly satisfied as to the great advantages for trade of the path which you have opened, and think that we ought to go to the Barotse, in order to make the way from us to Loanda shorter; but with whom am I to live there? If you were coming with us, I would remove to-morrow, but now you are going to the white man's country to bring Ma Robert, and when you return, you will find me near to the spot on which you wish to dwell." I had then no idea that any healthy spot existed in the country, and thought only of a convenient central situation, adapted for intercourse with the adjacent tribes and with the coast, such as that near to the confluence of the Leeba and Leeambye.

The fever is certainly a drawback to this otherwise important missionary field. The great humidity produced by heavy rains and inundations, the exuberant vegetation caused by fervid heat in rich moist soil, and the prodigious amount of decaying vegetable matter, annually exposed after the inundations to the rays of a torrid sun, with a flat surface often covered by forest through which the winds cannot pass, all combine to render the climate far from salubrious for any portion of the human family. But the fever, thus caused and rendered virulent, is almost the only disease prevalent in it. There is no consumption or scrofula, and but little insanity. Smallpox and measles visited the country some thirty years ago and cut off many, but they have since made no return, although the former has been almost constantly in one part or another of the coast. Singularly enough, the people used inoculation for this disease; and in one village, where they seem to have chosen a malignant case from which to inoculate the rest, nearly the whole village was cut off. I have seen but one case of hydrocephalus, a few of epilepsy, none of cholera or cancer, and many diseases common in England, are here quite unknown.   It is true that I suffered severely from fever, but my experience cannot be taken as a fair criterion in the matter.   Compelled to sleep on the damp ground month after month, exposed to drenching showers, and getting the lower extremities wetted two or three times every day, living on native food (with the exception of sugarless coffee, during the journey to the north and the latter half of the return journey), and that food the manioc-roots and meal, which contain so much uncombined starch that the eyes become affected (as in the case of animals fed for experiment on pure gluten or starch), and being exposed during many hours each day in comparative inaction to the direct rays of the sun, the thermometer standing above 96° in the shade—these constitute a more pitiful hygiène than any missionaries who may follow will ever have to endure. I do not mention these privations as if I considered them to be "*sacrifices*," for I think that the word ought never to be applied to anything we can do for Him, who came down from heaven and died for us; but I suppose it is necessary to notice them, in order that no unfavourable opinion may be formed from my experience as to what that of others might be, if less exposed to the vicissitudes of the weather and change of diet.

I believe that the interior of this country presents a much more inviting field for the philanthropist than does the west coast, where missionaries of the Church Missionary, United Presbyterian, and other societies, have long laboured with most astonishing devotedness and never-flagging zeal.   There the fevers are much more virulent and more speedily fatal than here; for from 8° south they almost invariably take the intermittent or least fatal type; and their effect being to enlarge the spleen, a complaint which is best treated by change of climate, we have the remedy at hand by passing the 20th parallel on our way south.   But I am not to be understood as intimating that any of the numerous tribes are anxious for instruction: they are not the inquiring spirits we read of in other countries; they do not desire the gospel, because they know nothing about either it, or its benefits; but there is no impediment in the way of instruction.   Every head-man would be proud of a European visitor or resident in his territory, and there is perfect security for life and property all over the interior country. The great barriers which have kept Africa shut are the unhealthiness of the coast, and the exclusive, illiberal disposition of the border tribes. It has not within the historic period been cut into, by deep arms of the sea, and only a small fringe of its population have come into contact with the rest of mankind. Race has much to do in the present circumstances of nations; yet it is probable that the unhealthy coast-climate has reacted on the people, and aided both in perpetuating their own degradation, and preventing those more inland from having intercourse with the rest of the world. It is to be hoped that these obstacles will be overcome by the more rapid means of locomotion possessed in the present age, if a good highway can become available from the coast into the interior.

Having found it impracticable to open up a carriage-path to the west, it became a question as to which part of the east coast we should direct our steps. The Arabs had come from Zanzibar through a peaceful country. They assured me that the powerful chiefs beyond the Cazembe on the N.E., viz. Moatutu, Moaroro, and Mogogo, chiefs of the tribes Batutu, Baroro, and Bagogo, would have no objection to my passing through their country. They described the population there, as located in small villages like the Balonda, and that no difficulty is experienced in travelling amongst them. They mentioned also that, at a distance of ten days beyond Cazembe, their path winds round the end of Lake Tanganyenka. But when they reach this lake a little to the north-west of its southern extremity, they find no difficulty in obtaining canoes to carry them over. They sleep on islands, for it is said to require three days in crossing, and may thus be forty or fifty miles broad. Here they punt the canoes the whole way, showing that it is shallow. There are many small streams in the path, and three large rivers. This then appeared to me to be the safest; but my present object being a path admitting of water rather than land carriage, this route did not promise so much as that by way of the Zambesi or Leeambye. The Makololo knew all the country eastwards as far as the Kafue, from having lived in former times near the confluence of that river with the Zambesi, and they all advised this path in preference to that by the way of

Zanzibar. The only difficulty that they assured me of was that in the falls of Victoria. Some recommended my going to Sesheke, and crossing over in a N.E. direction to the Kafue, which is only six days distant, and descending that river to the Zambesi. Others recommended me to go on the south bank of the Zambesi until I had passed the falls, then get canoes and proceed further down the river. All spoke strongly of the difficulties of travelling on the north bank, on account of the excessively broken and rocky nature of the country near the river on that side. And when Ponuane, who had lately headed a foray there, proposed that I should carry canoes along that side, till we reached the spot where the Leeambye becomes broad and placid again; others declared that, from the difficulties he himself had experienced in forcing the men of his expedition to do this, they believed that mine would be sure to desert me, if I attempted to impose such a task upon them. Another objection to travelling on either bank of the river, was the prevalence of the tsetse, which is so abundant, that the inhabitants can keep no domestic animals except goats.

While pondering over these different paths, I could not help regretting my being alone. If I had enjoyed the company of my former companion, Mr. Oswell, one of us might have taken the Zambesi, and the other gone by way of Zanzibar. The latter route was decidedly the easiest, because all the inland tribes were friendly, while the tribes in the direction of the Zambesi were inimical, and I should now be obliged to lead a party, which the Batoka of that country view as hostile invaders, through an enemy's land; but as the prospect of permanent water conveyance was good, I decided on going down the Zambesi, and keeping on the north bank, because, in the map given by Bowdich, Tete, the farthest inland station of the Portuguese, is erroneously placed on that side. Being near the end of September, the rains were expected daily; the clouds were collecting, and the wind blew strongly from the east, but it was excessively hot. All the Makololo urged me strongly to remain till the ground should be cooled by the rains; and as it was probable that I should get fever if I commenced my journey now, I resolved to wait. The parts of the country about 17° and 18° suffer from drought and become dusty. It is but the commencement of the humid region to the north, and partakes occasionally of the character of both the wet and dry regions. Some idea may be formed of the heat in October by the fact, that the thermometer (protected) stood, in the shade of my waggon, at 100° through the day. It rose to 110° if unprotected from the wind, at dark it showed 89°, at 10 o'clock 80°, and then gradually sunk till sunrise, when it was 70°. That is usually the period of greatest cold in each twenty-four hours, in this region. The natives during the period of greatest heat keep in their huts, which are always pleasantly cool by day, but close and suffocating by night. Those who are able to afford it, sit guzzling beer or boyaloa; the perspiration produced by copious draughts seems to give enjoyment, the evaporation causing a feeling of coolness. The attendants of the chief, on these occasions, keep up a continuous roar of bantering, raillery, laughing, and swearing. The dance is kept up, in the moonlight, till past midnight. The women stand clapping their hands continuously, and the old men sit admiringly, and say, "It is really very fine!" As crowds came to see me, I employed much of my time in conversation, that being a good mode of conveying instruction. In the public meetings for worship the people listened very attentively, and behaved with more decorum than formerly. They really form a very inviting field for a missionary. Surely the oft-told tale of the goodness and love of our Heavenly Father, in giving up His own Son to death for us sinners, will, by the power of His Holy Spirit, beget love in some of these heathen hearts.

1st October.—Before Ben Habib started for Loanda, he asked the daughter of Sebituane in marriage. This is the plan the Arabs adopt for gaining influence in a tribe, and they have been known to proceed thus cautiously to form connections, and gradually gain so much influence, as to draw all the tribe over to their religion. I never heard of any persecution, although the Arabs with whom I came in contact seemed much attached to their religion. This daughter of Sebituane, named Manchunyane, was about twelve years of age. As I was the bosom friend of her father, I was supposed to have a voice in her disposal, and, on being asked, objected to her being taken away, we knew not whither, and where we might never see her again. As her name implies, she was only a little black, and, besides being as fair as any of the Arabs, had quite the Arab features; but I have no doubt that Ben Habib will renew his suit more successfully on some other occasion. In these cases of marriage, the consent of the young women is seldom asked. A maidservant of Sekeletu, however, pronounced by the Makololo to be goodlooking, was at this time sought in marriage by five young men. Sekeletu, happening to be at my waggon when one of these preferred his suit, very coolly ordered all five to stand in a row before the young woman, that she might make her choice. Two refused to stand, apparently, because they could not brook the idea of a repulse, although willing enough to take her, if Sekeletu had acceded to their petition without reference to her will. Three dandified fellows stood forth, and she unhesitatingly decided on taking one who was really the best looking. It was amusing to see the mortification exhibited on the black faces of the unsuccessful candidates, while the spectators greeted them with a hearty laugh.

During the whole of my stay with the Makololo, Sekeletu supplied my wants abundantly, appointing some cows to furnish me with milk, and, when he went out to hunt, sent home orders for slaughtered oxen to be given. That the food was not given in a niggardly spirit, may be inferred from the fact, that, when I proposed to depart on the 20th of October, he protested against my going off in such a hot sun. "Only wait," said he, "for the first shower, and then I will let you go." This was reasonable, for the thermometer, placed upon a deal box in the sun, rose to 138°. It stood at 108° in the shade by day, and 96° at sunset. If my experiments were correct, the blood of a European is of a higher temperature than that of an African. The bulb, held under my tongue, stood at 100°, under that of the natives, at 98°. There was much sickness in the town, and no wonder, for part of the water left by the inundation, still formed a large pond in the centre. Even the plains between Linyanti and Sesheke had not yet been freed from the waters of the inundation. They had risen higher than usual, and for a long time, canoes passed from the one place to the other, a distance of upwards of 120 miles, in nearly a straight line. We found many patches of stagnant water, which, when disturbed by our passing through them, evolved strong effluvia of sulphuretted hydrogen. At other times these spots exhibit an efflorescence of the nitrate of soda ; they also contain abundance of lime, probably from decaying vegetable matter, and from these may have emanated the malaria which caused the present sickness. I have often remarked this effluvium in sickly spots, and cannot help believing but that it has some connection with fever, though I am quite aware of Dr. MacWilliams's unsuccessful efforts to discover sulphuretted hydrogen by the most delicate tests, in the Niger expedition.

I had plenty of employment, for, besides attending to the severer cases, I had perpetual calls on my attention. The town contained, at least, 7000 inhabitants, and every one thought that he might come, and at least look at me. In talking with some of the more intelligent in the evenings, the conversation having turned from inquiries respecting eclipses of the sun and moon to that other world where Jesus reigns, they let me know that my attempts to enlighten them had not been without some small effect. "Many of the children," said they, "talk about the strange things you bring to their ears, but the old men show a little opposition by saying, 'Do we know what he is talking about?'" Ntlaria and others, complain of treacherous memories, and say, "When we hear words about other things, we hold them fast; but when we hear you tell much more wonderful things than any we have ever heard before, we don't know how it is, they run away from our hearts." These are the more intelligent of my Makololo friends. On the majority, the teaching produces no appreciable effect; they assent to the truth with the most perplexing indifference, adding, "But we don't know," or, "We do not understand." My medical intercourse with them enabled me to ascertain their moral status, better than a mere religious teacher could do. They do not attempt to hide the evil, as men often do, from their spiritual instructors; but I have found it difficult to come to a conclusion on their character. They sometimes perform actions remarkably good, and sometimes as strangely the opposite. I have been unable to ascertain the motive for the good, or account for the callousness of conscience with which they perpetrate the bad. After long observation, I came to the conclusion that they are just such a strange mixture of good and evil, as men are everywhere else. There is not among them an approach to that constant stream of benevolence flowing from the rich to the poor which we have in England, nor yet the unostentatious attentions which we have among our own poor to each other. Yet there are frequent instances of genuine kindness and liberality, as well as actions of an opposite character. The rich show kindness to the poor, in expectation of services, and a poor person who has no relatives, will seldom be supplied even with water in illness, and, when dead, will be dragged out to be devoured by the hyænas, instead of being buried. Relatives alone will condescend to touch a dead body. It would be easy to enumerate instances of inhumanity which I have witnessed. An interesting-looking girl came to my waggon one day, in a state of nudity, and almost a skeleton. She was a captive from another tribe, and had been neglected by the man who claimed her. Having supplied her wants, I made inquiry for him, and found that he had been unsuccessful in raising a crop of corn, and had no food to give her. I volunteered to take her; but he said he would allow me to feed her and make her fat, and then take her away. I protested against this heartlessness; and as he said he could "not part with his child," I was precluded from attending to her wants. In a day or two she was lost sight of. She had gone out a little way from the town, and, being too weak to return, had been cruelly left to perish. Another day I saw a poor boy going to the water to drink, apparently in a starving condition. This case I brought before the chief in council, and found that his emaciation was ascribed to disease and want combined. He was not one of the Makololo, but a member of a subdued tribe. I showed them that any one professing to claim a child, and refusing proper nutriment, would be guilty of his death. Sekeletu decided that the owner of this boy should give up his alleged right, rather than destroy the child. When I took him, he was so far gone as to be in the cold stage of starvation, but was soon brought round by a little milk given three or four times a day. On leaving Linyanti, I handed him over to the charge of his chief Sekeletu, who feeds his servants very well. On the other hand, I have seen instances in which both men and women have taken up little orphans, and carefully reared them as their own children. By a selection of cases of either kind, it would not be difficult to make these people appear excessively good or uncommonly bad.

I still possessed some of the coffee which I had brought from Angola, and some of the sugar which I had left in my waggon. So long as the sugar lasted, Sekeletu favoured me with his company at meals; but the sugar soon came to a close. The

Makololo, as formerly mentioned, were well acquainted with the sugar-cane, as it is cultivated by the Barotse, but never knew that sugar could be got from it. When I explained the process by which it was produced, Sekeletu asked if I could not buy him an apparatus for the purpose of making sugar. He said that he would plant the cane largely, if he only had the means of making the sugar from it. I replied, that I was unable to purchase a mill, when he instantly rejoined, "Why not take ivory to buy it?" As I had been living at his expense, I was glad of the opportunity to show my gratitude by serving him; and when he and his principal men understood that I was willing to execute a commission, Sekeletu gave me an order for a sugar-mill, and for all the different varieties of clothing that he had ever seen, especially a mohair coat, a good rifle, beads, brass-wire, &c. &c., and wound up by saying, "and any other beautiful thing you may see in your own country." As to the quantity of ivory required to execute the commission, I said I feared that a large amount would be necessary. Both he and his councillors replied, "The ivory is all your own; if you leave any in the country it will be your own fault." He was also anxious for horses. The two I had left with him when I went to Loanda, were still living, and had been of great use to him in hunting the giraffe and eland, and he was now anxious to have a breed. This, I thought might be obtained at the Portuguese settlements. All were very much delighted with the donkeys we had brought from Loanda. As we found that they were not affected by the bite of the tsetse, and there was a prospect of the breed being continued, it was gratifying to see the experiment of their introduction so far successful. The donkeys came as frisky as kids all the way from Loanda, until we began to descend the Leeambye. There we came upon so many interlacing branches of the river, and were obliged to drag them through such masses of tangled aquatic plants, that we half drowned them, and were at last obliged to leave them somewhat exhausted at Naliele. They excited the unbounded admiration of my men by their knowledge of the different kinds of plants, which, as they remarked, "the animals had never before seen in their own country;" and when the donkeys indulged in their music, they startled the inhabitants more than if they had been lions. We never rode them, nor yet the horse which had been given by the Bishop, for fear of hurting them by any work.

Although the Makololo were so confiding, the reader must not imagine that they would be so to every individual who might visit them. Much of my influence depended upon the good name given me by the Bakwains, and that I secured only through a long course of tolerably good conduct. No one ever gains much influence in this country without purity and uprightness. The acts of a stranger are keenly scrutinized by both young and old, and seldom is the judgment pronounced, even by the heathen, unfair or uncharitable. I have heard women speaking in admiration of a white man, because he was pure, and never was guilty of any secret immorality. Had he been, they would have known it, and, untutored heathen though they be, would have despised him in consequence. Secret vice becomes known throughout the tribe; and while one unacquainted with the language may imagine a peccadillo to be hidden, it is as patent to all as it would be in London, had he a placard on his back.

27th October, 1855. The first continuous rain of the season commenced during the night, the wind being from the N.E., as it always was on like occasions at Kolobeng. The rainy season was thus begun, and I made ready to go. The mother of Sekeletu prepared a bag of ground-nuts, by frying them in cream with a little salt, as a sort of sandwiches for my journey. This is considered food fit for a chief. Others ground the maize from my own garden into meal, and Sekeletu pointed out Sekwébu and Kanyata, as the persons who should head the party intended to form my company. Sekwebu had been captured by the Matebele when a little boy, and the tribe in which he was a captive, had migrated to the country near Tete: he had travelled along both banks of the Zambesi several times, and was intimately acquainted with the dialects spoken there. I found him to be a person of great prudence and sound judgment, and his subsequent loss at the Mauritius has been, ever since, a source of sincere regret. He at once recommended our keeping well away from the river, on account of the tsetse and rocky country, assigning also as a reason for it, that the Leeambye beyond the falls turns round to the N.N.E. Mamire, who had married the mother of Sekeletu, on coming to bid me farewell before starting, said, "You

2 L

are now going among people who cannot be trusted, because we have used them badly, but you go with a different message from any they ever heard before, and Jesus will be with you, and help you, though among enemies; and if he carries you safely and brings you and Ma Robert back again, I shall say he has bestowed a great favour upon me. May we obtain a path whereby we may visit and be visited by other tribes, and by white men!" On telling him my fears that he was still inclined to follow the old marauding system, which prevented intercourse, and that he, from his influential position, was especially guilty in the late forays, he acknowledged all rather too freely for my taste, but seemed quite aware that the old system was far from right. Mentioning my inability to pay the men who were to accompany me, he replied, "A man wishes, of course, to appear among his friends after a long absence with something of his own to show: the whole of the ivory in the country is yours, so you must take as much as you can, and Sekeletu will furnish men to carry it." These remarks of Mamire are quoted literally, in order to show the state of mind of the most influential in the tribe. And as I wish to give the reader a fair idea of the other side of the question as well, it may be mentioned, that Motibe parried the imputation of the guilt of marauding by every possible subterfuge. He would not admit that they had done wrong, and laid the guilt of the wars in which the Makololo had engaged, on the Boers, the Matebele, and every other tribe except his own. When quite a youth, Motibe's family had been attacked by a party of Boers: he hid himself in an anteater's hole, but was drawn out and thrashed with a whip of hippopotamus-hide. When enjoined to live in peace, he would reply, "Teach the Boers to lay down their arms first." Yet Motibe on other occasions seemed to feel the difference between those who are Christians indeed, and those who are so only in name. In all our discussions we parted good friends.

CHAPTER XXVI.

On the 3rd of November we bade adieu to our friends at Linyanti, accompanied by Sekeletu and about 200 followers. We were all fed at his expense, and he took cattle for this purpose from every station we came to. The principal men of the Makololo; Lebeóle, Ntlarié, Nkwatléle, &c., were also of the party. We passed through the patch of the tsetse, which exists between Linyanti and Seshéke, by night. The majority of the company went on by daylight, in order to prepare our beds. Sekeletu and I, with about forty young men, waited outside the tsetse till dark. We then went forward, and about ten o'clock it became so pitchy dark, that both horses and men were completely blinded. The lightning spread over the sky, forming eight or ten branches at a time, in shape exactly like those of a tree. This, with great volumes of sheet-lightning, enabled us at times to see the whole country. The intervals between the flashes were so densely dark, as to convey the idea of stone-blindness. The horses trembled, cried out, and turned round, as if searching for each other, and every new flash revealed the men taking different directions, laughing, and stumbling against each other. The thunder was of

2 L 2

that tremendously loud kind only to be heard in tropical countries, and which, friends from India have assured me, is louder in Africa than any they have ever heard elsewhere. Then came a pelting rain, which completed our confusion. After the intense heat of the day, we soon felt miserably cold, and turned aside to a fire we saw in the distance. This had been made by some people on their march; for this path is seldom without numbers of strangers passing to and from the capital. My clothing having gone on, I lay down on the cold ground, expecting to spend a miserable night, but Sekeletu kindly covered me with his own blanket and lay uncovered himself. I was much affected by this little act of genuine kindness. If such men must perish by the advance of civilization, as certain races of animals do before others, it is a pity. God grant that ere this time comes, they may receive that gospel, which is a solace for the soul in death!

While at Sesheke, Sekeletu supplied me with twelve oxen— three of which were accustomed to being ridden upon—hoes, and beads to purchase a canoe, when we should strike the Leeambye beyond the falls. He likewise presented abundance of good fresh butter and honey, and did everything in his power to make me comfortable for the journey. I was entirely dependent on his generosity, for the goods I originally brought from the Cape, were all expended by the time I set off from Linyanti to the west coast. I there drew 70l. of my salary, paid my men with it, and purchased goods for the return journey to Linyanti. These being now all expended, the Makololo again fitted me out, and sent me on to the east coast. I was thus dependent on their bounty, and that of other Africans, for the means of going from Linyanti to Loanda, and again from Linyanti to the east coast; and I feel deeply grateful to them. Coin would have been of no benefit, for gold and silver are quite unknown. We were here joined by Moriantsáne, uncle of Sekeletu, and head-man of Sesheke, and, entering canoes on the 13th, some sailed down the river to the confluence of the Chobe, while others drove the cattle along the banks, spending one night at Mparia, the island at the confluence of the Chobe, which is composed of trap, having crystals of quartz in it, coated with a pellicle of green copper ore. Attempting to proceed down the river next day, we were detained some hours by a strong east wind, raising waves so large as to threaten to swamp the canoes. The river is here very large and deep, and contains two considerable islands, which from either bank seem to be joined to the opposite shore. While waiting for the wind to moderate, my friends related the traditions of these islands, and, as usual, praised the wisdom of Sebituane in balking the Batoka, who formerly enticed wandering tribes to them, and starved them, by compelling the chiefs to remain by his side till all his cattle and people were ferried over. The Barotse believe that at certain parts of the river a tremendous monster lies hid, and that it will catch a canoe and hold it fast and motionless, in spite of the utmost exertions of the paddlers. While near Nameta, they even objected to pass a spot supposed to be haunted, and proceeded along a branch instead of the main stream. They believe that some of them possess a knowledge of the proper prayer to lay the monster. It is strange to find fables similar to those of the more northern nations even in the heart of Africa. Can they be the vestiges of traditions of animals which no longer exist? The fossil bones which lie in the calcareous tufa of this region will yet, we hope, reveal the ancient fauna.

Having descended about ten miles, we came to the island of Nampéne, at the beginning of the rapids, where we were obliged to leave the canoes and proceed along the banks on foot. The next evening we slept opposite the island of Chondo, and, then crossing the Lekóne or Lekwine, early the following morning were at the island of Sekóte, called Kalái. This Sekote was the last of the Batoka chiefs whom Sebituane rooted out. The island is surrounded by a rocky shore and deep channels, through which the river rushes with great force. Sekote, feeling secure in his island home, ventured to ferry over the Matebele enemies of Sebituane. When they had retired, Sebituane made one of those rapid marches which he always adopted in every enterprise. He came down the Leeambye from Naliele, sailing by day along the banks, and during the night in the middle of the stream, to avoid the hippopotami. When he reached Kalai, Sekote took advantage of the larger canoes they employ in the rapids, and fled during the night to the opposite bank. Most of his people were slain or taken captive, and the island has ever since been under the Makololo. It is large enough to contain a considerable town. On the northern side I found the kotla of the

elder Sekote, garnished with numbers of human skulls mounted
on poles: a large heap of the crania of hippopotami, the tusks
untouched except by time, stood on one side.   At a short distance,
under some trees, we saw the grave of Sekote, ornamented with
seventy large elephants' tusks, planted round it with the points
turned inwards, and there were thirty more placed over the resting-
places of his relatives.   These were all decaying from the effects
of the sun and weather; but a few, which had enjoyed the shade,
were in a pretty good condition.   I felt inclined to take a specimen of the tusks of the hippopotami, as they were the largest I
had ever seen; but feared that the people would look upon me as
a "resurrectionist" if I did, and regard any unfavourable event
which might afterwards occur, as a punishment for the sacrilege.
The Batoka believe that Sekote had a pot of medicine buried here,
which, when opened, would cause an epidemic in the country.
These tyrants acted much on the fears of their people.

As this was the point from which we intended to strike off to
the north-east, I resolved on the following day to visit the falls of
Victoria, called by the natives Mosioatunya, or more anciently
Shongwe.   Of these we had often heard since we came into the
country: indeed one of the questions asked by Sebituane was,
"Have you smoke that sounds in your country?"   They did
not go near enough to examine them, but, viewing them with
awe at a distance, said, in reference to the vapour and noise,
"Mosi oa tunya" (smoke does sound there).   It was previously called Shongwe, the meaning of which I could not
ascertain.   The word for a "pot" resembles this, and it may mean
a seething caldron; but I am not certain of it.   Being persuaded
that Mr. Oswell and myself were the very first Europeans who
ever visited the Zambesi in the centre of the country, and that
this is the connecting link between the known and unknown
portions of that river, I decided to use the same liberty as the
Makololo did, and gave the only English name I have affixed to
any part of the country.   No better proof of previous ignorance
of this river could be desired, than that an untravelled gentleman,
who had spent a great part of his life in the study of the geography of Africa, and knew everything written on the subject
from the time of Ptolemy downwards, actually asserted in the
'Athenæum,' while I was coming up the Red Sea, that this

magnificent river, the Leeambye, had "no connection with the Zambesi, but flowed under the Kalahari Desert, and became lost;" and "that, as all the old maps asserted, the Zambesi took its rise in the very hills to which we have now come." This modest assertion smacks exactly as if a native of Timbuctu should declare, that the "Thames" and the "Pool" were different rivers, he having seen neither the one nor the other. Leeambye and Zambesi mean the very same thing, viz. the RIVER.

Sekeletu intended to accompany me, but, one canoe only having come instead of the two he had ordered, he resigned it to me. After twenty minutes' sail from Kalai, we came in sight, for the first time, of the columns of vapour, appropriately called "smoke," rising at a distance of five or six miles, exactly as when large tracts of grass are burned in Africa. Five columns now arose, and bending in the direction of the wind, they seemed placed against a low ridge covered with trees; the tops of the columns at this distance appeared to mingle with the clouds. They were white below, and higher up became dark, so as to simulate smoke very closely. The whole scene was extremely beautiful; the banks and islands dotted over the river are adorned with sylvan vegetation of great variety of colour and form. At the period of our visit several trees were spangled over with blossoms. Trees have each their own physiognomy. There, towering over all, stands the great burly baobab, each of whose enormous arms would form the trunk of a large tree, beside groups of graceful palms, which, with their feathery-shaped leaves depicted on the sky, lend their beauty to the scene. As a hieroglyphic they always mean "far from home," for one can never get over their foreign air in a picture or landscape. The silvery mohonono, which in the tropics is in form like the cedar of Lebanon, stands in pleasing contrast with the dark colour of the motsouri, whose cypress-form is dotted over at present with its pleasant scarlet fruit. Some trees resemble the great spreading oak, others assume the character of our own elms and chestnuts; but no one can imagine the beauty of the view from anything witnessed in England. It had never been seen before by European eyes; but scenes so lovely must have been gazed upon by angels in their flight. The only want felt, is that of mountains in the background. The falls are bounded on three sides by ridges 300 or 400 feet in height, which are covered

with forest, with the red soil appearing among the trees. When
about half a mile from the falls, I left the canoe by which we had
come down thus far, and embarked in a lighter one, with men well
acquainted with the rapids, who, by passing down the centre of
the stream in the eddies and still places caused by many jutting
rocks, brought me to an island situated in the middle of the river,
and on the edge of the lip over which the water rolls. In coming
hither, there was danger of being swept down by the streams
which rushed along on each side of the island; but the river was
now low, and we sailed where it is totally impossible to go when
the water is high. But though we had reached the island, and
were within a few yards of the spot, a view from which would solve
the whole problem, I believe that no one could perceive where
the vast body of water went; it seemed to lose itself in the
earth, the opposite lip of the fissure into which it disappeared,
being only 80 feet distant. At least I did not comprehend it until,
creeping with awe to the verge, I peered down into a large rent
which had been made from bank to bank of the broad Zambesi,
and saw that a stream of a thousand yards broad, leaped down a
hundred feet, and then became suddenly compressed into a space of
fifteen or twenty yards. The entire falls are simply a crack made
in a hard basaltic rock from the right to the left bank of the Zambesi, and then prolonged from the left bank away through thirty or
forty miles of hills. If one imagines the Thames filled with low
tree-covered hills immediately beyond the tunnel, extending as far
as Gravesend; the bed of black basaltic rock instead of London
mud; and a fissure made therein from one end of the tunnel to the
other, down through the keystones of the arch, and prolonged
from the left end of the tunnel through thirty miles of hills; the
pathway being 100 feet down from the bed of the river instead of
what it is, with the lips of the fissure from 80 to 100 feet apart;
then fancy the Thames leaping bodily into the gulf; and forced
there to change its direction, and flow from the right to the left
bank; and then rush boiling and roaring through the hills,—he may
have some idea of what takes place at this, the most wonderful
sight I had witnessed in Africa. In looking down into the fissure on
the right of the island, one sees nothing but a dense white cloud,
which, at the time we visited the spot, had two bright rainbows on
it. (The sun was on the meridian, and the declination about equal

to the latitude of the place.) From this cloud rushed up a great
jet of vapour exactly like steam, and it mounted 200 or 300
feet high; there condensing, it changed its hue to that of dark
smoke, and came back in a constant shower, which soon wetted us
to the skin. This shower falls chiefly on the opposite side of the
fissure, and a few yards back from the lip, there stands a straight
hedge of evergreen trees, whose leaves are always wet. From
their roots a number of little rills run back into the gulf; but
as they flow down the steep wall there, the column of vapour,
in its ascent, licks them up clean off the rock, and away they
mount again. They are constantly running down, but never
reach the bottom.

On the left of the island we see the water at the bottom, a white
rolling mass moving away to the prolongation of the fissure, which
branches off near the left bank of the river. A piece of the rock
has fallen off a spot on the left of the island, and juts out from the
water below, and from it, I judged the distance which the water
falls to be about 100 feet. The walls of this gigantic crack are
perpendicular, and composed of one homogeneous mass of rock.
The edge of that side over which the water falls, is worn off two or
three feet, and pieces have fallen away, so as to give it somewhat
of a serrated appearance. That over which the water does not
fall, is quite straight, except at the left corner, where a rent
appears, and a piece seems inclined to fall off. Upon the whole,
it is nearly in the state in which it was left at the period of its
formation. The rock is dark brown in colour, except about ten
feet from the bottom, which is discoloured by the annual rise of
the water to that or a greater height. On the left side of the
island we have a good view of the mass of water which causes one
of the columns of vapour to ascend, as it leaps quite clear of the
rock, and forms a thick unbroken fleece all the way to the bottom.
Its whiteness gave the idea of snow, a sight I had not seen for
many a day. As it broke into (if I may use the term) pieces of
water, all rushing on in the same direction, each gave off several
rays of foam, exactly as bits of steel, when burnt in oxygen gas,
give off rays of sparks. The snow-white sheet seemed like myriads
of small comets rushing on in one direction, each of which left
behind its nucleus rays of foam. I never saw the appearance
referred to, noticed elsewhere. It seemed to be the effect of the

mass of water leaping at once clear of the rock, and but slowly breaking up into spray.

I have mentioned that we saw five columns of vapour ascending from this strange abyss. They are evidently formed by the compression suffered by the force of the water's own fall, into an unyielding wedge-shaped space. Of the five columns, two on the right, and one on the left of the island were the largest, and the streams which formed them seemed each to exceed in size the falls of the Clyde at Stonebyres, when that river is in flood. This was the period of low water in the Leeambye, but, as far as I could guess, there was a flow of five or six hundred yards of water, which, at the edge of the fall, seemed at least three feet deep. I write in the hope that others more capable of judging distances than myself will visit this scene, and I state simply the impressions made on my mind at the time. I thought, and do still think, the river above the falls to be one thousand yards broad; but I am a poor judge of distances on water, for I showed a naval friend what I supposed to be four hundred yards in the bay of Loanda, and, to my surprise, he pronounced it to be nine hundred. I tried to measure the Leeambye with a strong thread, the only line I had in my possession, but when the men had gone two or three hundred yards, they got into conversation, and did not hear us shouting that the line had become entangled. By still going on they broke it, and, being carried away down the stream, it was lost on a snag. In vain I tried to bring to my recollection the way I had been taught to measure a river, by taking an angle with the sextant. That I once knew it, and that it was easy, were all the lost ideas I could recall, and they only increased my vexation. However, I measured the river farther down by another plan, and then I discovered that the Portuguese had measured it at Tete, and found it a little over one thousand yards. At the falls it is as broad as at Tete, if not more so. Whoever may come after me will not, I trust, find reason to say I have indulged in exaggeration. With respect to the drawing, it must be borne in mind, that it was composed from a rude sketch as viewed from the island, which exhibited the columns of vapour only, and a ground plan. The artist has given a good idea of the scene, but, by way of explanation, he has shown more of the depth of the fissure than is visible, except by going close to the edge. The

left-hand column, and that farthest off, are the smallest, and all
ought to have been a little more tapering at the tops.

The fissure is said by the Makololo to be very much deeper
farther to the eastward; there is one part at which the walls
are so sloping, that people accustomed to it, can go down by
descending in a sitting position. The Makololo on one occasion,
pursuing some fugitive Batoka, saw them, unable to stop the im-
petus of their flight at the edge, literally dashed to pieces at the
bottom. They beheld the stream like a "white cord" at the
bottom, and so far down (probably 300 feet) that they became
giddy, and were fain to go away, holding on to the ground.

Now, though the edge of the rock over which the river falls, does
not show wearing more than three feet, and there is no appearance
of the opposite wall being worn out at the bottom in the parts
exposed to view, yet it is probable that, where it has flowed
beyond the falls, the sides of the fissure may have given way,
and the parts out of sight may be broader than the "white cord"
on the surface. There may even be some ramifications of the
fissure, which take a portion of the stream quite beneath the
rocks; but this I did not learn.

If we take the want of much wear on the lip of hard basaltic
rock as of any value, the period when this rock was riven, is
not geologically very remote. I regretted the want of proper
means of measuring and marking its width at the falls, in order
that, at some future time, the question whether it is progressive
or not, might be tested. It seemed as if a palm-tree could be
laid across it from the island. And if it is progressive, as it would
mark a great natural drainage being effected, it might furnish a
hope that Africa will one day become a healthy continent. It is
at any rate very much changed in respect to its lakes, within a
comparatively recent period.

At three spots near these falls, one of them the island in the
middle on which we were, three Batoka chiefs offered up prayers
and sacrifices to the Barimo. They chose their places of prayer
within the sound of the roar of the cataract, and in sight of the
bright bows in the cloud. They must have looked upon the
scene with awe. Fear may have induced the selection. The
river itself is, to them, mysterious. The words of the canoe-song
are—

"The Leeambye! Nobody knows,
Whence it comes and whither it goes."

The play of colours of the double iris on the cloud, seen by them elsewhere only as the rainbow, may have led them to the idea that this was the abode of Deity. Some of the Makololo who went with me near to Gonye, looked upon the same sign with awe. When seen in the heavens it is named "motsé oa barimo"—the pestle of the gods. Here they could approach the emblem, and see it stand steadily above the blustering uproar below—a type of Him who sits supreme—alone unchangeable, though ruling over all changing things. But not aware of His true character, they had no admiration of the beautiful and good in their bosoms. They did not imitate His benevolence, for they were a bloody imperious crew, and Sebituane performed a noble service, in the expulsion from their fastnesses of these cruel "Lords of the Isles."

Having feasted my eyes long on the beautiful sight, I returned to my friends at Kalai, and, saying to Sekeletu that he had nothing else worth showing in his country, his curiosity was excited to visit it the next day. I returned with the intention of taking a lunar observation from the island itself, but the clouds were unfavourable, consequently all my determinations of position refer to Kalai. (Lat. 17° 51' 54" S., long. 25° 41' E.) Sekeletu acknowledged to feeling a little nervous at the probability of being sucked into the gulf before reaching the island. His companions amused themselves by throwing stones down, and wondered to see them diminishing in size, and even disappearing, before they reached the water at the bottom.

I had another object in view in my return to the island. I observed that it was covered with trees, the seeds of which had probably come down with the stream from the distant north, and several of which I had seen nowhere else, and every now and then the wind wafted a little of the condensed vapour over it, and kept the soil in a state of moisture, which caused a sward of grass, growing as green as on an English lawn. I selected a spot—not too near the chasm, for there the constant deposition of the moisture nourished numbers of polypi of a mushroom shape and fleshy consistence—but somewhat back, and made a little garden. I there planted about a hundred peach and apricot stones, and a quantity of coffee-seeds. I had attempted fruit-trees before, but, when left in charge of my Makololo friends, they were always allowed to wither, after having vegetated, by being forgotten. I bargained for a hedge with one of the Makololo, and if he is faithful, I have great hopes of Mosioatunya's abilities as a nurseryman. My only source of fear is the hippopotami, whose footprints I saw on the island. When the garden was prepared, I cut my initials on a tree, and the date 1855. This was the only instance in which I indulged in this piece of vanity. The garden stands in front, and were there no hippopotami, I have no doubt but this will be the parent of all the gardens, which may yet be in this new country. We then went up to Kalai again.

On passing up we had a view of the hut on the island, where my goods had lain so long in safety. It was under a group of palm-trees, and Sekeletu informed me that, so fully persuaded were most of the Makololo of the presence of dangerous charms in the packages, that, had I not returned to tell them the contrary, they never would have been touched. Some of the diviners had been so positive in their decisions on the point, that the men who lifted a bag thought they felt a live kid in it. The diviners always quote their predictions when thay happen to tally with the event. They declared that the whole party which went to Loanda had perished; and as I always quoted the instances in which they failed, many of them refused to throw the "bola" (instruments of divination) when I was near. This was a noted instance of failure. It would have afforded me equal if not greater pleasure to have exposed the failure, if such it had been, of the European diviner whose paper lay a whole year on this island, but I was obliged to confess that he had been successful with his "bola," and could only comfort myself with the idea that, though Sir Roderick Murchison's discourse had lain so long within sight and sound of the magnificent falls, I had been "cut out" by no one in their discovery.

I saw the falls at low water, and the columns of vapour, when five or six miles distant. When the river is full, or in flood, the columns, it is said, can be seen ten miles off, and the sound is quite distinct somewhat beyond Kalai, or about an equal distance. No one can then go to the island in the middle. The next visitor must bear these points in mind in comparing his description with mine.

We here got information of a foray, which had been made by a Makololo man in the direction we were going. This instance of marauding was so much in accordance with the system which has been pursued in this country, that I did not wonder at it. But the man had used Sekeletu's name as having sent him, and, the proof being convincing, he would undoubtedly be fined. As that would be the first instance of a fine being levied for marauding, I looked upon it as the beginning of a better state of things. In tribes which have been accustomed to cattle-stealing, the act is not considered immoral, in the way that theft is. Before I knew the language well, I said to a chief, " You stole the cattle of so and so." " No, I did not steal them," was the reply, "I only *lifted* them." The word " *gapa* " is identical with the Highland term for the same deed.

Another point came to our notice here. Some Mambari had come down thus far, and induced the Batoka to sell a very large tusk which belonged to Sekeletu, for a few bits of cloth. They had gone among the Batoka who need hoes, and, having purchased some of these from the people near Sesheke, induced the others living farther east, to sell both ivory and children. They would not part with children for clothing or beads, but agriculture with wooden hoes is so laborious, that the sight of the hoes prevailed. The Makololo proposed to knock the Mambari on the head as the remedy, the next time they came ; but on my proposing that they should send hoes themselves, and thereby secure the ivory in a quiet way, all approved highly of the idea, and Pitsane and Mohorisi expatiated on the value of the ivory, their own willingness to go and sell it at Loanda, and the disgust with which the Mambari whom we met in Angola, had looked upon their attempt to reach the proper market. If nothing untoward happens, I think there is a fair prospect of the trade in slaves being abolished in a natural way in this quarter ; Pitsane and Mohorisi having again expressed their willingness to go away back to Loanda if Sekeletu would give them orders. This was the more remarkable, as both have plenty of food and leisure at home.

20th November.—Sekeletu and his large party having conveyed me thus far, and furnished me with a company of 114 men to carry the tusks to the coast, we bade adieu to the Makololo, and proceeded northwards to the Lekone. The country around is very beautiful, and was once well peopled with Batoka, who possessed enormous herds of cattle. When Sebituane came in former times, with his small but warlike party of Makololo, to this spot, a general rising took place of the Batoka through the whole country, in order to "eat him up;" but his usual success followed him, and, dispersing them, the Makololo obtained so many cattle, that they could not take any note of the herds of sheep and goats. The tsetse has been brought by buffaloes into some districts where formerly cattle abounded. This obliged us to travel the first few stages by night. We could not well detect the nature of the country in the dim moonlight; the path, however, seemed to lead along the high bank of what may have been the ancient bed of the Zambesi, before the fissure was made. The Lekone now winds in it, in an opposite direction to that in which the ancient river must have flowed.

Both the Lekone and Unguesi flow back towards the centre of the country, and in an opposite direction to that of the main stream. It was plain, then, that we were ascending, the further we went eastward. The level of the lower portion of the Lekone is about 200 feet above that of the Zambesi at the falls, and considerably more than the altitude of Linyanti; consequently, when the river flowed along this ancient bed, instead of through the rent, the whole country between this, and the ridge beyond Libebe westwards; Lake Ngami and the Zouga southwards; and eastwards beyond Nchokotsa, was one large fresh-water lake. There is abundant evidence of the existence and extent of this vast lake in the longitudes indicated, and stretching from 17° to 21° S. latitude. The whole of this space is paved with a bed of tufa, more or less soft, according as it is covered with soil, or left exposed to atmospheric influences. Wherever ant-eaters make deep holes in this ancient bottom, fresh-water shells are thrown out, identical with those now existing, in the Lake Ngami and the Zambesi. The Barotse valley was another lake of a similar nature, and one existed beyond Masiko, and a fourth near the Orange River. The whole of these lakes were let out by means of cracks or fissures made in the subtending sides, by the upheaval of the country. The fissure made at the Victoria Falls let out the water of this great valley, and left a small patch in what was probably its deepest portion, and is now called Lake Ngami. The Falls of Gonye furnished an outlet to the lake of the Barotse valley, and so of the other great lakes of remote times. The Congo also finds its way to the sea through a narrow fissure, and so does the Orange River in the west; while other rents made in the eastern ridge, as the Victoria Falls and those to the east of Tanganyenka, allowed the central waters to drain eastward. All the African lakes hitherto discovered are shallow, in consequence of being the mere *residua* of very much larger ancient bodies of water. There can be no doubt that this continent was, in former times, very much more copiously supplied with water than at present, but a natural process of drainage has been going on for ages. Deep fissures are made, probably by the elevation of the land, proofs of which are seen in modern shells embedded in marly tufa, all round the coast-line. Whether this process of desiccation is as rapid throughout the continent, as in a letter to the late Dean Buckland, in 1843, I showed to have been the case in the Bechuana country, it is not for me to say; but though there is a slight tradition of the waters having burst through the low hills south of the Barotse, there is none of a sudden upheaval accompanied by an earthquake. The formation of the crack of Mosioatunya is perhaps too ancient for that; yet, although information of any remarkable event is often transmitted in the native names, and they even retain a tradition which looks like the story of Solomon and the harlots, there is not a name like Tom Earthquake, or Sam Shake-the-ground, in the whole country. They have a tradition which may refer to the building of the Tower of Babel, but it ends in the bold builders getting their crowns cracked by the fall of the scaffolding; and that they came out of a cave called "Loey" (Noe?), in company with the beasts, and all point to it in one direction, viz. the N.N.E. Loey, too, is an exception in the language, as they use masculine instead of neuter pronouns to it.

If we take a glance back at the great valley, the form the rivers have taken imparts the idea of a lake slowly drained out, for they have cut out for themselves beds exactly like what we may see, in the soft mud of a shallow pool of rain-water, when that is let off by a furrow. This idea would probably not strike a person on coming first into the country, but more extensive acquaintance with the river-system, certainly would convey the impression.   None of the rivers in the valley of the Leeambye have slopes down to their beds.   Indeed, many parts are much like the Thames at the Isle of Dogs, only the Leeambye has to rise twenty or thirty feet before it can overflow some of its meadows. The rivers have each a bed of low water; a simple furrow cut sharply out of the calcareous tufa, which lined the channel of the ancient lake; and another of inundation.   When the beds of inundation are filled, they assume the appearance of chains of lakes.   When the Clyde fills the holms ("haughs") above Bothwell Bridge and retires again into its channel, it resembles the river we are speaking of, only here, there are no high lands sloping down towards the bed of inundation, for the greater part of the region is not elevated fifty feet above them.   Even the rocky banks of the Leeambye below Gonye, and the ridges bounding the Barotse valley, are not more than two or three hundred feet in altitude over the general dead level.   Many of the rivers are very tortuous in their course, the Chobe and Simah particularly so; and if we may receive the testimony of the natives, they form what anatomists call *anastamosis*, or a network of rivers. Thus, for instance, they assured me that, if they go up the Simah in a canoe, they can enter the Chobe and descend that river to the Leeambye; or they may go up the Kama and come down the Simah.   And so in the case of the Kafue.   It is reputed to be connected in this way with the Leeambye in the north, and to part with the Loangwa; and the Makololo went from the one, into the other, in canoes.   And even though the interlacing may not be quite to the extent believed by the natives, the country is so level and the rivers so tortuous, that I see no improbability in the conclusion, that here is a network of waters of a very peculiar nature.   The reason why I am disposed to place a certain amount of confidence in the native reports is this,—when Mr. Oswell and I discovered the Zambesi in the centre of the continent in 1851, being unable to ascend it at the time ourselves, we employed the natives to draw a map embodying their ideas of that river.   We then sent the native map home with the same view that I now mention their ideas of the river system—namely, in order to be an aid to others in farther investigations.   When I was able to ascend the Leeambye to 14° south, and subsequently

2 M

descend it, I found, after all the care I could bestow, that the alterations I was able to make in the original native plan, were very trifling. The general idea their map gave was wonderfully accurate; and now I give, in the larger map appended, their views of the other rivers, in the hope that they may prove helpful to any traveller who may pursue the investigation farther.

24th.—We remained a day at the village of Moyara. Here the valley in which the Lekone flows, trends away to the eastward, while our course is more to the N.E. The country is rocky and rough, the soil being red sand, which is covered with beautiful green trees, yielding abundance of wild fruits. The father of Moyara was a powerful chief, but the son now sits among the ruins of the town, with four or five wives and very few people. At his hamlet a number of stakes are planted in the ground, and I counted fifty-four human· skulls hung on their points. These were Matebele, who, unable to approach Sebituane on the island of Loyéla, had returned sick and famishing. Moyara's father took advantage of their reduced condition, and, after putting them to death, mounted their heads in the Batoka fashion. The old man who perpetrated this deed now lies in the middle of his son's huts, with a lot of rotten ivory over his grave. One cannot help feeling thankful that the reign of such wretches is over. They inhabited the whole of this side of the country, and were probably the barrier to the extension of the Portuguese commerce in this direction. When looking at these skulls, I remarked to Moyara, that many of them were those of mere boys. He assented readily and pointed them out as such. I asked why his father had killed boys. "To show his fierceness," was the answer. "Is it fierceness to .kill boys?" "Yes, they had no business here." When I told him that this probably would ensure his own death if the Matebele came again, he replied, "When I hear of their coming I shall hide the bones." He was evidently proud of these trophies of his father's ferocity, and I was assured by other Batoka, that few strangers ever returned from a visit to this quarter. If a man wished to curry favour with a Batoka chief, he ascertained when a stranger was about to leave, and waylaid him at a distance from the town, and when he brought the head back to the chief, it was mounted as a trophy; the different chiefs vieing with each other as to which should mount the greatest number of skulls in his village.

If, as has been asserted, the Portuguese ever had a chain of trading stations across the country from Caconda to Tete, it must have passed through these people, but the total ignorance of the Zambesi flowing from north to south in the centre of the country, and the want of knowledge of the astonishing falls of Victoria which excite the wonder of even the natives, together with the absence of any tradition of such a chain of stations, compel me to believe,, that they existed only on paper. This conviction is strengthened by the fact that, when a late attempt was made to claim the honour of crossing the continent for the Portuguese, the only proof advanced was the journey of two black traders formerly mentioned, adorned with the name of " *Portuguese.*" If a chain of stations had existed, a few hundred names of the same sort might easily have been brought forward; and such is the love of barter among all the central Africans that, had there existed a market for ivory, its value would have become known, and even that on the graves of the chiefs, would not have been safe.

When about to leave Moyara on the 25th, he brought a root which, when pounded and sprinkled over the oxen, is believed to disgust the tsetse, so that it flies off without sucking the blood. He promised to show me the plant or tree if I would give him an ox; but as we were travelling, and could not afford the time required for the experiment, so as not to be cheated (as I had too often been by my medical friends), I deferred the investigation till I returned. It is probably but an evanescent remedy, and capable of rendering the cattle safe during one night only. Moyara is now quite a dependant of the Makololo, and my new party, not being thoroughly drilled, forced him to carry a tusk for them. When I relieved him, he poured forth a shower of thanks, at being allowed to go back to sleep beneath his skulls.

Next day we came to Namilanga, or "The Well of Joy." It is a small well dug beneath a very large fig-tree, the shade of which renders the water delightfully cool. The temperature through the day was 104° in the shade and 94° after sunset, but the air was not at all oppressive. This well received its name from the fact, that in former times marauding parties, in returning with cattle, sat down here and were regaled with boyaloa, music, and the lullilooing of the women from the adjacent towns.

All the surrounding country was formerly densely peopled, though now desolate and still. The old head-man of this place told us that his father once went to Bambala, where white tradérs lived, when our informant was a child, and returned when he had become a boy of about ten years. He went again, and returned when it was time to knock out his son's teeth. As that takes place at the age of puberty, he must have spent at least five years in each journey. He added that many who went there never returned, because they liked that country better than this. They had even forsaken their wives and children; and children had been so enticed and flattered by the finery bestowed upon them there, that they had disowned their parents and adopted others. The place to which they had gone, which they named Bambala, was probably Dambarari, which was situated close to Zumbo. This was the first intimation we had of intercourse with the whites. The Barotse, and all the other tribes in the central valley, have no such tradition as this; nor have either the one or the other any account of a trader's visit to them in ancient times.

All the Batoka tribes follow the curious custom of knocking out the upper front teeth at the age of puberty. This is done by both sexes, and though the under teeth, being relieved from the attrition of the upper, grow long and somewhat bent out, and thereby cause the under lip to protrude in a most unsightly way, no young woman thinks herself accomplished until she has got rid of the upper incisors. This custom gives all the Batoka an uncouth, old-man like appearance. Their laugh is hideous, yet they are so attached to it, that even Sebituane was unable to eradicate the practice. He issued orders, that none of the children living under him should be subjected to the custom by their parents, and disobedience to his mandates was usually punished with severity; but notwithstanding this, the children would appear in the streets without their incisors, and no one would confess to the deed. When questioned respecting the origin of this practice, the Batoka reply, that their object is to be like oxen, and those who retain their teeth they consider to resemble zebras. Whether this is the true reason or not, it is difficult to say; but it is noticeable that the veneration for oxen which prevails in many tribes should here be associated with hatred to the zebra, as among the Bakwains; that this operation is performed at the same age that circumcision is in other tribes; and that here that ceremony is unknown.   The custom is so universal, that a person who has his teeth is considered ugly, and occasionally, when the Batoka borrowed my looking-glass, the disparaging remark would be made respecting boys or girls who still retained their teeth, "Look at the great teeth!"   Some of the Makololo give a more facetious explanation of the custom; they say that the wife of a chief having in a quarrel bitten her husband's hand, he, in revenge, ordered her front teeth to be knocked out, and all the men in the tribe followed his example; but this does not explain why they afterwards knocked out their own.

The Batoka of the Zambesi are generally very dark in colour, and very degraded and negro-like in appearance, while those who live on the high lands we are now ascending, are frequently of the colour of coffee and milk.   We had a large number of the Batoka of Mokwiné in our party, sent by Sekeletu to carry his tusks.   Their greater degradation was probably caused by the treatment of their chiefs—the barbarians of the islands.   I found them more difficult to manage than any of the rest of my companions, being much less reasonable and impressible than the others. My party consisted of the head-men afore-mentioned, Sekwebu, and Kanyata.   We were joined at the falls by another head-man of the Makololo, named Monahin, in command of the Batoka. We had also some of the Banajoa under Mosisinyane, and last of all, a small party of Bashubia and Barotse under Tuba Mokoro, which had been furnished by Sekeletu because of their ability to swim.   They carried their paddles with them, and, as the Makololo suggested, were able to swim over the rivers by night and steal canoes, if the inhabitants should be so unreasonable as to refuse to lend them.   These different parties assorted together into messes; any orders were given through their head-man, and when food was obtained he distributed it to the mess.   Each party knew its own spot in the encampment; and as this was always placed so that our backs should be to the east, the direction from whence the prevailing winds came, no time was lost in fixing the sheds of our encampment.   They each took it in turn to pull grass to make my bed, so I lay luxuriously.

November 26*th.*—As the oxen could only move at night, in consequence of a fear that the buffaloes in this quarter might have introduced the tsetse, I usually performed the march by day on foot, while some of the men brought on the oxen by night. On coming to the villages under Marimba, an old man, we crossed the Unguesi, a rivulet which, like the Lekone, runs backward. It falls into the Leeambye a little above the commencement of the rapids. The stratified gneiss, which is the underlying rock of much of this part of the country, dips towards the centre of the continent, but the strata are often so much elevated as to appear nearly on their edges. Rocks of augitic trap are found in various positions on it; the general strike is north and south, but when the gneiss was first seen, near to the basalt of the falls, it was easterly and westerly, and the dip towards the north, as if the eruptive force of the basalt had placed it in that position.

We passed the remains of a very large town, which, from the only evidence of antiquity afforded by ruins in this country, must have been inhabited for a long period; the millstones of gneiss, trap, and quartz, were worn down, two and a half inches perpendicularly. The ivory gravestones soon rot away. Those of Moyara's father, who must have died not more than a dozen years ago, were crumbling into powder; and we found this to be generally the case all over the Batoka country. The region around is pretty well covered with forest; but there is abundance of open pasturage, and as we are ascending in altitude we find the grass to be short, and altogether unlike the tangled herbage of the Barotse valley.

It is remarkable that we now meet with the same trees we saw in descending towards the west coast. A kind of sterculia, which is the most common tree at Loanda, and the baobab, flourish here; and the tree called moshuka, which we found near Tala Mungongo, was now yielding its fruit, which resembles small apples. The people brought it to us in large quantities: it tastes like a pear, but has a harsh rind, and four large seeds within. We found prodigious quantities of this fruit as we went along. The tree attains the height of 15 or 20 feet, and has leaves, hard and glossy, as large as one's hand. The tree itself is never found on the lowlands, but is mentioned with approbation at the end of the work of Bowdich. My men almost lived upon the fruit for many days.

The rains had fallen only partially: in many parts the soil was quite dry and the leaves drooped mournfully, but the fruit-trees are unaffected by a drought, except when it happens at the time of their blossoming.   The Batoka of my party declared that no one ever dies of hunger here.   We obtained baskets of manéko, a curious fruit, with a horny rind, split into five pieces: these sections, when chewed, are full of a fine glutinous matter, and sweet like sugar.   The seeds are covered with a yellow silky down, and are not eaten: the entire fruit is about the size of a walnut.   We got also abundance of the motsouri and mamosho. We saw the Batoka eating the beans called nju, which are contained in a large square pod; also the pulp between the seeds of nux vomica, and the motsintséla.   Other fruits become ripe at other seasons, as the motsikiri, which yields an oil, and is a magnificent tree, bearing masses of dark evergreen leaves; so that, from the general plenty, one can readily believe the statement made by the Batoka.   We here saw trees allowed to stand in gardens, and some of the Batoka even plant them—a practice seen nowhere else among natives.   A species of leucodendron abounds.   When we meet with it on a spot on which no rain has yet fallen, we see that the young ones twist their leaves round during the heat of the day, so that the edge only is exposed to the rays of the sun; they have then a half twist on the petiole.   The acacias in the same circumstances, and also the mopane (*Bauhinia*), fold their leaves together, and, by presenting the smallest possible surface to the sun, simulate the eucalypti of Australia.

CHAPTER XXVII.

Low hills — Black soldier-ants; their cannibalism — The plasterer and its chloroform — White ants, their usefulness — Mutokwane-smoking; its effects — Border territory — Healthy table-lands — Geological formation — Cicadæ — Trees — Flowers — River Kalomo — Physical conformation of country — Ridges, sanatoria — A wounded buffalo assisted — Buffalo-bird — Rhinoceros-bird — Leaders of herds — The honey-guide — The White Mountain — Mozuma river — Sebituane's old home — Hostile village — Prophetic frenzy — Food of the elephant — Ant-hills — Friendly Batoka — Clothing despised — Method of salutation — Wild fruits — The captive released — Longings for peace — Pingola's conquests — The village of Monze — Aspect of the country — Visit from the chief Monze and his wife — Central healthy stations — Friendly feelings of the people in reference to a white resident — Fertility of the soil — Bashukulompo mode of dressing their hair — Gratitude of the prisoner we released — Kindness and remarks of Monze's sister —Dip of the rocks — Vegetation — Generosity of the inhabitants — Their anxiety for medicine — Hooping-cough — Birds and rain.

November 27th.—STILL at Marimba's. In the adjacent country palms abound, but none of that species which yields the oil; indeed that is met with only near the coast. There are numbers of flowers and bulbs just shooting up from the soil. The surface is rough and broken into gullies; and though the country is parched, it has not that appearance, so many trees having put forth their fresh green leaves at the time the rains ought to have come. Among the rest, stands the mola, with its dark brownish-green colour and spreading oak-like form. In the distance there are ranges of low hills. On the north we have one called Kanjele, and to the east that of Kaonka, to which we proceed to-morrow. We have made a considerable détour to the north, both on account of our wish to avoid the tsetse, and to visit the people. Those of Kaonka are the last Batoka we shall meet, in friendship with the Makololo.

Walking down to the forest, after telling these poor people, for the first time in their lives, that the Son of God had so loved them as to come down from heaven to save them, I observed many regiments of black soldier-ants, returning from their marauding expeditions. These I have often noticed before in different parts of the country; and as we had even at Kolobeng an opportunity of observing their habits, I may give a short account of them here. They are black, with a slight tinge of grey, about half an inch in length, and on the line of march appear three or four abreast; when disturbed, they utter a distinct hissing or chirping sound. They follow a few leaders who never carry anything, and they seem to be guided by a scent left on the path by the leaders; for happening once to throw the water from my basin behind a bush where I was dressing, it lighted on the path by which a regiment had passed before I began my toilette, and when they returned they were totally at a loss to find the way home, though they continued searching for it nearly half an hour. It was found only by one making a long circuit round the wetted spot. The scent may have indicated also, the propriety of their going in one direction only. If a handful of earth is thrown on the path, at the middle of the regiment, either on its way home or abroad, those behind it are completely at a loss as to their further progress. Whatever it may be that guides them, they seem only to know that they are not to return, for they come up to the handful of earth, but will not cross it, though not a quarter of an inch high. They wheel round and regain their path again, but never think of retreating to the nest, or to the place where they have been stealing. After a quarter of an hour's confusion and hissing, one may make a circuit of a foot round the earth, and soon all follow in that roundabout way. When on their way to attack the abode of the white ants, the latter may be observed rushing about in a state of great perturbation. The black leaders, distinguished from the rest by their greater size, especially in the region of the sting, then seize the white ants one by one, and inflict a sting, which seems to inject a portion of fluid similar in effect to chloroform, as it renders them insensible but not dead, and only able to move one or two front legs. As the leaders toss them on one side, the rank and file seize them and carry them off.

One morning I saw a party going forth on what has been supposed to be a slave-hunting expedition. They came to a stick, which, being enclosed in a white-ant gallery, I knew contained numbers of this insect; but I was surprised to see the black soldiers passing without touching it. I lifted up the stick and broke a portion of the gallery, and then laid it across the path in the middle of the black regiment. The white ants, when uncovered, scampered about with great celerity, hiding themselves under the leaves, but attracted little attention from the black marauders, till one of the leaders caught them, and applying his sting, laid them in an instant on one side in a state of coma; the others then promptly seized them and rushed off. On first observing these marauding insects at Kolobeng, I had the idea, imbibed from a work of no less authority than Brougham's Paley, that they seized the white ants in order to make them slaves; but having rescued a number of captives, I placed them aside, and found that they never recovered from the state of insensibility into which they had been thrown by the leaders. I supposed then that the insensibility had been caused by the soldiers holding the necks of the white ants too tightly with their mandibles, as that is the way they seize them; but even the pupæ which I took from the soldier ants, though placed in a favourable temperature, never became developed. In addition to this, if any one examines the orifice by which the black ant enters his barracks, he will always find a little heap of hard heads and legs of the white ants, showing that these black ruffians are a grade lower than slave-stealers, being actually cannibals. Elsewhere, I have seen a body of them removing their eggs from a place in which they were likely to be flooded by the rains; I calculated their numbers to be 1260; they carried their eggs a certain distance, then laid them down, when others took them and carried them further on. Every ant in the colony seemed to be employed in this laborious occupation, yet there was not a white slave-ant among them. One cold morning, I observed a band of another species of black ant, returning each with a captive: there could be no doubt of their cannibal propensities, for the "brutal soldiery" had already deprived the white ants of their legs. The fluid in the stings of this species, is of an intensely acid taste.

I had often noticed the stupefaction produced by the injection of a fluid from the sting of certain insects before. It is particularly observable in a hymenopterous insect called the "*plasterer*" (*Pelopæus Eckloni*), which in its habits resembles somewhat the mason-bee. It is about an inch and a quarter in length, jet black in colour, and may be observed coming into houses, carrying in

its fore-legs a pellet of soft plaster about the size of a pea. When
it has fixed upon a convenient spot for its dwelling, it forms a cell
about the same length as its body, plastering the walls, so as to
be quite thin and smooth inside. When this is finished, all except
a round hole, it brings seven or eight caterpillars or spiders, each
of which is rendered insensible, but not killed, by the fluid from
its sting. These it deposits in the cell, and then one of its own
larvæ, which, as it grows, finds food quite fresh. The insects are
in a state of coma, but the presence of vitality prevents putridity,
or that drying up, which would otherwise take place in this
climate. By the time the young insect is full grown and its wings
completely developed, the food is done. It then pierces the wall
of its cell at the former door, or place last filled up by its parent,
flies off, and begins life for itself. The plasterer is a most useful
insect, as it acts as a check on the inordinate increase of caterpillars and spiders. It may often be seen with a caterpillar or
even a cricket much larger than itself, but they lie perfectly still
after the injection of chloroform, and the plasterer, placing a row
of legs on each side of the body, uses both legs and wings in
trailing the victim along. The fluid in each case is, I suppose,
designed to cause insensibility and likewise act as an antiseptic,
the death of the victims being without pain.

Without these black soldier-ants, the country would be overrun
by the white ants; they are so extremely prolific, and nothing can
exceed the energy with which they work. They perform a most
important part in the economy of nature, by burying vegetable
matter as quickly beneath the soil, as the ferocious red ant does
dead animal substances. The white ant keeps generally out of
sight, and works under galleries constructed by night, to screen
them from the observation of birds. At some given signal, however, I never could ascertain what, they rush out by hundreds,
and the sound of their mandibles cutting grass into lengths, may
be heard like a gentle wind murmuring through the leaves of the
trees. They drag these pieces to the doors of their abodes, and
after some hours' toil leave off work, and many of the bits
of grass may be seen collected around the orifice. They continue out of sight for perhaps a month, but they are never idle.
On one occasion, a good bundle of grass was laid down for my bed,
on a spot which was quite smooth and destitute of plants. The

ants at once sounded the call to a good supply of grass. I heard them incessantly nibbling and carrying away all that night; and they continued all next day (Sunday) and all that night too with unabated energy. They had thus been thirty-six hours at it, and seemed as fresh as ever. In some situations, if we remained a day, they devoured the grass beneath my mat, and would have eaten that too, had we not laid down more grass. At some of their operations, they beat time in a curious manner. Hundreds of them are engaged in building a large tube, and they wish to beat it smooth. At a signal, they all give three or four energetic beats on the plaster in unison. It produces a sound like the dropping of rain off a bush when touched. These insects are the chief agents employed in forming a fertile soil. But for their labours, the tropical forests, bad as they are now with fallen trees, would be a thousand times worse. They would be impassable on account of the heaps of dead vegetation lying on the surface, and emitting worse effluvia than the comparatively small unburied collections do now. When one looks at the wonderful adaptations throughout creation, and the varied operations carried on with such wisdom and skill, the idea of second causes looks clumsy. We are viewing the direct handiworks of Him who is the one and only Power in the universe; wonderful in counsel; in whom we all live and move and have our being.

The Batoka of these parts are very degraded in their appearance, and are not likely to improve, either physically or mentally, while so much addicted to smoking the mutokwane (*Cannabis sativa*). They like its narcotic effects, though the violent fit of coughing, which follows a couple of puffs of smoke, appears distressing, and causes a feeling of disgust in the spectator. This is not diminished on seeing the usual practice of taking a mouthful of water, and squirting it out together with the smoke, then uttering a string of half-incoherent sentences, usually in self-praise. This pernicious weed is extensively used in all the tribes of the interior. It causes a species of frenzy, and Sebituane's soldiers, on coming in sight of their enemies, sat down and smoked it, in order that they might make an effective onslaught. I was unable to prevail on Sekeletu and the young Makololo to forego its use, although they cannot point to an old man in the tribe who has been addicted to this indulgence. I believe it was the proximate cause of Sebituane's last illness, for it sometimes occasions pneumonia. Never having tried it, I cannot describe the pleasurable effects it is said to produce, but the hachshish in use among the Turks is simply an extract of the same plant, and that, like opium, produces different effects on different individuals. Some view everything as if looking in through the wide end of a telescope, and others, in passing over a straw, lift up their feet as if about to cross the trunk of a tree. The Portuguese in Angola have such a belief in its deleterious effects that the use of it by a slave is considered a crime.

November 28*th.*—The inhabitants of the last of Kaonka's villages, complained of being plundered by the independent Batoka. The tribes in front of this are regarded by the Makololo as in a state of rebellion. I promised to speak to the rebels on the subject, and enjoined on Kaonka the duty of giving them no offence. According to Sekeletu's order, Kaonka gave us the tribute of maize-corn and ground-nuts, which would otherwise have gone to Linyanti. This had been done at every village, and we thereby saved the people the trouble of a journey to the capital. My own Batoka had brought away such loads of provisions from their homes that we were in no want of food.

After leaving Kaonka we travelled over an uninhabited, gently undulating, and most beautiful district, the border territory between those who accept, and those who reject, the sway of the Makololo. The face of the country appears as if in long waves, running north and south. There are no rivers, though water stands in pools in the hollows. We were now come into the country which my people all magnify as a perfect paradise. Sebituane was driven from it by the Matebele. It suited him exactly for cattle, corn, and health. The soil is dry, and often a reddish sand; there are few trees, but fine large shady ones stand dotted here and there over the country where towns formerly stood. One of the fig family I measured, and found to be forty feet in circumference; the heart had been burned out, and some one had made a lodging in it, for we saw the remains of a bed and a fire. The sight of the open country, with the increased altitude we were attaining, was most refreshing to the spirits. Large game abound. We see in the distance buffaloes, elands, hartebeest, gnus, and elephants, all very tame, as no one disturbs them. Lions, which always accompany other large animals, roared about us, but as it was moonlight there was no danger. In the evening, while standing on a mass of granite, one began to roar at me, though it was still light. The temperature was pleasant, as the rains, though not universal, had fallen in many places. It was very cloudy, preventing observations. The temperature at 6 A.M. was 70°, at midday 90°, in the evening 84°. This is very pleasant on the high lands, with but little moisture in the air.

The different rocks to the westward of Kaonka's, talcose gneiss, and white mica schist, generally dip towards the west, but at Kaonka's, large rounded masses of granite, containing black mica, began to appear. The outer rind of it inclines to peel off, and large crystals project on the exposed surface.

In passing through some parts where a good shower of rain has fallen, the stridulous piercing notes of the cicadæ are perfectly deafening; a drab-coloured cricket joins the chorus with a sharp sound, which has as little modulation as the drone of a Scottish bagpipe. I could not conceive how so small a thing could raise such a sound; it seemed to make the ground over it thrill. When cicadæ, crickets, and frogs unite, their music may be heard at the distance of a quarter of a mile.

A tree attracted my attention as new, the leaves being like those of an acacia, but the ends of the branches from which they grew resembled closely oblong fir-cones. The corn poppy was abundant, and many of the trees, flowering bulbs and plants, were identical with those in Pungo Andongo. A flower, as white as the snowdrop, now begins to appear, and farther on, it spots the whole sward with its beautiful pure white. A fresh crop appears every morning, and if the day is cloudy they do not expand till the afternoon. In an hour or so they droop and die. They are named by the natives, from their shape, "Tlaku ea pitse," hoof of zebra. I carried several of the somewhat bulbous roots of this pretty flower till I reached the Mauritius.

On the 30th we crossed the river Kalomo, which is about 50 yards broad, and is the only stream that never dries up on this ridge. The current is rapid, and its course is towards the south, as it joins the Zambesi at some distance below the falls. The Unguesi and Lekone, with their feeders, flow westward, this river

to the south, and all those to which we are about to come, take
an easterly direction. We were thus at the apex of the ridge,
and found that, as water boiled at 202°, our altitude above the
level of the sea was over 5000 feet. Here the granite crops out
again in great rounded masses which change the dip of the gneiss
and mica schist rocks from the westward to the eastward. In
crossing the western ridge, I mentioned the clay-shale or keele
formation, a section of which we have in the valley of the
Quango : the strata there lie nearly horizontal, but on this ridge
the granite seems to have been the active agent of elevation, for
the rocks, both on its east and west, abut against it. Both
eastern and western ridges are known to be comparatively
salubrious, and in this respect, as well as in the general aspect
of the country, they resemble that most healthy of all healthy
climates, the interior of South Africa, near and adjacent to the
Desert. This ridge has neither fountain nor marsh upon it,
and east of the Kalomo we look upon treeless undulating plains
covered with short grass. From a point somewhat near to
the great falls, this ridge or oblong mound trends away to the
N.E., and there treeless elevated plains again appear. Then
again the ridge is said to bend away from the falls to the
S.E., the Mashona country, or rather their mountains, appearing,
according to Mr. Moffat, about four days east of Matlokotloko, the
present residence of Mosilikatse. In reference to this ridge
he makes the interesting remark, "I observed a number of the
Angora goat, most of them being white ; and their long soft hair
covering their entire bodies to the ground made them look like
animals moving along without feet." *

It is impossible to say how much farther to the N. these
subtending ridges may stretch. There is reason to believe that,
though the same general form of country obtains, they are
not flanked by abrupt hills between the latitude 12° S. and the
equator. The inquiry is worthy the attention of travellers.
As they are known to be favourable to health, the Makololo,
who have been nearly all cut off by fevers in the valley, declaring that here they never had a headache, they may even be
recommended as a sanatorium for those whose enterprise leads

---

* Moffat's ' Visit to Mosilikatse,'—Royal Geog. Soc. Journal, vol. xxvi. p. 96.

them into Africa, either for the advancement of scientific knowledge, or for the purposes of trade or benevolence. In the case of
the eastern ridge, we have water-carriage, with only one short rapid
as an obstruction, right up to its base; and if a quick passage
can be effected during the healthy part of the year, there would
be no danger of loss of health during a long stay on these high
lands afterwards. How much further do these high ridges extend?
The eastern one seems to bend in considerably towards the great
falls; and the strike of the rocks indicating that, further to
the N.N.E. than my investigations extend, it may not, at a few
degrees of latitude beyond, be more than 300 or 350 miles from
the coast. They at least merit inquiry, for they afford a prospect
to Europeans, of situations superior in point of salubrity to any of
those on the coast: and so on the western side of the continent;
for it is a fact that many parts in the interior of Angola, which
were formerly thought to be unhealthy on account of their distance
inland, have been found, as population advanced, to be the most
healthy spots in-the country. Did the great Niger expedition
turn back when near such a desirable position for its stricken
and prostrate members?

The distances from top to top of the ridges may be about
10° of longitude, or 600 geographical miles. I cannot hear of a
hill *on* either ridge, and there are scarcely any in the space
enclosed by them. The Monakadze is the highest, but that is
not more than a thousand feet above the flat valley. On account
of this want of hills in the part of the country which, by gentle
undulations, leads one insensibly up to an altitude of 5000 feet
above the level of the sea, I have adopted the agricultural term
ridges, for they partake very much of the character of the oblong
mounds with which we are all familiar. And we shall yet see
that the mountains which are met with outside these ridges, are
only a low fringe, many of which are not of much greater altitude
than even the bottom of the great central valley. If we leave out
of view the greater breadth of the central basin at other parts, and
speak only of the comparatively narrow part formed by the bend
to the westward of the eastern ridge, we might say that the form of
this region is a broad furrow in the middle, with an elevated ridge
about 200 miles broad on either side, the land sloping thence,
on both sides, to the sea. If I am right in believing the granite

to be the cause of the elevation of this ridge, the direction in which the strike of the rocks trends to the N.N.E. may indicate that the same geological structure prevails farther north, and two or three lakes which exist in that direction, may be of exactly the same nature with lake Ngami; having been diminished to their present size by the same kind of agency as that which formed the falls of Victoria.

We met an elephant on the Kalomo which had no tusks. This is as rare a thing in Africa, as it is to find them with tusks in Ceylon. As soon as she saw us she made off. It is remarkable to see the fear of man operating even on this huge beast. Buffaloes abound, and we see large herds of them feeding in all directions by day. When much disturbed by man, they retire into the densest parts of the forest, and feed by night only. We secured a fine large bull by crawling close to a herd: when shot, he fell down, and the rest, not seeing their enemy, gazed about, wondering where the danger lay. The others came back to it, and, when we showed ourselves, much to the amusement of my companions, they lifted him up with their horns, and, half supporting him in the crowd, bore him away. All these wild animals usually gore a wounded companion and expel him from the herd; even zebras bite and kick an unfortunate or a diseased one. It is intended by this instinct, that none but the perfect and healthy ones should propagate the species. In this case they manifested their usual propensity to gore the wounded, but our appearance at that moment caused them to take flight, and this, with the goring being continued a little, gave my men the impression that they were helping away their wounded companion. He was shot between the fourth and fifth ribs; the ball passed through both lungs and a rib on the opposite side, and then lodged beneath the skin. But though it was two ounces in weight, yet he ran off some distance, and was secured only by the people driving him into a pool of water and killing him there with their spears. The herd ran away in the direction of our camp, and then came bounding past us again. We took refuge on a large ant-hill, and as they rushed by us at full gallop, I had a good opportunity of seeing that the leader of a herd of about sixty, was an old cow; all the others allowed her a full half-length in their front. On her withers sat about twenty buffalo-birds (*Textor erythrorhynchus*,

2 N

Smith), which act the part of guardian spirits to the animals. When the buffalo is quietly feeding, this bird may be seen hopping on the ground picking up food, or sitting on its back ridding it of the insects with which their skins are sometimes infested. The sight of the bird being much more acute than that of the buffalo, it is soon alarmed by the approach of any danger, and, flying up, the buffaloes instantly raise their heads to discover the cause, which has led to the sudden flight of their guardian. They sometimes accompany the buffaloes in their flight on the wing, at other times they sit as above described.

Another African bird, namely, the *Buphaga Africana*, attends the rhinoceros for a similar purpose. It is called "kala" in the language of the Bechuanas: when these people wish to express their dependence upon another, they address him as "my rhinoceros," as if they were the birds. The satellites of a chief go by the same name. This bird cannot be said to depend entirely on the insects on that animal, for its hard hairless skin is a protection against all except a few spotted ticks; but it seems to be attached to the beast, somewhat as the domestic dog is to man; and while the buffalo is alarmed by the sudden flying up of its sentinel, the rhinoceros, not having keen sight, but an acute ear, is warned by the cry of its associate, the *Buphaga Africana*. The rhinoceros feeds by night, and its sentinel is frequently heard in the morning uttering its well-known call, as it searches for its bulky companion. One species of this bird, observed in Angola, possesses a bill of a peculiar scoop or stone forceps form, as if intended only to tear off insects from the skin; and its claws are as sharp as needles, enabling it to hang on to an animal's ear, while performing a useful service within it. This sharpness of the claws allows the bird to cling to the nearly insensible cuticle without irritating the nerves of pain on the true skin, exactly as a burr does to the human hand; but in the case of the *Buphaga Africana* and *erythrorhyncha*, other food is partaken of, for we observed flocks of them roosting on the reeds, in spots where neither tame nor wild animals were to be found.

The most wary animal in a herd is generally the "leader." When it is shot, the others often seem at a loss what to do, and stop in a state of bewilderment. I have seen them then attempt to follow each other and appear quite confused, no one knowing for half a minute or more where to direct the flight.   On one occasion I happened to shoot the leader, a young zebra mare, which at some former time had been bitten on the hind leg by a carnivorous animal, and, thereby made unusually wary, had in consequence become a leader.   If they see either one of their own herd or any other animal taking to flight, wild animals invariably flee.   The most timid thus naturally leads the rest.   It is not any other peculiarity, but simply this provision, which is given them for the preservation of the race.   The great increase of wariness, which is seen to occur, when the females bring forth their young, causes all the leaders to be at that time females; and there is a probability that the separation of sexes into distinct herds, which is annually observed in many antelopes, arises from the simple fact that the greater caution of the she antelopes is partaken of only by the young males, and their more frequent flights now, have the effect of leaving the old males behind.   I am inclined to believe this, because, though the antelopes, as the pallahs, &c., are frequently in separate herds, they are never seen in the act of expelling the males.   There may be some other reason in the case of the elephants; but the male and female elephants are never seen in one herd.   The young males remain with their dams only until they are full grown, and so constantly is the separation maintained, that any one familiar with them, on seeing a picture with the sexes mixed, would immediately conclude that the artist had made it from his imagination, and not from sight.

December 2, 1855.—We remained near a small hill, called Maundo, where we began to be frequently invited by the honey-guide (*Cuculus indicator*).   Wishing to ascertain the truth of the native assertion that this bird is a deceiver, and by its call sometimes leads to a wild beast and not to honey, I inquired, if any of my men had ever been led by this friendly little bird to anything else, than what its name implies.   Only one of the 114 could say he had been led to an elephant instead of a hive, like myself with the black rhinoceros mentioned before.   I am quite convinced that the majority of people who commit themselves to its guidance are led to honey, and to it alone.

On the 3rd we crossed the river Mozuma, or river of Dila, having travelled through a beautifully undulating pastoral country.

To the south, and a little east of this, stands the hill Taba Cheu, or "White Mountain," from a mass of white rock, probably dolo-mite, on its top. But none of the hills are of any great altitude. When I heard this mountain described at Linyanti, I thought the glistening substance might be snow, and my informants were so loud in their assertions of its exceeding great altitude, that I was startled with the idea; but I had quite forgotten that I was speaking with men who had been accustomed to plains, and knew nothing of very high mountains. When I inquired what the white sub-stance was, they at once replied it was a kind of rock. I expected to have come nearer to it, and would have ascended it; but we were led to go to the north-east. Yet I doubt not that the native testimony of its being stone, is true. The distant ranges of hills which line the banks of the Zambesi on the south-east, and land-scapes which permit the eye to range over twenty or thirty miles at a time, with short grass under our feet, were especially refreshing sights to those who had travelled for months together, over the confined views of the flat forest, and among the tangled rank herbage of the great valley.

The Mozuma, or river of Dila, was the first watercourse which indicated that we were now on the slopes towards the eastern coast. It contained no flowing water, but revealed in its banks what gave me great pleasure at the time; pieces of lignite, possibly indicating the existence of a mineral, namely, coal, the want of which in the central country I had always deplored. Again and again we came to the ruins of large towns, containing the only hieroglyphics of this country, worn millstones, with the round ball of quartz with which the grinding was effected. Great numbers of these balls were lying about, showing that the depopulation had been the result of war, for, had the people removed in peace, they would have taken the balls with them.

At the river of Dila, we saw the spot where Sebituane lived, and Sekwebu pointed out the heaps of bones of cattle, which the Makololo had been obliged to slaughter, after performing a march with great herds captured from the Batoka, through a patch of the fatal tsetse. When Sebituane saw the symptoms of the poison, he gave orders to his people to eat the cattle. He still had vast numbers; and when the Matebele, crossing the Zambesi opposite this part, came to attack him, he invited the

Batoka to take repossession of their herds, he having so many as to be unable to guide them in their flight. The country was at that time exceedingly rich in cattle, and, besides pasturage, it is all well adapted for the cultivation of native produce. Being on the eastern slope of the ridge, it receives more rain than any part of the westward. Sekwebu had been instructed to point out to me the advantages of this position for a settlement, as that which all the Makololo had never ceased to regret. It needed no eulogy from Sekwebu; I admired it myself, and the enjoyment of good health in fine open scenery, had an exhilarating effect on my spirits. The great want was population, the Batoka having all taken refuge in the hills. We were now in the vicinity of those whom the Makololo deem rebels, and felt some anxiety as to how we should be received.

On the 4th we reached their first village. Remaining at a distance of a quarter of a mile, we sent two men to inform them who we were, and that our purposes were peaceful. The head-man came and spoke civilly, but when nearly dark, the people of another village arrived and behaved very differently. They began by trying to spear a young man who had gone for water. Then they approached us, and one came forward howling at the top of his voice in the most hideous manner; his eyes were shot out, his lips covered with foam, and every muscle of his frame quivered. He came near to me, and, having a small battle-axe in his hand, alarmed my men lest he might do violence; but they were afraid to disobey my previous orders, and to follow their own inclination by knocking him on the head. I felt a little alarmed, too, but would not show fear before my own people or strangers, and kept a sharp look-out on the little battle-axe. It seemed to me a case of extacy or prophetic frenzy, voluntarily produced. I felt it would be a sorry way to leave the world, to get my head chopped by a mad savage, though that perhaps would be preferable to hydrophobia or delirium tremens. Sekwebu took a spear in his hand, as if to pierce a bit of leather, but in reality to plunge it into the man if he offered violence to me. After my courage had been sufficiently tested, I beckoned with the head to the civil head-man to remove him, and he did so by drawing him aside. This man pretended not to know what he was doing. I would fain have felt his pulse, to ascertain whether the violent trembling were not

feigned, but had not much inclination to go near the battle-axe
again.   There was, however, a flow of perspiration, and the ex-
citement continued fully half an hour, then gradually ceased.
This paroxysm is the direct opposite of hypnotism, and it is singular that it has not been tried in Europe as well as clairvoyance.
This second batch of visitors took no pains to conceal their
contempt for our small party, saying to each other in a tone of
triumph, "They are quite a God-send!" literally, "God has
apportioned them to us."   "They are lost among the tribes!"
"They have wandered in order to be destroyed, and what can they
do without shields among so many?"   Some of them asked if
there were no other parties.   Sekeletu had ordered my men not to
take their shields, as in the case of my first company.   We were
looked upon as unarmed, and an easy prey.   We prepared against
a night attack by discharging and reloading our guns, which were
exactly the same in number (five) as on the former occasion, as I
allowed my late companions to retain those which I purchased at
Loanda.   We were not molested, but some of the enemy tried to lead
us towards the Bashukulompo, who are considered to be the fiercest
race in this quarter.   As we knew our direction to the confluence
of the Kafue and Zambesi, we declined their guidance, and the
civil head-man of the evening before, then came along with us.
Crowds of natives hovered round us in the forest; but he ran forward and explained; and we were not molested.   That night we
slept by a little village under a low range of hills, which are called
Chizamena.   The country here is more woody than on the high
lands we had left, but the trees are not in general large.   Great
numbers of them have been broken off by elephants, a foot or two
from the ground: they thus seem pollarded from that point.   This
animal never seriously lessens the number of trees; indeed I have
often been struck by the very little damage he does in a forest.
His food consists more of bulbs, tubers, roots, and branches, than
anything else.   Where they have been feeding, great numbers of
trees, as thick as a man's body, are seen twisted down or broken
off, in order that they may feed on the tender shoots at the tops.
They are said sometimes to unite in wrenching down large trees.
The natives in the interior believe that the elephant never touches
grass, and I never saw evidence of his having grazed until we came
near to Tete, and then he had fed on grass in seed only; this

seed contains so much farinaceous matter, that the natives collect it for their own food.

This part of the country abounds in ant-hills. In the open parts they are studded over the surface exactly as haycocks are in harvest, or heaps of manure in spring, rather disfiguring the landscape. In the woods they are as large as round haystacks, 40 or 50 feet in diameter at the base, and at least 20 feet high. These are more fertile than the rest of the land, and here they are the chief garden-ground for maize, pumpkins, and tobacco.

When we had passed the outskirting villages, which alone consider themselves in a state of war with the Makololo, we found the Batoka, or Batonga, as they here call themselves, quite friendly. Great numbers of them came from all the surrounding villages, with presents of maize and masuka, and expressed great joy at the first appearance of a white man, and harbinger of peace. The women clothe themselves better than the Balonda, but the men go *in puris naturalibus*. They walk about without the smallest sense of shame. They have even lost the tradition of the "figleaf." I asked a fine large-bodied old man, if he did not think it would be better to adopt a little covering. He looked with a pitying leer, and laughed with surprise at my thinking him at all indecent: he evidently considered himself above such weak superstition. I told them that on my return I should have my family with me, and no one must come near us in that state. "What shall we put on? we have no clothing." It was considered a good joke when I told them that, if they had nothing else, they must put on a bunch of grass.

The further we advanced, the more we found the country swarming with inhabitants. Great numbers came to see the white man, a sight they had never beheld before. They always brought presents of maize and masuka. Their mode of salutation is quite singular. They throw themselves on their backs on the ground, and, rolling from side to side, slap the outside of their thighs as expressions of thankfulness and welcome, uttering the words, "Kina bomba." This method of salutation was to me very disagreeable, and I never could get reconciled to it. I called out "Stop, stop! I don't want that;" but they, imagining I was dissatisfied, only tumbled about more furiously, and slapped their thighs with greater vigour. The men being totally unclothed, this performance imparted to my mind a painful sense of their extreme degrada-tion. My own Batoka were much more degraded than the Barotse, and more reckless. We had to keep a strict watch, so as not to be involved by their thieving from the inhabitants, in whose country and power we were. We had also to watch the use they made of their tongues, for some within hearing of the villagers would say, "I broke all the pots of that village," or, "I killed a man there." They were eager to recount their soldier deeds, when they were in company with the Makololo in former times, as a conquering army. They were thus placing us in danger by their remarks. I called them together, and spoke to them about their folly; and gave them a pretty plain intimation that I meant to insist upon as complete subordination as I had secured in my former journey, as being necessary for the safety of the party. Happily it never was needful to resort to any other measure for their obedience, as they all believed that I would enforce it.

In connection with the low state of the Batoka, I was led to think on the people of Kuruman, who were equally degraded and equally depraved. There a man scorned to shed a tear. It would have been "tlolo," or transgression. Weeping, such as Dr. Kane describes among the Esquimaux, is therefore quite unknown in that country. But I have witnessed instances like this: Baba, a mighty hunter—the interpreter who accompanied Captain Harris, and who was ultimately killed by a rhinoceros—sat listening to the gospel in the church at Kuruman, and the gracious words of Christ, made to touch his heart, evidently by the Holy Spirit, melted him into tears; I have seen him and others sink down to the ground weeping. When Baba was lying mangled by the furious beast which tore him off his horse, he shed no tear, but quietly prayed as long as he was conscious. I had no hand in his instruction: if these Batoka ever become like him, and they may, the influence that effects it must be divine.

A very large portion of this quarter is covered with masuka-trees, and the ground was so strewed with the pleasant fruit, that my men kept eating it constantly, as we marched along. We saw a smaller kind of the same tree named Molondo, the fruit of which is about the size of marbles, having a tender skin, and slight acidity of taste mingled with its sweetness. Another tree which is said to yield good fruit is named Sombo, but it was not ripe at this season.

December 6th.—We passed the night near a series of villages. Before we came to a stand under our tree, a man came running to us with hands and arms firmly bound with cords behind his back, entreating me to release him. When I had dismounted, the head-man of the village advanced, and I inquired the prisoner's offence. He stated that he had come from the Bashukulompo as a fugitive, and he had given him a wife and garden, and a supply of seed; but on refusing a demand for more, the prisoner had threatened to kill him, and had been seen the night before, skulking about the village, apparently with that intention. I declined interceding, unless he would confess to his father-in-law, and promise amendment. He at first refused to promise to abstain from violence, but afterwards agreed. The father-in-law then said that he would take him to the village and release him, but the prisoner cried out bitterly, " He will kill me there; don't leave me, white man." I ordered a knife, and one of the villagers released him on the spot. His arms were cut by the cords, and he was quite lame from the blows he had received.

These villagers supplied us abundantly with ground-nuts, maize, and corn. All expressed great satisfaction on hearing my message, as I directed their attention to Jesus as their Saviour, whose word is "Peace on earth and good will to men." They called out, "We are tired of flight; give us rest and sleep." They of course did not understand the full import of the message, but it was no wonder that they eagerly seized the idea of peace. Their country has been visited by successive scourges during the last half-century, and they are now " a nation scattered and peeled." When Sebituane came, the cattle were innumerable, and yet these were the remnants only, left by a chief called Pingola, who came from the north-east. He swept across the whole territory inhabited by his cattle-loving countrymen, devouring oxen, cows, and calves, without retaining a single head. He seems to have been actuated by a simple love of conquest, and is an instance of what has occurred two or three times in every century in this country, from time immemorial. A man of more energy or ambition than his fellows, rises up and conquers a large territory, but as soon as he dies, the power he built up is gone, and his reign, having been one of terror, is not perpetuated. This, and the want of literature, have prevented the establishment of any great empire in the interior of Africa. Pingola effected his conquests, by carrying numbers of smith's bellows with him. The arrow-heads were heated before shooting into a town, and when a wound was inflicted on either man or beast, great confusion ensued. After Pingola, came Sebituane, and after him the Matebele of Mosilikatse; and these successive inroads have reduced the Batoka to a state, in which they naturally rejoice at the prospect of deliverance and peace.

We spent Sunday the 10th at Monze's village, who is considered the chief of all the Batoka we have seen. He lives near the hill Kisekise, whence we have a view of at least thirty miles of open undulating country, covered with short grass, and having but few trees. These open lawns would in any other land, as well as this, be termed pastoral, but the people have now no cattle, and only a few goats and fowls. They are located all over the country in small villages, and cultivate large gardens. They are said to have adopted this wide-spread mode of habitation, in order to give alarm should any enemy appear. In former times they lived in large towns. In the distance (S.E.) we see ranges of dark mountains along the banks of the Zambesi, and are told of the existence there of the rapid named Kansala, which is said to impede the navigation. The river is reported to be placid above that as far as the territory of Sinamane, a Batoka chief, who is said to command it after it emerges smooth again below the falls. Kansala is the only rapid reported in the river until we come to Kebrabasa, twenty or thirty miles above Tete. On the north, we have mountains appearing above the horizon, which are said to be on the banks of the Kafue.

The chief Monze came to us on Sunday morning, wrapped in a large cloth, and rolled himself about in the dust, screaming "Kina bomba," as they all do. The sight of great naked men wallowing on the ground, though intended to do me honour, was always very painful; it made me feel thankful that my lot had been cast in such different circumstances from that of so many of my fellow-men. One of his wives accompanied him; she would have been comely if her teeth had been spared; she had a little battle-axe in her hand, and helped her husband to scream. She was much excited, for she had never seen a white man before. We rather liked Monze, for he soon felt at home amongst us, and kept up conversation during much of the day. One head-man of a village after another arrived, and each of them supplied us liberally with maize, ground-nuts, and corn. Monze gave us a goat and a fowl, and appeared highly satisfied with a present of some handkerchiefs I had got in my supplies left at the island. Being of printed cotton, they excited great admiration; and when I put a gaudy-coloured one as a shawl about his child, he said that he would send for all his people to make a dance about it. In telling them that my object was to open up a path, whereby they might, by getting merchandize for ivory, avoid the guilt of selling their children, I asked Monze, with about 150 of his men, if they would like a white man to live amongst them and teach them. All expressed high satisfaction at the prospect of the white man and his path: they would protect both him and his property. I asked the question, because it would be of great importance to have stations in this healthy region, whither agents oppressed by sickness might retire, and which would serve, moreover, as part of a chain of communication between the interior and the coast. The answer does not mean much more than what I know, by other means, to be the case,—that a white man *of good sense* would be welcome and safe in all these parts. By uprightness, and laying himself out for the good of the people, he would be known all over the country as a *benefactor* of the race. None desire Christian instruction, for of it they have no idea. But the people are now humbled by the scourgings they have received, and seem to be in a favourable state for the reception of the Gospel. The gradual restoration of their former prosperity in cattle, simultaneously with instruction, would operate beneficially upon their minds. The language is a dialect of the other negro languages in the great valley; and as many of the Batoka living under the Makololo understand both it and the Sichuana, missionaries could soon acquire it through that medium.

Monze had never been visited by any white man, but had seen black native traders, who, he said, came for ivory, not for slaves. He had heard of white men passing far to the east of him to

Cazembe, referring, no doubt, to Pereira, Lacerda, and others, who have visited that chief.

The streams in this part are not perennial; I did not observe one suitable for the purpose of irrigation. There is but little wood; here and there you see large single trees, or small clumps of evergreens, but the abundance of maize and ground-nuts we met with, shows that more rain falls than in the Bechuana country, for there they never attempt to raise maize, except in damp hollows on the banks of rivers. The pasturage is very fine for both cattle and sheep. My own men, who know the land thoroughly, declare that it is all garden-ground together, and that the more tender grains, which require richer soil than the native corn, need no care here. It is seldom stony.

The men of a village came to our encampment, and, as they followed the Bashukulompo mode of dressing their hair, we had an opportunity of examining it for the first time. A circle of hair at the top of the head, eight inches or more in diameter, is woven into a cone eight or ten inches high, with an obtuse apex, bent, in some cases, a little forward, giving it somewhat the appearance of a helmet. Some have only a cone, four or five inches in diameter at the base. It is said that the hair of animals is added, but the sides of the cone are woven something like basket-work. The headman of this village, instead of having his brought to a point, had it prolonged into a wand, which extended a full yard from the crown of his head. The hair on the forehead, above the ears, and behind, is all shaven off, so they appear somewhat as if a cap of liberty were cocked upon the top of the head. After the weaving is performed it is said to be painful, as the scalp is drawn tightly up; but they become used to it. Monze informed me that all his people were formerly ornamented in this way, but he discouraged it. I wished him to discourage the practice of knocking out the teeth, too, but he smiled, as if in that case the fashion would be too strong for him, as it was for Sebituane.

Monze came on Monday morning, and, on parting, presented us with a piece of a buffalo which had been killed the day before by lions. We crossed the rivulet Makoe, which runs westward into the Kafue, and went northwards in order to visit Semalembue, an influential chief there. We slept at the village

Bashukulompo mode of wearing the hair.

of Monze's sister, who also passes by the same name. Both he and his sister are feminine in their appearance, but disfigured by the foolish custom of knocking out the upper front teeth.

It is not often that jail-birds turn out well, but the first person who appeared to welcome us at the village of Monze's sister, was the prisoner we had released in the way. He came with a handsome present of corn and meal, and, after praising our kindness to the villagers who had assembled around us, asked them, "What do you stand gazing at? don't you know that they have

mouths like other people?" He then set off and brought large
bundles of grass and wood for our comfort, and a pot to cook
our food in.

December 12th.—The morning presented the appearance of a
continuous rain from the north, the first time we had seen it
set in from that quarter in such a southern latitude. In the
Bechuana country, continuous rains are always from the north-
east or east, while in Londa and Angola they are from the north.
At Pungo Andongo, for instance, the whitewash is all removed
from the north side of the houses. It cleared up, however, about
midday, and Monze's sister conducted us a mile or two upon the
road. On parting, she said that she had forwarded orders to a
distant village, to send food to the point where we should sleep.
In expressing her joy at the prospect of living in peace, she said
it would be so pleasant "to sleep without dreaming of any one
pursuing them with a spear."

In our front we had ranges of hills called Chamai, covered with
trees. We crossed the rivulet Nakachinta, flowing eastwards
into the Zambesi, and then passed over ridges of rocks of the
same mica schist which we found so abundant in Golungo Alto;
here they were surmounted by reddish porphyry and finely laminated felspathic grit with trap. The dip, however, of these rocks,
is not towards the centre of the continent as in Angola, for
ever since we passed the masses of granite on the Kalomo,
the rocks, chiefly of mica schist, dip away from them, taking an
easterly direction. A decided change of dip occurs again when
we come near the Zambesi, as will be noticed further on. The
hills which flank that river, now appeared on our right as a high
dark range, while those near the Kafue, have the aspect of a low
blue range, with openings between. We crossed two never-failing
rivulets also flowing into the Kafue. The country is very fertile,
but vegetation is nowhere rank. The boiling point of water
being 204°, showed that we were not yet as low down as Linyanti;
but we had left the masuka-trees behind us, and many others
with which we had become familiar. A feature common to the
forests of Angola and Benguela, namely the presence of orchilla-
weed and lichens on the trees, with mosses on the ground, began
to appear; but we never, on any part of the eastern slope, saw
the abundant crops of ferns which are met with everywhere in

Angola. The orchilla-weed and mosses, too, were in but small quantities.

As we passed along, the people continued to supply us with food in great abundance. They had by some means or other got a knowledge that I carried medicine, and somewhat to the disgust of my men, who wished to keep it all to themselves, brought their sick children for cure. Some of them I found had hooping-cough, which is one of the few epidemics that range through this country.

In passing through the woods, I, for the first time, heard the bird called Mokwa reza, or "Son-in-law of God" (Micropogon sulphuratus?), utter its cry, which is supposed by the natives to be "pula, pula" (rain, rain). It is said to do this only before heavy falls of rain. It may be a cuckoo, for it is said to throw out the eggs of the white-backed Senegal crow, and lay its own instead. This, combined with the cry for rain, causes the bird to be regarded with favour. The crow, on the other hand, has a bad repute, and when rain is withheld, its nest is sought for and destroyed, in order to dissolve the charm by which it is supposed to seal up the windows of heaven. All the other birds now join in full chorus in the mornings; and two of them, at least, have fine loud notes.

CHAPTER XXVIII.

13*th.*—THE country is becoming very beautiful, and furrowed by deep valleys; the underlying rocks, being igneous, have yielded fertile soil. There is great abundance of large game. The buffaloes select open spots, and often eminences, as standing-places through the day. We crossed the Mbai, and found in its bed, rocks of pink marble. Some little hills near it are capped by marble of beautiful whiteness, the underlying rock being igneous. Violent showers occur frequently on the hills, and cause such sudden sweeping floods in these rivulets, that five of our men, who had gone to the other side for firewood, were obliged to swim back. The temperature of the air is lowered considerably by the daily rains. Several times the thermometer at sunrise has been as low as 68°, and 74° at sunset. Generally, however, it stood at from 72° to 74° at sunrise, 90° to 96° at midday, and 80° to 84° at sunset. The sensation, however, as before remarked, was not disagreeable.

14*th.*—We entered a most beautiful valley, abounding in large game. Finding a buffalo lying down, I went to secure him for our food. Three balls did not kill him, and, as he turned round as if for a charge, we ran for the shelter of some rocks. Before we gained them, we found that three elephants, probably attracted by the strange noise, had cut off our retreat on that side: they, however, turned short off, and allowed us to gain the rocks. We then saw that the buffalo was moving off quite briskly, and in order not to be entirely balked, I tried a long shot at the last of the elephants, and, to the great joy of my people, broke his fore-leg. The young men soon brought him to a stand, and one shot in the brain despatched him. I was right glad to see the joy manifested at such an abundant supply of meat.

On the following day, while my men were cutting up the elephant, great numbers of the villagers came to enjoy the feast. We were on the side of a fine green valley, studded here and there with trees, and cut by numerous rivulets. I had retired from the noise, to take an observation among some rocks of laminated grit, when I beheld an elephant and her calf at the end of the valley, about two miles distant. The calf was rolling in the mud, and the dam was standing fanning herself with her great ears. As I looked at them through my glass, I saw a long string of my own men appearing on the other side of them, and Sekwebu came and told me that these had gone off, saying, "Our father will see to-day what sort of men he has got." I then went higher up the side of the valley, in order to have a distinct view of their mode of hunting. The goodly beast, totally unconscious of the approach of an enemy, stood for some time suckling her young one, which seemed about two years old; they then went into a pit containing mud, and smeared themselves all over with it, the little one frisking about his dam, flapping his ears and tossing his trunk incessantly, in elephantine fashion. She kept flapping her ears and wagging her tail, as if in the height of enjoyment. Then began the piping of her enemies, which was performed by blowing into a tube, or the hands closed together, as boys do into a key. They call out to attract the animal's attention—

> " O chief! chief! we have come to kill you.
> O chief! chief! many more will die besides you, &c.
> The gods have said it," &c. &c.

Both animals expanded their ears and listened, then left their bath as the crowd rushed towards them. The little one ran forward towards the end of the valley, but, seeing the men there, returned to his dam. She placed herself on the danger side of her calf, and passed her proboscis over it again and again, as if to assure it of safety. She frequently looked back to the men, who kept up an incessant shouting, singing, and piping; then looked at her young one and ran after it, sometimes sideways, as if her feelings were divided between anxiety to protect her offspring, and desire to revenge the temerity of her persecutors. The men kept about a hundred yards in her rear, and some, that distance from her flanks, and continued thus until she was obliged to cross a rivulet. The time spent in descending and getting up the opposite bank, allowed of their coming up to the edge, and discharging their spears at about twenty yards distance. After the first discharge, she appeared with her sides red with blood, and, beginning to flee for her own life, seemed to think no more of her young. I had previously sent off Sekwebu with orders to spare the calf. It ran very fast, but neither young nor old ever enter into a gallop; their quickest pace is only a sharp walk. Before Sekwebu could reach them, the calf had taken refuge in the water, and was killed. The pace of the dam gradually became slower. She turned with a shriek of rage, and made a furious charge back among the men. They vanished at right angles to her course, or sideways, and, as she ran straight on, she went through the whole party, but came near no one, except a man who wore a piece of cloth on his shoulders. Bright clothing is always dangerous in these cases. She charged three or four times, and, except in the first instance, never went farther than 100 yards. She often stood after she had crossed a rivulet, and faced the men, though she received fresh spears. It was by this process of spearing and loss of blood that she was killed, for at last, making a short charge, she staggered round and sank down dead in a kneeling posture. I did not see the whole hunt, having been tempted away by both sun and moon appearing unclouded. I turned from the spectacle of the destruction of noble animals, which might be made so useful in Africa, with a feeling of sickness, and it was not relieved by the recollection that the ivory was mine, though that was the case. I regretted to see them killed, and more especially

FEMALE ELEPHANT PURSUED WITH JAVELINS, PROTECTING HER YOUNG.

the young one, the meat not being at all necessary at that time; but it is right to add, that I did not feel sick when my own blood was up the day before. We ought perhaps to judge those deeds more leniently in which we ourselves have no temptation to engage. Had I not been previously guilty of doing the very same thing, I might have prided myself on superior humanity, when I experienced the nausea in viewing my men kill these two.

The elephant first killed was a male, not full grown; his height at the withers 8 feet 4 inches; circumference of the fore foot 44 inches × 2 = 7 feet 4 inches. The female was full grown, and measured in height 8 feet 8 inches; circumference of the fore foot 48 inches × 2 = 8 feet (96 inches). We afterwards found, that full-grown male elephants of this region ranged in height at the withers from 9 feet 9 inches to 9 feet 10 inches; and the circumference of the fore foot to be 4 feet 9½ inches × 2 = 9 feet 7 inches. These details are given because the general rule has been observed, that twice the circumference of the impression made by the fore foot on the ground is the height of the animal. The print on the ground being a little larger than the foot itself, would thus seem to be an accurate mode of measuring the size of any elephant that has passed; but the above measurements show, that it is applicable only to full-grown animals. The greater size of the African elephant in the south, would at once distinguish it from the Indian one; but here they approach more nearly to each other in bulk, a female being about as large as a common Indian male. But the ear of the African is an external mark which no one will mistake even in a picture. That of the female now killed, was 4 feet 5 inches in depth, and 4 feet in horizontal breadth. I have seen a native creep under one so as to be quite covered from the rain. The ear of the Indian variety is not more than a third of this size. The representation of elephants on ancient coins shows that this important characteristic was distinctly recognised of old. Indeed, Cuvier remarked that it was better known by Aristotle than by Buffon.

Having been anxious to learn whether the African elephant is capable of being tamed, through the kindness of my friend Admiral Smyth, I am enabled to give the reader conclusive evidence on this point. In the two medals furnished from his work, ' A descriptive Catalogue of his Cabinet of Roman and Imperial

large brass Medals,' the size of the ears will be at once noted as those of the true African elephant. They were even more docile than the Asiatic, and were taught various feats, as walking on ropes, dancing, &c. One of the coins is of Faustina senior, the other of Septimius Severus, and struck A.D. 197. These elephants were brought from Africa to Rome. The attempt to tame this most useful animal has never been made at the Cape, nor has one ever been exhibited in England. There is only one very young calf of the species in the British Museum.

The abundance of food in this country, as compared with the south, would lead one to suppose that animals here must attain a much greater size; but actual measurement now confirms the impression made on my mind by the mere sight of the animals, that those in the districts north of 20° were smaller than the same races existing southward of that latitude. The first time that Mr. Oswell and myself saw full-grown male elephants on the river Zouga, they seemed no larger than the females, (which are always smaller than males,) we had met on the Limpopo. There they attain a height of upwards of 12 feet. At the Zouga the height of one I measured was 11 feet 4 inches, and in this district 9 feet 10 inches. There is, however, an increase in the size of the tusks as we approach the equator. Unfortunately, I never made measurements of other animals in the south; but the appearance of the animals themselves in the north, at once produced the impression on my mind referred to, as to their decrease in size. When we first saw koodoos, they were so much smaller than those we had been accustomed to in the south, that we doubted whether they were not a new kind of antelope; and the leche, seen nowhere south of 20°, is succeeded by the poku as we go north. This is, in fact, only a smaller species of that antelope, with a more reddish colour. A great difference in size prevails also among domestic animals; but the influence of locality on them is not so well marked. The cattle of the Batoka, for instance, are exceedingly small and very beautiful, possessing generally great breadth between the eyes and a very playful disposition. They are much smaller than the aboriginal cattle in the south; but it must be added that those of the Barotse valley, in the same latitudes as the Batoka, are large. The breed may have come from the west, as the cattle within the influence of the sea air, as at Little Fish Bay, Benguela, Ambriz, and along that coast, are very large. Those found at Lake Ngami, with large horns and standing 6 feet high, probably come from the same quarter. The goats are also small, and domestic fowls throughout this country are of a very small size, and even dogs, except where the inhabitants have had an opportunity of improving the breed by importation from the Portuguese. As the Barotse cattle are an exception to this general rule, so are the Barotse dogs, for they are large savage-looking animals, though in reality very cowardly. It is a little remarkable, that a decrease in size should occur where food is the most abundant; but tropical climates seem unfavourable for the full development of either animals or man. It is not from want of care in the breeding, for the natives always choose the larger and stronger males for stock, and the same arrangement prevails in nature, for it is only by overcoming their weaker rivals, that the wild males obtain possession of the herd. Invariably they show the scars received in battle. The elephant we killed yesterday had an umbilical hernia as large as a child's head, probably caused by the charge of a rival. The cow showed scars received from men; two of the wounds in her side were still unhealed, and there was an orifice six inches long and open in her proboscis, and, as it was about a foot from the point, it must have interfered with her power of lifting water.

In estimating the amount of food necessary for these and other large animals, sufficient attention has not been paid to the kinds chosen. The elephant, for instance, is a most dainty feeder, and particularly fond of certain sweet-tasted trees and fruits. He chooses the mohonono, the mimosa, and other trees which contain much saccharine matter, mucilage, and gum. He may be seen putting his head to a lofty palmyra, and swaying it to and fro to shake off the seeds; he then picks them up singly and eats them.   Or he may be seen standing by the masuka and other fruit trees, patiently picking off the sweet fruits one by one.   He also digs up bulbs and tubers, but none of these are thoroughly digested. Bruce remarked upon the undigested bits of wood seen in their droppings, and he must have observed, too, that neither leaves nor seeds are changed, by passing through the alimentary canal.   The woody fibre of roots and branches is dropped in the state of tow, the nutritious matter alone having been extracted.   This capability of removing all the nourishment, and the selection of those kinds of food which contain great quantities of mucilage and gum, accounts for the fact that herds of elephants produce but small effect upon the vegetation of a country—quality being more requisite than quantity.   The amount of internal fat found in them makes them much prized by the inhabitants, who are all very fond of it, both for food and ointment.

After leaving the elephant valley, we passed though a very beautiful country, but thinly inhabited by man.   The underlying rock is trap, and dykes of talcose gneiss.   The trap is often seen tilted on its edge, or dipping a little either to the north or south.   The strike is generally to the N.E., the direction we are going.   About Losito we found the trap had given place to hornblende schist, mica schist, and various schorly rocks.   We had now come into the region, in which the appearance of the rocks, conveys the impression of a great force having acted along the bed of the Zambesi.   Indeed I was led to the belief, from seeing the manner in which the rocks have been thrust away on both sides from its bed, that the power which formed the crack of the falls, had given direction to the river below, and opened a bed for it all the way from the falls to beyond the gorge of Lupata.

Passing the rivulet Losito, and through the ranges of hills, we reached the residence of Semalembue on the 18th.   His village is situated at the bottom of ranges through which the Kafue finds a passage, and close to the bank of that river. The Kafue, sometimes called Kahowhe or Bashukulompo river, is upwards of 200 yards wide here, and full of hippopotami, the young of which may be seen perched on the necks of their dams.   At this point we had reached about the same level as Linyanti.

Semalembue paid us a visit soon after our arrival, and said that he had often heard of me, and now that he had the pleasure of seeing me, he feared that I should sleep the first night at his village hungry. This was considered the handsome way of introducing a present, for he then handed five or six baskets of meal and maize, and an enormous one of ground-nuts. Next morning he gave about twenty baskets more of meal. I could make but a poor return for his kindness, but he accepted my apologies politely, saying that he knew there were no goods in the country from which I had come, and, in professing great joy at the words of peace I spoke, he said, "Now I shall cultivate largely, in the hope of eating and sleeping in peace." It is noticeable that all whom we have yet met, eagerly caught up the idea of living in peace as the probable effect of the gospel. They require no explanation of the existence of the Deity. Sekwebu makes use of the term "Reza," and they appear to understand at once. Like negroes in general, they have a strong tendency to worship, and I heard that Semalembue gets a good deal of ivory from the surrounding tribes, on pretence of having some supernatural power. He transmits this to some other chiefs on the Zambesi, and receives in return English cotton goods which come from Mozambique by Babisa traders. My men here began to sell their beads and other ornaments for cotton cloth. Semalembue was accompanied by about forty people, all large men. They have much wool on their heads, which is sometimes drawn all together up to the crown, and tied there in a large tapering bunch. The forehead, and round by the ears, is shaven close to the base of this tuft. Others draw out the hair on one side, and twist it into little strings. The rest is taken over, and hangs above the ear, which gives the appearance of having a cap cocked jauntily on the side of the head.

The mode of salutation is by clapping the hands. Various parties of women came from the surrounding villages to see the white man, but all seemed very much afraid. Their fear, which I seldom could allay, made them, when addressed, clap their hands with increasing vigour. Sekwebu was the only one of the Makololo who knew this part of the country; and this was the region which to his mind was best adapted for the residence of a tribe. The natives generally have a good idea of the nature of the soil and pasturage, and Sekwebu expatiated with great eloquence on the capabilities of this part for supplying the wants of the Makololo. There is certainly abundance of room at present in the country for thousands and thousands more of population.

We passed near the Losito, a former encampment of the Matebele, with whom Sekwebu had lived. At the sight of the bones of the oxen they had devoured, and the spot where savage dances had taken place, though all deserted now, the poor fellow burst out into a wild Matebele song. He pointed out also a district about two days and a half west of Semalembue, where Sebituane had formerly dwelt. There is a hot fountain on the hills there, named "Nakalombo," which may be seen at a distance, emitting steam. "There," said Sekwebu, "had your Molekane (Sebituane) been alive, he would have brought you to live with him. You would be on the bank of the river, and by taking canoes you would at once sail down to the Zambesi and visit the white people at the sea."

This part is a favourite one with the Makololo, and probably it would be a good one in which to form a centre of civilization. There is a large flat district of country to the north, said to be peopled by the Bashukulompo and other tribes, who cultivate the ground to a great extent, and raise vast quantities of grain, ground-nuts, sweet potatoes, &c. They also grow sugar-cane. If they were certain of a market, I believe they would not be unwilling to cultivate cotton too, but they have not been accustomed to the peaceful pursuits of commerce. All are fond of trade, but they have been taught none, save that in ivory and slaves.

The Kafue enters a narrow gorge close by the village of Semalembue; as the hill on the north is called Bolengwe, I apply that name to the gorge (lat. 15° 48' 19" S., long. 28° 22' E.). Semalembue said, that he ought to see us over the river, so he accompanied us to a pass about a mile south of his village, and when we entered among the hills, we found the ford of the Kafue. On parting with Semalembue I put on him a shirt, and he went away with it apparently much delighted.

The ford was at least 250 yards broad, but rocky and shallow. After crossing it in a canoe we went along the left bank, and were completely shut in by high hills. Every available spot between the river and the hills is under cultivation; and the residence of the people here is intended to secure safety for

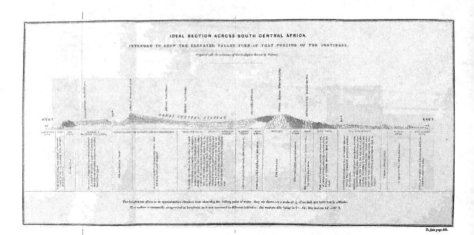

IDEAL SECTION ACROSS SOUTH CENTRAL AFRICA,

INTENDED TO SHOW THE ELEVATED VALLEY FORM OF THAT PORTION OF THE CONTINENT.

Prepared with the assistance of the Geological Society of Dublin.

WEST

GREAT CENTRAL PLATEAU

EAST

The heights are given as an approximation obtained from observing the boiling point of water: they are drawn on a scale of 1⁄20 of an inch per 1000 feet in altitude.
The section is immensely exaggerated as longitude, as it was traversed in different latitudes: the western side being in 8°–11°, the eastern 14°–16° S.

To face page 250.

WEST.

RAL PLATEAU.

Sea.

CALCAREOUS TUFA.	TRAP.	MICA SCHIST.	ND TRAP.	TUFA.	RADIATED ZEOLITE.
With modern shells, and similar to those now found in the sea adjacent, with strongly magnetic iron ore.		Dipping East.	of ferruginous conglomerate on the surface; hardened sandstone, with mudrepore holes, banks of gravel, and occasionally trap; south of 12°, large patches of soft calcareous tufa, with pebbles of jasper, agates, &c., lie on various horizontal traps, amygdaloids, with analcime and mesotype, which is burst through by basaltic rocks forming hills, and showing that the bottom of the valley consists of old silurian schists; there are also various granitic rocks cropping through the trap.		

ed from observing the boiling po

ngitude, as it was traversed in di

themselves and their gardens from their enemies; there is
plenty of garden-ground outside the hills; here they are obliged
to make pitfalls, to protect the grain against the hippopotami.
As these animals had not been disturbed by guns, they were
remarkably tame, and took no notice of our passing. We again
saw numbers of young ones, not much larger than terrier dogs,
sitting on the necks of their dams, the little saucy-looking heads
cocking up between the old one's ears; as they become a
little older, they sit on the withers. Needing meat, we shot a
full-grown cow, and found, as we had often done before, the flesh
to be very much like pork. The height of this animal was 4 feet
10 inches, and from the point of the nose to the root of the tail
10 feet 6. They seem quarrelsome, for both males and females
are found covered with scars, and young males are often killed by
the elder ones: we met an instance of this near the falls.

We came to a great many little villages among the hills, as if
the inhabitants had reason to hide themselves from the observation of their enemies. While detained cutting up the hippopotamus, I ascended a hill called Mabue asula (stones smell badly),
and though not the highest in sight, it was certainly not 100 feet
lower than the most elevated. The boiling point of water showed
it to be about 900 feet above the river, which was of the
level of Linyanti. These hills seemed to my men of prodigious
altitude, for they had been accustomed to ant-hills only. The
mention of mountains that pierced the clouds, made them draw in
their breath and hold their hands to their mouths. And when I
told them that their previous description of Taba cheu had led
me to expect something of the sort, I found that the idea of a
cloud-capped mountain had never entered into their heads. The
mountains certainly look high, from having abrupt sides. But
I had recognised the fact by the point of ebullition of water,
that they are of a considerably lower altitude than the top of the
ridge we had left. They constitute in fact a sort of low fringe on
the outside of the eastern ridge, exactly as the (apparently) high
mountains of Angola (Golungo Alto) form an outer low fringe to
the western ridge. I was much struck by the similarity of conformation and nature of the rocks on both sides of the continent.
But there is a difference in the structure of the subtending
ridges, as may be understood by the annexed ideal geological
section.

We can see from this hill five distinct ranges, of which Bolengo is the most westerly, and Komanga is the most easterly. The second is named Sekonkamena, and the third Funze. Very many conical hills appear among them, and they are generally covered with trees. On their tops we have beautiful white quartz rocks, and some have a capping of dolomite. On the west of the second range we have great masses of kyanite or disthene, and on the flanks of the third and fourth a great deal of specular iron-ore which is magnetic, and rounded pieces of black iron-ore, also strongly magnetic, and containing a very large percentage of the metal. The sides of these ranges are generally very precipitous, and there are rivulets between, which are not perennial. Many of the hills have been raised by granite, exactly like that of the Kalomo. Dykes of this granite, may be seen thrusting up immense masses of mica schist and quartz or sandstone schist, and making the strata fold over them on each side, as clothes hung upon a line. The uppermost stratum is always dolomite, or bright white quartz. Semalembue intended that we should go a little to the north-east, and pass through the people called Babimpe, and we saw some of that people, who invited us to come that way on account of its being smoother; but feeling anxious to get back to the Zambesi again, we decided to cross the hills towards its confluence with the Kafue. The distance, which in a straight line is but small, occupied three days. The precipitous nature of the sides of this mass of hills, knocked up the oxen and forced us to slaughter two, one of which, a very large one and ornamented with upwards of thirty pieces of its own skin detached and hanging down, Sekeletu had wished us to take to the white people as a specimen of his cattle. We saw many elephants among the hills, and my men ran off and killed three. When we came to the top of the outer range of the hills, we had a glorious view. At a short distance below us we saw the Kafue, wending away over a forest-clad plain to the confluence, and on the other side of the Zambesi beyond that, lay a long range of dark hills. A line of fleecy clouds appeared lying along the course of that river at their base. The plain below us, at the left of the Kafue, had more large game on it than anywhere else I had seen in Africa. Hundreds of buffaloes and zebras grazed on the open spaces, and there stood lordly elephants feeding majestically, nothing moving apparently but the proboscis. I wished that I had been able to take a photograph of a scene, so seldom beheld, and which is destined, as guns increase, to pass away from earth. When we descended we found all the animals remarkably tame. The elephants stood beneath the trees, fanning themselves with their large ears, as if they did not see us at 200 or 300 yards distance. The number of animals was quite astonishing, and made me think, that here I could realize an image of that time, when Megatheria fed undisturbed in the primeval forests. We saw great numbers of red-coloured pigs (*Potamochoerus*), standing gazing at us in wonder. The people live on the hills, and, having no guns, seldom disturb the game. They have never been visited, even by half-castes; but Babisa traders have come occasionally. Continuous rains kept us for some time on the banks of the Chiponga, and here we were unfortunate enough to come among the tsetse. Mr. I. E. Gray, of the British Museum, has kindly obliged me with a drawing of the insect, with the ravages of which I have unfortunately been too familiar. (For description see pp. 80–83.) No. 1 is the insect somewhat smaller

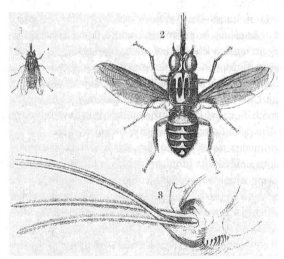

1. The Tsetse.—2. The same magnified.—3. The proboscis.

than life, from the specimen having contracted in drying; they are a little larger than the common house-fly. No. 2 is the insect magnified; and No. 3 shows the magnified proboscis and poison-bulb at the root.

We tried to leave one morning, but the rain coming on afresh brought us to a stand, and after waiting an hour, wet to the skin, we were fain to retrace our steps to our sheds. These rains were from the east, and the clouds might be seen on the hills, exactly as the "Table-cloth" on Table Mountain. · This was the first wetting we had got since we left Sesheke, for I had gained some experience in travelling. In Londa we braved the rain, and as I despised being carried in our frequent passage through running water, I was pretty constantly drenched; but now, when we saw a storm coming, we invariably halted. The men soon pulled grass sufficient to make a little shelter for themselves by placing it on a bush, and having got my camp-stool and umbrella, with a little grass under my feet, I kept myself perfectly dry. We also lighted large fires, and the men were not chilled by streams of water running down their persons, and abstracting the heat, as they would have been had they been exposed to the rain. When it was over, they warmed themselves by the fires, and we travelled on comfortably. The effect of this care was, that we had much less sickness than with a smaller party in journeying to Loanda. Another improvement made from my experience, was avoiding an entire change of diet. In going to Loanda I took little or no European food, in order not to burden my men and make them lose spirit, but trusted entirely to what might be got by the gun, and the liberality of the Balonda; but on this journey I took some flour which had been left in the waggon, with some got on the island, and baked my own bread all the way in an extemporaneous oven made by an inverted pot. With these precautions, aided, no doubt, by the greater healthiness of the district over which we passed, I enjoyed perfect health.

When we left the Chiponga on the 30th we passed along the range of hills on our left, which are composed of mica and clay-slate. At the bottom we found a forest of large silicified trees, all lying as if the elevation of the range had made them fall away from it, and towards the river. An ordinary-sized tree, standing on end, measured 22 inches in diameter: there were 12 laminæ to the inch. These are easily counted, because there is usually a scale of pure silica between each, which has not been so much affected by the weather as the rest of the ring itself: the edges of the rings thus stand out plainly. Mr. Quekett, having kindly examined some specimens, finds that it is " silicified *coniferous wood* of the ARAUCARIAN type; and the nearest allied wood that he knows of is that found, also in a fossil state, in New South Wales." The numbers of large game were quite astonishing. I never saw elephants so tame as those near the Chiponga: they stood close to our path without being the least afraid. This is different from their conduct where they have been accustomed to guns, for there they take alarm at the distance of a mile, and begin to run if a shot is fired even at a longer distance. My men killed another here, and rewarded the villagers of the Chiponga for their liberality in meal, by loading them with flesh. We spent a night at a baobab, which was hollow and would hold twenty men inside. It had been used as a lodging-house by the Babisa.

As we approached nearer the Zambesi, the country became covered with broad-leaved bushes, pretty thickly planted, and we had several times to shout to elephants to get out of our way. At an open space, a herd of buffaloes came trotting up to look at our oxen, and it was only by shooting one that I made them retreat. The meat is very much like that of an ox, and this one was very fine. The only danger we actually encountered was from a female elephant, with three young ones of different sizes. Charging through the centre of our extended line, and causing the men to throw down their burdens in a great hurry, she received a spear for her temerity. I never saw an elephant with more than one calf before. We knew that we were near our Zambesi again, even before the great river burst upon our sight, by the numbers of water-fowl we met. I killed four geese with two shots, and, had I followed the wishes of my men, could have secured a meal of water-fowl for the whole party. I never saw a river with so much animal life around and in it, and, as the Barotse say, "Its fish and fowl are always fat." When our eyes were gladdened by a view of its goodly broad waters, we found it very much larger than it is even above the falls. One might try to make his voice heard across it in vain. Its flow was more rapid than near Sesheke, being often four and a half miles an hour, and, what I never saw before, the water was discoloured and of a deep

brownish red.   In the great valley, the Leeambye never becomes
of this colour.   The adjacent country, so far north as is known, is
all level, and the soil, being generally covered with dense herbage,
is not abraded; but on the eastern ridge the case is different;
the grass is short, and, the elevation being great, the soil is washed
down by the streams, and hence the discoloration which we now
view.   The same thing was observed on the western ridge.   We
never saw discoloration till we reached the Quango; that obtained its matter from the western slope of the western ridge,
just as this part of the Zambesi receives its soil from the eastern
slope of the eastern ridge.   It carried a considerable quantity of
wreck of reeds, sticks, and trees.   We struck upon the river
about eight miles east of the confluence with the Kafue, and
thereby missed a sight of that interesting point.   The cloudiness
of the weather was such, that but few observations could be made
for determining our position, so, pursuing our course, we went
down the left bank, and came opposite the island of Menye makaba.   The Zambesi contains numerous islands; this was about a
mile and a half or two miles long, and upwards of a quarter of
a mile broad.   Besides human population, it has a herd of buffaloes that never leave it.   In the distance they seemed to be
upwards of sixty.   The human and brute inhabitants understand
each other; for when the former think they ought to avenge the
liberties committed on their gardens, the leaders of the latter
come out boldly to give battle.   They told us that the only time
in which they can thin them, is when the river is full and part of
the island flooded.   They then attack them from their canoes.
The comparatively small space to which they have confined
themselves, shows how luxuriant the vegetation of this region is;
for were they in want of more pasture, as buffaloes can swim well
and the distance 'from this bank to the island is not much more
than 200 yards, they might easily remove hither.   The opposite
bank is much more distant.

Ranges of hills appear now to run parallel with the Zambesi,
and are about fifteen miles apart.   Those on the north approach
nearest to the river.   The inhabitants on that side are the
Batonga, those on the south bank are the Banyai.   The hills
abound in buffaloes, and elephants are numerous, and many are
killed by the people on both banks.   They erect stages on

high trees overhanging the paths by which the elephants come, and then use a large spear with a handle nearly as thick as a man's wrist, and four or five feet long. When the animal comes beneath they throw the spear, and if it enters between the ribs above, as the blade is at least twenty inches long by two broad, the motion of the handle, as it is aided by knocking against the trees, makes frightful gashes within, and soon causes death. They kill them also by means of a spear, inserted in a beam of wood, which, being suspended on the branch of a tree by a cord attached to a latch fastened in the path, and intended to be struck by the animal's foot, leads to the fall of the beam, and, the spear being poisoned, causes death in a few hours.

We were detained by continuous rains several days at this island. The clouds rested upon the tops of the hills as they came from the eastward, and then poured down plenteous showers on the valleys below. As soon as we could move, Tomba Nyama, the head-man of the island, volunteered the loan of a canoe to cross a small river, called the Chongwe, which we found to be about fifty or sixty yards broad and flooded. All this part of the country was well known to Sekwebu, and he informed us that, when he passed through it as a boy, the inhabitants possessed abundance of cattle, and there were no tsetse. The existence of the insect now, shows that it may return in company with the larger game. The vegetation along the bank was exceedingly rank, and the bushes so tangled that it was difficult to get on. The paths had been made by the wild animals alone, for the general pathway of the people is the river, in their canoes. We usually followed the footpaths of the game, and of these there was no lack. Buffaloes, zebras, pallahs, and waterbucks abound, and there is also a great abundance of wild pigs, koodoos, and the black antelope. We got one buffalo, as he was rolling himself in a pool of mud. He had a large piece of skin torn off his flank, it was believed by an alligator.

We were struck by the fact that, as soon as we came between the ranges of hills which flank the Zambesi, the rains felt warm. At sunrise the thermometer stood at from 82° to 86°; at midday, in the coolest shade, namely, in my little tent, under a shady tree, at 96° to 98°; and at sunset it was 86°. This is different from anything we experienced in the interior, for these rains always bring

down the mercury to 72° or even 68°. There, too, we found a
small black coleopterous insect, which stung like the mosquito,
but injected less poison; it put us in mind of that insect, which
does not exist in the high lands we had left.

January 6th, 1856.—Each village we passed, furnished us with
a couple of men to take us to the next. They were useful in
showing us the parts least covered with jungle. When we came
near a village, we saw men, women, and children employed in
weeding their gardens, they being great agriculturists. Most
of the men are muscular, and have large ploughman hands.
Their colour is the same admixture, from very dark, to light olive,
that we saw in Londa. Though all have thick lips and flat noses,
only the more degraded of the population possess the ugly negro
physiognomy. They mark themselves by a line of little raised
cicatrices, each of which is a quarter of an inch long; they
extend from the tip of the nose to the root of the hair on the
forehead. It is remarkable that I never met with an Albino in
crossing Africa, though, from accounts published by the Portuguese, I was led to expect that they were held in favour as
doctors by certain chiefs. I saw several in the south: one at Kuruman is a full-grown woman, and a man having this peculiarity
of skin, was met with in the colony. Their bodies are always
blistered on exposure to the sun, as the skin is more tender than
that of the blacks. The Kuruman woman lived some time at
Kolobeng, and generally had on her bosom and shoulders the
remains of large blisters. She was most anxious to be made
black, but nitrate of silver, taken internally, did not produce its
usual effect. During the time I resided at Mabotsa, a woman
came to the station with a fine boy, an Albino. The father had
ordered her to throw him away, but she clung to her offspring
for many years. He was remarkably intelligent for his age. The
pupil of the eye was of a pink colour, and the eye itself was
unsteady in vision. The hair, or rather wool, was yellow, and the
features were those common among the Bechuanas. After I left
the place, the mother is said to have become tired of living apart
from the father, who refused to have her while she retained the
son. She took him out one day, and killed him close to the
village of Mabotsa, and nothing was done to her by the authorities.
From having met with no Albinos in Londa, I suspect they are

there also put to death. We saw one dwarf only in Londa, and brands on him showed he had once been a slave; and there is one dwarf woman at Linyanti. The general absence of deformed persons, is partly owing to their destruction in infancy, and partly to the mode of life being a natural one, so far as ventilation and food are concerned. They use but few unwholesome mixtures as condiments, and, though their undress exposes them to the vicissitudes of the temperature, it does not harbour vomites. It was observed, that, when smallpox and measles visited the country, they were most severe on the half-castes who were clothed. In several tribes a child which is said to "tlola," transgress, is put to death. "Tlolo," or transgression, is ascribed to several curious cases. A child who cut the upper front teeth before the under, was always put to death among the Bakaa, and, I believe, also among the Bakwains. In some tribes, a case of twins renders one of them liable to death; and an ox, which, while lying in the pen, beats the ground with its tail, is treated in the same way. It is thought to be calling death to visit the tribe. When I was coming through Londa, my men carried a great number of fowls, of a larger breed than any they had at home. If one crowed before midnight, it had been guilty of "tlolo," and was killed. The men often carried them sitting on their guns, and, if one began to crow in a forest, the owner would give it a beating, by way of teaching it not to be guilty of crowing at unseasonable hours.

The women here are in the habit of piercing the upper lip, and gradually enlarging the orifice until they can insert a shell. The lip then appears drawn out beyond the perpendicular of the nose, and gives them a most ungainly aspect. Sekwebu remarked, "These women want to make their mouths like those of ducks;" and indeed it does appear as if they had the idea that female beauty of lip had been attained by the *Ornithorhynchus paradoxus* alone. This custom prevails throughout the country of the Maravi, and no one could see it without confessing, that fashion had never led women to a freak more mad. We had rains now every day, and considerable cloudiness, but the sun often burst through with scorching intensity. All call out against it then, saying, "O the sun! that is rain again." It was worth noticing that my companions never complained of the heat while on the

2 P

highlands, but when we descended into the lowlands of Angola, and here also, they began to fret on account of it. I myself felt an oppressive steaminess in the atmosphere, which I had not experienced on the higher lands.

As the game was abundant and my party very large, I had still to supply their wants with the gun. We slaughtered the oxen only when unsuccessful in hunting. We always entered into friendly relations with the head-men of the different villages, and they presented grain and other food freely. One man gave a basinful of rice, the first we met with in the country. It is never seen in the interior. He said he knew it was "white man's corn," and when I wished to buy some more, he asked me to give him a slave. This was the first symptom of the slave-trade on this side of the country. The last of these friendly head-men was named Mobala; and having passed him in peace, we had no anticipation of anything else; but after a few hours we reached Selole or Chilole, and found that he not only considered us enemies, but had actually sent an express to raise the tribe of Mburúma against us. All the women of Selole had fled, and the few people we met, exhibited symptoms of terror. An armed party had come from Mburuma in obedience to the call, but the head-man of the company, being Mburuma's brother, suspecting that it was a hoax, came to our encampment and told us the whole. When we explained our objects, he told us that Mburuma, he had no doubt, would receive us well. The reason why Selole acted in this foolish manner, we afterwards found to be this: an Italian named Simoens, and nicknamed Siriatomba (don't eat tobacco), had married the daughter of a chief called Sekokole, living north of Tete. He armed a party of fifty slaves with guns, and, ascending the river in canoes some distance beyond the island Meya makaba, attacked several inhabited islands beyond, securing a large number of prisoners, and much ivory. On his return, the different chiefs, at the instigation of his father-in-law, who also did not wish him to set up as a chief, united, attacked and dispersed the party of Simoens, and killed him while trying to escape on foot. Selole imagined that I was another Italian, or, as he expressed it, "Siriatomba risen from the dead." In his message to Mburuma he even said that Mobala, and all the villages beyond, were utterly destroyed by our fire-arms, but the sight of Mobala him-

self, who had come to the village of Selole, led the brother of
Mburuma to see at once that it was all a hoax. But for this, the
foolish fellow Selole might have given us trouble.

We saw many of the liberated captives of this Italian among
the villages here, and Sekwebu found them to be Matebele. The
brother of Mburuma had a gun, which was the first we had seen
in coming eastward. Before we reached Mburuma, my men
went to attack a troop of elephants, as they were much in need
of meat. When the troop began to run, one of them fell into a
hole, and before he could extricate himself, an opportunity was
afforded for all the men to throw their spears. When he rose
he was like a huge porcupine, for each of the seventy or eighty
men had discharged more than one spear at him. As they had
no more, they sent for me to finish him. In order to put him
at once out of pain, I went to within twenty yards, there being
a bank between us which he could not readily climb. I rested
the gun upon an anthill, so as to take a steady aim; but though
I fired twelve 2-ounce bullets, all I had, into different parts,
I could not kill him. As it was becoming dark, I advised my
men to let him stand, being sure of finding him dead in the
morning; but though we searched all the next day, and went
more than ten miles, we never saw him again. I mention
this to young men who may think that they will be able to hunt
elephants on foot, by adopting the Ceylon practice of killing them
by one ball in the brain. I believe that in Africa the practice
of standing before an elephant, expecting to kill him with one shot,
would be certain death to the hunter; and I would add, for the
information of those who may think that, because I met with a
great abundance of game here, they also might find rare sport,
that the tsetse exists all along both banks of the Zambesi, and
there can be no hunting by means of horses. Hunting on foot in
this climate is such excessively hard work, that I feel certain the
keenest sportsman would very soon turn away from it in disgust.
I myself was rather glad, when furnished with the excuse that I
had no longer any balls, to hand over all the hunting to my men,
who had no more love for the sport than myself, as they never
engaged in it, except when forced by hunger.

Some of them gave me a hint to melt down my plate, by asking
if it were not lead. I had two pewter plates and a piece of zinc,

which I now melted into bullets. I also spent the remainder of my handkerchiefs in buying spears for them. My men frequently surrounded herds of buffaloes and killed numbers of the calves. I, too, exerted myself greatly; but as I am now obliged to shoot with the left arm I am a bad shot, and this, with the lightness of the bullets, made me very unsuccessful. The more the hunger, the less my success, invariably.

I may here add an adventure with an elephant of one who has had more narrow escapes than any man living, but whose modesty has always prevented him from publishing anything about himself. When we were on the banks of the Zouga in 1850, Mr. Oswell pursued one of these animals into the dense, thick, thorny bushes met with on the margin of that river, and to which the elephant usually flees for safety. He followed through a narrow pathway, by lifting up some of the branches and forcing his way through the rest; but when he had just got over this difficulty, he saw the elephant, whose tail he had but got glimpses of before, now rushing towards him. There was then no time to lift up branches, so he tried to force the horse through them. He could not effect a passage; and, as there was but an instant between the attempt and failure, the hunter tried to dismount, but in doing this one foot was caught by a branch, and the spur drawn along the animal's flank; this made him spring away and throw the rider on the ground with his face to the elephant, which, being in full chase, still went on. Mr. Oswell saw the huge fore foot about to descend on his legs, parted them, and drew in his breath as if to resist the pressure of the other foot, which he expected would next descend on his body. He saw the whole length of the under part of the enormous brute pass over him; the horse got away safely. I have heard of but one other authentic instance in which an elephant went over a man without injury, and, for any one who knows the nature of the bush in which this occurred, the very thought of an encounter in it with such a foe is appalling. As the thorns are placed in pairs on opposite sides of the branches, and these turn round on being pressed against, one pair brings the other exactly into the position in which it must pierce the intruder. They cut like knives. Horses dread this bush extremely: indeed, most of them refuse to face its thorns.

On reaching Mburuma's village, his brother came to meet us.

We explained the reason of our delay, and he told us that we were looked upon with alarm. He said that Siriatomba had been killed near the village of Selole, and hence that man's fears. He added that the Italian had come talking of peace, as we did, but had kidnapped children and bought ivory with them, and that we were supposed to be following the same calling. I pointed to my men, and asked if any of these were slaves, and if we had any children among them, and I think we satisfied him that we were true men. Referring to our ill success in hunting the day before, he said, "The man at whose village you remained was in fault in allowing you to want meat, for had he only run across to Mburuma he would have given him a little meal, and, having sprinkled that on the ground as an offering to the gods, you would have found your elephant." The chiefs in these parts take upon themselves an office somewhat like the priesthood, and the people imagine that they can propitiate the Deity through them. In illustration of their ideas, it may be mentioned that, when we were among the tribes west of Semalembue, several of the people came forward and introduced themselves—one as a hunter of elephants, another as a hunter of hippopotami, a third as a digger of pitfalls—apparently wishing me to give them medicine for success in their avocations, as well as to cure the diseases of those to whom I was administering the drugs. I thought they attributed supernatural power to them, for, like all Africans, they have unbounded faith in the efficacy of charms; but I took pains to let them know that they must pray and trust to another power than mine for aid. We never saw Mburuma himself, and the conduct of his people indicated very strong suspicions, though he gave us presents of meal, maize, and native corn. His people never came near us, except in large bodies and fully armed. We had to order them to place their bows, arrows, and spears at a distance before entering our encampment. We did not, however, care much for a little trouble now, as we hoped that, if we could pass this time without much molestation, we might yet be able to return with ease, and without meeting sour, suspicious looks.

The soil, glancing everywhere with mica, is very fertile, and all the valleys are cultivated, the maize being now in ear and eatable. Ranges of hills, which line both banks of the river above this, now come close up to each bank, and form a narrow

gorge, which, like all others of the same nature, is called Mpata.
There is a narrow pathway by the side of the river, but we preferred a more open one in a pass among the hills to the east,
which is called Mohango. The hills rise to a height of 800 or
1000 feet, and are all covered with trees. The rocks were of
various coloured mica schist; and parallel with the Zambesi lay
a broad band of gneiss with garnets in it. It stood on edge, and
several dykes of basalt, with dolerite, had cut through it.

Mburuma sent two men as guides to the Loangwa. These men
tried to bring us to a stand, at a distance of about six miles from
the village, by the notice, "Mburuma says you are to sleep under
that tree." On declining to do this, we were told that we must
wait at a certain village for a supply of corn. As none appeared
in an hour, I proceeded on the march. It is not quite certain
that their intentions were hostile, but this seemed to disarrange
their plans, and one of them was soon observed running back to
Mburuma. They had first of all tried to separate our party, by
volunteering the loan of a canoe to convey Sekwebu and me,
together with our luggage, by way of the river, and, as it was
pressed upon us, I thought that this was their design. The next
attempt was to detain us in the pass, but, betraying no suspicion,
we civilly declined to place ourselves in their power in an unfavourable position. We afterwards heard that a party of Babisa
traders, who came from the north-east, bringing English goods
from Mozambique, had been plundered by this same people.

Elephants were still abundant, but more wild, as they fled with
great speed as soon as we made our appearance. The country
between Mburuma's and his mother's village was all hilly and
very difficult, and prevented us from travelling more than ten
miles a day. At the village of Ma Mburuma (mother of Mburuma), the guides, who had again joined us, gave a favourable
report, and the women and children did not flee. Here we found
that traders, called Bazunga, have been in the habit of coming in
canoes, and that I was named as one of them. These I supposed
to be half-caste Portuguese, for they said that the hair of their
heads and the skin beneath their clothing were different from
mine. Ma Mburuma promised us canoes to cross the Loangwa
in our front. It was pleasant to see great numbers of men,
women, and boys come, without suspicion, to look at the books,

watch, looking-glass, revolver, &c.   They are a strong, muscular race, and both men and women are seen cultivating the ground. The soil contains so much comminuted talc and mica from the adjacent hills, that it seems as if mixed with spermaceti.   They generally eat their corn only after it has begun to sprout from steeping it in water.   The deformed lips of the women make them look very ugly; I never saw one smile.   The people in this part seem to understand readily what is spoken about God, for they listen with great attention, and tell in return their own ideas of departed spirits.   The position of the village of Mburuma's mother was one of great beauty, quite enclosed by high, steep hills; and the valleys are all occupied by gardens of native corn and maize, which grow luxuriantly.   We were obliged to hurry along, for the oxen were bitten daily by the tsetse, which, as I have before remarked, now inhabits extensive tracts which once supported herds of cattle that were swept off by Mpakane and other marauders, whose devastations were well known to Sekwebu, for he himself had been an actor in the scenes. When he told me of them he always lowered his voice, in order that the guides might not hear that he had been one of their enemies.   But that we were looked upon with suspicion, on account of having come in the footsteps of invaders, was evident from our guides remarking to men in the gardens through which we passed, "They have words of peace—all very fine; but lies only, as the Bazunga are great liars."   They thought we did not understand them, but Sekwebu knew every word perfectly, and, without paying any ostensible attention to these complimentary remarks, we always took care to explain ever afterwards that we were not Bazunga, but Makōa (English).

CHAPTER XXIX.

Confluence of Loangwa and Zambesi — Hostile appearances — Ruins of a church — Turmoil of spirit — Cross the river — Friendly parting — Ruins of stone houses — The situation of Zumbo for commerce — Pleasant gardens — Dr. Lacerda's visit to Cazembe — Peirara's statement — Unsuccessful attempt to establish trade with the people of Cazembe — One of my men tossed by a buffalo — Meet a man with jacket and hat on — Hear of the Portuguese and native war — Holms and terraces on the banks of river — Dancing for corn — Beautiful country — Mpende's hostility — Incantations — A fight anticipated — Courage and remarks of my men — Visit from two old councillors of Mpende — Their opinion of the English — Mpende concludes not to fight us — His subsequent friendship — Aids us to cross the river — The country — Sweet potatoes — Bakwain theory of rain confirmed — Thunder without clouds — Desertion of one of my men — Other natives' ideas of the English — Dalama (gold) — Inhabitants dislike slave-buyers — Meet native traders with American calico — Game-laws — Elephant medicine — Salt from the sand — Fertility of soil — Spotted hyæna — Liberality and politeness of the people — Presents — A stingy white trader — Natives' remarks about him — Effect on their minds — Rain and wind now from an opposite direction — Scarcity of fuel — Trees for boat-building — Boroma — Freshets — Leave the river — Chicova, its geological features — Small rapid near Tete — Loquacious guide — Nyampungo, the rain-charmer — An old man — No silver — Gold-washing — No cattle.

14th.—WE reached the confluence of the Loangwa and the Zambesi, most thankful to God for his great mercies in helping us thus far. Mburuma's people had behaved so suspiciously, that, though we had guides from him, we were by no means sure that we should not be attacked in crossing the Loangwa. We saw them here collecting in large numbers, and, though professing friendship, they kept at a distance from our camp. They refused to lend us more canoes than two, though they have many. They have no intercourse with Europeans, except through the Babisa. They tell us that this was formerly the residence of the Bazunga, and maintain silence as to the cause of their leaving it. I walked about some ruins I discovered, built of stone, and found the remains of a church, and on one side lay a broken bell, with the letters I. H. S. and a cross, but no date. There were no inscriptions on stone, and the people could not tell what the Bazunga called their place. We found afterwards it was Zumbo.

I felt some turmoil of spirit in the evening, at the prospect of having all my efforts for the welfare of this great region and its teeming population, knocked on the head by savages to-morrow, who might be said to "know not what they do." It seemed such a pity that the important fact of the existence of the two healthy ridges which I had discovered, should not become known in Christendom, for a confirmation would thereby have been given to the idea that Africa is not open to the Gospel. But I read that Jesus said, "All power is given unto me in heaven and on earth: go ye, therefore, and teach all nations . . . . . and lo, *I am with you alway, even unto the end of the world.*" I took this as His word of honour, and then went out to take observations for latitude and longitude, which, I think, were very successful. (The church: lat. 15° 37' 22" S., long. 30° 32' E.)

15th. The natives of the surrounding country collected around us this morning, all armed. The women and children were sent away, and one of Mburuma's wives, who lives in the vicinity, was not allowed to approach, though she had come from her village to pay me a visit. Only one canoe was lent to us, though we saw two others tied to the bank. The part we crossed was about a mile from the confluence, and, as it was now flooded, it seemed upwards of half a mile in breadth. We passed all our goods first on to an island in the middle, then the remaining cattle and men; occupying the post of honour, I, as usual, was the last to enter the canoe. A number of the inhabitants stood armed all the time we were embarking. I showed them my watch, lens, and other things to keep them amused, until there only remained those who were to enter the canoe with me. I thanked them for their kindness, and wished them peace. After all, they may have been influenced only by the intention to be ready, in case I should play them some false trick, for they have reason to be distrustful of the whites. The guides came over to bid us adieu, and we sat under a mango-tree, fifteen feet in circumference. We found them more communicative now. They said that the land on both sides belonged to the Bazunga, and that they had left of old, on the approach of Changamera, Ngaba, and Mpakane. Sekwebu was with the last named, but he maintained that they never

came to the confluence, though they carried off all the cattle of
Mburuma. The guides confirmed this by saying that the Bazunga
were not attacked, but fled in alarm on the approach of the enemy.
This mango-tree he knew by its proper name, and we found seven
others and several tamarinds, and were informed that the chief
Mburuma sends men annually to gather the fruit, but, like many
Africans whom I have known, has not had patience to propagate
more trees. I gave them some little presents for themselves, a
handkerchief and a few beads, and they were highly pleased with
a cloth of red baize for Mburuma, which Sekeletu had given me to
purchase a canoe. We were thankful to part good friends.

Next morning we passed along the bottom of the range, called
Mazanzwe, and found the ruins of eight or ten stone houses.
They all faced the river, and were high enough up the flanks
of the hill Mazanzwe to command a pleasant view of the broad
Zambesi. These establishments had all been built on one plan—
a house on one side of a large court, surrounded by a wall; both
houses and walls had been built of soft gray sandstone cemented
together with mud. The work had been performed by slaves
ignorant of building, for the stones were not often placed so as to
cover the seams below. Hence you frequently find the joinings
forming one seam from the top to the bottom. Much mortar or
clay had been used to cover defects, and now trees of the fig
family grow upon the walls, and clasp them with their roots.
When the clay is moistened, masses of the walls come down
by wholesale. Some of the rafters and beams had fallen in, but
were entire, and there were some trees in the middle of the
houses as large as a man's body. On the opposite or south bank
of the Zambesi, we saw the remains of a wall on a height which
was probably a fort, and the church stood at a central point,
formed by the right bank of the Loangwa and the left of the
Zambesi.

The situation of Zumbo was admirably well chosen as a site
for commerce. Looking backwards we see a mass of high, dark
mountains, covered with trees; behind us rises the fine high
hill Mazanzwe, which stretches away northwards along the left
bank of the Loangwa; to the S.E. lies an open country with
a small round hill in the distance called Tofulo. The merchants, as they sat beneath the verandahs in front of their

houses, had a magnificent view of the two rivers at their confluence; of their church at the angle; and of all the gardens which
they had on both sides of the rivers.   In these they cultivated
wheat without irrigation, and, as the Portuguese assert, of a grain
twice the size of that at Tete.   From the guides we learnt that
the inhabitants had not imbibed much idea of Christianity, for
they used the same term for the church bell which they did for
a diviner's drum.   From this point the merchants had water
communication in three directions beyond—namely, from the
Loangwa to the N.N.W., by the Kafue to the W., and by the Zambesi to the S.W.   Their attention, however, was chiefly attracted
to the N. or Londa; and the principal articles of trade were ivory
and slaves.   Private enterprise was always restrained, for the
colonies of the Portuguese being strictly military, and the pay of
the commandants being very small, the officers have always been
obliged to engage in trade; and had they not employed their
power to draw the trade to themselves, by preventing private
traders from making bargains beyond the villages, and only at
regulated prices, they would have had no trade, as they themselves
were obliged to remain always at their posts.

Several expeditions went to the north as far as to Cazembe, and
Dr. Lacerda, himself Commandant of Tete, went to that chief's
residence.   Unfortunately he was cut off while there, and his
papers, taken possession of by a Jesuit who accompanied him, were
lost to the world.   This Jesuit probably intended to act fairly and
have them published; but soon after his return he was called
away by death himself, and the papers were lost sight of.   Dr.
Lacerda had a strong desire to open up communication with
Angola, which would have been of importance then, as affording
a speedier mode of communication with Portugal than by the way
of the Cape; but since the opening of the overland passage to
India, a quicker transit is effected from Eastern Africa to Lisbon
by way of the Red Sea.   Besides Lacerda, Cazembe was visited
by Peirara, who gave a glowing account of that chief's power,
which none of my inquiries have confirmed.   The people of
Matiamvo stated to me that Cazembe was a vassal of their chief;
and, from all the native visitors whom I have seen, he appears to
be exactly like Shinte and Katema, only a little more powerful.
The term "Emperor," which has been applied to him, seems totally

inappropriate. The statement of Peirara that twenty negroes were slaughtered in a day, was not confirmed by any one else, though numbers may have been killed on some particular occasion during the time of his visit, for we find throughout all the country north of 20°, which I consider to be real negro, the custom of slaughtering victims to accompany the departed soul of a chief, and human sacrifices are occasionally offered, and certain parts of the bodies are used as charms. It is on account of the existence of such rites, with the similarity of the language, and the fact that the names of rivers are repeated again and again from north to south through all that region, that I consider them to have been originally one family. The last expedition to Cazembe was somewhat of the same nature as the others, and failed in establishing a commerce, because the people of Cazembe, who had come to Tete to invite the Portuguese to visit them, had not been allowed to trade with whom they might. As it had not been free-trade there, Cazembe did not see why it should be free-trade at his town; he accordingly would not allow his people to furnish the party with food except at his price; and the expedition, being half-starved in consequence, came away voting unanimously that Cazembe was a great bore.

When we left the Loangwa we thought we had got rid of the hills; but there are some behind Mazanzwe, though five or six miles off from the river. Tsetse and the hills had destroyed two riding oxen, and when the little one that I now rode knocked up, I was forced to march on foot. The bush being very dense and high, we were going along among the trees, when three buffaloes, which we had unconsciously passed above the wind, thought that they were surrounded by men, and dashed through our line. My ox set off at a gallop, and when I could manage to glance back, I saw one of the men up in the air about five feet above a buffalo, which was tearing along with a stream of blood running down his flank. When I got back to the poor fellow, I found that he had lighted on his face, and, though he had been carried on the horns of the buffalo about twenty yards before getting the final toss, the skin was not pierced nor was a bone broken. When the beasts appeared, he had thrown down his load and stabbed one in the side. It turned suddenly upon him, and, before he could use a tree for defence, carried him off. We shampooed him well,

THE TRAVELLING PROCESSION INTERRUPTED

and then went on, and in about a week he was able to engage in the hunt again.

At Zumbo we had entered upon old grey sandstone, with shingle in it, dipping generally towards the south, and forming the bed of the river. The Zambesi is very broad here, but contains many inhabited islands. We slept opposite one on the 16th, called Shibanga. The nights are warm, the temperature never falling below 80°; it was 91° even at sunset. One cannot cool the water by a wet towel round the vessel, and we feel no pleasure in drinking warm water, though the heat makes us imbibe large quantities. We often noticed lumps of a froth-like substance on the bushes as large as cricket-balls, which we could not explain.

On the morning of the 17th, we were pleased to see a person coming from the island of Shibanga, with jacket and hat on. He was quite black, but had come from the Portuguese settlement at Tete or Nyungwé; and now for the first time we understood that the Portuguese settlement was on the other bank of the river, and that they had been fighting with the natives for the last two years. We had thus got into the midst of a Caffre war, without any particular wish to be on either side. He advised us to cross the river at once, as Mpende lived on this side. We had been warned by the guides of Mburuma against him, for they said that if we could get past Mpende we might reach the white men, but that he was determined that no white man should pass him. Wishing to follow this man's advice, we proposed to borrow his canoes; but being afraid to offend the lords of the river, he declined. The consequence was, we were obliged to remain on the enemy's side. The next island belonged to a man named Zungo, a fine frank fellow, who brought us at once a present of corn, bound in a peculiar way in grass. He freely accepted our apology for having no present to give in return, as he knew that there were no goods in the interior, and besides sent forward a recommendation to his brother-in-law Pangola. The country adjacent to the river is covered with dense bush, thorny and tangled, making one stoop or wait till the men broke or held the branches on one side. There is much rank grass, but it is not so high or rank as that of Angola. The maize, however, which is grown here is equal in size to that which the Americans sell for seed at the Cape. There is usually a holm adjacent to the river, studded with villages and gardens. The holms are but partially cultivated, and on the other parts grows rank and reedy grass. There is then a second terrace, on which trees and bushes abound; and I thought I could detect a third and higher steppe. But I never could discover terraces on the adjacent country, such as in other countries show ancient sea-beaches. The path runs sometimes on the one and sometimes on the other of these river terraces. Canoes are essentially necessary; but I find that they here cost too much for my means, and higher up, where my hoes might have secured one, I was unwilling to enter into a canoe and part with my men, while there was danger of their being attacked.

18th.—Yesterday we rested under a broad-spreading fig-tree. Large numbers of buffaloes and water-antelopes were feeding quietly in the meadows; the people have either no guns or no ammunition, or they would not be so tame. Pangola visited us, and presented us with food. In few other countries would 114 sturdy vagabonds be supported by the generosity of the head-men and villagers, and whatever they gave be presented with politeness. My men got pretty well supplied individually, for they went into the villages and commenced dancing. The young women were especially pleased with the new steps they had to show, though I suspect many of them were invented for the occasion, and would say, "Dance for me, and I will grind corn for you." At every fresh instance of liberality, Sekwebu said, "Did not I tell you that these people had hearts, while we were still at Linyanti?" All agreed that the character he had given was true, and some remarked, "Look! although we have been so long away from home, not one of us has become lean." It was a fact that we had been all well supplied either with meat by my gun or their own spears, or food from the great generosity of the inhabitants. Pangola promised to ferry us across the Zambesi, but failed to fulfil his promise. He seemed to wish to avoid offending his neighbour Mpende by aiding us to escape from his hands, so we proceeded along the bank. Although we were in doubt as to our reception by Mpende, I could not help admiring the beautiful country as we passed along. There is, indeed, only a small part under cultivation in this fertile valley, but my mind naturally turned to the comparison of it with Kolobeng, where we waited anxiously during months for rain, and only a mere thunder-shower followed. I shall never forget the dry, hot east winds of that region; the yellowish, sultry, cloudless sky; the grass and all the plants drooping from drought, the cattle lean, the people dispirited, and our own hearts sick from hope deferred. There we often heard in the dead of the night the shrill whistle of the rain-doctor calling for rain that would not come, while here we listened to the rolling thunder by night and beheld the swelling valleys adorned with plenty by day. We have rain almost daily, and everything is beautifully fresh and green. I felt somewhat as people do on coming ashore after a long voyage —inclined to look upon the landscape in the most favourable light. The hills are covered with forests, and there is often a long line of fleecy cloud lying on them about midway up; they are very beautiful. Finding no one willing to aid us in crossing the river, we proceeded to the village of the chief Mpende. A fine, large, conical hill now appeared to the N.N.E.; it is the highest I have seen in these parts, and at some points it appears to be two cones joined together, the northern one being a little lower than the southern. Another high hill stands on the same side to the N.E., and, from its similarity in shape to an axe on the top, is called Motemwa. Beyond it, eastward, lies the country of Kaimbwa, a chief who has been engaged in actual conflict with the Bazunga, and beat them too, according to the version of things here. The hills on the south bank are named Kamoenja. When we came to Mpende's village, he immediately sent to inquire who we were, and then ordered the guides who had come with us from the last village to go back and call their masters. He sent no message to us whatever. We had travelled very slowly up to this point, the tsetse-stricken oxen being now unable to go two miles an hour. We were also delayed by being obliged to stop at every village, and send notice of our approach to the head-man, who came and received a little information, and gave some food. If we had passed on without taking any notice of them, they would have considered it impolite, and we should have appeared more as enemies than friends. I consoled myself for the loss of time by the thought that these conversations tended to the opening of our future path.

23rd.—This morning, at sunrise, a party of Mpende's people came close to our encampment, uttering strange cries and waving some bright red substance towards us. They then lighted a fire with charms in it, and departed, uttering the same hideous screams as before. This was intended to render us powerless, and probably also to frighten us. Ever since dawn, parties of armed men have been seen collecting from all quarters, and numbers passed us while it was yet dark. Had we moved down the river at once, it would have been considered an indication of fear or defiance, and so would a retreat. I therefore resolved to wait, trusting in Him who has the hearts of all men in His hands. They evidently intended to attack us, for no friendly message was sent; and when three of the Batoka the night before entered the village to beg food, a man went round about each of them, making a noise like a lion. The villagers then called upon them to do homage, and, when they complied, the chief ordered some chaff to be given them, as if it had been food. Other things also showed unmistakeable hostility. As we were now pretty certain of a skirmish, I ordered an ox to be slaughtered, as this is a means which Sebituane employed for inspiring courage. I have no doubt that we should have been victorious; indeed, my men, who were far better acquainted with fighting than any of the people on the Zambesi, were rejoicing in the prospect of securing captives to carry the tusks for them. "We shall now," said they, "get both corn and clothes in plenty." They were in a sad state, poor fellows! for the rains we had encountered had made their skin-clothing drop off piecemeal, and they were looked upon with disgust by the well-fed and well-clothed Zambesians. They were, however, veterans in marauding, and the head-men, instead of being depressed by fear, as the people of Mpende intended should be the case in using their charms, hinted broadly to me that I ought to allow them to keep Mpende's wives. The roasting of meat went on fast and furious, and some of the young men said to me, "You have seen us with elephants, but you don't know yet what we can do with men." I believe that, had Mpende struck the first blow, he would soon have found out that he never made a greater mistake in his life.

His whole tribe was assembled at about the distance of half a mile. As the country is covered with trees, we did not see them; but every now and then a few came about us as spies,

and would answer no questions. I handed a leg of the ox to two
of these, and desired them to take it to Mpende. After waiting
a considerable time in suspense, two old men made their appearance, and said they had come to inquire who I was. I replied,
"I am a Lekoa" (an Englishman). They said, "We don't know
that tribe. We suppose you are a Mozunga, the tribe with which
we have been fighting." As I was not yet aware that the term
Mozunga was applied to a Portuguese, and thought they meant
half-castes, I showed them my hair and the skin of my bosom,
and asked if the Bazunga had hair and skin like mine. As the
Portuguese have the custom of cutting the hair close, and are also
somewhat darker than we are, they answered, "No; we never saw
skin so white as that;" and added, "Ah! you must be one of
that tribe that loves (literally, *has heart to*) the black men." I,
of course, gladly responded in the affirmative. They returned to
the village, and we afterwards heard that there had been a long
discussion between Mpende and his councillors, and that one of
the men with whom we had remained to talk the day before had
been our advocate. He was named Sindese Oaléa. When we
were passing his village, after some conversation, he said to his
people, "Is that the man whom they wish to stop after he has
passed so many tribes? What can Mpende say to refusing him
a passage?" It was owing to this man, and the fact that I
belonged to the "friendly white tribe," that Mpende was persuaded to allow us to pass. When we knew the favourable
decision of the council, I sent Sekwebu to speak about the purchase of a canoe, as one of my men had become very ill, and I
wished to relieve his companions by taking him in a canoe.
Before Sekwebu could finish his story, Mpende remarked, "That
white man is truly one of our friends. See, how he lets me know
his afflictions!" Sekwebu adroitly took advantage of this turn
in the conversation, and said, "Ah! if you only knew him as well
as we do who have lived with him, you would understand that he
highly values your friendship and that of Mburuma, and, as he is
a stranger, he trusts in you to direct him." He replied, "Well,
he ought to cross to the other side of the river, for this bank is
hilly and rough, and the way to Tete is longer on this, than on
the opposite bank." "But who will take us across, if you do not?"
"Truly!" replied Mpende, "I only wish you had come sooner to

2 Q

tell me about him; but you shall cross." Mpende said frequently he was sorry he had not known me sooner, but that he had been prevented by his enchanter from coming near me; and he lamented that the same person had kept him from eating the meat which I had presented. He did everything he could afterwards to aid us on our course, and our departure was as different as possible from our approach to his village. I was very much pleased to find the English name spoken of with such great respect so far from the coast, and most thankful that no collision occurred to damage its influence.

24th.—Mpende sent two of his principal men to order the people of a large island below to ferry us across. The river is very broad, and, though my men were well acquainted with the management of canoes, we could not all cross over before dark. It is 1200 yards from bank to bank, and between 700 and 800 of deep water, flowing at the rate of $3\frac{3}{4}$ miles per hour. We landed first on an island, then, to prevent our friends playing false with us, hauled the canoes up to our bivouac, and slept in them. Next morning we all reached the opposite bank in safety. We observed as we came along the Zambesi that it had fallen two feet below the height at which we first found it, and the water, though still muddy enough to deposit a film at the bottom of vessels in a few hours, is not nearly so red as it was, nor is there so much wreck on its surface. It is therefore not yet the period of the central Zambesi inundation, as we were aware also from our knowledge of the interior. The present height of the water has been caused by rains outside the eastern ridge. The people here seem abundantly supplied with English cotton goods. The Babisa are the medium of trade, for we were informed that the Bazunga, who formerly visited these parts, have been prevented by the war from coming for the last two years. The Babisa are said to be so fond of a tusk that they will even sell a newly married wife for one. As we were now not far from the latitude of Mozambique, I was somewhat tempted to strike away from the river to that port, instead of going to the S.E. in the direction the river flows, but, the great object of my journey being to secure water carriage, I resolved to continue along the Zambesi, though it did lead me among the enemies of the Portuguese. The region to the north of the ranges of hills on our left is called Senga, from being the country of the Basenga, who are said to be great workers in iron, and to possess abundance of fine iron-ore, which, when broken, shows veins of the pure metal in its substance. It has been well roasted in the operations of nature. Beyond Senga lies a range of mountains called Mashinga, to which the Portuguese in former times went to wash for gold, and beyond that, are great numbers of tribes which pass under the general term Maravi. To the N.E. there are extensive plains destitute of trees, but covered with grass, and in some places it is marshy. The whole of the country to the north of the Zambesi is asserted to be very much more fertile than that to the south. The Maravi, for instance, raise sweet potatoes of immense size, but when these are planted on the southern bank they soon degenerate. The root of this plant (*convolvulus batala*) does not keep more than two or three days, unless it is cut into thin slices and dried in the sun, but the Maravi manage to preserve them for months by digging a pit and burying them therein enclosed in wood-ashes. Unfortunately, the Maravi, and all the tribes on that side of the country, are at enmity with the Portuguese, and, as they practise night attacks in their warfare, it is dangerous to travel among them.

29th.—I was most sincerely thankful to find myself on the south bank of the Zambesi, and, having nothing else, I sent back one of my two spoons and a shirt as a thank-offering to Mpende. The different head-men along this river act very much in concert, and if one refuses passage they all do, uttering the sage remark, "If so-and-so did not lend his canoes, he must have had some good reason." The next island we came to, was that of a man named Mozinkwa. Here we were detained some days by continuous rains, and thought we observed the confirmation of the Bakwain theory of rains. A double tier of clouds floated quickly away to the west, and as soon as they began to come in an opposite direction the rains poured down. The inhabitants who live in a dry region like that of Kolobeng are nearly all as weather-wise as the rainmakers, and any one living amongst them for any length of time, becomes as much interested in the motions of the clouds as they are themselves. Mr. Moffat, who was as sorely tried by droughts as we were, and had his attention directed in the same way, has noted the curious phenomenon of thunder

without clouds. Mrs. L. heard it once, but I never had that good
fortune. It is worth the attention of the observant. Humboldt
has seen rain without clouds, a phenomenon quite as singular.
I have been in the vicinity of the fall of three aërolites, none of
which I could afterwards discover. One fell into the lake Kuma-
dau with a report somewhat like a sharp peal of thunder. The
women of the Bakurutse villages there, all uttered a scream on
hearing it. This happened at midday, and so did another at
what is called the Great Chuai, which was visible in its descent,
and was also accompanied with a thundering noise. The third
fell near Kuruman and at night, and was seen as a falling star by
people at Motito and at Daniel's Kuil, places distant forty miles
on opposite sides of the spot. It sounded to me like the report
of a great gun, and a few seconds after, a lesser sound as if
striking the earth after a rebound. Does the passage of a few
such aërolites through the atmosphere to the earth by day cause
thunder without clouds?

We were detained here so long that my tent became again
quite rotten. One of my men, after long sickness, which I did
not understand, died here. He was one of the Batoka, and, when
unable to walk, I had some difficulty in making his companions
carry him. They wished to leave him to die when his case
became hopeless. Another of them deserted to Mozinkwa. He
said that his motive for doing so was that the Makololo had
killed both his father and mother, and, as he had neither wife
nor child, there was no reason why he should continue longer
with them. I did not object to his statements, but said if he
should change his mind he would be welcome to rejoin us, and
intimated to Mozinkwa that he must not be sold as a slave.
We are now among people inured to slave-dealing. We were
visited by men who had been as far as Tete or Nyungwe, and
were told that we were but ten days from that fort. One of
them, a Mashona man, who had come from a great distance to
the S.W., was anxious to accompany us to the country of the
white men; he had travelled far, and I found that he had also
knowledge of the English tribe, and of their hatred to the trade
in slaves. He told Sekwebu that the "English were men," an
emphasis being put upon the term *men*, which leaves the impression that others are, as they express it in speaking scornfully,

"only *things*." Several spoke in the same manner, and I found that from Mpende's downwards I rose higher every day in the estimation of my own people. Even the slaves gave a very high character to the English, and I found out afterwards that, when I was first reported at Tete, the servants of my friend the Commandant said to him in joke, "Ah! this is our brother who is coming; we shall all leave you and go with him." We had still, however, some difficulties in store for us before reaching that point.

The man who wished to accompany us came and told us before our departure that his wife would not allow him to go, and she herself came to confirm the decision. Here the women have only a small puncture in the upper lip, in which they insert a little button of tin. The perforation is made by degrees, a ring with an opening in it being attached to the lip, and the ends squeezed gradually together. The pressure on the flesh between the ends of the ring causes its absorption, and a hole is the result. Children may be seen with the ring on the lip, but not yet punctured. The tin they purchase from the Portuguese, and, although silver is reported to have been found in former times in this district, no one could distinguish it from tin. But they had a knowledge of gold, and for the first time I heard the word "dalama" (gold) in the native language. The word is quite unknown in the interior, and so is the metal itself. In conversing with the different people, we found the idea prevalent that those who had purchased slaves from them had done them an injury. "All the slaves of Nyungwe," said one, "are our children; the Bazunga have made a town at our expense." When I asked if they had not taken the prices offered them, they at once admitted it, but still thought that they had been injured by being so far tempted. From the way in which the lands of Zumbo were spoken of as still belonging to the Portuguese (and they are said to have been obtained by purchase), I was inclined to conclude that the purchase of land is not looked upon by the inhabitants in the same light as the purchase of slaves.

February 1st.—We met some native traders, and, as many of my men were now in a state of nudity, I bought some American calico marked "Lawrence Mills, Lowell," with two small tusks, and distributed it amongst the most needy. After leaving Mo-

zinkwa's we came to the Zingesi, a sand rivulet in flood (lat. 15°
38′ 34″ S., long. 31° 1′ E.). It was sixty or seventy yards wide,
and waist-deep. Like all these sand-rivers, it is for the most
part dry; but by digging down a few feet, water is to be found,
which is percolating along the bed on a stratum of clay. This
is the phenomenon which is dignified by the name of " a river
flowing underground." In trying to ford this I felt thousands
of particles of coarse sand striking my legs, and the slight disturbance of our footsteps caused deep holes to be made in the
bed. The water, which is almost always very rapid in them,
dug out the sand beneath our feet in a second or two, and we
were all sinking by that means so deep, that we were glad to
relinquish the attempt to ford it before we got halfway over;
the oxen were carried away down into the Zambesi. These
sand-rivers remove vast masses of disintegrated rock before it is
fine enough to form soil. The man who preceded me was only
thigh-deep, but the disturbance caused by his feet made it breast-
deep for me. The shower of particles and gravel which struck
against my legs, gave me the idea that the amount of matter
removed by every freshet must be very great. In most rivers
where much wearing is going on, a person diving to the bottom
may hear literally thousands of stones knocking against each
other. This attrition, being carried on for hundreds of miles in
different rivers, must have an effect greater than if all the pestles
and mortars and mills of the world, were grinding and wearing
away the rocks. The pounding to which I refer, may be heard
most distinctly in the Vaal River, when that is slightly in flood.
It was there I first heard it. In the Leeambye in the middle of
the country, where there is no discoloration and little carried
along but sand, it is not to be heard.

While opposite the village of a head-man called Mosusa, a
number of elephants took refuge on an island in the river.
There were two males, and a third not full-grown, indeed
scarcely the size of a female. This was the first instance I had
ever seen of a comparatively young one with the males, for they
usually remain with the female herd till as large as their dams.
The inhabitants were very anxious that my men should attack
them, as they go into the gardens on the islands, and do much
damage. The men went, but the elephants ran about half a

mile to the opposite end of the island, and swam to the mainland with their probosces above the water, and, no canoe being
near, they escaped. They swim strongly, with the proboscis
erect in the air. I was not very desirous to have one of these
animals killed, for we understood that when we passed Mpende,
we came into a country where the game-laws are strictly en-
forced. The lands of each chief are very well defined, the
boundaries being usually marked by rivulets, great numbers of
which flow into the Zambesi from both banks, and, if an elephant
is wounded on one man's land and dies on that of another, the
under half of the carcase is claimed by the lord of the soil; and so
stringent is the law, that the hunter cannot begin at once to cut
up his own elephant; but must send notice to the lord of the soil
on which it lies, and wait until that personage sends one autho-
rized to see a fair partition made. If the hunter should begin to
cut up before the agent of the landowner arrives, he is liable to
lose both the tusks and all the flesh. The hind leg of a buffalo
must also be given to the man on whose land the animal was
grazing, and a still larger quantity of the eland, which here and
everywhere else in the country is esteemed right royal food. In
the country above Zumbo we did not find a vestige of this law; and
but for the fact that it existed in the country of the Bamapela,
far to the south of this, I should have been disposed to regard it
in the same light as I do the payment for leave to pass—an im-
position levied on him who is seen to be weak because in the
hands of his slaves. The only game-laws in the interior are, that
the man who first wounds an animal, though he has inflicted but
a mere scratch, is considered the killer of it, the second is entitled
to a hind-quarter, and the third to a fore-leg. The chiefs are
generally entitled to a share as tribute; in some parts it is the
breast, in others the whole of the ribs and one fore-leg. I generally respected this law, although exceptions are sometimes made
when animals are killed by guns. The knowledge that he who
succeeds in reaching the wounded beast first, is entitled to a share,
stimulates the whole party to greater exertions in despatching
it. One of my men, having a knowledge of elephant medicine,
was considered the leader in the hunt; he went before the others,
examined the animals, and on his decision all depended. If he
decided to attack a herd, the rest went boldly on; but if he

declined, none of them would engage. A certain part of the
elephant belonged to him by right of the office he held, and such
was the faith in medicine held by the slaves of the Portuguese
whom we met hunting, that they offered to pay this man handsomely, if he would show them the elephant medicine.

When near Mosusa's village we passed a rivulet called Chowé,
now running with rain-water. The inhabitants there, extract a
little salt from the sand when it is dry, and all the people of the
adjacent country come to purchase it from them. This was the
first salt we had met with since leaving Angola, for none is to be
found in either the country of the Balonda or Barotse; but we
heard of salt-pans about a fortnight west of Naliele, and I got a
small supply from Mpololo while there. That had long since been
finished, and I had again lived two months without salt, suffering
no inconvenience except an occasional longing for animal food or
milk.

In marching along, the rich reddish-brown soil was so clammy,
that it was very difficult to walk. It is, however, extremely fertile,
and the people cultivate amazing quantities of corn, maize, millet,
ground-nuts, pumpkins, and cucumbers. We observed that, when
plants failed in one spot, they were in the habit of transplanting
them into another, and they had also grown large numbers of
young plants on the islands, where they are favoured by moisture
from the river, and were now removing them to the mainland.
The fact of their being obliged to do this shows that there is less
rain here than in Londa, for there we observed the grain in all
stages of its growth at the same time.

The people here build their huts in gardens on high stages.
This is necessary on account of danger from the spotted hyæna,
which is said to be very fierce, and also as a protection against
lions and elephants. The hyæna is a very cowardly animal,
but frequently approaches persons lying asleep, and makes an
ugly gash on the face. Mozinkwa had lost his upper lip in this
way, and I have heard of men being killed by them; children
too are sometimes carried off; for though he is so cowardly that
the human voice will make him run away at once, yet, when his
teeth are in the flesh, he holds on, and shows amazing power of
jaw. Leg-bones of oxen, from which the natives have extracted
the marrow and everything eatable, are by this animal crunched

up with the greatest ease, which he apparently effects by turning them round in his teeth till they are in a suitable position for being split.

We had now come among people who had plenty, and were really very liberal. My men never returned from a village without some corn or maize in their hands. The real politeness with which food is given by nearly all the interior tribes, who have not had much intercourse with Europeans, makes it a pleasure to accept. Again and again I have heard an apology made for the smallness of the present, or regret expressed that they had not received notice of my approach in time to grind more, and generally they readily accepted our excuse at having nothing to give in return, by saying that they were quite aware, that there are no white men's goods in the interior. When I had it in my power, I always gave something really useful. To Katema, Shinte, and others I gave presents which cost me about 2l. each, and I could return to them at any time without having a character for stinginess. How some men can offer three buttons, or some other equally contemptible gift, while they have abundance in their possession, is to me unaccountable. They surely do not know, when they write it in their books, that they are declaring they have compromised the honour of Englishmen. The people receive the offering with a degree of shame, and ladies may be seen to hand it quickly to the attendants, and, when they retire, laugh until the tears stand in their eyes, saying to those about them, "Is that a white man? then there are niggards among them too. Some of them are born without hearts!" One white trader, having presented an *old gun* to a chief, became a standing joke in the tribe: "The white man who made a present of a gun that was new, when his grandfather was sucking his great-grandmother." When these tricks are repeated, the natives come to the conclusion that people who show such a want of sense must be told their duty; they therefore let them know what they ought to give, and travellers then complain of being pestered with their "shameless begging." I was troubled by importunity on the confines of civilization only, and when I first came to Africa.

February 4*th.*—We were much detained by rains, a heavy shower without wind falling every morning about daybreak; it often cleared up after that, admitting of our moving on a few miles. A continuous rain of several hours then set in. The wind up to this point was always from the east, but both rain and wind now came so generally from the west, or opposite direction to what we had been accustomed to in the interior, that we were obliged to make our encampment face the east, in order to have them in our backs. The country adjacent to the river abounds in large trees; but the population is so numerous, that those left being all green, it is difficult to get dry firewood. On coming to some places, too, we were warned by the villagers not to cut the trees growing in certain spots, as they contained the graves of their ancestors. There are many tamarind-trees, and another very similar, which yields a fruit as large as a small walnut, of which the elephants are very fond. It is called Motondo, and the Portuguese extol its timber as excellent for building boats, as it does not soon rot in water.

On the 6th we came to the village of Boroma, which is situated among a number of others, each surrounded by extensive patches of cultivation. On the opposite side of the river we have a great cluster of conical hills called Chorichori. Boroma did not make his appearance, but sent a substitute who acted civilly. I sent Sekwebu in the morning to state that we intended to move on; his mother replied that, as she had expected that we should remain, no food was ready, but she sent a basket of corn and a fowl. As an excuse why Boroma did not present himself, she said that he was seized that morning by the Barimo, which probably meant that his lordship was drunk.

We marched along the river to a point opposite the hill Pinkwe (lat. 15° 39' 11″ S., long. 31° 48' E.), but the late abundant rains now flooded the Zambesi again, and great quantities of wreck appeared upon the stream. It is probable that frequent freshets, caused by the rains on this side of the ridge, have prevented the Portuguese near the coast, from recognising the one peculiar flood of inundation observed in the interior, and caused the belief that it is flooded soon after the commencement of the rains. The course of the Nile being in the opposite direction to this, it does not receive these subsidiary waters, and hence its inundation is recognised all the way along its course. If the Leeambye were prolonged southwards into the Cape Colony, its flood would be identical with that of the Nile. It would not be influenced by any streams in the Kalahari, for there, as in a corresponding part of the Nile, there would be no feeders. It is to be remembered that the great ancient river which flowed to the lake at Boochap took this course exactly, and probably flowed thither until the fissure of the falls was made.

This flood having filled the river, we found the numerous rivulets which flow into it, filled also, and when going along the Zambesi, we lost so much time in passing up each little stream till we could find a ford about waist-deep, and then returning to the bank, that I resolved to leave the river altogether, and strike away to the S.E. We accordingly struck off when opposite the hill Pinkwe, and came into a hard Mopane country. In a hole of one of the mopane-trees, I noticed that a squirrel (*Sciurus cepapi*) had placed a great number of fresh leaves over a store of seed. It is not against the cold of winter that they thus lay up food, but it is a provision against the hot season, when the trees have generally no seed. A great many silicified trees are met with lying on the ground all over this part of the country; some are broken off horizontally, and stand upright; others are lying prone and broken across into a number of pieces. One was 4 feet 8 inches in diameter, and the wood must have been soft like that of the baobab, for there were only six concentric rings to the inch. As the semi-diameter was only 28 inches, this large tree could have been but 168 years old. I found also a piece of palm-tree transformed into oxide of iron, and the pores filled with pure silica. These fossil trees lie upon soft grey sandstone containing banks of shingle, which forms the underlying rock of the country all the way from Zumbo to near Lupata. It is met with at Litubaruba and in Angola, with similar banks of shingle imbedded exactly like those now seen on the sea-beach, but I never could find a shell. There are many nodules and mounds of hardened clay upon it, which seem to have been deposited in eddies made round the roots of these ancient trees, for they appear of different colours in wavy and twisted lines. Above this, we have small quantities of calcareous marl.

As we were now in the district of Chicova, I examined the geological structure of the country with interest, because here, it has been stated, there once existed silver-mines. The general rock is the grey soft sandstone I have mentioned, but at the rivulet Bangue, we come upon a dyke of basalt six yards wide, running north and south. When we cross this, we come upon several others, some of which run more to the eastward. The sandstone is then found to have been disturbed, and at the rivulet called Nake we found it tilted up and exhibiting a section which was coarse sandstone above, sandstone-flag, shale, and lastly a thin seam of coal. The section was only shown for a short distance, and then became lost by a fault made by a dyke of basalt, which ran to the E.N.E. in the direction of Chicova.

This Chicova is not a kingdom, as has been stated, but a level tract, a part of which is annually overflowed by the Zambesi, and is well adapted for the cultivation of corn. It is said to be below the northern end of the hill Bungwe. I was very much pleased in discovering this small specimen of such a precious mineral as coal. I saw no indication of silver, and, if it ever was worked by the natives, it is remarkable that they have entirely lost the knowledge of it, and cannot distinguish between silver and tin. In connexion with these basaltic dykes, it may be mentioned that when I reached Tete I was informed of the existence of a small rapid in the river near Chicova; had I known this previously, I certainly would not have left the river without examining it. It is called Kebrabasa, and is described as a number of rocks, which jut out across the stream. I have no doubt but that it is formed by some of the basaltic dykes which we now saw, for they generally ran towards that point. I was partly influenced in leaving the river by a wish to avoid several chiefs in that direction, who levy a heavy tribute on those who pass up or down. Our path lay along the bed of the Nake for some distance, the banks being covered with impenetrable thickets. The villages are not numerous, but we went from one to the other and were treated kindly. Here they call themselves Bambiri, though the general name of the whole nation is Banyái. One of our guides was an inveterate talker, always stopping and asking for pay, that he might go on with a merry heart. I thought that he led us in the most difficult paths, in order to make us feel his value, for, after passing through one thicket after another, we always came into the bed of the Nake again, and as that was full of coarse sand, and the water only ankle-deep, and as hot as a footbath

from the powerful rays of the sun, we were all completely tired
out. He likewise gave us a bad character at every village we
passed, calling to them that they were to allow him to lead us
astray, as we were a bad set. Sekwebu knew every word he said,
and, as he became intolerable, I dismissed him, giving him six feet
of calico I had bought from native traders, and telling him that
his tongue was a nuisance. It is in general best, when a scolding
is necessary, to give it in combination with a present, and then
end it by good wishes. This fellow went off smiling, and my men
remarked, "His tongue is cured now." The country around the
Nake is hilly, and the valleys covered with tangled jungle. The
people who live in this district have reclaimed their gardens from
the forest, and the soil is extremely fertile. The Nake flows
northerly, and then to the east. It is 50 or 60 yards wide,
but during most of the year is dry, affording water only by
digging in the sand. We found in its bed masses of volcanic
rock, identical with those which I subsequently recognised as
such at Aden.

13th.—The head-man of these parts is named Nyampungo. I
sent the last fragment of cloth we had, with a request that we
should be furnished with a guide to the next chief. After a long
conference with his council, the cloth was returned with a promise
of compliance, and a request for some beads only. This man is
supposed to possess the charm for rain, and other tribes send to
him to beg it. This shows that what we inferred before was correct, that less rain falls in this country than in Londa. Nyampungo behaved in quite a gentlemanly manner, presented me
with some rice, and told my people to go amongst all the villages
and beg for themselves. An old man, father-in-law of the chief,
told me that he had seen books before, but never knew what they
meant. They pray to departed chiefs and relatives, but the idea
of praying to God seemed new, and they heard it with reverence.
As this was an intelligent old man, I asked him about the silver,
but he was as ignorant of it as the rest, and said, "We never dug
silver, but we have washed for gold in the sands of the rivers
Mazoe and Luia, which unite in the Luenya." I think that this
is quite conclusive on the question of no silver having been dug by
the natives of this district. Nyampungo is afflicted with a kind
of disease called Sesenda, which I imagine to be a species of

leprosy common in this quarter, though they are a cleanly people. They never had cattle. The chief's father had always lived in their present position, and, when I asked him why he did not possess these useful animals, he said, "Who would give us the medicine to enable us to keep them?" I found out the reason afterwards in the prevalence of tsetse, but of this he was ignorant, having supposed that he could not keep cattle because he had no medicine.

CHAPTER XXX.

An elephant-hunt — Offering and prayers to the Barimo for success — Native
mode of expression — Working of game-laws — A feast — Laughing
hyænas — Numerous insects — Curious notes of birds of song — Caterpillars — Butterflies — Silica — The fruit Mokoronga and elephants —
Rhinoceros adventure — Korwé bird — Its nest — A real confinement —
Honey and bees'-wax — Superstitious reverence for the lion — Slow tra-
velling — Grapes — The Ue — Monína's village — Native names — Govern-
ment of the Banyai — Electing a chief — Youths instructed in "Bonyái"
— Suspected of falsehood — War-dance — Insanity and disappearance of
Monahin — Fruitless search — Monina's sympathy — The sand-river
Tangwe — The ordeal „Muavi : its victims — An unreasonable man —
"Woman's rights" — Presents — Temperature — A winding course to
shun villages — Banyai complexion and hair — Mushrooms — The tubers,
Mokuri — The tree Shekabakadzi — Face of the country — Pot-holes —
Pursued by a party of natives — Unpleasant threat — Aroused by a
company of soldiers — A civilised breakfast — Arrival at Tete.

14th.—WE left Nyampungo this morning. The path wound
up the Molinge, another sand-river which flows into the Nake.
When we got clear of the tangled jungle which covers the banks
of these rivulets, we entered the Mopane country, where we could
walk with comfort. When we had gone on a few hours, my men
espied an elephant, and were soon in full pursuit. They were in
want of meat, having tasted nothing but grain for several days.
The desire for animal food made them all eager to slay him, and,
though an old bull, he was soon killed. The people of Nyampungo had never seen such desperadoes before. One rushed up
and hamstrung the beast while still standing, by a blow with an
axe. Some Banyai elephant-hunters happened to be present
when my men were fighting with him. One of them took out
his snuff-box, and poured out all its contents at the root of a
tree, as an offering to the Barimo for success. As soon as the
animal fell, the whole of my party engaged in a wild savage
dance round the body, which quite frightened the Banyai, and
he who made the offering said to me, "I see you are travelling
with people who don't know how to pray : I therefore offered

the only thing I had in their behalf, and the elephant soon fell."
One of Nyampungo's men who remained with me, ran a little
forward, when an opening in the trees gave us a view of the
chase, and uttered loud prayers for success in the combat. I
admired the devout belief they all possessed in the actual existence of unseen beings, and prayed that they might yet know
that benignant One who views us all as His own. My own
people, who are rather a degraded lot, remarked to me as I
came up, "God gave it to us. He said to the old beast, 'Go
up there; men are come who will kill and eat you.'" These
remarks are quoted to give the reader an idea of the native
mode of expression.

As we were now in the country of stringent game-laws, we
were obliged to send all the way back to Nyampungo, to give
information to a certain person who had been left there by the
real owner of this district to watch over his property, the owner
himself living near the Zambesi. The side upon which the elephant fell, had a short broken tusk; the upper one, which was
ours, was large and thick. The Banyai remarked on our good
luck. The men sent to give notice, came back late in the afternoon of the following day. They brought a basket of corn, a
fowl, and a few strings of handsome beads, as a sort of thank-
offering for our having killed it on their land, and said they had
thanked the Barimo besides for our success, adding "There it is;
eat it and be glad." Had we begun to cut it up before we got
this permission, we should have lost the whole. They had brought
a large party to eat their half, and they divided it with us in a
friendly way. My men were delighted with the feast, though, by
lying unopened a whole day, the carcase was pretty far gone.
An astonishing number of hyænas collected round, and kept up
a loud laughter for two whole nights. Some of them do make
a very good imitation of a laugh. I asked my men what the
hyænas were laughing at; as they usually give animals credit for
a share of intelligence; they said, that they were laughing because
we could not take the whole, and that they would have plenty
to eat as well as we.

On coming to the part where the elephant was slain, we passed
through grass so tall that it reminded me of that in the valley of
Cassange. Insects are very numerous after the rains commence.

While waiting by the elephant, I observed a great number of insects, like grains of fine sand, moving on my boxes. On examination with a glass, four species were apparent; one of green and gold preening its wings, which glanced in the sun with metallic lustre, another clear as crystal, a third of the colour of vermilion, and a fourth black. These are probably some of those which consume the seeds of every plant that grows. Almost every kind has its own peculiar insect, and when the rains are over, very few seeds remain untouched. The rankest poisons, as the Kongwhane and Euphorbia, are soon devoured—the former has a scarlet insect; and even the fiery bird's-eye pepper, which will keep off many others from their own seeds, is itself devoured by a maggot. I observed here, what I had often seen before, that certain districts abound in centipedes. Here they have light reddish bodies and blue legs; great myriapedes are seen crawling everywhere. Although they do no harm, they excite in man a feeling of loathing. Perhaps our appearance produces a similar feeling in the elephant and other large animals. Where they have been much disturbed, they certainly look upon us with great distrust, as the horrid biped that ruins their peace. In the quietest parts of the forest there is heard a faint but distinct hum, which tells of insect joy. One may see many whisking about in the clear sunshine in patches among the green glancing leaves; but there are invisible myriads working with never-tiring mandibles on leaves, and stalks, and beneath the soil. They are all brimful of enjoyment. Indeed the universality of organic life may be called a mantle of happy existence encircling the world, and imparts the idea of its being caused by the consciousness of our benignant Father's smile on all the works of His hands.

The birds of the tropics have been described as generally wanting in power of song. I was decidedly of opinion that this was not applicable to many parts in Londa, though birds there are remarkably scarce. Here the chorus, or body of song, was not much smaller in volume than it is in England. It was not so harmonious, and sounded always as if the birds were singing in a foreign tongue. Some resemble the lark, and indeed there are several of that family; two have notes not unlike those of the thrush. One brought the chaffinch to my mind, and another

2 R

the robin; but their songs are intermixed with several curious abrupt notes unlike anything English. One utters deliberately "peek, pak, pok;" another has a single note like a stroke on a violin-string. The mokwa reza gives forth a screaming set of notes like our blackbird when disturbed, then concludes with what the natives say is "pula, pula" (rain, rain), but more like "weep, weep, weep." Then we have the loud cry of francolins, the "pumpuru, pumpuru" of turtle-doves, and the "chiken, chiken, chik, churr, churr" of the honey-guide. Occasionally near villages we have a kind of mocking bird, imitating the calls of domestic fowls. These African birds have not been wanting in song, they have only lacked poets to sing their praises, which ours have had from the time of Aristophanes downwards. Ours have both a classic and a modern interest to enhance their fame. In hot dry weather, or at midday when the sun is fierce, all are still: let, however, a good shower fall, and all burst forth at once into merry lays and loving courtship. The early mornings and the cool evenings are their favourite times for singing. There are comparatively few with gaudy plumage, being totally unlike, in this respect, the birds of the Brazils. The majority have decidedly a sober dress, though collectors, having generally selected the gaudiest as the most valuable, have conveyed the idea that the birds of the tropics for the most part possess gorgeous plumage.

15th.—Several of my men have been bitten by spiders and other insects, but no effect except pain has followed. A large caterpillar is frequently seen, called lezuntabuea. It is covered with long grey hairs, and, the body being dark, it resembles a porcupine in minature. If one touches it, the hairs run into the pores of the skin, and remain there, giving sharp pricks. There are others which have a similar means of defence; and when the hand is drawn across them, as in passing a bush on which they happen to be, the contact resembles the stinging of nettles. From the great number of caterpillars seen, we have a considerable variety of butterflies. One particular kind flies more like a swallow than a butterfly. They are not remarkable for the gaudiness of their colours.

In passing along we crossed the hills Vungue or Mvungwe, which we found to be composed of various eruptive rocks. At one part we have breccia of altered marl or slate in quartz, and various amygdaloids. It is curious to observe the different forms which silica assumes. We have it in claystone porphyry here, in minute round globules, no larger than turnip-seed, dotted thickly over the matrix; or crystallised round the walls of cavities, once filled with air, or other elastic fluid; or it may appear in similar cavities as tufts of yellow asbestos, or as red, yellow, or green crystals, or in laminæ so arranged as to appear like fossil wood. Vungue forms the watershed between those sand rivulets which run to the N.E. and others which flow southward, as the Kapopo, Ue, and Due, which run into the Luia.

We found that many elephants had been feeding on the fruit called Mokoronga. This is a black-coloured plum, having purple juice. We all ate it in large quantities, as we found it delicious. The only defect it has, is the great size of the seed in comparison with the pulp. This is the chief fault of all uncultivated wild fruits. The Mokoronga exists throughout this part of the country most abundantly, and the natives eagerly devour it, as it is said to be perfectly wholesome, or, as they express it, "It is pure fat," and fat is by them considered the best of food. Though only a little larger than a cherry, we found that the elephants had stood picking them off patiently by the hour. We observed the footprints of a black rhinoceros (*Rhinoceros bicornis*, Linn.) and her calf. We saw other footprints among the hills of Semalembue, but the black rhinoceros is remarkably scarce in all the country north of the Zambesi. The white rhinoceros (*Rhinoceros simus* of Burchell), or Mohóhu of the Bechuanas, is quite extinct here, and will soon become unknown in the country to the south. It feeds almost entirely on grasses, and is of a timid unsuspecting disposition: this renders it an easy prey, and they are slaughtered without mercy on the introduction of fire-arms. The black possesses a more savage nature, and, like the ill-natured in general, is never found with an ounce of fat in its body. From its greater fierceness and wariness, it holds its place in a district much longer than its more timid and better conditioned neighbour. Mr. Oswell was once stalking two of these beasts, and as they came slowly to him, he, knowing that there is but little chance of hitting the small brain of this animal by a shot in the head, lay expecting one of them to give his shoulder, till he was within a few yards.

2 R 2

THE RHINOCEROS.   CHAP. XXX.

The hunter then thought that by making a rush to his side he might succeed in escaping, but the rhinoceros, too quick for that, turned upon him, and though he discharged his gun close to the animal's head he was tossed in the air. My friend was insensible for some time, and on recovering found large wounds on the thigh and body: I saw that on the former part still open and five inches long. The white, however, is not always quite safe, for one, even after it was mortally wounded, attacked Mr. Oswell's horse, and thrust the horn through to the saddle, tossing at the time both horse and rider. I once saw a white rhinoceros give a buffalo which was gazing intently at myself a poke in the chest, but it did not wound it, and seemed only a hint to get out of the way. Four varieties of the rhinoceros are enumerated by naturalists, but my observation led me to conclude that there are but two; and that the extra species have been formed from differences in their sizes, ages, and the direction of the horns, as if we should reckon the short-horned cattle a different species from the Alderneys or the Highland breed. I was led to this, from having once seen a black rhinoceros with a horn bent downwards, like that of the kuabaoba, and also because the animals of the two great varieties differ very much in appearance at different stages of their growth. I find, however, that Dr. Smith, the best judge in these matters, is quite decided as to the propriety of the subdivision into three or four species. For common readers it is sufficient to remember that there are two well-defined species, that differ entirely in appearance and food. The absence of both these rhinoceroses among the reticulated rivers in the central valley may easily be accounted for, they would be such an easy prey to the natives in their canoes at the periods of inundation; but one cannot so readily account for the total absence of the giraffe and the ostrich on the high open lands of the Batoka, north of the Zambesi, unless we give credence to the native report which bounds the country still further north by another network of waters near Lake Shuia, and suppose that it also prevented their progress southwards. The Batoka have no name for the giraffe or the ostrich in their language; yet, as the former exists in considerable numbers in the angle formed by the Leeambye and Chóbe, they may have come from the north along the western ridge. The Chobe would seem to have been too narrow to act as an obstacle to the giraffe, supposing it to have come into that district from the south; but the broad river into which that stream flows, seems always to have presented an impassable barrier to both the giraffe and the ostrich, though they abound on its southern border, both in the Kalahari Desert and the country of Mashona.

We passed through large tracts of Mopane country, and my men caught a great many of the birds called Korwé (*Tockus erythrorhynchus*) in their breeding-places, which were in holes in the mopane-trees. On the 19th we passed the nest of a korwe, just ready for the female to enter: the orifice was plastered on both sides, but a space was left of a heart shape, and exactly the size of the bird's body. The hole in the tree was in every case found to be prolonged some distance upwards above the opening, and thither the korwe always fled to escape being caught. In another nest we found that one white egg, much like that of a pigeon, was laid, and the bird dropped another when captured. She had four besides in the ovarium. The first time that I saw this bird was at Kolobeng, where I had gone to the forest for some timber. Standing by a tree, a native looked behind me and exclaimed, "There is the nest of a korwe." I saw a slit only, about half an inch wide and three or four inches long, in a slight hollow of the tree. Thinking the word korwe denoted some small animal, I waited with interest to see what he would extract; he broke the clay which surrounded the slit, put his arm into the hole, and brought out a *Tockus*, or *red-beaked hornbill*, which he killed. He informed me that when the female enters her nest she submits to a real confinement. The male plasters up the entrance, leaving only a narrow slit by which to feed his mate, and which exactly suits the form of his beak. The female makes a nest of her own feathers, lays her eggs, hatches them, and remains with the young till they are fully fledged. During all this time, which is stated to be two or three months, the male continues to feed her and the young family. The prisoner generally becomes quite fat, and is esteemed a very dainty morsel by the natives, while the poor slave of a husband gets so lean that, on the sudden lowering of the temperature which sometimes happens after a fall of rain, he is benumbed, falls down, and dies. I never had an opportunity of ascertaining the actual length of the confinement, but on passing the same tree at Kolobeng about eight days afterwards, the hole was plastered up again, as if, in the short time that had elapsed, the disconsolate husband had secured another wife. We did not disturb her, and my duties prevented me from returning to the spot. This is the month in which the female enters the nest. We had seen one of these, as before mentioned, with the plastering not quite finished; we saw many completed; and we received the very same account here that we did at Kolobeng, that the bird comes forth when the young are fully fledged, at the period when the corn is ripe; indeed, her appearance abroad with her young is one of the signs they have for knowing when it ought to be so. As that is about the end of April, the time is between two and three months. She is said sometimes to hatch two eggs, and, when the young of these are full-fledged, other two are just out of the egg-shells: she then leaves the nest with the two elder, the orifice is again plastered up, and both male and female attend to the wants of the young which are left. On several occasions I observed a branch bearing the marks of the male having often sat upon it when feeding his mate, and the excreta had been expelled a full yard from the orifice, and often proved a means of discovering the retreat.

The honey-guides were very assiduous in their friendly offices, and enabled my men to get a large quantity of honey; but though bees abound, the wax of these parts forms no article of trade. In Londa it may be said to be fully cared for, as you find hives placed upon trees in the most lonesome forests. We often met strings of carriers laden with large blocks of this substance, each 80 or 100 lbs. in weight, and pieces were offered to us for sale at every village; but here we never saw a single artificial hive. The bees were always found in the natural cavities of mopane-trees. It is probable that the good market for wax afforded to Angola by the churches of Brazil, led to the gradual development of that branch of commerce there. I saw even on the banks of the Quango as much as sixpence paid for a pound. In many parts of the Batoka country, bees exist in vast numbers; and the tribute due to Sekeletu is often paid in large jars of honey; but having no market nor use for the wax, it is thrown away. This was the case also with ivory at the Lake Ngami, at the period of its discovery. The reports brought by my other party from Loanda of the value of wax, had induced some of my present companions to bring small quantities of it to Tete, but, not knowing the proper mode of preparing it, it was so dark coloured that no one would purchase it; I afterwards saw a little at Kilimane, which had been procured from the natives somewhere in this region.

Though we are now approaching the Portuguese settlement, the country is still full of large game. My men killed six buffalo calves out of a herd we met. The abundance of these animals, and also of antelopes, shows the insufficiency of the bow and arrow to lessen their numbers. There are also a great many lions and hyænas, and there is no check upon the increase of the former, for the people, believing that the souls of their chiefs enter into them, never attempt to kill them; they even believe that a chief may metamorphose himself into a lion, kill any one he chooses, and then return to the human form; therefore when they see one they commence clapping their hands, which is the usual mode of salutation here. The consequence is, that lions and hyænas are so abundant, that we see little huts made in trees, indicating the places where some of the inhabitants have slept when benighted in the fields. As numbers of my men frequently left the line of march in order to take out the korwes from their nests, or follow the honey-guides, they excited the astonishment of our guides, who were constantly warning them of the danger they thereby incurred from lions. I was often considerably ahead of the main body of my men on this account, and was obliged to stop every hour or two, but, the sun being excessively hot by day, I was glad of the excuse for resting. We could make no such prodigious strides as officers in the Arctic regions are able to do. Ten or twelve miles a day were a good march for both the men and myself, and it was not the length of the marches, but continuing day after day to perform the same distance, that was so fatiguing. It was in this case much longer than appears on the map, because we kept out of the way of villages. I drank less than the natives when riding, but all my clothing was now constantly damp from the moisture which was imbibed in large quantities at every pond. One does not stay on these occasions to prepare water with alum or anything else, but drinks any amount without fear. I never felt the atmosphere so steamy as on the low-lying lands of the Zambesi, and yet it was becoming cooler than it was on the highlands.

We crossed the rivulets Kapopo and Ue, now running, but usually dry. There are great numbers of wild grape-vines growing in this quarter; indeed they abound everywhere along the banks of the Zambesi. In the Batoka country there is a variety which yields a black grape of considerable sweetness. The leaves are very large and harsh, as if capable of withstanding the rays of this hot sun; but the most common kinds—one with a round leaf and a greenish grape, and another with a leaf closely resembling that of the cultivated varieties, and with dark or purple fruit—have large seeds, which are strongly astringent and render it a disagreeable fruit. The natives eat all the varieties; and I tasted vinegar made by a Portuguese from these grapes. Probably a country which yields the wild vines so very abundantly, might be a fit one for the cultivated species. At this part of the journey so many of the vines had run across the little foot-path we followed, that one had to be constantly on the watch to avoid being tripped. The ground was covered with rounded shingle, which was not easily seen among the grass. Pedestrian-ism may be all very well for those whose obesity requires much exercise, but for one who was becoming as thin as a lath, through the constant perspiration caused by marching day after day in the hot sun, the only good I saw in it was, that it gave an honest sort of man a vivid idea of the treadmill.

Although the rains were not quite over, great numbers of pools were drying up, and the ground was in many parts covered with small, green, cryptogamous plants, which gave it a mouldy appearance and a strong smell. As we sometimes pushed aside the masses of rank vegetation which hung over our path, we felt a sort of hot blast on our faces. Everything looked unwhole-some, but we had no fever. The Ue flows between high banks of a soft red sandstone streaked with white, and pieces of tufa. The crumbling sandstone is evidently alluvial, and is cut into, 12 feet deep. In this region, too, we met with pot-holes, six feet deep and three or four in diameter. In some cases they form convenient wells; in others they are full of earth; and in others still, the people have made them into graves for their chiefs.

On the 20th we came to Monína's village (close to the sand-river Tangwe, lat. 16° 13′ 38″ S., long. 32° 32′ E.). This man is very popular among the tribes on account of his liberality. Boróma, Nyampúngo, Monína, Jira, Katolósa (Monomotápa), and Súsa, all acknowledge the supremacy of one called Nyatéwe, who is reported to decide all disputes respecting land. This confederation is exactly similar to what we observed in Londa and other parts of Africa. Katolósa is "the Emperor Monomotapa" of history, but he is a chief of no great power, and acknowledges the supremacy of Nyatéwe. The Portuguese formerly honoured Monomotapa with a guard, to fire off numbers of guns on the occasion of any funeral, and he was also partially subsidized. The only evidence of greatness possessed by his successor, is his having about a hundred wives. When he dies, a disputed succession and much fighting are expected. In reference to the term Monomotapa, it is to be remembered that Mono, Moéne, Mona, Mana, or Moréna, mean simply *chief*, and considerable confusion has arisen from naming different people by making a plural of the chief's name. The names Monomoízes, spelt also Monemuíges and Monomuízes, and Monomotápistas, when applied to these tribes are exactly the same as if we should call the Scotch the Lord Douglases. Motápe was the chief of the Bambíri, a tribe of the Banyai, and is now represented in the person of Katolósa. He was probably a man of greater energy than his successor, yet only an insignificant chief. Monomoízes was formed from Moiza or Muiza, the singular of the word Babísa or Aiza, the proper name of a large tribe to the north. In the transformation of this name the same error has been committed as in the others; and mistakes have occurred in many other names by inattention to the meaning, and predilection for the letter *r*. The river Loangwa, for instance, has been termed Arroangoa; and the Luenya, the Ruanha. The Bazizúlu, or Mashóna, are spoken of as the Morurúrus.

The government of the Banyai is rather peculiar, being a sort of feudal republicanism. The chief is elected, and they choose the son of the deceased chief's sister in preference to his own offspring. When dissatisfied with one candidate, they even go to a distant tribe for a successor, who is usually of the family of the late chief, a brother, or a sister's son, but never his own son or daughter. When first spoken to on the subject, he answers as if he thought himself unequal to the task and unworthy of the honour, but, having accepted it, all the wives, goods, and children of his predecessor belong to him, and he takes care to keep them in a dependent position. When any one of them becomes tired of this state of vassalage and sets up his own village, it is not unusual for the elected chief to send a number of the young men, who congregate about himself, to visit him. If he does not receive them with the usual amount of clapping of hands and humility, they, in obedience to orders, at once burn his village. The children of the chief have fewer privileges than common free men. They may not be sold, but, rather than choose any one of them for a chief at any future time, the free men would prefer to elect one of themselves who bore only a very distant relationship to the family. These free men are a distinct class who can never be sold; and under them there is a class of slaves whose appearance as well as position is very degraded. Monina had a great number of young men about him from twelve to fifteen years of age. These were all sons of free men, and bands of young lads like them in the different districts, leave their parents about the age of puberty, and live with such men as Monina for the sake of instruction. When I asked the nature of the instruction I was told "Bonyái," which I suppose may be understood as indicating manhood, for it sounds as if we should say, "to teach an American, Americanism," or "an Englishman to be English." While here they are kept in subjection to rather stringent regulations. They must salute carefully by clapping their hands on approaching a superior, and when any cooked food is brought, the young men may not approach the dish, but an elder divides a portion to each. They remain unmarried, until a fresh set of youths is ready to occupy their place under the same instruction. The parents send servants with their sons to cultivate gardens to supply them with food, and also tusks to Monina to purchase clothing for them. When the lads return to the village of their parents, a case is submitted to them for adjudication, and if they speak well on the point, the parents are highly gratified.

When we told Monina that we had nothing to present but some hoes, he replied that he was not in need of those articles,

and that he had absolute power over the country in front,
and if he prevented us from proceeding, no one would say anything to him. His little boy Borómo having come to the
encampment to look at us, I gave him a knife, and he went off
and brought a pint of honey for me. The father came soon
afterwards, and I offered him a shirt. He remarked to his
councillors, "It is evident, that this man has nothing, for, if
he had, his people would be buying provisions, but we don't
see them going about for that purpose." His council did not
agree in this. They evidently believed that we had goods, but
kept them hid, and we felt it rather hard to be suspected of
falsehood. It was probably at their suggestion that in the
evening a war-dance was got up, about a hundred yards from
our encampment, as if to put us in fear and force us to bring
forth presents. Some of Monina's young men had guns, but
most were armed with large bows, arrows, and spears. They
beat their drums furiously, and occasionally fired off a gun. As
this sort of dance is never got up unless there is an intention to
attack, my men expected an assault. We sat and looked at them
for some time, and then, as it became dark, lay down, all ready
to give them a warm reception. But an hour or two after dark
the dance ceased, and, as we then saw no one approaching us, we
went to sleep. During the night, one of my head-men, Monahin,
was seen to get up, look towards the village, and say to one who
was half awake, "Don't you hear what these people are saying?
Go and listen!" He then walked off in the opposite direction
and never returned. We had no guard set, but every one lay
with his spear in his hand. The man to whom he spoke appears
to have been in a dreamy condition, for it did not strike him
that he ought to give the alarm. Next morning I found to my
sorrow that Monahin was gone, and not a trace of him could be
discovered. He had an attack of pleuritis some weeks before,
and had recovered, but latterly complained a little of his head.
I observed him in good spirits on the way hither, and in crossing
some of the streams, as I was careful not to wet my feet, he
aided me, and several times joked at my becoming so light. In
the evening he sat beside my tent until it was dark, and did not
manifest any great alarm. It was probably either a sudden fit
of insanity, or, having gone a little way out from the camp, he

may have been carried off by a lion, as this part of the country is full of them. I incline to the former opinion, because sudden insanity occurs when there is any unusual strain upon their minds. Monahin was in command of the Batoka of Mokwiné in my party, and he was looked upon with great dislike by all that chief's subjects. The only difficulties I had with them arose in consequence of being obliged to give orders through him. They said Mokwine is reported to have been killed by the Makololo, but Monahin is the individual who put forth his hand and slew him. When one of these people kills in battle, he seems to have no compunction afterwards, but when he makes a foray on his own responsibility, and kills a man of note, the common people make remarks to each other, which are reported to him, and bring the affair perpetually to his remembrance. This iteration on the conscience causes insanity, and when one runs away in a wide country like this, the fugitive is never heard of. Monahin had lately become afraid of his own party from over-hearing their remarks, and said more than once to me, " They want to kill me." I believe if he ran to any village they would take care of him. I felt his loss greatly, and spent three days in searching for him. He was a sensible and most obliging man. I sent in the morning to inform Monina of this sad event, and he at once sent to all the gardens around, desiring the people to look for him, and, should he come near, to bring him home. He evidently sympathised with us in our sorrow, and, afraid lest we might suspect him, added, " We never catch nor kidnap people here. It is not our custom. It is considered as guilt among all the tribes." I gave him credit for truthfulness, and he allowed us to move on without further molestation.

After leaving his village we marched in the bed of a sand-river a quarter of a mile broad, called Tangwe. Walking on this sand is as fatiguing as walking on snow. The country is flat, and covered with low trees, but we see high hills in the distance. A little to the south we have those of the Lobole. This region is very much infested by lions, and men never go any distance into the woods alone. Having turned aside on one occasion at midday, and gone a short distance among grass a little taller than myself, an animal sprung away from me which was certainly not an antelope, but I could not distinguish whether it was a lion

or a hyæna. This abundance of carnivora made us lose all hope
of Monahin. We saw footprints of many black rhinoceroses, buffaloes, and zebras.

After a few hours we reached the village of Nyakóba. Two
men, who accompanied us from Monina to Nyakoba's, would not
believe us when we said that we had no beads. It is very trying
to have one's veracity doubted, but, on opening the boxes, and
showing them that all I had was perfectly useless to them, they
consented to receive some beads off Sekwebu's waist, and I
promised to send four yards of calico from Tete. As we came
away from Monina's village, a witch-doctor, who had been sent
for, arrived, and all Monina's wives went forth into the fields
that morning fasting. There they would be compelled to drink
an infusion of a plant named "goho," which is used as an ordeal.
This ceremony is called "muavi," and is performed in this way.
When a man suspects that any of his wives have bewitched him,
he sends for the witch-doctor, and all the wives go forth into the
field, and remain fasting till that person has made an infusion
of the plant. They all drink it, each one holding up her hand
to heaven in attestation of her innocency. Those who vomit it
are considered innocent, while those whom it purges are pronounced guilty, and put to death by burning. The innocent
return to their homes, and slaughter a cock as a thank-offering
to their guardian spirits. The practice of ordeal is common
among all the negro nations north of the Zambesi. This sum-
mary procedure excited my surprise, for my intercourse with the
natives here had led me to believe, that the women were held in
so much estimation that the men would not dare to get rid of
them thus. But the explanation I received was this. The
slightest imputation makes them eagerly desire the test; they
are conscious of being innocent, and have the fullest faith in the
muavi detecting the guilty alone; hence they go willingly, and
even eagerly, to drink it. When in Angola, a half-caste was
pointed out to me, who is one of the most successful merchants
in that country; and the mother of this gentleman, who was
perfectly free, went, of her own accord, all the way from Ambaca to Cassange, to be killed by the ordeal, her rich son
making no objection. The same custom prevails among the
Barotse, Bashubia, and Batoka, but with slight variations. The

Barotse, for instance, pour the medicine down the throat of a cock or of a dog, and judge of the innocence or guilt of the person accused, according to the vomiting or purging of the animal. I happened to mention to my own men the water-test for witches formerly in use in Scotland : the supposed witch, being bound hand and foot, was thrown into a pond ; if she floated, she was considered guilty, taken out, and burned ; but if she sank and was drowned, she was pronounced innocent. The wisdom of my ancestors excited as much wonder in their minds, as their custom did in mine.

The person whom Nyakoba appointed to be our guide, having informed us of the decision, came and bargained that his services should be rewarded with a hoe. I had no objection to give it, and showed him the article ; he was delighted with it, and went off to show it to his wife. He soon afterwards returned, and said that, though he was perfectly willing to go, his wife would not let him. I said, " Then bring back the hoe ;" but he replied, " I want it." " Well, go with us, and you shall have it." " But my wife won't let me." I remarked to my men, " Did you ever hear such a fool ? " They answered, " Oh, that is the custom of these parts ; the wives are the masters." And Sekwebu informed me that he had gone to this man's house, and heard him saying to his wife, " Do you think that I would ever leave you ? " then, turning to Sekwebu, he asked, " Do you think I would leave this pretty woman ? Is she not pretty ? " Sekwebu had been making inquiries among the people, and had found that the women indeed possessed a great deal of influence. We questioned the guide whom we finally got from Nyakoba, an intelligent young man, who had much of the Arab features, and found the statements confirmed. When a young man takes a liking to a girl of another village, and the parents have no objection to the match, he is obliged to come and live at their village. He has to perform certain services for the mother-in-law, such as keeping her well supplied with firewood ; and when he comes into her presence he is obliged to sit with his knees in a bent position, as putting out his feet towards the old lady would give her great offence. If he becomes tired of living in this state of vassalage, and wishes to return to his own family, he is obliged to leave all his children behind—they belong to the wife. This is only a more stringent enforcement of the law from which emanates the practice which prevails so very extensively in Africa, known to Europeans as "buying wives." Such virtually it is, but it does not appear quite in that light to the actors. So many head of cattle or goats are given to the parents of the girl, "to give her up," as it is termed, *i. e.* to forego all claim on her offspring, and allow an entire transference of her and her seed into another family. If nothing is given, the family from which she has come can claim the children as part of itself: the payment is made to sever this bond. In the case supposed, the young man has not been able to advance anything for that purpose; and, from the temptations placed here before my men, I have no doubt that some prefer to have their daughters married in that way, as it leads to the increase of their own village. My men excited the admiration of the Bambiri, who took them for a superior breed on account of their bravery in elephant-hunting, and wished to get them as sons-in-law on the conditions named, but none yielded to the temptation.

We were informed that there is a child belonging to a half-caste Portuguese in one of these tribes, and the father had tried in vain to get him from the mother's parents. We saw several things to confirm the impression of the higher position which women hold here; and, being anxious to discover if I were not mistaken, when we came amongst the Portuguese I inquired of them, and was told that they had ascertained the same thing; and that, if they wished a man to perform any service for them, he would reply, "Well, I shall go and ask my wife." If she consented, he would go, and perform his duty faithfully; but no amount of coaxing or bribery would induce him to do it if she refused. The Portuguese praised the appearance of the Banyai, and they certainly are a fine race.

We got on better with Nyakoba than we expected. He has been so much affected by the sesenda that he is quite decrepit, and requires to be fed. I at once showed his messenger that we had nothing whatever to give. Nyakoba was offended with him for not believing me, and he immediately sent a basket of maize and another of corn, saying that he believed my statement, and would send men with me to Tete who would not lead me to any other village.

The birds here sing very sweetly, and I thought I heard the canary, as in Londa. We had a heavy shower of rain, and I observed that the thermometer sank 14° in one hour afterwards. From the beginning of February we experienced a sensible diminution of temperature. In January the lowest was 75°, and that at sunrise; the average at the same hour (sunrise) being 79°; at 3 P.M., 90°; and at sunset, 82°. In February it fell as low as 70° in the course of the night, and the average height was 88°. Only once did it rise to 94°, and a thunderstorm followed this; yet the sensation of heat was greater now than it had been at much higher temperatures on more elevated lands.

We passed several villages by going roundabout ways through the forest. We saw the remains of a lion that had been killed by a buffalo, and the horns of a putokwane (black antelope), the finest I had ever seen, which had met its death by a lion. The drums beating all night in one village near which we slept, showed that some person in it had finished his course. On the occasion of the death of a chief, a trader is liable to be robbed, for the people consider themselves not amenable to law until a new one is elected. We continued a very winding course, in order to avoid the chief Katolósa, who is said to levy large sums upon those who fall into his hands. One of our guides was a fine tall young man, the very image of Ben-Habib the Arab. They were carrying dried buffalo's meat to the market at Tête as a private speculation.

A great many of the Banyai are of a light coffee-and-milk colour, and indeed this colour is considered handsome throughout the whole country,—a fair complexion being as much a test of beauty with them as with us. As they draw out their hair into small cords a foot in length, and entwine the inner bark of a certain tree round each separate cord, and dye this substance of a reddish colour, many of them put me in mind of the ancient Egyptians. The great mass of dressed hair which they possess, reaches to the shoulders, but, when they intend to travel, they draw it up to a bunch, and tie it on the top of the head. They are cleanly in their habits.

As we did not come near human habitations, and could only take short stages on account of the illness of one of my men, I had an opportunity of observing the expedients my party resorted to in order to supply their wants. Large white edible mushrooms are found on the anthills, and are very good. The mokúri, a tuber which abounds in the Mopane country, they discovered by percussing the ground with stones; and another tuber, about the size of a turnip, called "bonga," is found in the same situations. It does not determine to the joints like the mokuri, and in winter has a sensible amount of salt in it. A fruit called "ndongo" by the Makololo, "dongolo" by the Bambiri, resembles in appearance a small plum, which becomes black when ripe, and is good food, as the seeds are small. Many trees are known by tradition, and one receives curious bits of information in asking about different fruits that are met with. A tree named "shekabakádzi" is superior to all others for making fire by friction. As its name implies, women may even readily make fire by it when benighted.

The country here is covered over with well-rounded shingle and gravel of granite, gneiss, with much talc in it, mica schist, and other rocks which we saw *in situ* between the Kafue and Loangwa. There are great mounds of soft red sand slightly coherent, which crumble in the hand with ease. The gravel and the sand drain away the water so effectually, that the trees are exposed to the heat during a portion of the year, without any moisture; hence they are not large, like those on the Zambesi, and are often scrubby. The rivers are all of the sandy kind, and we pass over large patches between this and Tete, in which, in the dry season, no water is to be found. Close on our south, the hills of Lokóle rise to a considerable height, and beyond them flows the Mazóe with its golden sands. The great numbers of pot-holes on the sides of sandstone ridges, when viewed in connection with the large banks of rolled shingle and washed sand which are met with on this side of the eastern ridge, may indicate that the sea in former times rolled its waves along its flanks. Many of the hills between the Kafue and Loangwa, have their sides of the form seen in mud banks left by the tide. The pot-holes appear most abundant on low grey sandstone ridges here; and as the shingle is composed of the same rocks as the

2 s

hills west of Zumbo, it looks as if a current had dashed along from the south-east in the line in which the pot-holes now appear, and if the current was deflected, by those hills, towards the Maravi country, north of Tete, it may have hollowed the rounded water-worn caverns, in which these people store their corn, and also hide themselves from their enemies. I could detect no terraces on the land, but, if I am right in my supposition, the form of this part of the continent must once have resembled the curves or indentations seen on the southern extremity of the American continent. In the indentation to the S.E., S., S. W., and W. of this, lie the principal gold-washings ; and the line of the current, supposing it to have struck against the hills of Mburuma, shows the washings in the N. and N.E. of Tete.

We were tolerably successful in avoiding the villages, and slept one night on the flanks of the hill Zimika, where a great number of deep pot-holes afforded an abundant supply of good rain-water. Here, for the first time, we saw hills with bare, smooth, rocky tops, and we crossed over broad dykes of gneiss and syenitic porphyry : the directions in which they lay were N. and S. As we were now near to Tete, we were congratulating ourselves on having avoided those who would only have plagued us ; but next morning some men saw us, and ran off to inform the neighbouring villages of our passing. A party immediately pursued us, and, as they knew we were within call of Katolósa (Monomotápa), they threatened to send information to that chief of our offence, in passing through the country without leave. We were obliged to give them two small tusks, for, had they told Katolosa of our supposed offence, we should in all probability have lost the whole. We then went through a very rough stony country without any path. Being pretty well tired out in the evening of the 2nd of March, I remained at about eight miles distance from Téte, Tétte, or Nyungwé. My men asked me to go on ; I felt too fatigued to proceed, but sent forward to the Commandant the letters of recommendation with which I had been favoured in Angola by the Bishop and others, and lay down to rest. Our food having been exhausted, my men had been subsisting for some time on roots and honey. About two o'clock in the morning of the 3rd we were aroused by two officers and a company of soldiers, who had been sent with the materials for a civilized breakfast and a

" masheela" to bring me to Tete. (Commandant's house: lat. 16° 9′ 3″ S., long. 33° 28′ E.) My companions thought that we were captured by the armed men, and called me in alarm.   When I understood the errand on which they had come, and had partaken of a good breakfast, though I had just before been too tired to sleep, all my fatigue vanished. It was the most refreshing breakfast I ever partook of, and I walked the last eight miles without the least feeling of weariness, although the path was so rough that one of the officers remarked to me, " This is enough to tear a man's life out of him." The pleasure experienced in partaking of that breakfast was only equalled by the enjoyment of Mr. Gabriel's bed on my arrival at Loanda. It was also enhanced by the news that Sebastopol had fallen, and the war was finished.

NOTE. — Having neglected, in referring to the footprints of the rhinoceros, to mention what may be interesting to naturalists, I add it here in a note; that wherever the footprints are seen, there are also marks of the animal having ploughed up the ground and bushes with his horn. This has been supposed to indicate that he is subject to " fits of ungovernable rage ;" but when seen, he appears rather to be rejoicing in his strength. He acts as a bull sometimes does when he gores the earth with his horns. The rhinoceros, in addition to this, stands on a clump of bushes ; bends his back down, and scrapes the ground with his feet, throwing it out backwards, as if to stretch and clean his toes, in the same way that a dog may be seen to do on a little grass : this is certainly not rage.

CHAPTER XXXI.

I WAS most kindly received by the Commandant Tito Augusto d'Aráujo Sicard, who did everything in his power to restore me from my emaciated condition ; and as this was still the unhealthy period at Kilimane, he advised me to remain with him until the following month. He also generously presented my men with abundant provisions of millet; and by giving them lodgings in a house of his own, until they could erect their own huts, he preserved them from the bite of the tampans, here named Carapatos.* We had heard frightful accounts of this insect while among the

---

* Another insect, resembling a maggot, burrows into the feet of the natives and sucks their blood. Mr. Westwood says, " The tampan is a large species of mite, closely allied to the poisonous bug (as it is called) of Persia, *Argos reflexus*, respecting which such marvellous accounts have been recorded, and which the statement respecting the carapato or tampan would partially confirm." Mr. W. also thinks that the poison-yielding larvæ called N'gwa is a " species of chrysomelidæ. The larvæ of the British species of that family exude a fetid yellow thickish fluid when alarmed, but he has not heard that any of them are at all poisonous."

Banyai, and Major Sicard assured me that to strangers its bite
is more especially dangerous, as it sometimes causes fatal fever.
It may please our homœopathic friends to hear that, in curing the
bite of the tampan, the natives administer one of the insects
bruised in the medicine employed.

The village of Tete is built on a long slope down to the river,
the fort .being close to the water. The rock beneath is grey
sandstone, and has the appearance of being crushed away from
the river: the strata have thus a crumpled form. The hollow
between each crease is a street, the houses being built upon the
projecting fold. The rocks at the top of the slope are much
higher than the fort, and of course completely command it.
There is then a large valley, and beyond that, an oblong hill
called Karueira. The whole of the adjacent country is rocky
and broken, but every available spot is under cultivation. The
stone houses in Tetè are cemented with mud instead of lime, and
thatched with reeds and grass. The rains, having washed out the
mud between the stones, give all the houses a rough untidy
appearance. No lime was known to be found, nearer than
Mozambique; some used in making seats in the verandahs,
had actually been brought all that distance. The Portuguese,
evidently, knew nothing of the pink and white marbles, which I
found at the Mbai, and another rivulet, named the Unguesi, near
it, and of which I brought home specimens; nor yet of the
dolomite which lies so near to Zumbo; they might have
burned the marble into lime without going so far as Mozambique. There are about thirty European houses; the rest are
native, and of wattle and daub. A wall about ten feet high
is intended to enclose the village, but most of the native inhabitants prefer to live on different spots outside. There are
about 1200 huts in all, which with European households would
give a population of about 4500 souls. Only a small proportion of these, however, live on the spot; the majority are engaged in agricultural operations in the adjacent country. Generally there are not more than 2000 people resident, for, compared
with what it was, Tete is now a ruin. The number of Portuguese is very small; if we exclude the military, it is under
twenty. Lately, however, 105 soldiers were sent from Portugal
to Senna, where in one year twenty-five were cut off by fever.

They were then removed to Tete, and here they enjoy much better
health, though, from the abundance of spirits distilled from various
plants, wild fruits, and grain, in which pernicious beverage they
largely indulge, besides partaking chiefly of unwholesome native
food, better health could scarcely have been expected.   The
natives here understand the method of distillation by means of
gun-barrels, and a succession of earthen pots filled with water to
keep them cool.   The general report of the fever here is that,
while at Kilimane the fever is continuous, at Tete a man re-
covers in about three days.   The mildest remedies only are used
at first, and, if that period be passed, then the more severe.

The fort of Tete has been the salvation of the Portuguese power
in this quarter.   It is a small square building, with a thatched
apartment for the residence of the troops; and though there are
but few guns, they are in a much better state than those of any
fort in the interior of Angola.   The cause of the decadence of
the Portuguese power in this region is simply this.   In former
times considerable quantities of grain, as wheat, millet, and maize,
were exported, also coffee, sugar, oil, and indigo, besides gold-
dust and ivory.   The cultivation of grain was carried on by
means of slaves, of whom the Portuguese possessed a large number.   The gold-dust was procured by washing at various points
on the north, south, and west of Tete.   A merchant took all his
slaves with him to the washings, carrying as much calico and
other goods as he could muster.   On arriving at the washing-
place he made a present to the chief, of the value of about a
pound sterling.   The slaves were then divided into parties, each
headed by a confidential servant, who not only had the supervision
of his squad while the washing went on, but bought dust from the
inhabitants, and made a weekly return to his master.   When
several masters united at one spot, it was called a "Bara," and
they then erected a temporary church, in which a priest from one
of the missions performed mass.   Both chiefs and people were
favourable to these visits, because the traders purchased grain for
the sustenance of the slaves with the goods they had brought.
They continued at this labour until the whole of the goods
were expended, and by this means about 130 lbs. of gold were
annually produced.   Probably more than this was actually obtained, but, as it was an article easily secreted, this alone was

submitted to the authorities for taxation.   At present the whole amount of gold obtained annually by the Portuguese is from 8 to 10 lbs. only.   When the slave-trade began, it seemed to many of the merchants a more speedy mode of becoming rich, to sell off the slaves, than to pursue the slow mode of gold-washing and agriculture, and they continued to export them, until they had neither hands to labour nor to fight for them.   It was just the story of the goose and the golden egg.   The coffee and sugar plantations and gold-washings were abandoned, because the labour had been exported to the Brazils.   Many of the Portuguese then followed their slaves, and the Government was obliged to pass a law to prevent further emigration, which, had it gone on, would have depopulated the Portuguese possessions altogether.   A clever man of Asiatic (Goa) and Portuguese extraction, called Nyaude, now built a stockade at the confluence of the Luenya and Zambesi ; and when the Commandant of Tete sent an officer with his company to summon him to his presence, Nyaude asked permission of the officer to dress himself, which being granted, he went into an inner apartment, and the officer ordered his men to pile their arms. A drum of war began to beat a note which is well known to the inhabitants.   Some of the soldiers took the alarm on hearing this note, but the officer, disregarding their warning, was, with his whole party, in a few minutes disarmed and bound hand and foot.   The Commandant of Tete then armed the whole body of slaves and marched against the stockade of Nyaude, but when they came near to it, there was the Luenya still to cross.   As they did not effect this speedily, Nyaude despatched a strong party under his son Bonga across the river below the stockade, and up the left bank of the Zambesi until they came near to Tete.   They then attacked Tete, which was totally undefended save by a few soldiers in the fort, plundered and burned the whole town except the house of the Commandant and a few others, with the church and fort.   The women and children fled into the church, and it is a remarkable fact, that none of the natives of this region will ever attack a church.   Having rendered Tete a ruin, Bonga carried off all the cattle and plunder to his father.   News of this having been brought to the army before the stockade, a sudden panic dispersed the whole ; and as the fugitives took roundabout ways in their flight, Katolosa, who had hitherto pretended to be friendly with the Portuguese, sent out his men to capture as many of them as they could. They killed many for the sake of their arms. This is the account which both natives and Portuguese give of the affair.

Another half-caste from Macao, called Kisaka or Choutama, on the opposite bank of the river, likewise rebelled. His father having died, he imagined that he had been bewitched by the Portuguese, and he therefore plundered and burnt all the plantations of the rich merchants of Tete on the north bank. As I have before remarked, that bank is the most fertile, and there the Portuguese had their villas and plantations to which they daily retired from Tete. When these were destroyed, the Tete people were completely impoverished. An attempt was made to punish this rebel, but it also was unsuccessful, and he has lately been pardoned by the home Government. One point in the narrative of this expedition is interesting. They came to a field of sugarcane so large, that 4000 men eating it during two days did not finish the whole. The Portuguese were thus placed between two enemies, Nyaude on the right bank and Kisaka on the left, and not only so, but Nyaude, having placed his stockade on the point of land on the right banks of both the Luenya and Zambesi, and washed by both these rivers, could prevent intercourse with the sea. The Luenya rushes into the Zambesi with great force, when the latter is low, and in coming up the Zambesi boats must cross it and the Luenya separately, even going a little way up that river, so as not to be driven away by its current in the bed of the Zambesi, and dashed on the rock which stands on the opposite shore. In coming up to the Luenya for this purpose, all boats and canoes came close to the stockade to be robbed. Nyaude kept the Portuguese shut up in their fort at Tete during two years, and they could only get goods sufficient to buy food, by sending to Kilimane by an overland route along the north bank of the Zambesi. The mother country did not in these "Caffre wars" pay the bills, so no one either became rich or blamed the missionaries.

The merchants were unable to engage in trade; and commerce, which the slave-trade had rendered stagnant, was now completely obstructed. The present Commandant of Tete, Major Sicard, having great influence among the natives from his good character, put a stop to the war more than once by his mere presence on the spot. We heard of him among the Banyai as a man with whom they would never fight, because "he had a good heart." Had I come down to this coast instead of going to Loanda in 1853, I should have come among the belligerents while the war was still raging, and should probably have been cut off. My present approach was just at the conclusion of the peace; and when the Portuguese authorities here were informed, through the kind offices of Lord Clarendon and Count de Lavradio, that I was expected to come this way, they all declared that such was the existing state of affairs that no European could possibly pass through the tribes. Some natives at last came down the river to Tete and said, alluding to the sextant and artificial horizon, that "the Son of God had come," and that he was "able to take the sun down from the heavens and place it under his arm!" Major Sicard then felt sure that this was the man mentioned in Lord Clarendon's despatch.

On mentioning to the Commandant that I had discovered a small seam of coal, he stated that the Portuguese were already aware of nine such seams, and that five of them were on the opposite bank of the river. As soon as I had recovered from my fatigue I went to examine them. We proceeded in a boat to the mouth of the Lofúbu or Revúbu, which is about two miles below Tete, and on the opposite or northern bank. Ascending this about four miles against a strong current of beautifully clear water, we landed near a small cataract, and walked about two miles through very fertile gardens to the seam, which we found to be in one of the feeders of the Lofubu, called Muatize or Motize. The seam is in the perpendicular bank, and dips into the rivulet, or in a northerly direction. There is first of all, a seam 10 inches in diameter, then some shale, below which there is another seam, 58 inches of which are seen, and, as the bottom touches the water of the Muatize, it may be more. This part of the seam is about 30 yards long. There is then a fault. About 100 yards higher up the stream, black vesicular trap is seen, penetrating in thin veins the clay shale of the country, converting it into porcellanite, and partially crystallizing the coal with which it came into contact. On the right bank of the Lofubu there is another feeder entering that river near its confluence with the Muatize, which is called the Morongózi, in which there is another and still larger bed of coal exposed. Further up the Lofubu, there are other seams in the rivulets Inyavu and Makare; also several spots in the Maravi country have the coal cropping out. This has evidently been brought to the surface by volcanic action at a later period than the coal formation.

I also went up the Zambesi and visited a hot spring called Nyamborónda, situated in the bed of a small rivulet named Nyaondo, which shows that igneous action is not yet extinct. We landed at a small rivulet called Mokorozi, then went a mile or two to the eastward, where we found a hot fountain at the bottom of a high hill. A little spring bubbles up on one side of the rivulet Nyaondo, and a great quantity of acrid steam rises up from the ground adjacent, about 12 feet square of which is so hot, that my companions could not stand on it with their bare feet. There are several little holes from which the water trickles, but the principal spring is in a hole a foot in diameter, and about the same in depth. Numbers of bubbles are constantly rising. The steam feels acrid in the throat, but is not inflammable, as it did not burn when I held a bunch of lighted grass over the bubbles. The mercury rises to 158° when the thermometer is put into the water in the hole, but after a few seconds it stands steadily at 160°. Even when flowing over the stones, the water is too hot for the hand. Little fish frequently leap out of the stream in the bed of which the fountain rises, into the hot water, and get scalded to death. We saw a frog which had performed that experiment, and was now cooked. The stones over which the water flows are encrusted with a white salt, and the water has a saline taste. The ground has been dug out near the fountain by the natives, in order to extract the salt it contains. It is situated among rocks of syenitic porphyry in broad dykes, and gneiss tilted on edge, and having a strike to the N.E. There are many specimens of half-formed pumice, with greenstone and lava. Some of the sandstone strata are dislocated by a hornblende rock and by basalt; the sandstone nearest to the basalt being converted into quartz.

The country around, as indeed all the district lying N. and N.W. of Tete, is hilly, and, the hills being covered with trees, the scenery is very picturesque. The soil of the valleys is very fruitful and well cultivated. There would not be much difficulty in working the coal. The Lofubu is about 60 yards broad; it flows perennially, and at its very lowest period, which is after September, there is water about 18 inches deep, which could be navigated in flat-bottomed boats. At the time of my visit it was full, and the current was very strong. If the small cataract referred to were to be avoided, the land-carriage beyond would only be about two miles. The other seams further up the river may, after passing the cataract, be approached more easily than that in the Muatize; as the seam, however, dips down into the stream, no drainage of the mine would be required, for if water were come to, it would run into the stream. I did not visit the others, but I was informed that there are seams in the independent native territory, as well as in that of the Portuguese. That in the Nake, is in the Banyai country, and indeed I have no doubt but that the whole country between Zumbo and Lupata is a coalfield of at least $2\frac{1}{4}°$ of latitude in breadth, having many faults, made during the time of the igneous action. The grey sandstone rock having silicified trees lying on it, is of these dimensions. The plantation in which the seam of coal exists, would be valued among the Portuguese at about 60 dollars or 12l., but much more would probably be asked if a wealthy purchaser appeared. They could not, however, raise the price very much higher, because estates containing coal might be had from the native owners at a much cheaper rate. The wages of free labourers, when employed in such work as gold-washing, agriculture, or digging coal, is 2 yards of unbleached calico per day. They might be got to work cheaper if engaged by the moon, or for about 16 yards per month. For masons and carpenters even, the ordinary rate is 2 yards per day. This is called 1 braça. Tradesmen from Kilimane demand 4 braças, or 8 yards, per day. English or American unbleached calico is the only currency used. The carriage of goods up the river to Tete, adds about 10 per cent. to their cost. The usual conveyance is by means of very large canoes and launches built at Senna.

The amount of merchandise brought up during the five months of peace previous to my visit, was of the value of 30,000 dollars, or about 6000l. The annual supply of goods for trade is about 15,000l., being calico, thick brass-wire, beads, gunpowder, and guns. The quantity of the latter is, however, small, as the Government of

Mozambique made that article contraband, after the commencement of the war. Goods, when traded with in the tribes around
the Portuguese, produce a profit of only about 10 per cent., the
articles traded in being ivory and gold-dust. A little oil and wheat
are exported, but nothing else. Trade with the tribes beyond the
exclusive ones is much better. Thirty brass rings cost 10s. at Senna,
1l. at Tete, and 2l. beyond the tribes in the vicinity of Tete ; these
are a good price for a penful of gold-dust of the value of 2l. The
plantations of coffee, which, previous to the commencement of the
slave-trade, yielded one material for exportation, are now deserted,
and it is difficult to find a single tree. The indigo (*Indigofera
argentea*, the common wild indigo of Africa) is found growing
everywhere, and large quantities of the senna-plant * grow in the
village of Tete and other parts; but neither indigo nor senna is
collected. Calumba-root, which is found in abundance in some
parts further down the river, is bought by the Americans, it is said,
to use as a dye-stuff. A kind of sarsaparilla, or a plant which is
believed by the Portuguese to be such, is found from Londa to
Senna, but has never been exported.

The price of provisions is low, but very much higher than previous to the commencement of the war. Two yards of calico are
demanded for six fowls ; this is considered very dear, because, before
the war, the same quantity of calico was worth 24 fowls. Grain
is sold in little bags made from the leaves of the palmyra, like
those in which we receive sugar. They are called panjas, and each
panja weighs between 30 and 40 lbs. The panja of wheat at Tete
is worth a dollar, or 5s.; but the native grain may be obtained
among the islands below Lupata, at the rate of three panjas for two
yards of calico. The highest articles of consumption are tea and
coffee—the tea being often as high as 15s. a pound. Food is
cheaper down the river below Lupata, and, previous to the war, the
islands which stud the Zambesi were all inhabited, and, the soil
being exceedingly fertile, grain and fowls could be got to any
amount. The inhabitants disappeared before their enemies the
Landeens, but are beginning to return since the peace. They
have no cattle, the only place where we found no tsetse being
the district of Tete itself; and the cattle in the possession of

---

* These appear to belong to *Cassia acutifolia*, or true senna of commerce,
found in various parts of Africa and India.—*Dr. Hooker.*

the Portuguese are a mere remnant of what they formerly owned.

When visiting the hot fountain, I examined what were formerly the gold-washings in the rivulet Mokoroze, which is nearly on the 16th parallel of latitude. The banks are covered with large groves of fine mango-trees, among which the Portuguese lived while superintending the washing for the precious metal. The process of washing is very laborious and tedious. A quantity of sand is put into a wooden bowl with water; a half rotatory motion is given to the dish, which causes the coarser particles of sand to collect on one side of the bottom. These are carefully removed with the hand, and the process of rotation renewed until the whole of the sand is taken away, and the gold alone remains. It is found in very minute scales, and, unless I had been assured to the contrary, I should have taken it to be mica, for, knowing the gold to be of greater specific gravity than the sand, I imagined that a stream of water would remove the latter and leave the former; but here the practice is, to remove the whole of the sand by the hand. This process was, no doubt, a profitable one to the Portuguese, and it is probable that, with the improved plan by means of mercury, the sands would be lucrative. I had an opportunity of examining the gold-dust from different parts to the east and north-east of Tete. There are six well-known washing-places. These are called Mashínga, Shindúndo, Missála, Kapáta, Máno, and Jáwa. From the description of the rock I received, I suppose gold is found both in clay-shale and quartz. At the range Mushinga to the N.N.W. the rock is said to be so soft, that the women pound it into powder in wooden mortars previous to washing.

Round towards the westward, the old Portuguese indicate a station which was near to Zumbo on the river Panyáme, and called Dambarári, near which much gold was found. Further west, lay the now unknown kingdom of Abútua, which was formerly famous for the metal; and then, coming round towards the east, we have the gold-washings of the Mashóna, or Bazizúlu, and further east, that of Maníca, where gold is found much more abundantly than in any other part, and which has been supposed by some to be the Ophir of King Solomon. I saw the gold from this quarter as large as grains of wheat; that found in the rivers which run into the coalfield, being in very minute scales. If we place one leg of the compasses at Tete, and extend the other three and a half degrees, bringing it round from the north-east of Tete by west, and then to the south-east, we nearly touch or include all the known gold-producing country. As the gold on this circumference is found in coarser grains than in the streams running towards the centre, or Tete, I imagine that the real gold-field lies round about the coal-field; and, if I am right in the conjecture, then we have coal encircled by a gold-field, and abundance of wood, water, and provisions—a combination not often met with in the world. The inhabitants are not unfavourable to washings, conducted on the principle formerly mentioned. At present they wash only when in want of a little calico. They know the value of gold perfectly well, for they bring it for sale in goose-quills, and demand 24 yards of calico for one penful. When the rivers in the district of Manica and other gold-washing places have been flooded, they leave a coating of mud on the banks. The natives observe the spots which dry soonest, and commence digging there, in firm belief that gold lies beneath. They are said not to dig deeper than their chins, believing that if they did so the ground would fall in and kill them. When they find a *piece* or flake of gold, they bury it again, from the superstitious idea that this is the seed of the gold, and, though they know the value of it well, they prefer losing it rather than the whole future crop. This conduct seemed to me so very unlikely in men who bring the dust in quills, and even put in a few seeds of a certain plant as a charm to prevent their losing any of it in the way, that I doubted the authority of my informant; but I found the report verified by all the Portuguese who know the native language and mode of thinking, and give the statement for what it is worth. If it is really practised, the custom may have been introduced by some knowing one who wished to defraud the chiefs of their due; for we are informed in Portuguese history that in former times, these pieces or flakes of gold were considered the perquisites of the chiefs.

Major Sicard, the Commandant, whose kindness to me and my people was unbounded, presented a rosary made of the gold of the country, the workmanship of a native of Tete, to my little daughter; also specimens of the gold-dust of three different places, which, with the coal of Muatize and Morongoze, are deposited in the Museum of Practical Geology, Jermyn-street, London.

All the cultivation is carried on with hoes in the native manner, and considerable quantities of *Holcus sorghum*, maize, *Pennisetum typhoideum*, or lotsa of the Balonda, millet, rice, and wheat, are raised, as also several kinds of beans—one of which, called "litloo" by the Bechuanas, yields under-ground, as well as the *Arachis hypogœa*, or ground-nut; with cucumbers, pumpkins, and melons. The wheat is sown in low-lying places which are annually flooded by the Zambesi. When the waters retire, the women drop a few grains in a hole made with a hoe, then push back the soil with the foot. One weeding alone is required before the grain comes to maturity. This simple process represents all our subsoil-ploughing, liming, manuring, and harrowing, for in four months after planting, a good crop is ready for the sickle, and has been known to yield a hundred-fold. It flourished still more at Zumbo. No irrigation is required, because here there are gentle rains, almost like mist, in winter, which go by the name of "wheat-showers," and are unknown in the interior, where no winter rain ever falls. The rains at Tete come from the east, though the prevailing winds come from the S.S.E. The finest portion of the flour does not make bread nearly so white as the seconds, and here the boyaloa (pombe), or native beer, is employed to mix with the flour instead of yeast. It makes excellent bread. At Kilimane, where the cocoa-nut palm abounds, the toddy from it, called "sura," is used for the same purpose, and makes the bread still lighter.

As it was necessary to leave most of my men at this place, Major Sicard gave them a portion of land on which to cultivate their own food, generously supplying them with corn in the mean time. He also said that my young men might go and hunt elephants in company with his servants, and purchase goods with both the ivory and dried meat, in order that they might have something to take with them on their return to Sekeletu. The men were delighted with his liberality, and soon sixty or seventy of them set off to engage in this enterprise. There was no calico to be had at this time in Tete, but the Commandant handsomely furnished my men with clothing. I was in a state of want myself, and, though I pressed him to take payment in ivory for both myself and men, he refused all recompence. I shall ever remember his kindness with deep gratitude. He has written me, since my arrival in England, that my men had killed four elephants in the course of two months after my departure.

On the day of my arrival I was visited by all the gentlemen of the village, both white and coloured, including the padre. Not one of them had any idea as to where the source of the Zambesi lay. They sent for the best travelled natives, but none of them knew the river even as far as Kansála. The father of one of the rebels who had been fighting against them, had been a great traveller to the south-west, and had even heard of our visit to Lake Ngami; but he was equally ignorant with all the others that the Zambesi flowed in the centre of the country. They had, however, more knowledge of the country to the north of Tete than I had. One man, who had gone to Cazembe with Major Monteiro, stated that he had seen the Luapúra or Loapula flowing past the town of that chieftain into the Luaméji or Leeambye, but imagined that it found its way, somehow or other, into Angola. The fact that sometimes rivers were seen to flow like this towards the centre of the country, led geographers to the supposition that inner Africa was composed of elevated sandy plains, into which rivers ran and were lost. One of the gentlemen present, Senhor Candido, had visited a lake 45 days to the N.N.W. of Tete, which is probably the Lake Maravi of geographers, as in going thither they pass through the people of that name. The inhabitants of its southern coast are named Shiva; those on the north, Mujao; and they call the lake Nyanja or Nyanje, which simply means a large water, or bed of a large river. A high mountain stands in the middle of it, called Murómbo or Murombola, which is inhabited by people who have much cattle. He stated that he crossed the Nyanja at a narrow part, and was 36 hours in the passage. The canoes were punted the whole way, and, if we take the rate about two miles per hour, it may be sixty or seventy miles in breadth. The country all round was composed of level plains covered with grass, and, indeed, in going thither they travelled seven or eight days without wood, and cooked their food with grass and stalks of native corn alone. The people sold their cattle at a very cheap rate. From the southern extremity of the lake, two rivers issue forth: one, named after itself, the Nyanja, which passes into the sea on the east coast under another name; and the Shire, which flows into the Zambesi, a little below Senna. The Shire is named Shirwa at its point of departure from the lake, and Senhor Candido was informed, when there, that the lake was simply an expansion of the river Nyanja, which comes from the north and encircles the mountain Murómbo, the meaning of which is junction or union, in reference to the water having parted at its northern extremity, and united again at its southern. The Shire flows through a low, flat, marshy country, but abounding in population, and they are said to be brave. The Portuguese are unable to navigate the Shire up to the lake Nyanja, because of the great abundance of a water-plant which requires no soil, and which they name " alfacinya " (*Pistia stratiotes*), from its resemblance to a lettuce. This completely obstructs the progress of canoes. In confirmation of this I may state that, when I passed the mouth of the Shire, great quantities of this same plant were floating from it into the Zambesi, and many parts of the banks below were covered with the dead plants.

Senhor Candido stated that slight earthquakes have happened several times in the country of the Maravi, and at no great distance from Tete. The motion seems to come from the eastward, and never to have lasted more than a few seconds. They are named in the Maravi tongue "shiwo," and in that of the people of Tete " shitakotéko," or " *shivering.*" This agrees exactly with what has taken place in the coast of Mozambique—a few slight shocks of short duration, and all appearing to come from the east. At Senna, too, a single shock has been felt several times, which shook the doors and windows and made the glasses jingle. Both Tete and Senna have hot springs in their vicinity, but the shocks seemed to come not from them, but from the east and proceed to the west. They are probably connected with the active volcanoes in the island of Bourbon.

As Senhor Candido holds the office of judge in all the disputes of the natives and knows their language perfectly, his statement may be relied on that all the natives of this region have a clear idea of a Supreme Being, the maker and governor of all things. He is named " Morimo," " Molungo," " Reza," " Mpámbe," in the different dialects spoken. The Barotse name him "Nyámpi," and the Balonda "Zámbi." All promptly acknowledge him as the ruler over all. They also fully believe in the soul's continued existence apart from the body, and visit the graves of relatives,

2 T

making offerings of food, beer, &c.. When undergoing the ordeal, they hold up their hands to the Ruler of Heaven, as if appealing to him to assert their innocence. When they escape, or recover from sickness, or are delivered from any danger, they offer a sacrifice of a fowl or a sheep, pouring out the blood as a libation to the soul of some departed relative. They believe in the transmigration of souls ; and also that while persons are still living they may enter into lions and alligators, and then return again to their own bodies.

While still at Tete the son of Monomotapa paid the Commandant a visit. He is named Mozungo, or "White Man," has a narrow tapering head, and probably none of the ability or energy his father possessed. He was the favourite of his father, who hoped that he would occupy his place. A strong party, however, in the tribe placed Katalosa in the chieftainship, and the son became, as they say, a child of this man. The Portuguese have repeatedly received offers of territory if they would only attend the interment of the departed chief with troops, fire off many rounds of cartridges over the grave, and then give éclat to the instalment of the new chief. Their presence would probably influence the election, for many would vote on the side of power, and a candidate might feel it worth while to grant a good piece of land, if thereby he could secure the chieftainship to himself. When the Portuguese traders wish to pass into the country beyond Katalosa, they present him with about thirty-two yards of calico and some other goods, and he then gives them leave to pass in whatever direction they choose to go. They must, however, give certain quantities of cloth to a number of inferior chiefs beside, and they are subject to the game-laws. They have thus a body of exclusive tribes around them, preventing direct intercourse between them and the population beyond. It is strange that, when they had the power, they did not insist on the free navigation of the Zambesi. I can only account for this in the same way in which I accounted for a similar state of things in the west. All the traders have been in the hands of slaves, and have wanted that moral courage which a free man, with free servants on whom he can depend, usually possesses. If the English had been here, they would have insisted on the free navigation of this pathway as an indispensable condition of friendship. The present system

is a serious difficulty in the way of developing the resources of
the country, and might prove fatal to an unarmed expedition.
If this desirable and most fertile field of enterprise is ever to be
opened up, men must proceed on a different plan from that
which has been followed, and I do not apprehend there would be
much difficulty in commencing a new system, if those who
undertook it insisted that it is not our custom to pay for a highway which has not been made by man. The natives themselves
would not deny that the river is free to those who do not trade
in slaves. If, in addition to an open frank explanation, a small
subsidy were given to the paramount chief, the willing consent of
all the subordinates would soon be secured.

On the 1st of April I went to see the site of a former establishment of the Jesuits, called Micombo, about ten miles S.E. of Tete.
Like all their settlements I have seen, both judgment and taste
had been employed in the selection of the site. A little stream
of mineral water had been collected in a tank and conducted to
their house, before which was a little garden for raising vegetables
at times of the year when no rain falls. It is now buried in a
deep shady grove of mango-trees. I was accompanied by
Captain Nunes, whose great-grandfather, also a Captain in the
time of the Marquis of Pombal, received sealed orders, to be
opened only on a certain day. When that day arrived, he found
the command to go with his company, seize all the Jesuits of this
establishment, and march them as prisoners to the coast. The
riches of the fraternity, which were immense, were taken possession of by the state. Large quantities of gold had often been
sent to their superiors at Goa, enclosed in images. The Jesuits
here do not seem to have possessed the sympathies of the people
as their brethren in Angola did. They were keen traders in
ivory and gold-dust. All praise their industry. Whatever they
did, they did it with all their might, and probably their successful
labours in securing the chief part of the trade to themselves, had
excited the envy of the laity. None of the natives here can read;
and though the Jesuits are said to have translated some of the
prayers into the language of the country, I was unable to obtain
a copy. The only religious teachers now in this part of the
country are two gentlemen of colour, natives of Goa. The
one who officiates at Tete, named Pedro Antonio d'Araujo, is a

graduate in Dogmatic Theology and Moral Philosophy. There is but a single school in Tete, and it is attended only by the native Portuguese children, who are taught to read and write. The black population is totally uncared for. The soldiers are marched every Sunday to hear·mass, and but few others attend church. During the period of my stay, a kind of theatrical representation of our Saviour's passion and resurrection was performed. The images and other paraphernalia used were of great value, but the present riches of the church are nothing to what it once possessed. The Commandant is obliged to lock up all the gold and silver in the fort for safety, though not from any apprehension of its being stolen by the people, for they have a dread of sacrilege.

The state of religion and education is, I am sorry to say, as low as that of commerce ; but the European Portuguese value education highly, and send their children to Goa and elsewhere for instruction in the higher branches. There is not a single book-seller's shop, however, in either eastern or western Africa. Even Loanda, with its 12,000 or 14,000 souls, cannot boast of one store for the sale of food for the mind.

On the 2nd the Zambesi suddenly rose several feet in height. Three such floods are expected annually, but this year there were four. This last was accompanied by discoloration, and must have been caused by another great fall of rain east of the ridge. We had observed a flood of discoloured water when we reached the river at the Kafue; it then fell two feet, and from subsequent rains again rose so high, that we were obliged to leave it when opposite the hill Pinkwe. About the 10th of March the river rose several feet with comparatively clear water, and it continued to rise until the 21st, with but a very slight discolora-tion. This gradual rise was the greatest, and was probably caused by the water of inundation in the interior. The sudden rise which happened on the 2nd, being deeply discoloured, showed again the effect of rains at a comparatively short distance. The fact of the river rising three or four times annually, and the one flood of inundation being mixed with the others, may account for the Portuguese not recognising the phenomenon of the periodical inundation, so well known in the central country.

The independent natives cultivate a little cotton, but it is not at all equal, either in quantity or quality, to what we found in

Angola. The pile is short, and it clings to the seed so much that they use an iron roller to detach it. The soil, however, is equal to the production of any tropical plant or fruit. The natives have never been encouraged to cultivate cotton for sale, nor has any new variety been introduced. We saw no palm-oil trees, the oil which is occasionally exported being from the ground-nut. One of the merchants of Tete had a mill of the rudest construction for grinding this nut, which was driven by donkeys. It was the only specimen of a machine I could exhibit to my men. A very superior kind of salad-oil is obtained from the seeds of cucumbers, and is much used in native cookery.

An offer, said to have been made by the ' Times,' having excited attention even in this distant part, I asked the Commandant if he knew of any plant fit for the production of paper. He procured specimens of the fibrous tissue of a species of aloe, named Congé, and some also from the root of a wild date, and, lastly, of a plant named Buáze, the fibres of which, though useless for the manufacture of paper, are probably a suitable substitute for flax. I submitted a small quantity of these fibres to Messrs. Pye, Brothers, of London, who have invented a superior mode for the preparation of such tissues for the manufacturer. They most politely undertook the examination, and have given a favourable opinion of the Buáze, as may be seen in the note below.*

* 80, *Lombard Street*, 20*th March*, 1857.

Dear Sir,—We have now the pleasure to return you the specimens of fibrous plants from the Zambesi river, on which you were desirous to see the effects of our treatment; we therefore enclose you,

No. 1. Buáze, in the state received from you.
1 A. Do.   as prepared by us.
1 B. The tow which has come from it in hackling.

No. 2. Congé, as received from you.
2 A. Do.   as prepared by us.

With regard to both these fibres, we must state that the *very minute quantity* of each specimen has prevented our subjecting them to anything like the full treatment of our process, and we can therefore only give you an *approximate* idea of their value.

The Buáze evidently possesses a very strong and fine fibre, assimilating to flax in its character, but we believe, when treated *in quantity* by our process, it would show both a stronger and finer fibre than flax; but being unable to apply the rolling or pressing processes with any efficiency to so very small a quantity, the gums are not yet so perfectly extracted as they would be, nor the fibre opened out to so fine a quality as it would then exhibit.   This

A representation of the plant is given in the annexed woodcut, as a help to its identification. I was unable to procure either the

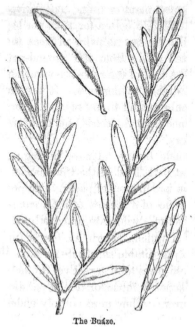

The Buaze.

flowers or fruit, but, as it is not recognised at sight by that accomplished botanist and eminent traveller, Dr. J. D. Hooker, it may safely be concluded that it is quite unknown to botanists. It is stated by the Portuguese to grow in large quantities in the Maravi country north of the Zambesi, but it is not cultivated, and the only known use it has been put to, is in making threads on which the natives string their beads. Elsewhere the split tendons of animals are employed for this purpose. This seems to be of equal strength, for a firm thread of it feels like catgut in the hand, and would rather cut the fingers than break.

This is even yet more the case with the Congé, which, being naturally a harsh fibre, full of gums, wants exactly that powerful treatment which our process is calculated to give it, but which cannot be applied to such miniature specimens. We do not therefore consider this as more than half treated, its fibre consequently remaining yet harsh, and coarse, and stiff, as compared with what it would be if treated *in quantity*.

Judging that it would be satisfactory to you to be in possession of the best practical opinion to be obtained on such a subject, we took the liberty of forwarding your little specimens to Messrs. Marshall, of Leeds, who have kindly favoured us with the following observations on them :—

" We have examined the samples you sent us yesterday, and think the Congé or aloe fibre would be of no use to us, but the Buazé fibre appears to resemble flax, and as prepared by you will be equal to flax worth 50*l*. or 60*l*. per ton, but we could hardly speak positively to the value unless we had 1 cwt. or 2 cwt. to try on our machinery. However, we think the result is promising, and we hope further inquiry will be made as to the probable supply of the material."

We are, dear Sir,

Your very obedient servants,

The Rev. Dr. Livingstone.   PYE, BROTHERS.

Having waited a month for the commencement of the healthy
season at Kilimane, I would have started at the beginning of
April, but tarried a few days in order that the moon might make
her appearance, and enable me to take lunar observations on my
way down the river. A sudden change of temperature happening
on the 4th, simultaneously with the appearance of the new moon,
the Commandant and myself, with nearly every person in the
house, were laid up with a severe attack of fever. I soon recovered by the use of my wonted remedies, but Major Sicard and
his little boy were confined much longer. There was a general
fall of 4° of temperature from the middle of March, 84° at 9 A.M.
and 87° at 9 P.M.; the greatest heat being 90° at mid-day, and
the lowest 81° at sunrise. It afforded me pleasure to attend the
invalids in their sickness, though I was unable to show a tithe of
the gratitude I felt for the Commandant's increasing kindness.
My quinine and other remedies were nearly all expended, and
no fresh supply was to be found here, there being no doctors at
Tete, and only one apothecary with the troops, whose stock of
medicine was also small. The Portuguese, however, informed
me that they had the cinchona bark growing in their country—
that there was a little of it to be found at Tete—whole forests of
it at Senna and near the delta of Kilimane. It seems quite a
providential arrangement, that the remedy for fever should be
found in the greatest abundance where it is most needed. On
seeing the leaves, I stated that it was not the *Cinchona longifolia*,
from which it is supposed the quinine of commerce is extracted,
but the name and properties of this bark made me imagine that
it was a cinchonaceous tree. I could not get the flower, but when
I went to Senna I tried to bring away a few small living trees
with earth in a box. They, however, all died when we came to
Kilimane. Failing in this mode of testing the point, I submitted
a few leaves and seed-vessels to my friend, Dr. Hooker, who
kindly informs me that they belong " apparently to an apocy-
neous plant, very nearly allied to the Malouetia Heudlotii (of
Decaisne), a native of Senegambia." Dr. H. adds, " Various
plants of this natural order are reputed powerful febrifuges, and
some of them are said to equal the cinchona in their effects."
It is called in the native tongue Kumbanzo.
    The flowers are reported to be white. The pods are in pairs, a

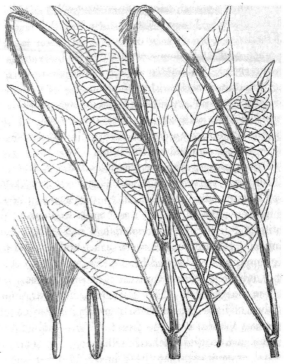

The Kumbanzo leaves, pods, and seeds.

foot or fifteen inches in length, and contain a groove on their inner sides. The thick soft bark of the root is the part used by the natives, the Portuguese use that of the tree itself. I immediately began to use a decoction of the bark of the root, and my men found it so efficacious, that they collected small quantities of it for themselves, and kept it in little bags for future use. Some of them said that they knew it in their own country, but I never happened to observe it. The decoction is given after the first paroxysm of the complaint is over. The Portuguese believe it to have the same effects as the quinine, and it may prove a substitute for that invaluable medicine.

There are numbers of other medicines in use among the natives, but I have always been obliged to regret want of time to ascertain which were useful, and which of no value. We find a medicine in use by a tribe in one part of the country, and the same plant employed by a tribe a thousand miles distant. This surely must arise from some inherent virtue in the plant. The Boers under Potgeiter visited Delgoa Bay for the first time about ten years ago, in order to secure a port on the east coast for their republic. They had come from a part of the interior where the disease called croup occasionally prevails. There was no appearance of the disease amongst them at the period of their visit, but the Portuguese inhabitants of. that bay found that they had left it among them, and several adults were cut off by a form of the complaint called *Laryngismus stridulus*, the disease of which the great Washington died. Similar cases have occurred in the South Sea Islands. Ships have left diseases, from which no one on board was suffering at the time of their visit. Many of the inhabitants here, were cut down, usually in three days from their first attack, until a native doctor adopted the plan of scratching the root of the tongue freely with a certain root, and giving a piece of it to be chewed. The cure may have been effected by the scarification only, but the Portuguese have the strongest faith in the virtues of the root, and always keep some of it within reach.

There are also other plants which the natives use in the treatment of fever, and some of them produce *diaphoresis* in a short space of time. It is certain that we have got the knowledge of the most potent febrifuge in our pharmacopœia from the natives of another country. We have no cure for cholera and some other diseases. It might be worth the investigation of those who visit Africa to try and find other remedies in a somewhat similar way to that in which we found the quinine.*

* I add the native names of a few of their remedies in order to assist the inquirer :—Mupanda panda : this is used in fever for producing perspiration ; the leaves are named Chirussa ; the roots dye red and are very astringent. Goho or Goŏ : this is the ordeal medicine ; it is both purgative and emetic. Mutuva or Mutumbue : this plant contains so much oil that it serves as lights in Londa ; it is an emollient drink for the cure of coughs, and the pounded leaves answer as soap to wash the head. Nyamucu ucu has a curious softening effect on old dry grain. Mussakasi is believed to remove the effects of the Goŏ. Mudama is a stringent vermifuge. Mapubuza dyes a red colour. Musikizi yields an oil. Shinkondo : a virulent poison ; the Maravi use it in their ordeal, and it is very fatal. Kanunka utare is said to expel serpents and rats by its pungent smell, which is not at all disagreeable to man ; this is probably a kind of *Zanthoxylon*, perhaps the Z. melancantha of Western

The only other metal, besides gold, we have in abundance in this region, is iron, and that is of excellent quality. In some places it is obtained from what is called the specular iron ore, and also from black oxide. The latter has been well roasted in the operations of nature, and contains a large proportion of the metal. It occurs generally in tears or rounded lumps, and is but slightly magnetic. When found in the beds of rivers, the natives know of its existence by the quantity of oxide on the surface, and they find no difficulty in digging it with pointed sticks. They consider English iron as "rotten;" and I have seen, when a javelin of their own iron lighted on the cranium of a hippopotamus, it curled up like the proboscis of a butterfly, and the owner would prepare it for future use by straightening it *cold* with two stones. I brought home some of the hoes which Sekeletu gave me to purchase a canoe, also some others obtained in Kilimane, and they have been found of such good quality that

Africa, as it is used to expel rats and serpents there. Mussonzoa dyes cloth black. Mussio: the beans of this also dye black. Kangome, with flowers and fruit like Mocha coffee ; the leaves are much like those of the sloe, and the seeds are used as coffee or eaten as beans. Kanembe-embé: the pounded leaves used as an extemporaneous glue for mending broken vessels. Katunguru is used for killing fish. Mutavea Nyerere: an active caustic. Mudiacoro: also an external caustic, and used internally. Kapande: another ordeal plant, but used to produce *diaphoresis*. Karumgasura: also diaphoretic. Munyazi yields an oil, and is one of the ingredients for curing the wounds of poisoned arrows. Uombue: a large root, employed in killing fish. Kakumate: used in intermittents. Musheteko: applied to ulcers ; and the infusion also internally in amenorrhœa. Inyákanyánya: this is seen in small dark-coloured crooked roots of pleasant aromatic smell and slightly bitter taste, and is highly extolled in the treatment of fever ; it is found in Maníca. Eskinencia: used in croup and sore-throat. Itaca, or Itaka: for diaphoresis in fever ; this root is brought as an article of barter by the Arabs to Kilimane ; the natives purchase it eagerly. Mukundukundu: a decoction used as a febrifuge in the same way as quinine ; it grows plentifully at Shupanga, and the wood is used as masts for launches. I may here add the recipe of Brother Pedro of Zumbo for the cure of poisoned wounds, in order to show the similarity of practice among the natives of the Zambesi, from whom in all probability he acquired his knowledge, and the Bushmen of the Kalahari. It consists of equal parts of the roots of the Calumba, Musheteko, Abutua, Batatinya, Paregekanto, Itaka, or Kapande, put into a bottle and covered with common castor-oil. As I have before observed, I believe the oily ingredient is the effectual one, and ought to be tried by any one who has the misfortune to get wounded by a Bushman's or Banyai arrow.

Nunes, to treat me as they would himself. From every one of these gentlemen I am happy to acknowledge that I received most disinterested kindness, and I ought to speak well for ever of Portuguese hospitality. I have noted each little act of civility received, because somehow or other we have come to hold the Portuguese character in rather a low estimation. This may have arisen partly from the pertinacity with which some of them have pursued the slave-trade, and partly from the contrast which they now offer to their illustrious ancestors—the foremost navigators of the world. If my specification of their kindnesses will tend to engender a more respectful feeling to the nation, I shall consider myself well rewarded. We had three large canoes in the company which had lately come up with goods from Senna. They are made very large and strong, much larger than any we ever saw in the interior, and might strike with great force against a rock and not be broken. The men sit at the stern when paddling, and there is usually a little shed made over a part of the canoe to shade the passengers from the sun. The boat in which I went was furnished with such a covering, so I sat quite comfortably,

CHAPTER XXXII.

Leave Tete and proceed down the river — Pass the stockade of Bonga — Gorge of Lupata — " Spine of the world " — Width of river — Islands — War drum at Shiramba — Canoe navigation — Reach Senna — Its ruinous state — Landeens levy fines upon the inhabitants — Cowardice of native militia — State of the revenue — No direct trade with Portugal — Attempts to revive the trade of Eastern Africa — Country round Senna — Gorongozo, a Jesuit station — Manica, the best gold region in Eastern Africa — Boatbuilding at Senna — Our departure — Capture of a rebel stockade — Plants Alfacinya and Njefu at the confluence of the Shire — Landeen opinion of the whites — Mazaro, the point reached by Captain Parker — His opinion respecting the navigation of the river from this to the ocean — Lieut. Hoskins' remarks on the same subject — Fever, its effects — Kindly received into the house of Colonel Nunes at Kilimane. — Forethought of Captain Nolloth and Dr. Walsh — Joy embittered — Deep obligations to the Earl of Clarendon, &c. — On developing resources of the interior — Desirableness of Missionary Societies selecting healthy stations. — Arrangements on leaving my men — Retrospect — Probable influence of the discoveries on slavery — Supply of cotton, sugar, &c., by free labour — Commercial stations — Development of the resources of Africa a work of time — Site of Kilimane — Unhealthiness — Death of a shipwrecked crew from fever — The Captain saved by quinine — Arrival of H. M. brig " Frolic" — Anxiety of one of my men to go to England — Rough passage in the boats to the ship — Sekwebu's alarm — Sail for Mauritius — Sekwebu on board ; he becomes insane ; drowns himself — Kindness of Major-General C. M. Hay — Escape shipwreck — Reach home.

WE left Tete at noon on the 22nd, and in the afternoon arrived at the garden of Senhor A. Manoel de Gomes, son-in-law and nephew of Bonga. The Commandant of Tete had sent a letter to the rebel Bonga, stating that he ought to treat me kindly, and he had deputed his son-in-law to be my host. Bonga is not at all equal to his father Nyaude, who was a man of great ability. He is also in bad odour with the Portuguese, because he receives all runaway slaves and criminals. He does not trust the Portuguese, and is reported to be excessively superstitious. I found his son-in-law, Manoel, extremely friendly, and able to converse in a very intelligent manner. He was in his garden when we arrived, but soon dressed himself respectably, and gave us a good tea and dinner.

in a small flat-bottomed steamer during the whole year as far as
Tete. At this time, a steamer of large size could have floated
easily. The river was measured at the latter place by the
Portuguese, and found by them to be 1050 yards broad. The
body of water flowing past when I was there was very great, and
the breadth it occupied when amongst the islands, had a most
imposing effect. I could not get a glimpse of either shore. All
the right bank beyond Lupata is low and flat: on the north, the
ranges of hills and dark lines below them are seen, but from the
boat it is impossible to see the shore. I only guess the breadth
of the river to be two miles, it is probably more. Next day we
landed at Shiramba for breakfast, having sailed 8½ hours from
Lupata. This was once the residence of a Portuguese brigadier,
who spent large sums of money in embellishing his house and
gardens: these we found in entire ruin, as his half-caste son had
destroyed all and then rebelled against the Portuguese, but with
less success than either Nyaude or Kisaka, for he had been seized
and sent a prisoner to Mozambique a short time before our visit.
All the southern shore has been ravaged by the Caffres, who are
here named Landeens, and most of the inhabitants who remain,
acknowledge the authority of Bonga and not of the Portuguese.
When at breakfast, the people of Shiramba commenced beating
the drum of war. Lieutenant Miranda, who was well acquainted
with the customs of the country, immediately started to his feet,
and got all the soldiers of our party under arms: he then
demanded of the natives why the drum was beaten while we were
there. They gave an evasive reply; and as they employ this
means of collecting their neighbours when they intend to rob
canoes, our watchfulness may have prevented their proceeding
further.

We spent the night of the 26th on the island called Nkuesi,
opposite a remarkable saddle-shaped mountain, and found that
we were just on the 17th parallel of latitude. The sail down the
river was very fine; the temperature becoming low, it was pleasant
to the feelings; but the shores being flat and far from us, the
scenery was uninteresting. We breakfasted on the 27th at Pita,
and found some half-caste Portuguese had established themselves
there, after fleeing from the opposite bank to escape Kisaka's
people, who were now ravaging all the Maganja country. On the

2 U

afternoon of the 27th we arrived at Senna. (Commandant Isidore's house, 300 yards S.W. of the mud fort on the banks of the river: lat. 17° 27' 1" S., long. 35° 10' E.) We found Senna to be twenty-three and a half hours' sail from Tete. We had the current entirely in our favour, but met various parties in large canoes toiling laboriously against it. They use long ropes and pull the boats from the shore. They usually take about twenty days to ascend the distance we had descended in about four. The wages paid to boatmen are considered high. Part of the men who had accompanied me, gladly accepted employment from Lieutenant Miranda, to take a load of goods in a canoe from Senna to Tete.

I thought the state of Tete quite lamentable, but that of Senna was ten times worse. At Tete there is some life; here everything is in a state of stagnation and ruin. The fort, built of sun-dried bricks, has the grass growing over the walls, which have been patched in some places by paling. The Landeens visit the village periodically, and levy fines upon the inhabitants, as they consider the Portuguese a conquered tribe, and very rarely does a native come to trade. Senhor Isidore, the Commandant, a man of considerable energy, had proposed to surround the whole village with palisades as a protection against the Landeens, and the villagers were to begin this work the day after I left. It was sad to look at the ruin manifest in every building, but the half-castes appear to be in league with the rebels and Landeens; for when any attempt is made by the Portuguese to coerce the enemy or defend themselves, information is conveyed at once to the Landeen camp, and, though the Commandant prohibits the payment of tribute to the Landeens, on their approach the half-castes eagerly ransom themselves. When I was there, a party of Kisaka's people were ravaging the fine country on the opposite shore. They came down with the prisoners they had captured, and forthwith the half-castes of Senna went over to buy slaves. Encouraged by this, Kisaka's people came over into Senna fully armed and beating their drums, and were received into the house of a native Portuguese. They had the village at their mercy, yet could have been driven off by half a dozen policemen. The Commandant could only look on with bitter sorrow. He had soldiers, it is true, but it is notorious that the native militia of both Senna and Kilimane never think of standing to fight, but invariably run away, and leave their officers to be killed. They are brave only among the peaceable inhabitants. One of them sent from Kilimane with a packet of letters or expresses, arrived while I was at Senna. He had been charged to deliver them with all speed, but Senhor Isidore had in the mean time gone to Kilimane, remained there a fortnight, and reached Senna again before the courier came. He could not punish him. We gave him a passage in our boat, but he left us in the way to visit his wife, and, "on urgent private business," probably gave up the service altogether, as he did not come to Kilimane all the time I was there. It is impossible to describe the miserable state of decay into which the Portuguese possessions here have sunk. The revenues are not equal to the expenses, and every officer I met told the same tale, that he had not received one farthing of pay for the last four years. They are all forced to engage in trade for the support of their families. Senhor Miranda had been actually engaged against the enemy during these four years, and had been highly lauded in the Commandant's despatches to the Home Government; but when he applied to the Governor of Kilimane for part of his four years' pay, he offered him twenty dollars only. Miranda resigned his commission in consequence. The common soldiers sent out from Portugal received some pay in calico. They all marry native women, and the soil being very fertile, the wives find but little difficulty in supporting their husbands. There is no direct trade with Portugal. A considerable number of Banians, or natives of India, come annually in small vessels with cargoes of English and Indian goods from Bombay. It is not to be wondered at then, that there have been attempts made of late years by speculative Portuguese in Lisbon, to revive the trade of Eastern Africa by means of mercantile companies. One was formally proposed, which was modelled on the plan of our East India Company; and it was actually imagined that all the forts, harbours, lands, &c., might be delivered over to a company, which would bind itself to develop the resources of the country, build schools, make roads, improve harbours, &c., and after all leave the Portuguese the option of resuming possession.

Another effort has been made to attract commercial enterprise to this region, by offering any mining company permission to search for the ores and work them. Such a company, however, would gain but little in the way of protection or aid from the government of Mozambique, as that can but barely maintain a hold on its own small possessions; the condition affixed of importing at the company's own cost a certain number of Portuguese from the island of Madeira or the Azores, in order to increase the Portuguese population in Africa, is impolitic. Taxes would also be levied on the minerals exported. It is noticeable that all the companies which have been proposed in Portugal have this put prominently in the preamble, " and for the abolition of the inhuman slave-trade." This shows, either that the statesmen in Portugal are enlightened and philanthropic, or it may be meant as a trap for English capitalists; I incline to believe the former. If the Portuguese really wish to develop the resources of the rich country beyond their possessions, they ought to invite the co-operation of other nations on equal terms with themselves. Let the pathway into the interior be free to all; and, instead of wretched forts, with scarcely an acre of land around them which can be called their own, let real colonies be made. If, instead of military establishments, we had civil ones, and saw emigrants going out with their wives, ploughs, and seeds, rather than military convicts with bugles and kettle-drums, we might hope for a return of prosperity to Eastern Africa.

The village of Senna stands on the right bank of the Zambesi. There are many reedy islands in front of it, and there is much bush in the country adjacent. The soil is fertile; but the village, being in a state of ruin, and having several pools of stagnant water, is very unhealthy. The bottom rock is the akose of Brongniart, or granitic grit, and several conical hills of trap have burst through it. One standing about half a mile west of the village is called Baramuana, which has another behind it; hence the name, which means " carry a child on the back." It is 300 or 400 feet high, and on the top lie two dismounted cannon, which were used to frighten away the Landeens, who in one attack upon Senna killed 150 of the inhabitants. The prospect from Baramuana is very fine; below, on the eastward, lies the Zambesi, with the village of Senna; and some twenty or thirty miles beyond stands the lofty mountain Morumbála, probably 3000 or 4000 feet high. It is of an oblong shape, and from its physiognomy, which can be distinctly seen when the sun is in the west, is evidently igneous. On the northern end there is a hot sulphurous fountain, which my Portuguese friends refused to allow me to visit, because the mountain is well peopled, 'and the mountaineers are at present not friendly with the Portuguese. They have plenty of garden-ground and running water on its summit. My friends at Senna declined the responsibility of taking me into danger. To the north of Morumbala we have a fine view of the mountains of the Maganja; they here come close to the river and terminate in Morumbala. Many of them are conical, and the Shíre is reported to flow amongst them, and to run on the Senna side of Morumbala, before joining the Zambesi. On seeing the confluence afterwards, close to a low range of hills beyond Morumbala, I felt inclined to doubt the report, as the Shire must then flow parallel with the Zambesi, from which Morumbala seems distant only twenty or thirty miles. All around to the south-east, the country is flat, and covered with forest, but near Senna a number of little abrupt conical hills diversify the scenery. To the west and north the country is also flat forest, which gives it a sombre appearance; but just in the haze of the horizon south-west by south, there rises a mountain range equal in height to Morumbala, and called Nyamónga. In a clear day, another range beyond this may be seen, which is Gorongózo, once a station of the Jesuits. Gorongozo is famed for its clear cold waters and healthiness, and there are some inscriptions engraved on large square slabs on the top of the mountain, which have probably been the work of the fathers. As this lies in the direction of a district between Manica and Sofála, which has been conjectured to be the Ophir of King Solomon, the idea that first sprang up in my mind was, that these monuments might be more ancient than the Portuguese; but on questioning some persons who had seen them, I found that they were in Roman characters, and did not deserve a journey of six days to see them.

Manica lies three days north-west of Gorongozo, and is the best gold country known in Eastern Africa. The only evidence the Portuguese have of its being the ancient Ophir, is, that at

Sofala, its nearest port, pieces of wrought gold have been dug up near the fort, and in the gardens. They also report the existence of hewn stones in the neighbourhood, but these cannot have been abundant, for all the stones of the fort of Sofala are said to have been brought from Portugal. Natives whom I met in the country of Sekeletu, from Manica, or Manoa, as they call it, state that there are several caves in the country, and walls of hewn stone, which they believe to have been made by their ancestors; and there is, according to the Portuguese, a small tribe of Arabs there, who have become completely like the other natives. Two rivers, the Motirikwe and Sabía, or Sabe, run through their country into the sea. The Portuguese were driven out of the country by the Landeens, but now talk of re-occupying Manica.

The most pleasant sight I witnessed at Senna was the negroes of Senhor Isidore building boats, after the European model, without any one to superintend their operations. They had been instructed by a European master, but now go into the forest and cut down the motondo-trees, lay down the keel, fit in the ribs, and make very neat boats and launches, valued at from 20*l.* to 100*l.* Senhor Isidore had some of them instructed also in carpentry at Rio Janeiro, and they constructed for him the handsomest house in Kilimane, the woodwork being all of country trees, some of which are capable of a fine polish, and very durable. A medical opinion having been asked by the Commandant respecting a better site for the village, which, lying on the low bank of the Zambesi, is very unhealthy, I recommended imitation of the Jesuits, who had chosen the high healthy mountain of Gorongozo, and to select a new site on Morumbala, which is perfectly healthy, well watered, and where the Shire is deep enough for the purpose of navigation at its base. As the next resource, I proposed removal to the harbour of Mitilone, which is at one of the mouths of the Zambesi, a much better port than Kilimane, and where, if they must have the fever, they would be in the way of doing more good to themselves and the country than they can do in their present situation. Had the Portuguese possessed this territory as a real colony, this important point would not have been left unoccupied; as it is, there is not even a native village placed at the entrance of this splendid river to show the way in.

On the 9th of May sixteen of my men were employed to carry government goods in canoes up to Tete. They were much pleased at getting this work. On the 11th the whole of the inhabitants of Senna, with the Commandant, accompanied us to the boats. A venerable old man, son of a judge, said they were in much sorrow on account of the miserable state of decay into which they had sunk, and of the insolent conduct of the people of Kisaka, now in the village. We were abundantly supplied with provisions by the Commandant and Senhor Ferrão, and sailed pleasantly down the broad river. About thirty miles below Senna, we passed the mouth of the river Zangwe on our right, which farther up goes by the name of Pungwe ; and about five miles farther on our left, close to the end of a low range into which Morumbala merges, we crossed the mouth of the Shire, which seemed to be about 200 yards broad. A little inland from the confluence there is another rebel stockade, which was attacked by Ensign Rebeiro with three European soldiers, and captured ; they disarmed the rebels and threw the guns into the water. This Ensign and Miranda volunteered to disperse the people of Kisaka, who were riding roughshod over the inhabitants of Senna ; but the offer was declined, the few real Portuguese fearing the disloyal half-castes among whom they dwelt. Slavery and immorality have here done their work; nowhere else does the European name stand at so low an ebb; but what can be expected? Few Portuguese women are ever taken to the colonies, and here I did not observe that honourable regard for the offspring which I noticed in Angola. The son of a late Governor of Tete was pointed out to me in the condition and habit of a slave. There is neither priest nor school at Senna, though there are ruins of churches and convents.

On passing the Shire, we observed great quantities of the plant Alfacinya, already mentioned, floating down into the Zambesi. It is probably the *Pistia stratiotes*, a gigantic "duck-weed." It was mixed with quantities of another aquatic plant, which the Barotse named "Njéfu," containing in the petiole of the leaf a pleasant-tasted nut. This was so esteemed by Sebituane, that he made it part of his tribute from the subjected tribes. Dr. Hooker kindly informs me that the njefu "is probably a species of *Trapa*, the nuts of which are eaten in the south of

Europe and in India. Government derives a large revenue from
them in Kashmir, amounting to 12,000l. per annum for 128,000
ass-loads ! The ancient Thracians are said to have eaten them
largely. In the south of France they are called water-chesnuts."
The existence of these plants in such abundance in the Shire,
may show that it flows from large collections of still water. We
found them growing in all the still branches and lagoons of the
Leeambye in the far north, and there also we met a beautiful
little floating plant, the *Azolla nilotica*, which is found in the
upper Nile. They are seldom seen in flowing streams.

A few miles beyond the Shire we left the hills entirely, and
sailed between extensive flats. The banks seen in the distance
are covered with trees. We slept on a large inhabited island,
and then came to the entrance of the river Mutu (lat. 18° 3' 37"
S., long. 35° 46' E.) : the point of departure is called Mazáro, or
"mouth of the Mutu." The people who live on the north are
called Baróro, and their country Bororo. The whole of the right
bank is in subjection to the Landeens, who, it was imagined, would
levy a tribute upon us, for this they are accustomed to do to
passengers. I regret that we did not meet them, for, though they
are named Caffres, I am not sure whether they are of the Zulu
family or of the Mashona. I should have liked to form their
acquaintance, and to learn what they really think of white men.
I understood from Sekwebu, and from one of Changamera's
people who lives at Linyanti, and was present at the attack on
Senna, that they consider the whites as a conquered tribe.

The Zambesi at Mazaro is a magnificent river, more than
half a mile wide and without islands. The opposite bank is
covered with forests of fine timber; but the delta which begins
here, is only an immense flat covered with high coarse grass
and reeds, with here and there a few mango and cocoa-nut
trees. This was the point which was reached by the late
lamented Captain Parker, who fell at the Sulina mouth of the
Danube. I had a strong desire to follow the Zambesi further,
and ascertain where this enormous body of water found its way
into the sea; but, on hearing from the Portuguese that he had
ascended to this point and had been highly pleased with the
capabilities of the river, I felt sure that his valuable opinion
must be in possession of the Admiralty. On my arrival in

England I applied to Captain Washington, Hydrographer to the Admiralty, and he promptly furnished the document for publication by the Royal Geographical Society.

The river between Mazaro and the sea must, therefore, be judged of from the testimony of one more competent to decide on its merits than a mere landsman like myself.

On the Quilimane and Zambesi Rivers. From the Journal of the late Capt. HYDE PARKER, R.N., H.M. Brig " Pantaloon."

" THE Lúabo is the main outlet of the Great Zambesi. In the rainy season — January and February principally—the whole country is overflowed, and the water escapes by the different rivers as far up as Quilimane; but in the dry season neither Quilimane nor Olinda communicates with it. The position of the river is rather incorrect in the Admiralty chart, being six miles too much to the southward and also considerably to the westward. Indeed, the coast from here up to Tongamiara seems too far to the westward. The entrance to the Luabo river is about two miles broad, and is easily distinguishable, when abreast of it, by a bluff (if I may so term it) of high straight trees, very close together, on the western side of the entrance. The bar may be said to be formed by two series of sandbanks,— that running from the eastern point runs diagonally across (opposite?) the entrance and nearly across it. Its western extremity is about two miles outside the west point.

" The bank running out from the west point projects to the southward three miles and a half, passing not one quarter of a mile from the eastern or cross bank. This narrow passage is the *bar passage*. It breaks completely across at low water, except under very extraordinary circumstances. At this time— low water—a great portion of the banks are uncovered; in some places they are seven or eight feet above water.

" On these banks there is a break at all times, but in fine weather, at high water, a boat may cross near the east point. There is very little water, and, in places, a nasty race and bubble, so that caution is requisite. The best directions for going in over the regular bar passage, according to my experience, are as follows :—Steer down well to the eastward of the bar passage, so as to avoid the outer part of the western shoals,

on which there is usually a bad sea. When you get near the
cross-bar, keep along it till the bluff of trees on the west side of
the entrance bears N.E.; you may then steer straight for it. This
will clear the end of the *cross-bar*, and, directly you are within
that, the water is smooth. The worst sea is generally just
without the bar passage.

"Within the points the river widens at first and then contracts
again. About three miles from the Tree Bluff is an island; the
passage up the river is the right-hand side of it, and deep. The
plan will best explain it. The rise and fall of the tide at the
entrance of the river being at springs twenty feet, any vessel can
get in at that time, but, with all these conveniences for traffic,
there is none here at present. The water in the river is fresh
down to the bar with the ebb-tide, and in the rainy season it is
fresh at the surface quite outside. In the rainy season, at the
full and change of the moon, the Zambesi frequently overflows
its banks, making the country for an immense distance one
great lake, with only a few small eminences above the water.
On the banks of the river the huts are built on piles, and at
these times the communication is only in canoes; but the
waters do not remain up more than three or four days at a
time. The first village is about eight miles up the river, on the
western bank, and is opposite to another branch of the river
called 'Musélo,' which discharges itself into the sea about five
miles to the eastward.

"The village is extensive, and about it there is a very large
quantity of land in cultivation; calavances, or beans, of different
sorts, rice, and pumpkins, are the principal things. I saw also
about here some wild cotton, apparently of very good quality,
but none is cultivated. The land is so fertile as to produce
almost any (thing?) without much trouble.

"At this village is a very large house, mud-built, with a court-
yard. I believe it to have been used as a barracoon for slaves,
several large cargoes having been exported from this river. I
proceeded up the river as far as its junction with the Quilimane
river, called 'Boca do Rio,' by my computation between 70 and
80 miles from the entrance. The influence of the tides is felt
about 25 or 30 miles up the river. Above that, the stream, in
the dry season, runs from $1\frac{1}{2}$ to $2\frac{1}{2}$ miles an hour, but in the

rains much stronger. The banks of the river, for the first 30 miles, are generally thickly clothed with trees, with occasional open glades. There are many huts and villages on both sides, and a great deal of cultivation. At one village, about 17 miles up on the eastern bank, and distinguished by being surrounded by an immense number of bananas and plantain-trees, a great quantity of excellent peas are cultivated, also cabbages, tomatos, onions, &c. Above this there are not many inhabitants on the left or west bank, although it is much the finest country, being higher, and abounding in cocoa-nut palms; the eastern bank being sandy and barren. The reason is, that some years back the Landeens, or Caffres, ravaged all this country, killing the men and taking the women as slaves, but they have never crossed the river; hence the natives are afraid to settle on the west bank, and the Portuguese owners of the different " prasos " have virtually lost them. The banks of the river continue mostly sandy, with few trees, except some cocoa-nut palms, until the southern end of the large plantation of Nyangué, formed by the river about 20 miles from Maruru. Here the country is more populous and better cultivated, the natives a finer race, and the huts larger and better constructed. Maruru belongs to Señor Asevédo, of Quilimane, well known to all English officers on the east coast for his hospitality.

" The climate here is much cooler than nearer the sea, and Asevedo has successfully cultivated most European as well as tropical vegetables. The sugar-cane thrives, as also coffee and cotton, and indigo is a weed. Cattle here are beautiful, and some of them might show with credit in England. The natives are intelligent, and under a good government this fine country might become very valuable. Three miles from Maruru is Mesan, a very pretty village among palm and mango trees. There is here a good house belonging to a Señor Ferrão; close by is the canal (Mútu) of communication between the Quilimane and Zambesi rivers, which in the rainy season is navigable (?). I visited it in the month of October, which is about the dryest time of the year; it was then a dry canal, about 30 or 40 yards wide, overgrown with trees and grass, and, at the bottom, at least 16 or 17 feet above the level of the Zambesi, which was running beneath. In the rains, by the marks I saw, the entrance

rise of the river must be very nearly 30 feet, and the volume of
water discharged by it (the Zambesi) enormous.

"Above Maruru the country begins to become more hilly, and
the high mountains of Boruru are in sight; the first view of
these is obtained below Nyangue, and they must be of considerable height, as from this they are distant above 40 miles.
They are reported to contain great mineral wealth; gold and
copper being found in the range, as also *coal* (?). The natives
(Landeens) are a bold, independent race, who do not acknowledge the Portuguese authority, and even make them pay for
leave to pass unmolested. Throughout the whole course of the
river, hippopotami were very abundant, and at one village a
chase by the natives was witnessed. They harpoon the animal
with a barbed lance, to which is attached, by a cord 3 or 4
fathoms long, an inflated bladder. The natives follow in their
canoes, and look out to fix more harpoons as the animal rises to
blow, and, when exhausted, despatch him with their lances. It
is, in fact, nearly similar to a whale-hunt. Elephants and lions
are also abundant on the western side; the latter destroy many
of the blacks annually, and are much feared by them. Alligators
are said to be numerous, but I did not see any.

"The voyage up to Maruru occupied seven days, as I did not
work the men at the oar, but it might be done in four; we returned to the bar in two and a half days.

"There is another mouth of the Zambesi, seven miles to the
westward of Luabo, which was visited by the 'Castor's' pinnace;
and I was assured by Lieutenant Hoskins that the bar was
better than the one I visited."

The conclusions of Captain Parker are strengthened by those
of Lieutenant A. H. Hoskins, who was on the coast at the same
time, and also visited this spot. Having applied to my friend
for his deliberate opinion on the subject, he promptly furnished
the following note in January last:—

"The Zambesi appears to have five principal mouths, of which
the Luabo is the most southern and most navigable; Cumana,
and two whose names I do not know, not having myself visited
it, lying between it and the Quilimane, and the rise and fall at
spring-tides on the bar of the Luabo is 22 feet; and as, in the

passage, there is NEVER less than four feet (I having crossed it
at dead low-water—springs), this would give an average depth
sufficient for any commercial purposes. The rise and fall is six
feet greater, the passages narrower and more defined, consequently deeper and more easily found than that of the Quilimane
river. The river above the bar is very tortuous, but deep; and
it is observable that the influence of the tide is felt much higher
in this branch than in the others; for whereas in the Catrina
and Cumana I have obtained drinkable water a very short distance from the mouth, in the Luabo I have ascended 70 miles
without finding the saltness perceptibly diminished. This would
facilitate navigation, and I have no hesitation in saying that
little difficulty would be experienced in conveying a steam-vessel
of the size and capabilities of the gunboat I lately commanded
as high as the branching off of the Quilimane river (Mazáro),
which, in the dry season, is observed many yards above the
Luabo (main stream); though I have been told by the Portuguese that the freshes which come down in December and March
fill it temporarily. These freshes deepen the river considerably
at that time of the year, and freshen the water many miles from
the coast. The population of the delta, except in the immediate
neighbourhood of the Portuguese, appeared to be very sparse.
Antelopes and hippopotami were plentiful; the former tame and
easily shot. I inquired frequently of both natives and Portuguese, if slavers were in the habit of entering there to ship their
cargoes, but could not ascertain that they have ever done so in
any except the Quilimane. With common precaution the rivers
are not unhealthy; for, during the whole time I was employed
in them (off and on during eighteen months), in open boats and
at all times of the year, frequently absent from the ship for a
month or six weeks at a time, I had not, in my boat's crew of
fourteen men, more than two, and those mild, cases of fever.
Too much importance cannot be ascribed to the use of quinine,
to which I attribute our comparative immunity, and with which
our judicious commander, Commodore Wyvill, kept us amply
supplied. I hope these few remarks may be of some little use
in confirming your views of the utility of that magnificent river.

" A. H. H. HOSKINS."

It ought to be remembered that the testimony of these gentlemen is all the more valuable, because they visited the river when the water was at its lowest, and the surface of the Zambesi was not, as it was now, on a level with and flowing into the Mutu, but 16 feet beneath its bed. The Mutu, at the point of departure, was only 10 or 12 yards broad, shallow, and filled with aquatic plants. Trees and reeds along the bank overhang it so much, that, though we had brought canoes and a boat from Tete, we were unable to enter the Mutu with them, and left them at Mazaro. During most of the year, this part of the Mutu is dry, and we were even now obliged to carry all our luggage by land for about fifteen miles. As Kilimane is called, in all the Portuguese documents, the capital of the rivers of Senna, it seemed strange to me that the capital should be built at a point where there was no direct water conveyance to the magnificent river whose name it bore; and on inquiry, I was informed that the whole of the Mutu was large in days of yore, and admitted of the free passage of great launches from Kilimane all the year round; but that now this part of the Mutu had been filled up.

I was seized by a severe tertian fever at Mazaro, but went along the right bank of the Mutu to the N.N.E. and E. for about 15 miles. We then found that it was made navigable by a river called the Pangázi, which comes into it from the north. Another river, flowing from the same direction, called the Luáre, swells it still more; and, last of all, the Likuáre, with the tide, make up the river of Kilimane. The Mutu at Mazaro is simply a connecting link, such as is so often seen in Africa, and neither its flow nor stoppage affects the river of Kilimane. The waters of the Pangazi were quite clear compared with those of the Zambesi.*

* I owe the following information, of a much later date, also to the politeness of Captain Washington. H. M. sloop "Grecian" visited the coast in 1852-3, and the master remarks that "the entrance to the Luabo is in lat. 18° 51' S., long. 36° 12' E., and may be known by a range of hummocks on its eastern side, and very low land to the S.W. The entrance is narrow, and, as with all the rivers on this coast, is fronted by a bar, which renders the navigation, particularly for boats, very dangerous with the wind to the south of east or west. Our boats proceeded 20 miles up this river, 2 fathoms on the bar, then 2½—4—6—7 fathoms. It was

My fever became excessively severe, in consequence of travelling in the hot sun, and the long grass blocking up the narrow
path, so as to exclude the air.　The pulse beat with amazing
force, and felt as if thumping against the crown of the head.
The stomach and spleen swelled enormously, giving me, for the
first time, an appearance which I had been disposed to laugh at
among the Portuguese.　At Interra we met Senhor Asevedo, a
man who is well known by all who ever visited Kilimane, and
who was presented with a gold chronometer watch by the Admiralty, for his attentions to English officers.　He immediately
tendered his large sailing launch, which had a house in the stern.
This was greatly in my favour, for it anchored in the middle of
the stream, and gave me some rest from the mosquitoes, which

navigable further up, but they did not proceed.　It is quite possible for
a moderate-sized vessel to cross the bar at spring-tides, and be perfectly
landlocked and hidden amongst the trees.

"The Maiüdo, in 18° 52' S., 36° 12' E., *is not mentioned in Horsburgh, nor
laid down in the Admiralty chart*, but is, nevertheless, one of some importance, and appears to be one of the principal stations for shipping slaves,
as the boats found two barracoons, about 20 miles up, bearing every
indication of having been very recently occupied, and which had good
presumptive evidence that the ' Cauraigo,' a brig under American colours,
had embarked a cargo from thence but a short time before.　This river is
fronted by a portion of the Elephant Shoals, at the distance of three or
four miles outside.　The eastern bank is formed by level sea-cliffs (as seen
from the ship it has that appearance), high for this part of the coast, and
conspicuous.　The western side is composed of thick trees, and terminates
in dead wood, from which we called it ' Dead-wood Point.'　After crossing
the bar it branches off in a W. and N.W. direction, the latter being the
principal arm, up which the boats went some 30 miles, or about 10
beyond the barracoon.　Fresh water can be obtained almost immediately
inside the entrance, as the stream runs down very rapidly with the ebb-
tide.　The least water crossing the bar (low-water—springs) was 1½ fathom,
one cast only therefrom from 2 to 5 fathoms, another 7 fathoms nearly
the whole way up.

"The Catrina, lat. 18° 50' S., long. 36° 24' E.　The external appearance of
this river is precisely similar to that of the Maiudo, so much so, that it is
difficult to distinguish them by any feature of the land.　The longitude
is the best guide, or, in the absence of observation, perhaps the angles
contained by the extremes of land will be serviceable.　Thus, at nine
miles off the Maiudo the angle contained by the above was seven points,
the bearing being N.E. W. of N.W. (?); whilst off the Catrina, at the same
distance from shore (about nine miles), the angle was only 3½ to 4 points,
being N. to N.W.　As we did not send the boats up this river, no information was obtained."

in the whole of the delta are something frightful. Sailing comfortably in this commodious launch along the river of Kilimane, we reached that village (lat. 17° 53′ 8″ S., long. 36° 40′ E.) on the 20th of May, 1856, which wanted only a few days of being four years since I started from Cape Town. Here I was received into the house of Colonel Galdino Jose Nunes, one of the best men in the country. I had been three years without hearing from my family; letters having frequently been sent, but somehow or other, with but a single exception, they never reached me. I received, however, a letter from Admiral Trotter, conveying information of their welfare, and some newspapers, which were a treat indeed. Her Majesty's brig the "Frolic" had called to inquire for me in the November previous, and Captain Nolloth of that ship had most considerately left a case of wine; and his surgeon, Dr. Jas. Walsh, divining what I should need most, left an ounce of quinine. These gifts made my heart overflow. I had not tasted any liquor whatever during the time I had been in Africa; but when reduced in Angola to extreme weakness, I found much benefit from a little wine, and took from Loanda one bottle of brandy in my medicine-chest, intending to use it if it were again required; but the boy who carried it whirled the box upside down, and smashed the bottle, so I cannot give my testimony either in favour of or against the brandy.

But my joy on reaching the east coast was sadly embittered by the news that Commander MacLune, of H. M. brigantine "Dart," on coming in to Kilimane to pick me up, had, with Lieutenant Woodruffe and five men, been lost on the bar. I never felt more poignant sorrow. It seemed as if it would have been easier for me to have died for them, than that they should all be cut off from the joys of life in generously attempting to render me a service. I would here acknowledge my deep obligations to the Earl of Clarendon; to the Admiral at the Cape; and others, for the kind interest they manifested in my safety; even the inquiries made were very much to my advantage. I also refer with feelings of gratitude to the Governor of Mozambique for offering me a passage in the schooner "Zambesi," belonging to that province; and I shall never forget the generous hospitality of Colonel Nunes and his nephew, with whom I remained. One of the discoveries I have made is that there are vast numbers of good people in the world, and I do most devoutly tender my unfeigned thanks to that Gracious One who mercifully watched over me in every position, and influenced the hearts of both black and white to regard me with favour.

With the united testimony of Captain Parker and Lieutenant Hoskins, added to my own observation, there can be no reasonable doubt but that the real mouth of the Zambesi is available for the purposes of commerce. The delta is claimed by the Portuguese, and the southern bank of the Luabo, or Cuama, as this part of the Zambesi is sometimes called, is owned by independent natives of the Caffre family. The Portuguese are thus near the main entrance to the new central region; and, as they have of late years shown, in an enlightened and liberal spirit, their desire to develop the resources of Eastern Africa by proclaiming Mozambique a free port, it is to be hoped that the same spirit will lead them to invite mercantile enterprise up the Zambesi, by offering facilities to those who may be led to push commerce into the regions lying far beyond their territory. Their wish to co-operate in the noble work of developing the resources of the rich country beyond, could not be shown better than by placing a village with Zambesian pilots at the harbour of Mitilone, and erecting a lighthouse for the guidance of seafaring men. If this were done, no nation would be a greater gainer by it than the Portuguese themselves, and assuredly no other needs a resuscitation of its commerce more. Their kindness to me personally makes me wish for a return of their ancient prosperity; and the most liberal and generous act of the enlightened young king H. M. Don Pedro, in sending out orders to support my late companions at the public expense of the province of Mozambique until my return to claim them, leads me to hope for encouragement in every measure for either the development of commerce, the elevation of the natives, or abolition of the trade in slaves.

As far as I am myself concerned, the opening of the new central country is a matter for congratulation only in so far as it opens up a prospect for the elevation of the inhabitants. As I have elsewhere remarked, I view the end of the geographical feat as the beginning of the missionary enterprise. I take the latter term in its most extended signification, and include every

effort made for the amelioration of our race; the promotion of
all those means by which God in His providence is working, and
bringing all His dealings with man to a glorious consummation.
Each man in his sphere, either knowingly or unwittingly, is
performing the will of our Father in heaven. Men of science,
searching after hidden truths, which when discovered will, like
the electric telegraph, bind men more closely together—soldiers
battling for the right against tyranny—sailors rescuing the victims of oppression from the grasp of heartless men-stealers—
merchants teaching the nations lessons of mutual dependence—
and many others, as well as missionaries, all work in the same
direction, and all efforts are overruled for one glorious end.

If the reader has accompanied me thus far, he may perhaps
be disposed to take an interest in the objects I propose to myself,
should God mercifully grant me the honour of doing something
more for Africa. As the highlands on the borders of the central
basin are comparatively healthy, the first object seems to be to
secure a permanent path thither, in order that Europeans may
pass as quickly as possible through the unhealthy region near
the coast. The river has not been surveyed, but at the time
I came down there was abundance of water for a large vessel,
and this continues to be the case during four or five months of
each year. The months of low-water still admit of navigation
by launches, and would permit small vessels equal to the
Thames steamers to ply with ease in the deep channel. If a
steamer were sent to examine the Zambesi, I would recommend
one of the lightest draught, and the months of May, June, and
July for passing through the delta; and this not so much for
fear of want of water, as the danger of being grounded on a
sand or mud bank, and the health of the crew being endangered
by the delay.

In the months referred to, no obstruction would be incurred in
the channel below Tete. Twenty or thirty miles above that
point we have a small rapid, of which I regret my inability to
speak, as (mentioned already) I did not visit it. But taking the
distance below this point, we have, in round numbers, 300 miles
of navigable river. Above this rapid we have another reach of
300 miles, with sand, but no mudbanks in it, which brings us to
the foot of the eastern ridge. Let it not, however, be thought

that a vessel by going thither would return laden with ivory and gold-dust. The Portuguese of Tete pick up all the merchandize of the tribes in their vicinity, and, though I came out by traversing the people with whom the Portuguese have been at war, it does not follow that it will be perfectly safe for others to go in whose goods may be a stronger temptation to cupidity than anything I possessed. When we get beyond the hostile population mentioned, we reach a very different race. On the latter my chief hopes at present rest. All of them, however, are willing and anxious to engage in trade, and, while eager for this, none have ever been encouraged to cultivate the raw materials of commerce. Their country is well adapted for cotton; and I venture to entertain the hope that by distributing seeds of better kinds than that which is found indigenous, and stimulating the natives to cultivate it by affording them the certainty of a market for all they may produce, we may engender a feeling of mutual dependence between them and ourselves. I have a two-fold object in view, and believe that, by guiding our missionary labours so as to benefit our own country, we shall thereby more effectually and permanently benefit the heathen. Seven years were spent at Kolobeng in instructing my friends there; but the country being incapable of raising materials for exportation, when the Boers made their murderous attack and scattered the tribe for a season, none sympathised except a few Christian friends. Had the people of Kolobeng been in the habit of raising the raw materials of English commerce, the outrage would have been felt in England; or, what is more likely to have been the case, the people would have raised themselves in the scale by barter, and have become, like the Basutos of Moshesh and people of Kuruman, possessed of fire-arms, and the Boers would never have made the attack at all. We ought to encourage the Africans to cultivate for our markets, as the most effectual means, next to the Gospel, of their elevation.

It is in the hope of working out this idea that I propose the formation of stations on the Zambesi beyond the Portuguese territory, but having communication through them with the coast. A chain of stations admitting of easy and speedy intercourse, such as might be formed along the flank of the eastern ridge, would be in a favourable position for carrying out the

2 x 2

objects in view. The London Missionary Society has resolved to have a station among the Makololo on the north bank, and another on the south among the Matebele. The Church—Wesleyan, Baptist, and that most energetic body, the Free Church—could each find desirable locations among the Batoka and adjacent tribes. The country is so extensive there is no fear of clashing. All classes of Christians find that sectarian rancour soon dies out when they are working together among and for the real heathen. Only let the healthy locality be searched for, and fixed upon, and then there will be free scope to work in the same cause in various directions, without that loss of men which the system of missions on the unhealthy coasts entails. While respectfully submitting the plan to these influential societies, I can positively state that, when fairly in the interior, there is perfect security for life and property among a people who will at least listen and reason.

Eight of my men begged to be allowed to come as far as Kilimane, and, thinking that they would there see the ocean, I consented to their coming, though the food was so scarce in consequence of a dearth, that they were compelled to suffer some hunger. They would fain have come further; for when Sekeletu parted with them, his orders were that none of them should turn until they had reached Ma Robert and brought her back with them. On my explaining the difficulty of crossing the sea, he said, "Wherever you lead, they must follow." As I did not know well how I should get home myself, I advised them to go back to Tete, where food was abundant, and there await my return. I bought a quantity of calico and brass wire with ten of the smaller tusks which we had in our charge, and sent the former back as clothing to those who remained at Tete. As there were still twenty tusks left, I deposited them with Colonel Nunes, that, in the event of anything happening to prevent my return, the impression might not be produced in the country, that I had made away with Sekeletu's ivory. I instructed Colonel Nunes, in case of my death, to sell the tusks and deliver the proceeds to my men; but I intended, if my life should be prolonged, to purchase the goods ordered by Sekeletu in England with my own money, and pay myself on my return out of the price of the ivory. This I explained to the men fully, and they, understanding the matter, replied, "Nay, father, you will not die; you will return to take us back to Sekeletu." They promised to wait till I came back, and, on my part, I assured them that nothing but death would prevent my return. This I said, though while waiting at Kilimane a letter came from the Directors of the London Missionary Society, stating that "they were restricted in their power of aiding plans connected only remotely with the spread of the Gospel, and that the financial circumstances of the Society were not such as to afford any ground of hope that it would be in a position, within any definite period, to enter upon untried, remote, and difficult fields of labour." This has been explained since as an effusion caused by temporary financial depression; but feeling perfect confidence in my Makololo friends, I was determined to return and trust to their generosity. The old love of independence, which I had so strongly before joining the Society, again returned. It was roused by a mistaken view of what this letter meant, for the Directors, immediately on my reaching home, saw the great importance of the opening, and entered with enlightened zeal on the work of sending the Gospel into the new field. It is to be hoped that their constituents will not only enable them to begin, but to carry out their plans; and that no material depression will ever again be permitted, nor appearance of spasmodic benevolence recur. While I hope to continue the same cordial co-operation and friendship which have always characterised our intercourse, various reasons induce me to withdraw from pecuniary dependence on any Society. I have done something for the heathen, but for an aged mother, who has still more sacred claims than they, I have been able to do nothing, and a continuance of the connection would be a perpetuation of my inability to make any provision for her declining years. In addition to "clergyman's sore throat," which partially disabled me from the work, my father's death imposed new obligations; and a fresh source of income having been opened to me without my asking, I had no hesitation in accepting what would enable me to fulfil my duty to my aged parent as well as to the heathen.

If the reader remembers the way in which I was led, while teaching the Bakwains, to commence exploration, he will, I think, recognise the hand of Providence. Anterior to that, when

Mr. Moffat began to give the Bible—the Magna Charta of all the rights and privileges of modern civilization—to the Bechuanas, Sebituane went north, and spread the language into which he was translating the sacred oracles, in a new region larger than France. Sebituane, at the same time, rooted out hordes of bloody savages among whom no white man could have gone, without leaving his skull to ornament some village. He opened up the way for me —let us hope also for the Bible. Then, again, while I was labouring at Kolobeng, seeing only a small arc of the cycle of Providence; I could not understand it, and felt inclined to ascribe our successive and prolonged droughts to the wicked one. But when forced by these, and the Boers, to become explorer, and open a new country in the north rather than set my face southwards, where missionaries are not needed; the gracious Spirit of God influenced the minds of the heathen to regard me with favour; the Divine hand is again perceived. Then, I turned away westwards, rather than in the opposite direction, chiefly from observing that some native Portuguese, though influenced by the hope of a reward from their Government to cross the continent, had been obliged to return from the east without accomplishing their object. Had I gone at first in the eastern direction, which the course of the great Leeambye seemed to invite, I should have come among the belligerents near Tete, when the war was raging at its height, instead of, as it happened, when all was over. And again, when enabled to reach Loanda, the resolution to do my duty by going back to Linyanti, probably saved me from the fate of my papers in the " Forerunner." And then, last of all, this new country is partially opened to the sympathies of Christendom, and I find that Sechele himself has, though unbidden by man, been teaching his own people. In fact, he has been doing all, that I was prevented from doing, and I have been employed in exploring—a work I had no previous intention of performing. I think, that I see the operation of the unseen hand in all this, and I humbly hope, that it will still guide me to do good in my day and generation in Africa.

Viewing the success awarded to opening up the new country, as a development of Divine Providence in relation to the African family, the mind naturally turns to the probable influence it may have on negro slavery; and more especially on the practice of it by a large portion of our own race. We now demand increased supplies of cotton and sugar, and then reprobate the means our American brethren adopt to supply our wants. We claim a right to speak about this evil, and also to act in reference to its removal, the more especially because we are of one blood. It is on the Anglo-American race that the hopes of the world for liberty and progress rest. Now it is very grievous to find one portion of this race practising the gigantic evil, and the other aiding, by increased demands for the produce of slave-labour, in perpetuating the enormous wrong. The Mauritius, a mere speck on the ocean, yields sugar, by means of guano, improved machinery, and free labour, equal in amount to one-fourth part of the entire consumption of Great Britain. On that island, land is excessively dear, and far from rich: no crop can be raised except by means of guano, and labour has to be brought all the way from India. But in Africa the land is cheap, the soil good, and free labour is to be found on the spot. Our chief hopes rest with the natives themselves; and if the point to which I have given prominence, of healthy inland commercial stations, be realized, where all the produce raised may be collected, there is little doubt but that slavery among our kinsmen across the Atlantic will, in the course of some years, cease to assume the form of a necessity to even the slaveholders themselves. Natives alone can collect produce from the more distant hamlets, and bring it to the stations contemplated. This is the system pursued so successfully in Angola. If England had possessed that strip of land, by civilly declining to enrich her " Frontier colonists" by " Caffre wars," the inborn energy of English colonists would have developed its resources, and the exports would not have been 100,000l. as now, but one million at least. The establishment of the necessary agency must be a work of time, and greater difficulty will be experienced on the eastern, than on the western side of the continent, because in the one region we have a people who know none but slave-traders, while in the other we have tribes who have felt the influence of the coast missionaries, and of the great Niger expedition; one invaluable benefit it conferred was the dissemination of the knowledge of English love of commerce and English hatred of slavery, and it therefore was no failure. But on the east, there is a river which may become a good pathway to a central population who are friendly to the English; and if we can conciliate the less amicable people on the river, and introduce commerce, an effectual blow will be struck at the slave-trade in that quarter. By linking the Africans there to ourselves, in the manner proposed, it is hoped that their elevation will eventually be the result. In this hope and proposed effort, I am joined by my brother Charles, who has come from America, after seventeen years' separation, for the purpose. We expect success through the influence of that Spirit who already aided the efforts to open the country, and who has since turned the public mind towards it. A failure may be experienced by sudden rash speculation, over-stocking the markets there, and raising the prices against ourselves. But I propose to spend some more years of labour, and shall be thankful if I see the system fairly begun in an open pathway which will eventually benefit both Africa and England.

The village of Kilimane stands on a great mud bank, and is surrounded by extensive swamps and rice-grounds. The banks of the river are lined with mangrove-bushes, the roots of which, and the slimy banks on which they grow, are alternately exposed to the tide and sun. The houses are well built of brick and lime; the latter from Mozambique. If one digs down two or three feet in any part of the site of the village, he comes to water: hence the walls built on this mud bank gradually subside; pieces are sometimes sawn off the doors below, because the walls in which they are fixed have descended into the ground, so as to leave the floors higher than the bottom of the doors. It is almost needless to say that Kilimane is very unhealthy. A man of plethoric temperament is sure to get fever; and, concerning a stout person, one may hear the remark, " Ah! he will not live long, he is sure to die.".

A Hamburgh vessel was lost near the bar before we came down. The men were much more regular in their habits than English sailors, so I had an opportunity of observing the fever, acting as a slow poison. They felt " out of sorts " only, but gradually became pale, bloodless, and emaciated, then weaker and weaker, till at last they sank more like oxen bitten by tsetse than any disease I ever saw. The captain, a strong robust young man, remained in perfect health for about three months, but was at last knocked down suddenly, and made as helpless as a child, by this terrible disease. He had imbibed a foolish prejudice against quinine, our sheet-anchor in the complaint. This is rather a professional subject, but I introduce it here, in order to protest against the prejudice as almost entirely unfounded. Quinine is invaluable in fever, and never produces any unpleasant effects in any stage of the disease, *if exhibited in combination with an aperient.* The captain was saved by it, without his knowledge, and I was thankful that the mode of treatment so efficacious among natives, promised so fair among Europeans.

. After waiting about six weeks at this unhealthy spot, in which, however, by the kind attentions of Colonel Nunes and his nephew, I partially recovered from my tertian, H. M. brig " Frolic " arrived off Kilimane. As the village is twelve miles from the bar, and the weather was rough, she was at anchor ten days before we knew of her presence, about seven miles from the entrance to the port. She brought abundant supplies for all my need; and 150*l.* to pay my passage home, from my kind friend Mr. Thompson, the Society's agent at the Cape. The Admiral at the Cape kindly sent an offer of a passage to the Mauritius, which I thankfully accepted. Sekwebu and one attendant alone remained with me now. He was very intelligent, and had been of the greatest service to me; indeed, but for his good sense, tact, and command of the language of the tribes through which we passed, I believe we should scarcely have succeeded in reaching the coast. I naturally felt grateful to him; and as his chief wished *all* my companions to go to England with me, and would probably be disappointed if none went, I thought it would be beneficial for him to see the effects of civilization, and report them to his countrymen; I wished also to make some return for his very important services. Others had petitioned to come, but I explained the danger of a change of climate and food, and with difficulty restrained them. The only one who now remained begged so hard to come on board ship, that I greatly regretted, that the expense prevented my acceding to his wish to visit England. I said to him, " You will die if you go to such a cold country as mine." " That is nothing," he reiterated; " let me die at your feet."

When we parted from our friends at Kilimane, the sea on the bar was frightful even to the seamen. This was the first time Sekwebu had seen the sea. Captain Peyton had sent two boats in case of accident. The waves were so high that, when the cutter was in one trough, and we in the pinnace in another, her mast was hid. We then mounted to the crest of the wave, rushed down the slope, and struck the water again with a blow which felt as if she had struck the bottom. Boats must be singularly well constructed to be able to stand these shocks. Three breakers swept over us. The men lift up their oars, and a wave comes sweeping over all, giving the impression that the boat is going down, but she only goes beneath the top of the wave, comes out on the other side, and swings down the slope, and a man bales out the water with a bucket. Poor Sekwebu looked at me when these terrible seas broke over, and said, "Is this the way you go? Is this the way you go?" I smiled, and said, "Yes; don't you see it is?" and tried to encourage him. He was well acquainted with canoes, but never had seen aught like this. When we reached the ship—a fine, large brig of sixteen guns and a crew of one hundred and thirty—she was rolling so, that we could see a part of her bottom. It was quite impossible for landsmen to catch the ropes and climb up, so a chair was sent down, and we were hoisted in as ladies usually are, and received so hearty an English welcome from Captain Peyton and all on board, that I felt myself at once at home in everything, except my own mother-tongue. I seemed to know the language perfectly, but the words I wanted, would not come at my call. When I left England I had no intention of returning, and directed my attention earnestly to the languages of Africa, paying none to English composition. With the exception of a short interval in Angola, I had been three and a half years without speaking English, and this, with thirteen years of previous partial disuse of my native tongue, made me feel sadly at a loss on board the "Frolic."

We left Kilimane on the 12th of July, and reached the Mauritius on the 12th of August, 1856. Sekwebu was picking up English, and becoming a favourite with both men and officers. He seemed a little bewildered, everything on board a man-of-war being so new and strange; but he remarked to me several times, "Your countrymen are very agreeable," and "What a strange country this is—all water together." He also said, that he now understood why I used the sextant. When we reached the Mauritius a steamer came out to tow us into the harbour. The constant strain on his untutored mind seemed now to reach a climax, for during the night he became insane. I thought at first that he was intoxicated. He had descended into a boat, and, when I attempted to go down and bring him into the ship, he ran to the stern, and said, "No! no! it is enough that I die alone. You must not perish; if you come I shall throw myself into the water." Perceiving that his mind was affected, I said, "Now, Sekwebu, we are going to Ma Robert." This struck a chord in his bosom, and he said, "O yes; where is she, and where is Robert?" and he seemed to recover. The officers proposed to secure him by putting him in irons, but, being a gentleman in his own country, I objected, knowing that the insane often retain an impression of ill-treatment, and I could not bear to have it said in Sekeletu's country that I had chained one of his principal men, as they had seen slaves treated. I tried to get him on shore by day, but he refused. In the evening a fresh accession of insanity occurred—he tried to spear one of the crew, then leaped overboard, and, though he could swim well, pulled himself down hand under hand, by the chain cable. We never found the body of poor Sekwebu.

At the Mauritius I was most hospitably received by Major-General C. M. Hay, and he generously constrained me to remain with him till, by the influence of the good climate and quiet English comfort, I got rid of an enlarged spleen from African fever. In November I came up the Red Sea; escaped the danger of shipwreck through the admirable management of Captain Powell, of the Peninsular and Oriental Steam Company's ship "Candia;" and on the 12th of December was once more in dear old England. The Company most liberally refunded my passage-money. I have not mentioned half the favours bestowed, but I may just add that no one has cause for more abundant gratitude to his fellow-men and to his Maker than I have; and may God grant that the effect on my mind be such that I may be more humbly devoted to the service of the Author of all our mercies!

APPENDIX.

APPENDIX.—LATITUDES AND LONGITUDES OF POSITIONS.

Positions.	Latitude. South. ° ′ ″	Longitude. East. ° ′ ″	Date.	No. of Sets of Lunar Distances. W.	E.	Remarks.
Manakalongwe Pass	22 55 52	..	1853 Jan. 26			
Letloche	22 38 0	..	Jan. 28			
Kanne	22 26 56	..	Jan. 31			
Lotlokane, where the first Palmyra trees occur	21 27 47	..	Feb. 11, 12			
Hence path to Nchokotsa N.N.W., thence to Kobe N.W.						
Kobe (1st group)	20 53 14	24 52 0	Feb. 18, 19			
Kama Kama, from whence travelled in magnetic meridian (1st group)	19 52 31					
Fever Ponds (1st group)	19 15 53	24 55 0	Mar. 2			
Ten miles S. of hill N'gwa (1st group)	18 38 0	24 26 0	Mar. 11, 28			
N'gwa Hill (a central occultation of B. A. C. 2364 Gemini)	18 27 50	24 13 36	Apr. 14			
N'gwa Valley, half-mile N. of hill	18 27 20	24 13 36	Apr. 15, 16			
E. of and in parallel of Waggon Station of 1851	18 20 0	..	Apr. 17			
Waggon Station on the Chobe, 3 miles S. of Sekeletu's Town	18 20 0	23 50 0	Apr. 17			
Sekeletu's Town (1st group)	18 17 20	23 50 9	{ June 13, July 14, 17 }	..	..	Boiling point of water=205½° : Alt. =3521 feet.
Island Mahonta. The Chobe runs here in 17° 58″	17 58 0	(24 6)	Apr. 26			At a well-known Baobab-tree 9′ S. of Mahonta island.
Banks of Sanshureh River, a branch of the Chobe (1st group)	18 4 27	24 6 20	1855 Apr. 26	..	1	
Town of Sesheke on the Zambesi	17 31 38	25 13 0	Aug. 31	..		
Sekhosi's Town on the Zambesi (about 25 miles W. of Sesheke)	17 29 13	..	1853 Jul.26, 27		1	
Cataract of Nambwe	17 17 16	..	July 31			
Confluence of Njoko and Zambesi	17 7 31	..	1855 Aug. 22		1	
Cataract of Bombwe	16 56 33	..	1853 Aug. 21		1	
Kale Cataract	16 49 52	..	1855 Aug. 1			
Falls of Gonye	16 38 50	23 55 0	{ 1853 Aug. 2, 1855 Aug. 19 }	1	2	
Nameta	16 12 9	..	Aug. 17		2	

Place	Lat. °	′	″	Long. °	′	″	Date	No.	Remarks
Loyela, S. end of this island, town of Mamochisane	15	27	30				Aug. 9	⋮	
Naliele or Nariele, chief town of Barotse (occultation of ♃) (1st group)	15	24	17	23	5	54	Aug. 10, 13		
Linangelo, old town of Santuru (site nearly swallowed up)	15	18	40				Aug. 19		
Katongo (near Slave Merchants' Stockade)	15	16	33				Aug. 30		
Point of Junction of Nariele Branch with the Main Stream	15	15	43				Aug. 29		Boiling point of water = 203° = 4741 ft.
Quando Village	15	6	8				Aug. 28		
Town of Libonta	14	59	0				Aug. 21		
Island of Tongane	14	38	6				Aug. 23		
Cowrie Island	14	20	5				Aug. 24		
Junction of the Loeti with the Main Stream (Leeambye, Zambesi)	14	18	57				Aug.	⋮	
Confluence of the Leeba or Lonta with the Leeambye (1st group)	14	10	52	23	35	40	Aug. 24, 25	⋮	
Kabompo, near the Leeba	12	37	35	22	47	0	{1854 Jan. 1 / 1855 July 3}	3	
Village about 2′ N.W. of the Leeba after leaving Kabompo town: the hill Peeri, or Piri, bearing S.S.E., distant about 6′									
Village of Soana Molopo, 3′ from Lokalueje river	12	6	6	22	57	0	1854 Feb. 1		
Village of Quendende, about 2′ S.E. of the ford of the Lotembwa, and about 9′ from the town of Katema	11	49	22	22	42	0	Feb. 7		
Banks of the Lovoa	11	41	17				Feb. 11	2	
Lofuje River flows into the Leeba; Nyamoana's village	11	40	54				June 20		
Confluence of the Makondo and Leeba Rivers	12	52	35	22	49	0	July 7	3	
Katema's Town, 5′ S. of Lake Dilolo, the source of the Lotembwa, one of the principal feeders of the Leeba	13	23	12				July 13		
Lake Dilolo (station about half a mile S. of the lake)	11	35	49	22	27	0	1854 Feb. 17	2	Boiling point of water = 203° = 4741 ft.
	11	32	1				1855 June 18	2	
Village near the ford of the river Kasai, Kasye, or Loke. The ford is in latitude 11° 17′	11	15	55				1854 Feb. 28	⋮	

Positions.	Latitude, South.			Longitude, East.			Date.	No. of Sets of Lunar Distances		Remarks.
	°	'	"	°	'	"		W.	E.	
Manakalongwe Pass	22	55	52			..	1853 Jan. 26			
Letloche	22	38	0			..	Jan. 28			
Kanne	22	36	56			..	Jan. 31			
Letlokane, where the first Palmyra trees occur Hence path to Nchokotsa N.N.W., thence to Kobe N.W.	21	27	47			..	Feb. 11, 12			
Kobe (1st group)	20	53	14	24	52	0	Feb. 18, 19			
Kama Kama, from whence travelled in magnetic meridian (1st group)	19	52	31			..	Mar. 2			
Fever Ponds (1st group)	19	15	53	24	55	0	Mar. 11, 28			
Ten miles S. of hill N'gwa (1st group)	18	38	0	24	26	0	Apr. 14			
N'gwa Hill (a central occultation of B.A.C. 2364 Gemini)	18	27	50	24	13	36	Apr. 15, 16			
N'gwa Valley, half-mile N. of hill	18	27	20	24	13	36	Apr. 17			
E. of and in parallel of Waggon Station of 1851 ..	18	20	0			..	Apr. 17			
Waggon Station on the Chobe, 3 miles S. of Sekeletu's Town	18	20	0	23	50	0				
Sekeletu's Town (1st group)	18	17	20	23	50	0	{June 13} {July 14, 17}	..	..	Boiling point of water = 205½° : Alt. = 3521 feet.
Island Mahonta. The Chobe runs here in 17°58'	17	58	0	(24	6)		Apr. 26			
Banks of Sanshureh River, a branch of the Chobe (1st group)	18	4	27	24	6	20	Apr. 26	..	..	At a well-known Baobab-tree 9' S. of Mahonta Island.
Town of Sesheke on the Zambesi	17	31	38	25	13	0	1855 Aug. 31	..	1	
Sekhosi's Town on the Zambesi (about 25 miles W. of Sesheke)	17	29	18			..	1853 Jul.26, 27			
Cataract of Namhwe	17	17	16			..	July 31			
Confluence of Njoko and Zambesi	17	7	31			..	1855 Aug. 22	..	1	
Cataract of Bombwe	15	56	33			..	1853 Aug. 1			
Kale Cataract	16	49	52			..	1855 Aug. 21	..	1	
Falls of Gonye	16	38	50	23	55	0	{1853 Aug. 2} {1855 Aug. 19}	1	2	
Namta	16	13	9			..	Aug. 17	..	2	
Stori na Mei, or Island of Water	16	6	32			..	1853 Aug. 5			
Litaba Island, town of Loyela, S. end of this island, town of Mosmo-chisane	15	53	0			..	Aug. 7			
Naliele or Nariele, chief town of Barotse (occultation of ♃) (1st group)	15	27	30			..	Aug. 9			
Linangolo, old town of Santaru (site nearly swallowed up)	15	24	17	23	5	54	Aug. 10, 13			
Katongo (near Slave Merchants' Stockade) ..	15	18	40			..	Aug. 19			
Point of Junction of Nariele Branch with the Main Stream	15	16	33			..	Aug. 30			
Quando Village	15	15	43			..	Aug. 29			
Town of Libonta	15	6	8			..	Aug. 28			
Island of Tongane	14	59	0			..	Aug. 21			
Cowrie Island	14	38	6			..	Aug. 23			
Junction of the Loeti with the Main Stream (Leeambye, Zambesi)	14	20	5			..	Aug. 24			
Confluence of the Leeba or Lonta with the Leeambye (1st group)	14	18	57			..	Aug.	..	..	Boiling point of water = 203° = 4741 ft.
Kabompo, near the Leeba	14	10	52	23	35	40	Aug. 24, 25			
Village about 2' N.W. of the Leeba after leaving Kabompo town: the hill Peeri, or Piri, bearing S.S.E., distant about 6'	12	37	35	22	47	0	{1854 Jan. 1} {1855 July 3}	..	3	
Village of Soana Molopo, 3' from Lokalueje river	12	5	6	22	57	0	1854 Feb. 1			
Village of Quendende, about 2' S.E. of the ford of the Lotembwa, and about 9' from the town of Katema	11	49	22	22	42	0	Feb. 7			
Banks of the Lovoa	11	41	17			..	Feb. 11			
Lofuje River flows into the Leeba; Nyamoana's village	11	40	54			..	1855 June 20	2		
Confluence of the Makondo and Leeba Rivers ..	13	52	35	22	40	0	July 7	..	3	
Katema's Town, 5' S. of Lake Dilolo, the source of the Lotembwa, one of the principal feeders of the Leeba	13	23	12			..	July 13			
Lake Dilolo (station about half a mile S. of the lake)	11	35	49	22	27	0	1854 Feb. 17 1855 June 18	..	2 2	
Village near the ford of the river Kasai, Kasye, or Loke. The ford is in latitude 11° 17' ..	11	32	1			..	June 13	..	..	Boiling point of water = 203° = 4741 ft.
	11	15	55			..	1854 Feb. 28			

Latitudes and Longitudes of Positions—continued.

Positions.	Latitude. South.	Longitude. East.	Date.	No. of Sets of Lunar Distances. W.	No. of Sets of Lunar Distances. E.	Remarks.
Bango's Village, about 10' W. of the Loembwe	10 22 53	20 58 0	1855 May 28	..	.	The longitude doubtful.
Banks of the Stream Chihune	10 57 30	(20 53) *	1854 Mar. 8	..	..	
Ionga Panza's village	10 25 0	20 15 0‡	Mar. 20	..	..	
Ford of the River Quango	9 50 0	(18 27 0)	April 5	..	2	
Cassange, about 40 or 50 miles W. of the River Quango, and situated in a deep valley	9 37 30	17 49 0	Apr. 13, 17	3	..	Longitude not observed: Water boils— Top of =206°, height 3151 ft. Bottom of descent =208°=2097 ft. Bottom of East ascent = 205°=3680 ft. Top ,, = 202°=5278 ft. On the top of the rocks water boils at 204°=4210 ft.
Tala Mungongo, 2' E, of following station	9 42 37	(17 27)	Jan, 11, 14	..	..	
Banks of the Quize, near the source, 2' W. of the sudden descent which forms the valley of Cassange	9 42 37	17 25 0	1855 Jan. 10	1	..	
Sanza, on the River Quize (about 15 yds. wide)	9 37 46	16 59 0	Jan. 7	..	4	
Pungo Andongo, on the River Coanza	9 42 14	15 30 0	1854 Dec. 11	..	4	
On the River Coanza, 2' W. of Pungo Andongo	9 47 2	..	Dec. 22			
Candumba, 15 miles E. of Pungo Andongo, 300 yards N. of the Coanza	9 42 46	..	1855 Jan. 2			
Confluence of the Lombe and Coanza, 8' or 10' E. of Candumba, and at house of M. Pires, taken at about half a mile N. of confluence	9 41 26	..	Jan. 3	..	..	Here the Coanza takes its southern bend.
Golungo Alto, about midway between Ambaca and Loanda	9 8 30	14 51 0	1854 {Oct. 27, May 14}	..	..	
"Aguaes doces" in Cassange, 10' W. of Golungo Alto	9 15 2	..	Oct. 6, 7	..	2	At the confluence of the Luinha and Luee.
Confluence of the Luinha and Lucalla	9 26 23	..	..			
Confluence of the Lucalla and Coanza, Massangano town and fort	9 37 46	..	Oct. 11, 12	..	..	A prominent hill in Cazengo, called Zunga, is about 6' S.S.W. of 'Aguaes doces," and it bears N E, by E. from the house of the commandant at Massangano.
Ambaca, residence of the commandant of the district	9 16 35	15 23 0	Dec. 6	2	3	Water boils at 204½°=3945 ft. Between Lekone and Kalomo, Marimba 203¾°=4608 ft.
Kalai, near the Mosioatunya Falls	17 51 54	25 41 0	1855 Nov. 18	4	1	The lat. and long. doubtful. Top of ridge, water boils at 202°=5278 ft.
Lekone Rivulet	17 45 6	25 55 0	Nov. 20			
Kalomo River	(17 3 0)	..	Nov. 30	..	1	
Rivulet of Dela, called Mozuma	16 56 0	26 45 0	Dec. 2	3	3	

Station	Lat. S.	Long. E.	Date			Remarks
Elephant's Grave	(16 3 0)	(28 10)*	Dec. 14	1	··	= 4210 ft.
Kenia Hills, Rivulet Losito on their western flank	(15 56 0)	(28 1)†	Dec. 16	3	··	The latitude not observed.
6' E. of Bolengwe Gorge, and on the banks of the Kafue	15 48 19	28 22 0	Dec. 18	3	3	The latitude not observed.
7' or 8' N.E. or E.N.E. of the confluence of the Kafue and Zambesi, at a rivulet called Kambare	(15 49 0)	(28 34)‡	Dec. 29	··	4	The lat. not observed; water boils 205½°=3415 ft. Top of the hills Semalembue, water boils 204½°=4078 ft. Bottom of ditto, 205¾°=3288 ft.
Confluence of Kafue and Zambesi	15 53 0	··	··	··	··	
Banks of Zambesi, 8' or 10' below confluence	15 50 49	··	Dec. 30	··	··	Water boils at 209°=1571 ft.
Village of Ma-Mburuma, about 10 miles from Zumbo	15 36 57	30 22 0	1856 Jan. 12	1	1	
Zumbo Station, ruins of a church on the right bank of the Loangwa, about 300 yards from confluence with Zambesi		30 32 0	Jan. 13	2	3	Water boils at 209¼°=1440 ft.
Chilonda's Village, quarter of a mile N. of Zambesi, near the Kabaula Hill	15 37 22	30 52 0	Jan. 20	3	:1	
Opposite Hill Pinkwe	15 38 34	(32 5)§	Feb. 7	:1	2	Long. doubtful; the moon's alt. only 4°.
Moshua Rivulet	15 39 11	32 22 0‖	Feb. 9	··	··	
Tangwe Rivulet, or Sand River, ¾ mile broad	15 45 33	32 29 0	Feb. 20	··	··	
Tete or Nyungwe station, house of commandant	16 13 38	33 28 0	Mar. 2, 17	4	8	
Hot Spring Makorozi, about 10 m. up the river	16 9 3	··	Mar. 13	1	··	
Below Tete, island of Mozambique, on the Zambesi	15 59 35	32 51 0	April 23	··	··	
Island of Nkuesa	16 34 46	··	April 25	··	··	
Senna, 300 yards S.W. of the Mud Fort on the bank of the river	17 1 6	34 57 0¶	{April 27; May 8, 9}	2	6	
Islet of Shupanga	17 27 1	··	May 12	··	··	
Small islet in the middle of the Zambesi, and six or eight miles below Shupanga	17 51 38	··	May 13	··	··	
Mazaro or Mutu, where the Kilimane River branches off the Zambesi	17 59 21	35 57 0	May 14	2	2	
Kilimane Village, at the house of Señor Galdino Jose Nunes, colonel of militia	18 3 37	36 40 0**	June 13, 25, and 27.	1	6	
	17 53 8					

* Probably 20° 25'.—I. A. † Probably 20° 16'.—I. A. ‡ Probably 28° 56'.—I. A. § Probably 31° 46' 30''.—I. A.

‖ Probably 31° 56'.—I. A. ¶ Probably 35° 16' 15''.—I. A. ** Probably 36° 8''.—I. A.

Latitudes and Longitudes of Positions—*continued.*

Positions.	Latitude. South.	Longitude. East.	Date.	No. of S.ts of Lunar Distances.		Remarks.
	° ′ ″	° ′ ″		W.	E.	
Bango's Village, about 10′ W. of the Loembwe	10 22 53	20 58 0	1855 May 28			
Banks of the Stream Chiluue	10 57 20	(20 53) *	1854 Mar. 8	..	..	The longitude doubtful.
Ionga Panza's village	10 25 0	20 15 0†	Mar. 20			
Ford of the River Quango	9 50 0	(18 27 0)	April 5	..	..	
Cassange, about 40 or 50 miles W. of the River Quango, and situated in a deep valley	9 37 30	17 49 0	Apr. 13, 17	3	2	
Tala Mungongo, 2′ E. of following station	9 42 37	(17 27)	Jan. 11, 14	..	..	Longitude not observed : Water boils— Top of = 206°, height 3151 ft.
Banks of the Quize, near the source, 2′ W. of the sudden descent which forms the valley of Cassange	9 42 37	17 25 0	1855 Jan. 10	..	1	Bottom of descent = 208° = 2097 ft. Bottom of East ascent = 205° = 3680 ft.
Sanza, on the River Quize (about 15 yds. wide)	9 37 46	16 59 0	Jan. 7	..	4	Top ,, = 202° = 5278 ft.
Pungo Andongo, on the River Coanza	9 42 14	15 30 0	1854 Dec. 11	..	4	On the top of the rocks water boils at 204° = 4210 ft.
On the River Coanza, 2′ W. of Pungo Andongo	9 47 2		Dec. 22			
Candumba, 15 miles E. of Pungo Andongo, 300 yards N. of the Coanza	9 42 46	..	1855 Jan. 2			
Confluence of the Lombe and Coanza, 8′ or 10′ E. of Candumba, and at house of M. Pires, taken at about half a mile N. of confluence	9 41 26	..	Jan. 3	..	..	Here the Coanza takes its southern bend.
Golungo Alto, about midway between Ambaca and Loanda	9 8 30	14 51 0	1854 { Oct. 27 { May 14 }			
"Aguaes doces" in Cassange, 10′ W. of Golungo Alto	9 15 2	..	Oct. 6, 7	..	2	At the confluence of the Luinha and Luce.
Confluence of the Luinha and Lucalla	9 26 23	..				
Confluence of the Lucalla and Coanza, Massangano town and fort	9 37 46	..	Oct. 11, 12	..	..	A prominent hill in Cazengo, called Zunga, is about 6′ S.S.W. of "Aguaes doces," and it bears N.E. by E. from the house of the commandant at Massangano.
Ambaca, residence of the commandant of the district	9 16 35	15 26 0	Dec. 6			
Kulai, near the Mosiautunya Falls	17 51 54	25 41 0	1855 Nov. 18	2	3	Water boils at 204½° = 3845 ft. Between Lekone and Xalome, Marimba 203½° = 4608 ft.
Lekone Rivulet	17 45 6	25 55 0	Nov. 20	4	1	
Kalomo River	(17 3 0)		Nov. 30	..	1	The lat. and long. doubtful. Top of ridge, water boils at 202° = 5278 ft.
Rivulet of Dela, called Mozuma	16 56 0	26 45 0	Dec. 2	..	3	
Kise Kise Hills	16 27 20		Dec. 5			
Natwehinga Rivulet	16 11 24		Dec. 11	..	..	On eastern descent from ridge, water boils at 204° = 4210 ft.
Elephant's Grave	(16 3 0)	(28 10)	Dec. 14	1	1	The latitude not observed.
Kenia Hills, Rivulet Losito on their western flank	(15 56 0)	(28 1)	Dec. 16	3	..	The latitude not observed.
6′ E. of Bolengwe Gorge, and on the banks of the Kafue	15 48 19	28 22 0	Dec. 18	3	3	
7′ or 8′ N.E. or E.N.E. of the confluence of the Kafue and Zambesi, at a rivulet called Kambare	(15 49 0)	(28 34) ‡	Dec. 29	..	4	The lat. not observed ; water boils 205½° = 3415 ft. Top of the hills Semalembne, water boils 204½°
Confluence of Kafue and Zambesi	15 53 0	..				= 4078 ft. Bottom of ditto, 205½° = 3288 ft.
Banks of Zambesi, 8′ or 10′ below confluence	15 50 49	..	Dec. 30	..	..	Water boils at 209° = 1571 ft.
Village of Ma-Mburuma, about 10 miles from Zumbo	15 36 57	30 22 0	1856 Jan. 12	1	1	
Zumbo Station, ruins of a church on the right bank of the Loangwa, about 300 yards from confluence with Zambesi	15 37 22	30 32 0	an. 13	2	3	Water boils at 209½° = 1440 ft.
Chilonda's Village, quarter of a mile N. of Zambesi, near the Kalamba Hill	15 38 34	30 52 0	Jan. 20	3	..	
Opposite Hill Pinkwe	15 39 11	(32 5) §	Feb. 7	..	1	Long. doubtful ; the moon's alt. only 4°.
Moshua Rivulet	15 45 36	32 22 0‖	Feb. 9	1	2	
Tangwe Rivulet, or Sand River, ½ mile broad	16 13 38	32 29 0	Feb. 20			
Tete or Nyungwe station, house of commandant	16 9 3	33 28 0	Mar. 2, 17	4	6	
Hot Spring Makorozi, about 10 m. up the river	15 59 35	..	Mar. 15			
Below Tete, island of Mozambique, on the Zambesi	16 34 46	33 51 0	April 23	1	..	
Island of Nkuesa	17 1 6	..	April 25			
Senna, 300 yards S.W. of the Mud Fort on the bank of the river	17 27 1	34 57 0¶	{ April 27 { May 8, 9 }	2	6	
Islet of Shupanga	17 51 38	..	May 12			
Small islet in the middle of the Zambesi, and six or eight miles below Shupanga	17 59 21	..	May 13			
Mazaro or Mutu, where the Kilimane River branches off the Zambesi	18 3 37	35 57 0	May 14	2	2	
Kilimane Village, at the house of Señor Galdino Jose Nunes, colonel of militia	17 55 8	35 40 0**	June 13, 25, and 27.	1	6	

* Probably 20° 26′.—I. A.   † Probably 20° 19′.—I. A.   ‡ Probably 28° 56′.—I. A.   § Probably 31° 49′ 39″.—I. A.
‖ Probably 31° 56′.—I. A.   ¶ Probably 35° 10′ 15″.—I. A.   ** Probably 36° 59′ 8″.—I. A.

INDEX.

2 Y

2 Z

THE END.

LONDON:
PRINTED BY WILLIAM CLOWES AND SONS, STAMFORD STREET,
AND CHARING CROSS.

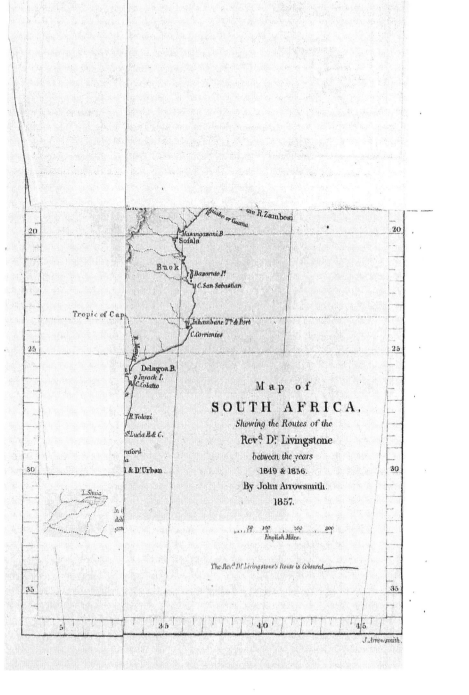

Map of

SOUTH AFRICA,

Showing the Routes of the

Rev.ᵈ Dr. Livingstone

between the years

1849 & 1856.

By John Arrowsmith.

1857.

English Miles.

The Rev.ᵈ Dr. Livingstone's Route is Coloured

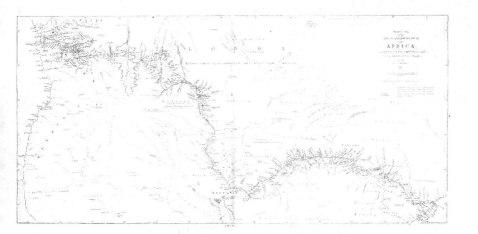

THE FAREWELL

LIVINGSTONE FESTIVAL.

THE festival in honour of Dr. Livingstone on his departure to explore the river Zambesi and the interior of South Africa, which originated in the Royal Geographical Society and was organized by the zeal of some members of that body at a few days' notice only, was held at the Freemasons' Tavern on the 13th February, 1858, Sir RODERICK MURCHISON in the Chair.

A wish having been expressed that a more ample account than appeared in the Daily Newspapers, should be preserved of the speeches made on that occasion, a record of them is now printed, to form a popular part of the Proceedings of the Royal Geographical Society; in order to mark the cordial spirit and right feeling with which the public were actuated in offering a farewell to the great and meritorious African Traveller.

It was intended to limit the number of his friends present to 250; but so great was the pressure for admission, that ample accommodation and good fare were provided for upwards of 350 persons, of whom a list is annexed so far as the names were inscribed.*

Their Excellencies the Ministers of Sweden and Norway and of Denmark; the Dukes of Argyll and *Wellington; the Earls of Shaftesbury, Grey, *Sheffield, and *Shelburne; Lords *Radstock and Ebury; the Bishops of *Oxford and *St. David's; the Honourables Captain J. *Denman, R.N.; A. *Kinnaird, M.P.; and E. B. Wrottesley; Count *Strzelecki; Sir B. *Brodie; Sir E. North *Buxton, M.P.; Sir J. *Clark; Sir Culling *Eardley; Sir William Fraser, M.P.; Sir Ralph *Howard and Sir Moreton *Peto, M.P.; Sir John Forbes; Sir Charles *Nicholson; Sir John *Rennie; Rear-Admirals H. Austin, Sir G. *Back, and H. D. *Trotter; Major-Generals Murray, Hay, and J. E. *Portlock, R.E.; Messrs. W. E. Baxter, M.P.; W. Buchanan, M.P.; A. M. Dunlop, M.P.; J. Kershaw, M.P.; W. S. *Lindsay, M.P.; E. Miall, M.P.; J. *Pilkington, M.P.; J. Richardson, M.P.; J. Slaney, M.P.; Colonel W. H. *Sykes, M.P.; and J. A. *Warre, M.P.; Aldermen Exall, Finnis, and Wire; Baron de *Forrester; Chevalier de *Forrester; Colonel Burgwyn (U.S.); Captains A. B. *Becher,

---

* Each name of a member of the Royal Geographical Society has a star affixed to it.

B

R. *Collinson, W. H. *Hall, and M. S. *Nolloth; Commanders * Bedingfeld
and Dayman, Royal Navy; Consuls Alcock, G. *Brand, and C. H.
*Dickson; Major Ditmas; Captains Burgess, and L. T. *Cave; Lieutenant
P. A. *Halkett, R.N.; and V. Zaroudny of the Imperial Russian Navy; the
Reverends W. Cardall, A. Church, D. S. *Halkett, J. Hill, J. Hutchinson,
C. Livingstone; T. *Marziot, W. Mitchell, J. F. Ogle of Patagonia, and
C. S. Stewart (U.S.); Doctors Aikin, Cape, Cooke, Copland, Diamond,
Gladstone, Hall, Hull, Bence Jones, J. *Kirk, E. Lankester, Waller Lewis,
David Livingstone, J. O. M'William, Charles Murchison, W. F. *Packman,
J. Percy, Lyon Playfair, C.B., Pointer, Price, William Sharpey, H. Norton
*Shaw, F. Sibson, W. Smith, J. Trounser, and G. *Webster; Professors
Bentley, Huxley, Maskelyne, R. Owen, Ramsay, Warington Smyth, and
J. *Tennant; Messrs. Henry Ancell, S. H. Angier, George A. Arbuthnot,
John *Arrowsmith, J. K. Aston, T. W. Aveline, T. *Baines, S. W. Baker,
Charles Barry, James *Bateman, J. D. Barry (Cape of Good Hope), Joshua
*Bates, J. *Betts, A. F. *Birch, J. W. *Birch, J. G. Blake, Wollaston *Blake,
H. G. *Bohn, F. W. Bond, J. Boord, G. T. Bosanquet, H. W. Bristow,
W. J. Brodribb, G. T. *Brooking, T. H. *Brooking, John *Brown, J. Brown,
W. J. Browne, H. *Browning, C. Capper, L. P. *Casella, S. *Cave, D. Chambers,
J. W. *Childers, C. Churchill, G. *Clowes, W. J. Cockerell, E. *Coghlan
H. W. Cole, R. *Cooke, Corscadden, Norman *Cowley, W. W. Crispin,
Croggon, W. F. *Cumming, J. *Cunningham, Deorman, C. Wentworth
*Dilke, H. *Donkin; T. Donkin, E. R. Dorrell, E. W. Dundas, J. Earle,
Edmonstone, W. Ewer, P. Fenton, A. *Findlay, A. G. *Findlay, F. Fitch,
A. P. Fletcher, C. *Fraser, J. P. Gassiot, J. Gayton, G. Gladstone, A. *Gordon,
J. *Gould, G. P. Green, W. N. Green, T. *Greene, J. Griffin, W. D. Griffith,
C. L. *Gruneisen, G. Hall, S. C. Hall, W. J. *Hamilton, J. Hammond, G. F.
*Harris, W. Helps, E. *Heneage, R. Hepburn, F. Hicks, T. Hicks, A. Hill,
J. Hill, P. Hill, Hind, J. Holmes, L. Hope, Hornblower, B. Hornby,
J. Hornby, H. H. Howell, J. W. Hulke, E. Hull, G. O. Irwin, T. Ivens,
J. James, W. P. Jervis, G. Johnstone, W. W. Kilpin, E. B. *Lawrence,
W. Laird, Macgregor *Laird, F. Leach, F. *Le Breton, P. Lecki, M. Lethem,
T. *Lee, T.*Letts, Ch. Lewell (of Finland), Leyland, W. *Lockhart (of China),
G. A. *Lloyd, W. Lovecroft, L. Lucas, E. M'Dermott, D. *M'Gregor, R. J.
Macintosh, P. *Macintyre, A. Macmillan, C. Makins, J. Marshall, Mont-
gomery *Martin, F. Marziot, A. Miall, D. W. Mitchell, F. D. *Mocatta, J. C.
Moore, C. E. Mudie, J. *Murray, R. W. Mylne, E. B. Neil, G. *Nelthropp,
H. *Nesbitt, G. Newman, D. Owen, W. *Phelps, J. S. Pigeon, J. Piggott, J. H.
*Plowes, F. L. *Price, W. C. Prince, E. J. *Ravenshawe, R. Rawlinson,
Trenham Reeks, J. *Reid, J. Reive, J. S. Renton, J. *Reynolds, G. T. Rose,
A. Rowlandson, A. Sim, H. S. Skeats, R. Slater, E. Osborne *Smith, F.
Smith, J. Sidney Smith, G. *Smith, R. Smith, T. Spalding, T. *Staveley,
W. C. *Street, A. Stuart, H. Sturt, A. *Swanzy, W. *Tait, J. Taylor, R.
Thornton, G. Tolstoy (of St. Petersburgh), W. *Trotter, E. O. and H. *Tudor,
A. *Vardon, Ch. *Verrey, G. Waugh; J. C. Webster, R. J. *Wheeler,
Charles *White, H. *White, John White, W. Foster *White, J. H. Wicht
(Cape of Good Hope), T. Wilcocks, C. Wilshire, W. H. Wilde, E. W. Wyon,
J. *Yeats; C. Baring *Young, and C. J. Young, Esqrs.

The gallery was filled with ladies, among whom were the Countess Grey and Miss Copley, the Countess of Carnarvon, Mrs. Ashley Warre, Miss Burdett Coutts and Mrs. Brown, Lady Back, Lady Franklin, Mrs. Baines, Miss Cracroft, Mrs. Dundas, Mrs. Gordon, Mrs. Greene, Mrs. Portlock, Mrs. and Miss Wrottesley, Mrs. Owen, Mrs. Twyford, Mrs. Livingstone, &c.

Each Toast was given with all the honours, and the band of the Grenadier Guards played suitable and chiefly Scottish airs.

The Duke of Sutherland also sent his Highland Piper to enliven the festival in honour of a countryman.

Grace was said before dinner by the Bishop of St. David's, and after dinner by the Bishop of Oxford.

The Toasts and Speeches were as follows:—

SIR RODERICK MURCHISON.—As a loyal subject of Her Majesty, I rise to propose the health of our beloved Sovereign. (*Loud cheers.*)

Reigning over many a distant land, and engaging as She does the affection and devotion of all her subjects, whether in the remotest of her Colonies or in these Islands, our gracious Queen has, through the wide spread beneficence of her rule, gained a *new title*, which must, I am sure, be most dear to her heart, and which specially connects Her Majesty with the object of this meeting; for Livingstone has told us that Victoria is known throughout the now protected races of South Africa, as the Queen of the people who love the Black Man. (*Loud cheers.*)

And as a striking proof of Her Majesty's desire to extend the blessings of Religion, Civilization, and Commerce to the great interior of South Africa, She has appointed our dear friend to be her Consul at those Portuguese Settlements from which he can successfully and efficiently carry out his noble mission. (*Great cheering.*)

Let me now add, Gentlemen, a piece of information which in these days of rapid diffusion of intelligence is unknown to you;—nay even to the great Journal of Printing House Square, and which will, I know, give unbounded pleasure to you all. Her Majesty, with that good taste and right feeling which is peculiarly her own, and which has ever characterized her private as well as public conduct, has selected this very day of our farewell festival to grant an interview to Livingstone and kindly to wish him God speed!

"The Queen, God bless her."
(*Enthusiastic cheers.*)

SIR R. MURCHISON.—Gentlemen, I now call on you to drink to the health of " H.R.H. the Prince Consort, H.R.H. the Prince of Wales, and the other members of the Royal Family." (*Cheers.*)

Whenever it has been my lot to occupy the Chair at a public meeting, I have invariably spoken of the Royal Consort as a Prince who, loving and encouraging science, letters, and art, is continually striving to do practical good service, by diffusing education and knowledge through all classes of the community. (*Cheers.*)

And as teaching by example is more efficacious than a thousand precepts, we are grateful to him for having soon after Livingstone's arrival in England conversed for some time with our great traveller in the presence of the younger members of the Royal Family; and specially we applaud his conduct for so guiding the education of his children, that in addition to the instruction usually given to Royal personages, the Prince of Wales and his brother have been taught by Faraday (*loud cheers*) and others, those great truths of Science upon the cultivation and diffusion of which, the present and future grandeur of the British Empire mainly depends. Let us then cordially drink to the health of His Royal Highness the Prince Consort, the Prince of Wales, and the other members of the Royal Family.

(*Loud cheers.*)

SIR R. MURCHISON.—It gives me true satisfaction, Gentlemen, to see that the object of our meeting is supported by the Representatives of two Foreign Sovereigns who have just reached our shores, who come from northern countries which are connected with us by many natural ties, and to whose rulers and people I am bound in affection for kindnesses received during my explorations of Scandinavia.

I allude to their Excellencies the Minister of the King of Sweden and Norway, Count Platen; and the Minister of the King of Denmark, Admiral Van Dockum. (*Loud cheering.*)

The representative of another Sovereign, who by his acts has shown his hearty concurrence in this exploration of South Africa, is unfortunately prevented by illness from attending; but that nobleman, the Count de Lavradio, with the enlarged views and right feeling which characterize the representative of the enlightened King of Portugal, has thus written to me:—

" I should have been happy to have profited by this good opportunity to announce personally to the distinguished friends of Dr. Livingstone, that my august Sovereign no sooner learnt that Dr.

Livingstone intended to explore the Zambesi than he issued the most positive orders to the authorities of Portuguese Africa to offer to the learned and courageous traveller all the protection and all the aid which he might need, and to receive him with all the attention due to his great merits.

"Be assured, my dear Sir Roderick," his Excellency adds, "that my Sovereign, as enlightened as he is virtuous ['We all know the merits of the young King,' interposed the Chairman (*loud cheers*)], rejoices whenever it is in his power to do anything to advance civilization and to afford some proof of his unalterable affection for his most ancient, most constant, and most natural ally, Great Britain." (*Loud cheers.*)

"I have full confidence," continued the Count, "that the new explorations of Livingstone will have great results for science, commerce, and the civilization of Africa. The infamous slave trade can never be brought to an end without first putting a stop to slavery in the interior of Africa, which will be the more easily brought about when the unfortunate Africans are instructed in the principles of religion and education, and are taught the true value of labour.

"I offer then my most ardent hopes for the prosperous journey of Livingstone and for the success of his researches, trusting that he may return safe, sound, and glorious, to receive the blessings of his countrymen and those of the enlightened men of all countries." (*Loud cheers.*)

Reverting now, Gentlemen, to the toast, "The Ministers of Foreign Powers who have honoured us by their presence," I drink to the health of our distinguished visitors Count Platen and Admiral Van Dockum. (*Great cheering.*)

COUNT PLATEN, in responding to the toast, said that he should ever take a deep interest in any enterprise which affected the prosperity of Great Britain, not only on account of the mutual relations which existed between England and that country of which he was the representative, but also from personal feeling; for perhaps the three happiest years of his life had been spent, if not upon English ground, at least upon English bottom, he having served three years in the British navy. (*Loud cheers.*) He could only add that, in common, he was sure, with all those to whom the toast referred, he most cordially concurred in the great objects of the expedition of their distinguished friend Dr. Livingstone, and, in the name of his colleague and himself, he most heartily wished him complete success, and a safe return to his native land. (*Loud cheers.*)

SIR R. MURCHISON.—On, no, former occasion did I ever propose the toast of the Navy and Army with a higher satisfaction than at the present moment; for never at any period of my life was I more proud of the heroism of my countrymen, whose noble bearing in India not only excites the heartfelt applause of every Englishman, but is, I know, extolled by foreign nations as a prowess scarcely if ever paralleled in the annals of war. (*Loud cheers.*)

And though the men of my old profession, the soldiers, have necessarily had to bear the brunt of this great spasmodic and unexampled Indian outburst, we all know how an intrepid band of blue jackets under William Peel have mainly contributed to the winning of victories a thousand miles distant from that element in which they are supreme, and will I trust for ever remain so. (*Loud cheering.*)

Gentlemen, in alluding to the Army let me say, that I cannot now wear a Peninsular medal, and recollect that I am one of those still surviving who had the honour to accompany our great Duke when he first set his foot on the shore of Portugal, without expressing to you the sincere gratification it gives me to see here, and sitting by the side of Livingstone, the son of that illustrious man (*great cheering*). My regard for the present Duke has indeed been recently raised into high respect, by knowing that it is the anxious study of my noble friend to search out and publish documents which, but for the devotedness of the son, might have lain long in obscurity—documents which now issuing from the press demonstrate, that the young Wellesley, the rising soldier of India, possessed even then much of the thoughtfulness, prescience, and wisdom which characterized the future Wellington. (*Loud cheers.*)

It would naturally be my wish to call upon the son of my revered commander to answer for the Army; but I have not forgotten military duty, and a senior officer is present—one, fortunately, who is directly and honourably connected with this festival; for it was General Murray Hay, who, commanding in the Mauritius, received Livingstone when he emerged from the east coast of Africa, and was the first of our countrymen who hospitably sheltered the houseless traveller. (*Loud cheers.*)

In like manner it gives me real pleasure to perceive that the Navy is represented by my gallant and good friend Admiral Trotter, whose name and exploits are interwoven with the cause of the civilization of Africa (*cheers*), and who, when recently on duty at the Cape Station, was most serviceable in enabling us to keep up our intercourse with the great traveller in the interior of Africa. (*Cheers.*)

I give you then the Navy and Army, and call on you to drink to the health of Admiral Trotter and General Murray Hay. (*Loud cheers.*)

REAR-ADMIRAL TROTTER.—I rise to return thanks for the Navy on the present occasion with peculiar pleasure, as I claim for our service the honour of having most powerfully operated in the same cause with our distinguished guest—I mean the civilization of Africa; and I believe Dr. Livingstone has lost no opportunity of proclaiming in his addresses, though that part of them to which I allude has not always been faithfully reported, that all hope of success in that great object over that vast continent depends, humanly speaking, on the extinction of the slave trade, and that the most powerful and indispensable means to this end is the British squadron on the coast of Africa: our efforts in this cause, in conjunction with the exertions of such men as Livingstone, will hereafter be classed amongst the noblest deeds of the Navy.—It is therefore, I say, with especial pleasure that I return thanks on the present occasion. (*Cheers.*)

MAJOR-GEN. MURRAY HAY.—Being the senior military officer present, it is my duty, Sir, to respond to the toast you have proposed, and the great and immortal man so justly eulogized by you, has taught us that to a soldier duty is a sacred word.

Distant employment prevented me from sharing personally the brilliant services of the army of the Crimea, but it is to me a great consolation to think that I was thereby enabled to form, I trust, a lasting friendship with our distinguished guest, Dr. Livingstone. On his arrival at Mauritius, I received him as a comrade from a hard fought and gallantly won battle ; for he too is a soldier, a soldier of the Cross. (*Cheers.*) The unanimous voice of this great nation has proclaimed, loudly proclaimed, that the British Army has gloriously upheld the renown of its predecessors and of its country, and that Army has received the reward dearest to the heart of a soldier in the applause and approbation of our gracious Queen and the thanks of a grateful country. (*Loud cheers.*)

SIR R. MURCHISON.—I rise, Gentlemen, to propose the toast of the evening—" Health to the excellent man who sits on my right hand, and success to his expedition." (*Vehement and long continued applause.*) When this farewell dinner to my distinguished friend was suggested ten days ago only, by a few ardent geographers, with a request that I would take the Chair, it might well have been supposed that in so brief a space of time it would be difficult to obtain an attendance worthy of the great occasion ; but I felt assured that the name of Livingstone alone would attract an assembly larger than any room in London could contain. (*Cheers.*) My anticipation, Gentlemen, was correct ; and it truly gratifies me to see that this impromptu " coup de voyageur " has brought together men of real distinction in all the great classes of the British public. (*Cheers.*) The only weak part of the programme, I said to my friends, would be that of your Chairman (*cries of " No, no "*) ; but at all events, you know, Gentlemen, that my geographical friends and myself have done our best to honour the great traveller and good missionary. (*Cheers.*)

At any public meeting held a year and a half ago, it would have been necessary to dwell upon the merits of Livingstone ; but now his name has become a household word among my countrymen, and no efforts of mine can raise him higher in that esteem which he has won for himself, and specially I rejoice to say by the sale of 30,000 copies of the work issued by the flourishing firm of Murray, Livingstone, and Co. (*laughter*), and by which he has secured independence for himself, and a provision for his wife and family. (*Cheers.*)

My eminent friend has not only made us thoroughly well acquainted with the character and disposition of the inhabitants and the nature of the animals and plants of the interior of Africa, but has realized that which no missionary has ever accomplished before ; since with consummate talent, perseverance, and labour he has laid down the longitude as well as latitude of places hitherto unknown to us, and has enriched every department of knowledge by his valuable and original discoveries. These are great claims upon the admiration of men of science ; but, great as they are, they fall far short of others which attach to the name of the missionary who, by his fidelity to his word, by his conscientious regard for his engagements, won the affections of the natives of Africa by the example which he set before them in his treatment of the poor people who followed him in his arduous researches through that great continent. (*Loud cheers.*)

Sitting by my side (laying his hand on Dr. Livingstone's shoulder) is the man who, knowing what he had to encounter—who having twenty or thirty times struggled with the fever of Africa—who, knowing when he reached the western coast, at St. Paul de Laonda, that a ship was ready to carry him to his native land, where his wife and children were anxiously awaiting his arrival, true to his plighted word, threw these considerations, which would have influenced an ordinary man, to the winds, and reconducted those poor natives who had accompanied him through the heart of the country back to their homes!—thus by his noble and courageous conduct leaving for himself in that country a glorious name, and proving to the people of Africa what an English Christian is. (*Loud and long continued cheering.*)

So much for the character of the man of whom, as a Scotchman, I am justly proud; and now a few words with regard to his present expedition, of which I may say that no enterprise could have been better organized than it has been, under the recommendation of my distinguished friend, aided by the countenance and hearty co-operation of Lord Clarendon, and the very judicious arrangements of Captain Washington, the Hydrographer of the Admiralty, on whom fortunately has fallen the chief labour of its organization. (*Loud cheers.*) The naval officer of the expedition is Commander Bedingfeld, a man well known to geographers for his successful explorations of the coast and rivers of Western Africa, especially the Congo, and my dear friend will no doubt receive substantial assistance from that gallant officer. (*Cheers.*) Dr. Kirk, of Edinburgh, an accomplished botanist, zoologist, and physiologist, also accompanies the expedition; whilst my clever young friend Richard Thornton will, I doubt not, do good service as the mining geologist. (*Cheers.*) Mr. Baines, too, whose previous travels in Africa and North Australia and striking sketches are well known to the public, will be there; and last but not least in usefulness among the members of the expedition let me mention Mrs. Livingstone. (*Loud and long continued cheering.*)

When I remember the efforts which have been made in the cause of Christianity and for the diffusion of knowledge by that exemplary lady (*loud cheers*), when I know how she, the daughter of that faithful missionary, the venerable Moffat, has educated her children, and when I see the spirit with which she is again going to cross the broad seas and to share all the toils and perils of her husband, I cannot but think that the services of Mrs. Livingstone (acquainted as she is with many of the languages of South Africa) will tend materially to the success of the expedition. (*Loud and protracted cheering.*)

But, Gentlemen, I would not, however, wish you to raise your hopes too high as to the immediate results of this expedition, which is in truth one of an exploratory character only. It is, in fact, merely the sowing of the seed which, under God's Providence, may produce an abundant harvest. We must not look to a sudden importation of indigo or of cotton, and those raw materials which

we manufacture in this country, nor must we expect suddenly to
light upon a new El Dorado; though I believe that my friend
may find districts which abound in gold and copper, and good thick
coal-seams.

Yet if, after all, those expectations to which the commercial world
looks should fail—if we gain nothing more than the implanting in
Africa of that good name which Dr. Livingstone is sure to leave
(*cheers*), and that accession to our knowledge which the discoveries
of our great explorer are certain to supply, and which it would be a
disgrace to Britain not to endeavour to obtain, even then I say that
the Livingstone expedition will have a great and a glorious issue.
(*Loud and long continued cheering.*) I propose, therefore, the health of
our eminent friend Dr. Livingstone, and success to his noble enterprise. (The toast was drunk with the utmost enthusiasm; and
after the cheering had ceased, at the suggestion of a gentleman in
the body of the room, three more hearty cheers were given for Mrs.
Livingstone.)

The name of Sekeletu, chief of Livingstone's Makololo friends,
was announced at the bottom of the room, and a cheer was claimed
for him.

DR. LIVINGSTONE, in rising to return thanks, showed unmistakeably
how much he was affected by the reception which he had met
with.

He said,—When I was in Africa I could not but look forward
with joyous anticipation to my arrival in my native land; but when
I remember how I have been received, and when I reflect that I am
now again returning to the scene of my former labours, I am at a
loss how to express in words the feelings of my heart. (*Loud cheers.*)
In former times, while I was performing what I considered to be
my duty in Africa, I felt great pleasure in the work; and now,
when I perceive that all eyes are directed to my future conduct, I
feel as if I were laid under a load of obligation to do better than I
have ever done as yet. (*Loud cheers.*) I expect to find for myself no
large fortune in that country (*renewed cheers*), nor do I expect to
explore any large portions of a new country; but I do hope to find
in that part of the country which I have partially explored, a pathway by means of the river Zambesi which may lead to highlands
where Europeans may form a healthful settlement, and where by
opening up communication and establishing commercial intercourse
with the natives of Africa they may slowly, but not the less surely,
impart to the people of that country the knowledge and the inesti-
mable blessings of Christianity. (*Loud cheers.*)

I am glad to have connected with me in this expedition my gallant friend Captain Bedingfeld (*hear, hear*), who knows not only what African rivers are, but also what are African fevers. (*A laugh.*) With his aid I may be able to determine the principles of the river system of that great continent; and if I find that system to be what I think it is, I propose to establish a depôt upon the Zambesi, and from that station more especially to examine into that river system, which, according to the statements of the natives, would afford a pathway to the country beyond, where cotton, indigo, and other raw material might be obtained to any amount.

I am happy also in being accompanied, as Sir Roderick has told you, by men experienced in geology, in botany, in art, and in photography, who will bring back to England, reports upon all those points, which I alone have attempted to deal with, and with very little means at my disposal. (*Loud cheers.*)

The success—if I may call it success—which has attended my former efforts (*renewed cheering*) to open up the country mainly depended upon my entering into the feelings and the wishes of the people of the interior of Africa. I found that the tribes in the interior of that country were just as anxious to have a path to the seaboard as I was to open a communication with the interior, and I am quite certain of obtaining the co-operation of those tribes in my next expedition. Should I succeed in my endeavour—should we be able to open a communication advantageous to ourselves with the natives of the interior of Africa, it would be our duty to confer upon them those great benefits of Christianity which have been bestowed upon ourselves. (*Cheers.*) Let us not make the same mistake in Africa that we have made in India (*renewed cheering*), but let us take to that country our Christianity with us. (*Cheers.*)

I confess that I am not sanguine enough to hope for any speedy result from this expedition, but I am sanguine as to its ultimate result. (*Cheers.*) I feel convinced that if we can establish a system of free labour in Africa, it will have a most decided influence upon slavery throughout the world. (*Loud cheers.*) Success, however, under Providence, depends upon us as Englishmen. I look upon Englishmen as perhaps the most freedom-loving people in the world, and I think that the kindly feeling which has been displayed towards me since my return to my native land has arisen from the belief that my efforts might at some future time tend to put an end to the odious traffic in slaves. (*Loud cheers.*) England has, unfortunately, been compelled to obtain cotton and other raw material from slave States (*cheers*), and has thus been the mainstay and support of slavery in America. Surely, then, it follows that if we can succeed in obtain-

ing the raw material from other sources than from the slave States
of America, we should strike a heavy blow at the system of slavery
itself.. (*Loud cheers.*)

I do not wish, any more than my friend Sir Roderick, to arouse
expectations in connexion with this expedition which may never be
realized, but what I want to do is to get in the thin end of the
wedge (*cheers*), and then leave it to be driven home by English
energy and English spirit. (*Loud cheers.*)

I cannot express to you in adequate language the sense which I
entertain of the kindness which I have received since my return to
this country, but I can assure you that I shall ever retain a grateful
recollection of the way you have received me on the eve of my
departure from my native land. (*Cheers.*)

Reference has been made in language most kind to Mrs. Livingstone. (*Cheers.*) Now, it is scarcely fair to ask a man to praise his
own wife (*laughter*), but I can only say that when I left her at the
Cape, telling her that I should return in two years, and when it
happened that I was absent four years and a half, I supposed that I
should appear before her with a damaged character. (*Laughter.*)
I was, however, forgiven. (*Laughter and cheering.*) My wife, who
has always been the main spoke in my wheel, will accompany me
in this expedition, and will be most useful to me. She is familiar
with the languages of South Africa, she is able to work, she is
willing to endure, and she well knows that in that country one
must put one's hand to everything. In the country to which I am
about to proceed she knows that at the missionary's station the wife
must be the maid-of-all-work within, while the husband must be
the jack-of-all-trades without, and glad am I indeed that I am to be
accompanied by my guardian angel. (*Loud cheering.*) Allow me,
in conclusion, to say one word in reference to our excellent chairman. In packing up my things a few days ago, I found the identical Address which he delivered to the Geographical Society in
1852, and which he had the impudence to send out to me in the
heart of Africa, where it lay upon an island a whole year before I
got it. In that Address my distinguished friend actually fore-
shadowed a great portion of my discoveries; and all I can now
say is, that I hope he will not do the same again. (*Laughter and
long continued applause.*)

The company then gave "Three times three for Mrs. Livingstone,"
and that lady, from the gallery, bowed in acknowledgment of the
compliment.

SIR R. MURCHISON.—I now call on my scientific friends and others to drink to the toast of " The Legislature which supplied the means, and the Government which prepared the measures, to carry out the Livingstone Expedition." (*Applause.*)

It was indeed most cheering to all geographers and philanthropists to witness the cordial spirit with which the House of Commons granted the sum asked for to promote the Livingstone Expedition— a sum, however, which after all I consider somewhat inadequate to the great object in view (*hear, hear*), but which, in unison with the wishes of the public, the Parliament will, I am confident, augment when needful. (*Cheers.*)

As to the acts of the Government I can truly say, that having had opportunities of observing and scrutinising them, including the warm sympathy and aid of Lord Palmerston and his associates, I cannot too highly commend their conduct. Lord Clarendon in particular took the most lively interest in promoting the welfare of Livingstone long before the traveller came home, by sending out orders to succour the unaided Missionary; and he has since zealously and sincerely laboured to promote by every means in his power the present expedition, and has also counselled Her Majesty to give to our friend that public appointment which will enable him to be really useful; it having been a principle with the noble Earl to lose no opportunity of raising the position of the poor African, and of rendering him the cultivator of substances of which Britain has need. (*Cheers.*)

In proposing this toast of the Legislature and Her Majesty's Government, I call upon the Duke of Argyll to speak for the Upper House of Parliament and the Government, and Mr. Baxter for the House of Commons; and if the band will only play " The Campbells are coming," we who know the powers of the Noble Duke are certain that a good speech will follow. (*Loud cheers.*)

The DUKE of ARGYLL.—I deem it a great honour, Gentlemen, to any Government and to any Parliament to be able to assist in that noble enterprise to which Dr. Livingstone has devoted his best energies, and to which he is now willing to devote his life. Perhaps no enterprise of modern times has attracted so large an amount of public attention; and this because it includes within itself almost every variety and degree of interest. First and foremost there is the interest which attaches to the character of the man; and it is right, Gentlemen, that this should be the first and foremost interest of all. The progress of the world depends upon its great men; and happy is that people which knows them when they appear. (*Cheers.*)

Dr. Livingstone has to-night told us, with that moderation and sobriety of expectation which is one of the most remarkable characteristics of his mind, that he looks for no great immediate results; but he hopes, he says, to be able to serve as the " small end of the wedge." Now, Gentlemen, I say that at all times and in all successful movements for the improvement of the human race, " the small ends of the wedge " have been individual men of great endowments for their special work. (Loud cheers.)

I will not dwell on some of those features in the character of Dr. Livingstone which have been referred to with so much feeling by our Chairman; but I think I cannot go far wrong when I say that one thing at least for which he is admired by his countrymen is for that lofty and enduring courage—that true British pluck—for there is no better word—of which we have lately seen many noble examples, but which has never been exhibited in a nobler form than that which—not under the strong incitement of a desire to preserve the lives of those nearest and dearest to him, or of the pride, the just pride of national dominion, but for objects hid in the far distant future—has sustained Dr. Livingstone for years through the deserts and the swamps of Africa. Then, as another great source of public interest, there is the love of natural science. I recognise around me the faces of many who are devoted to that science in its various branches: nor is there one of them who may not reasonably expect material additions to his knowledge from the researches of our guest. Dr. Livingstone has told us how our Chairman, in two great branches of inquiry in which he is almost equally distinguished, had in some degree anticipated and forestalled the result of his (Dr. Livingstone's) discoveries; and sharing as I am sure our Chairman does in the higher interests of this expedition, he cherishes also, I suspect, a secret hope that it may add another province to the already extended dominions of the Silurian king. (Laughter.) I see at this table my distinguished friend Professor Owen. He also, Gentlemen, is well able—no man more able—to appreciate the " higher ends " of our guest's exertions; but mingled with his interest in these, he too perhaps has an eye open to special pursuits—and to bones which may extend the range of his favourite " homologies." (Laughter.)

But the real source, Gentlemen, of the interest taken by the public in the enterprise of Dr. Livingstone, is the deep and abiding interest which they take in that great cause with which it is specially connected—that great cause to which their attention was roused in the last generation by the eloquence of Wilberforce and his associates— the cause of the African race. (Cheers.) I have been astonished during this last week to receive from America a Journal containing the report of a discussion which has lately taken place in the Senate of that great Republic, in which it was asserted that there were evident symptoms of a change of feeling upon this subject in England. And I was even more surprised to see the reply made to that assertion by another member of the same body, which was to the effect that he did not believe there was any change on the part of the people of this country, although he feared there was a change of policy on the part of its Government. Now, Gentlemen, there is nothing I am more anxious to say on this occasion than to give an emphatic denial to both assertions. (*Cheers.*) There is no change in the feeling of the people—as little is there any change in the policy of the Government. I need hardly say that as regards slavery, in America the Government of this country neither has, nor can have, any policy at all. There can be no doubt that any public or official interference on our part upon that subject would only tend to add to the many powerful motives already arrayed on the side of slavery, the just susceptibilities of national independence. But as regards the policy of the Government with reference to the Slave-trade, and generally towards the African race, it is the same as it has ever been since this country was awakened to her duty. I think I could appeal to the keenest opponent of Lord Palmerston whether, during his long and distinguished public career, there has been any subject on which he has shown more constantly his characteristic energy and tenacity of purpose. (*Cheers.*) I can sincerely say that the great motive which has induced him and my noble friend Lord Clarendon, and the other Members of the Government, to support the enterprise of Dr. Livingstone, has been the hope that it may tend to promote the civilization and improvement of the people of Africa. (*Loud applause.*)

Before I sit down, Gentlemen, I trust I may be allowed to refer for a moment to a matter which has been touched upon by our Chairman. I am proud of Dr. Livingstone not only as a Scotchman, but as a native of that part of the country with which I am more particularly connected. Dr. Livingstone has himself informed me that at a very recent period his family came from the little Island of Ulva, on the coast of Argyllshire, an island belonging to what Sir Walter Scott has called

> " the group of islets gay
> That guard famed Staffa round."

And I deem it, Gentlemen, a circumstance not altogether unworthy of remark, that Ulva stands in very close proximity to another island which was one of the earliest seats of Missionary enterprise in our own country. Most of you will probably recollect the famous sentence in which the great moralist and philosopher of England, Dr. Johnson, records his visit to that celebrated spot. I think I can remember it with substantial accuracy. " We were now treading that illustrious island whence roving tribes and rude barbarians derived the benefits of knowledge and the blessings of religion. The philosophy of that man is but little to be envied whose patriotism would not kindle on the plains of Marathon, or whose piety would not grow warmer among the ruins of Iona." If such be the feelings with which we should tread upon the spot which at the distance of so many centuries has been hallowed by the footsteps of the Christian Missionary, surely it is with something of the same feelings of reverence with which we should assemble here to-night, to bid God-speed to one whose name will be remembered in after ages, and perhaps by millions of the human race, as the first pioneer of civilization and the first harbinger of the Gospel. (*Loud and long-continued cheers.*)

MR. BAXTER, M.P., in responding for the House of Commons, said that he regretted that the duty had been committed to so feeble hands as his. He believed that this honour had been conferred on him as the representative on this auspicious occasion of that Scotland which had given birth to, and which was so justly proud of, Dr. Livingstone. He only wished that his excellent friend had been present to hear the general and repeated cheers which in December last greeted the Chancellor of the Exchequer's proposal that a sum of money should be advanced for the purposes of a new expedition. As for the Government and the House of Commons, they had only done what it was their duty to do, and what the country demanded of them, and he hoped that the 5000*l.* grant would prove but the earnest and foretaste of what this nation would yet do for the cause of discovery and colonization in Africa.

SIR BENJAMIN BRODIE.—I shall not occupy your time, Gentlemen, for more than a few minutes before I name the toast which I have undertaken to propose.

We recognize in Dr. Livingstone the intrepid and enterprising traveller, exploring regions which, in great part at least, had not been before explored by Europeans, contributing to the general stock an abundance of valuable information in geography, in natural history, in geology; associating with races of mankind of whom we had little or no previous knowledge, conversing with them in their own language, familiarising himself with their habits, institutions, and modes of thought; and thus promoting the advancement of that most important of all the sciences, the science of human nature. (*Cheers.*)

Nor was Dr. Livingstone thus occupied, as in the case of ordinary travellers, for a few months or for one or two years, but for many successive years. During this long period he continued his researches with unabated zeal; without being appalled by danger, or disheartened by the privations to which he was subjected, or the difficulties which he had to encounter; not the least of these being, repeated and severe attacks of bodily illness. (*Cheers.*)

But Dr. Livingstone is also presented to us under another aspect, as a Christian missionary, using his endeavours to extend the advantages of civilization, not after the fashion of the Roman conquerors of Gaul and Britain, by transplanting, at the cost of rapine and bloodshed, the arts and sciences of an older and more civilised people into the conquered country, but by communicating knowledge, promoting education, and inculcating the principles of a religion which enjoins the exercise of kindness, charity, and justice, which tells us that we are to forgive our enemies, and do unto others as we would that they should do unto us.

There are others in Africa engaged in the same pursuits, who, however occupied with their duties as missionaries, have found leisure from time to time to transmit to Europe important information on other subjects, and to whom science is much indebted; and I have to propose to you as a toast—" The members of the Missionary Societies who by their Christian labours have so much enlarged our acquaintance with Africa and its inhabitants." (*Cheers.*)

LORD EBURY said he sincerely regretted that his noble friend Lord Shaftesbury, who had taken such a deep interest in the career of Dr. Livingstone, should have left the room; for he could with so much greater propriety have responded to the toast which had just been proposed. The moral of the evening, however, was, that England expected of all her sons not only that they should do their duty, but that they should do it under the most adverse circumstances, and he could not shrink from attempting to perform this task to the best of his ability. If ever there was an occasion upon which the Missionary Societies might indulge in some pardonable degree of exultation, it was the present. (*Cheers.*) If they desired to view a successful monument of their labours, they might in truth point to the extraordinary man who sits beside the Chairman, and to the multitude of preeminently

C

honoured names in art and science, and, above all, the great work of
Missionary enterprise, which thronged this hall. (*Cheers.*) Humanly
speaking, theirs had been the task of giving to Dr. Livingstone the
means of displaying those wonderful qualifications which have con-
centrated such unbounded interest in his proceedings, both past and
future. It was for the public of England now to do its part,—to give
free scope to this great genius in the double work of civilization and
evangelization. They must have seen how Dr. Livingstone had successfully encountered all the trials of adversity, fatigue, sickness,
weariness, hope deferred, peril of death. There yet remained one
more trial, to some the sorest of all, namely, that of comparative ease,
and the praise of all men. Believing, as the Missionary Society did,
that his faith in Christ is firmly fixed, they doubted not he would go
through this trial also without fail; but they would, he trusted, continue to offer up constant prayers for him in his new and dangerous
position, that the blessing of the Almighty might still accompany him.
For himself he would only add, that having had the privilege of pre-
siding at the great missionary meeting which welcomed Dr. Livingstone back to this country at the termination of his unparalleled
labours, and having witnessed the enthusiasm which then abounded,
it would ever be a subject of the most gratifying remembrance that
he had been permitted to take a prominent part upon this scarcely
less memorable occasion, and have had the very distinguished
honour, for such he must ever call it, of wishing this great messenger of Gospel civilization God-speed, on behalf of the Missionary
Societies of Great Britain. (*Applause.*)

The BISHOP of OXFORD.—Mr. Chairman, the toast which has been
committed to me is one as to the propriety of which all present
have already expressed their opinion; for once and once only to-
night there has been expressed a general dissent to an observation
of yours, and that observation was that you were not the fittest
person to fill that chair. (*Loud cheers.*)

In proposing, therefore, Gentlemen, to you the health of our
Chairman, I know that I have with me the universal concurrence of
all the members of this great gathering. (*Cheers.*) In truth, Sir, for
reasons which connect themselves immediately with our important
object to-night, you are the fittest man amongst us to occupy that
post. For you as a most distinguished geologist and geographer,
and as the head of the Royal Geographical Society, have done more
by far than any who have not carefully examined the whole matter

can conceive, both to support our enterprising friend Dr. Livingstone during his arduous undertakings, and finally to crown them with success. (*Cheers.*)

Gentlemen, I need but draw your attention for a single moment to the pregnant words in which Dr. Livingstone has dedicated his recent volume to our Chairman in order to convince you of this. Weigh well these words, "as a token of gratitude for the kind interest he has always taken in the author's pursuits and welfare;" and then remember the simple-hearted, truth-speaking writer from whose pen they flowed, and you will be more able to estimate what were really our Chairman's services in this great undertaking. (*Cheers.*)

Truly it does need the combination of different men and different faculties before any such vast undertaking as this can be achieved. There must be, first, the physical, the intellectual, the moral, and the spirtual faculties combined in one person, which are so eminently combined in Dr. Livingstone, before the actual agent in such explorations can be provided. But then beyond these personal qualifications he must have support from home; there must be the mere physical support, as I may call it, of money, means, ships, companions, goods for presents, and the like; and then, far beyond these, there must be that internal consciousness of possessing the sympathy of hearty, generous, trusting friends at home; that inward stirring of a true national life within the individual; the reflection within himself of the outcoming towards him of the strong national life at home which makes the poet, or the hero, or the great explorer. In how many times of trial, difficulty, and despondency does the stirring of this inward life again invigorate the far-off man in the midst of his lonely wanderings in the desert! (*Cheers.*)

But then the existence of this home remembrance must, in a great degree, depend on there being at home some few who are able and willing generously to keep alive the home remembrance of the absent man and an interest in his work. For at home all things are moving so fast that things out of sight are soon things out of mind. The world round us goes at such speed, its objects, its cares, its pleasures, its amusements, its entanglements, shift and vary with such rapid and endless permutation, that unless there be some "Sacred prophet" evermore at hand to sing to us of the absent, he passes out of remembrance; and this work for Dr. Livingstone was done by our Chairman: from the chair of the Geographical Society, amongst men of science, amongst statesmen, he kept alive the interest which was due to Livingstone and his work. And how well

c 2

qualified above other men he was to do this, the rest of that
dedication shows : for it embalms the really remarkable fact
already alluded to, that our Chairman by his mere scientific de-
ductions had arrived at the true hypothesis as to the physical conformation of the African Continent which Livingstone verified by
actual observation. And so, for these discoveries, there were combined the various necessary conditions—(*Cheers*)—the Geographical
Society, headed by its President, to solicit the Government to keep
alive the interest of the public, and so to support the enterprising
traveller. He, too, combined in himself rare faculties for his work
of stepping out, if I may so express it, as to African explorations the
first track of civilized feet on the dangerous and untrodden snows,
which at any moment might be found to have merely loosely covered
fathomless abysses. He had the physical strength needed for such
work. He had the capacity for understanding the greatness of his
enterprise, and, Gentlemen, I believe it to be full of the truest
greatness. (*Cheers.*)

You will not think that I speak too strongly when I say that
I believe we owe a debt of unparalleled magnitude to our dark
brethren dwelling in that great continent. For we, as a nation,
were of old the great founders and the great conductors of the
accursed slave-trade. Complete at last, thank God! but late as
well as complete, was our repentance, and all that we can do we are
bound to do to remedy the wrongs we have inflicted. And fearful
have they been. How humiliating is it to us in our talk of the
onward march of civilization, and of piercing with our discoveries
into the heart of African barbarism, to learn from Dr. Livingstone
that he can trace by the presence of vice, and crime, and rapine,
and distrust, and insecurity of property and life, the very limits of
the past intercourse of the black savages of Africa with the white
Christians of Europe! (*Cheers.*) For it was not only on the coast
line that deep injury was inflicted by that accursed trade ; but far
within that coast line, wherever the agents of that traffic penetrated,
there were contamination and destruction. And how can this evil
be undone? Much may be done by our naval squadron, and for
doing anything by any means I am convinced that its vigorous
maintenance is essential; but the best successes of that blockade
can only create the calm necessary for the working of other influences, and amongst the very first, if not actually as the very first,
of those influences I esteem the establishment of lawful commerce.
(*Cheers.*)

Now, this Livingstone had the grasp of mind to perceive; to
see that he should be most effectually opening the way for the

future evangelisation of Africa, if he first opened a path by which lawful Christian commerce could pass and repass into those hitherto separated regions. (*Cheers.*)

Well, but in addition to this he had many other faculties, which all made up together the combination necessary to qualify him to act as the true discoverer of Africa. For, besides what I have named already, he had a clear, shrewd, strong understanding, great simplicity, great power of mastering languages, great courage, great power of influencing others, great gentleness by which he won on their affections, and, above all, he had, to qualify him for his work, downright, straightforward, sterling British truth and honesty. (*Great cheering.*)

For supporting, then, this man as he has supported him, we owe, I think, all thanks and honour to our Chairman, and I call upon you to drink with all the honours long life and happiness to him. (*Loud applause.*)

SIR RODERICK MURCHISON.—In returning you, Gentlemen, my warmest thanks for the flattering reception you have given to my name, and your kind acknowledgment of my services, let me say that I cannot have heard the band play the last air (" The Bannocks of Barley Meal "), preceded as it has been by so many good old Scottish tunes, without my heart overflowing, and being very proud that, like my friend Livingstone, I also am a Scotchman! (*Cheers.*)

I see indeed with pleasure sitting not far from me another Scotchman, the late Lord Mayor, Alderman Finnis, and near him Alderman Wire, both of whom were foremost in the good cause of welcoming our great traveller on his return, and in conferring on him the proud distinction of the freedom of the City of London.

But I pass from the personal considerations with which, in terms of much higher praise than I deserve, the Bishop of Oxford has been pleased to speak of my efforts in science, to the grand theme of the day, which his Lordship has illustrated with such fervid eloquence, and, if possible, still more to connect that theme with the special object of our present happy meeting. I will therefore just add this one phrase. I have before adverted to the wondrous exploits of Livingstone as a geographical traveller, and also to his noble moral bearing as a missionary; but I have still to point out one of the brightest features in his character when I say, that notwithstanding eighteen months of laudation so justly bestowed on him by all classes of his countrymen, and after receiving all the honours which the universities and cities of our country could shower upon him, he is still the same honest, true-hearted David Livingstone as when he issued from the wilds of Africa. (*Loud and protracted cheering.*)

PROFESSOR OWEN.—I rise to express the pleasure with which I avail myself of the opportunity I am favoured with of publicly acknowledging the deep sense of the obligation which, in common with all men of science, and more especially the cultivators of natural history, I feel towards the distinguished traveller we have this day assembled to honour. (*Cheers.*)

During the long and painful journeyings by which the great geographical discoveries were made that place the name of LIVINGSTONE among the foremost in that science — though harassed by every difficulty, enfeebled by sickness and encompassed by dangers—in perils of swamps and waters, in perils of noxious and destructive beasts, or of crafty and hostile men—yet no phenomenon of nature, whether meteoric or living, appears to have escaped the clear glance and self-possessed cognition of the determined explorer. (*Loud cheers.*)

In regard to zoology, I must state that I never perused the work of any traveller from which I had to take, from the same number of pages, so many extracts of new and original notices of the living habits of rare animals, as from the volume of African travels of which Mr. Murray now announces the "Thirtieth Thousand." In this work the South African colonist and the entomologist are alike benefited by the most precise and authentic evidence yet obtained of the terrible tsetse-fly, and its fatal effects on the ox, horse, dog, and other animals indispensable to colonising progress. The scientific staff about to accompany Livingstone in his second exploration of the Zambesi will doubtless, aided by his experience, clear up all the mystery of this most extraordinary property attributed to an insect no bigger than the house-fly. In the same unpretending volume we find a rich store of new facts in natural history, told with the charm of direct transcript from nature, and with the raciness of original power, and that humour which is so often the concomitant of great and simple minds. In regard to the singular economy of the ants and termites, with what interest we read of the unhooking of the wings by the insect itself after the nuptial flight, when the bride, her one holiday-excursion ended, lays down her "limber fans" of glistening gauze, and betakes herself henceforth to the duties of domestic life,—of the untiring activity of the workers, under the scorching sun, which unwearied-ness the deep-thinking Traveller illustrates by comparison with the beating of the heart; perhaps unconscious of the profound physiological truth embodied in this comparison of insect movements with the involuntary or reflex muscular action in higher animals! How mysterious seems that power of most rapid diffusion of a subtle penetrating effluvium, which Livingstone notices as the defence of certain ants, with experimental determinations of distance and rate of progress of the emanation! (*Applause.*) The same faculty of exact inquiry is manifested in the experiments, which remind us of those of Hunter—born, like Livingstone, in the parish of Kilbride—by which our traveller determined the independent source of the fluid secretion of the tree-insect, from which it dripped in such extraordinary quantity, both whilst attached to the twig and when insulated from its sap-vessels. The ornithologist has wondered at the seeming monstrous beaks of the hornbills, little dreaming of that strange economy manifested in the voluntary imprisonment of the incubating female, plastered up with her nest in the cleft of a tree, a fissure, only being left through which she can protrude the tip of her long bill to receive food from her attendant mate, and he, reciprocally, poke his into the procreative prison to tempt her with some dainty. (*Applause.*)

Of the ostrich much has been written; yet we wanted Livingstone's testimony of the vocal power of the wild male, roaring like the lion, and only, as our traveller tells us, distinguishable by being heard in broad day instead of by night. (*Continued applause.*) Of the king of beasts himself the volume contains the richest storehouse of facts, from direct and varied observations of him, in his native wilderness.

Perhaps, however, this is the part of our friend's book that has failed to give unmixed satisfaction to the British public. We dislike to have our settled notions disturbed by provokingly unvarnished, uncompromising assertions of facts that militate against a cherished prepossession. Some of us feel rather sore at our notions of the majesty of England's old emblematic beast being upset by the sum of our guest's opportunities of intimate acquaintance with the natural disposition and habits of the lion of South Africa. (*Laughter.*) Fearfully intimate, indeed, was part of his experience! That direful grip—which since has left one arm a dangling appendage—when the dishevelled mane of the irate monster was tossed about his victim's head, and the hot breath driven with deafening roar into his ear!—did it shake all respect for the traditional nobility of the lion out of the Doctor's mind? Certain it is, the sum of his recorded observations shows the lion to be a slothful, skulking, cruel beast of prey,—by no means the psychical compound we have delighted to associate with our national emblem. (*Laughter.*) Perhaps, however, I have a word of comfort for those who would still glorify its type. Species differ in habits. The British lion is not a mere heraldic monster, but was once a grim flesh-and-blood reality. I have had the satisfaction of determining that the *Felis spelæa* of our Yorkshire, Somersetshire, and Devonshire bone-caves was a veritable lion, surpassing in bulk, and with paws of twice the relative size, of those of the largest living lion of North or South Africa. The old British species has passed away— at least he now only shakes his mane and roars in metaphor (*continued laughter*); but the extinct antetype may have possessed all the qualities which his most ardent admirer would have ascribed to him. (*Cheers.*)

It is hard for the naturalist, when on his favourite topic, to forbear gleaning from Livingstone's full and rich storehouse of facts about buffaloes, rhinoceroses, elephants, and so forth. But the hour reminds me that time has fled apace—quickly because so pleasantly.

Our excellent Chairman has pointedly adverted to one quality in Livingstone—his inflexible adherence to his word. (*Cheers.*) It is shown in small as well as great things. When, eighteen years ago, the young missionary was preparing himself for his task, he devoted part of his short leisure in London to studying the series of comparative anatomy in the Hunterian Museum, then under my charge. On taking leave of me he promised to bear me in mind if any particular curiosity fell in his way. Such an one did in the course of his Zambesi travels—the tusk of an elephant with a spiral curve. It was a heavy one; and you may recall the difficulties of the progress of the weak, sick traveller, on the bullock's back. Every pound weight was of moment; but Livingstone said, "Owen shall have this tusk," and he placed it in my hands in London. (*Loud cheers.*)

In the perusal of the Missionary's Travels it is impossible not to infer the previous training of a strong and original mind richly and variously stored; not otherwise could science have been enriched by such precious records of wanderings in a previously untrod field of discovery. Our honoured guest may feel assured that whilst the cultivators of science yield to no class of minds in their appreciation and reverence of his dauntless dissemination of that higher wisdom which is not of this world, such feelings enhance their sense of obligation for his co-operation in the advancement of that lower wisdom which our great poet defines as " resting in the contemplation of natural causes and dimensions." (*Applause.*)

Every man to whom it has been given to add to human knowledge looks back with grateful feelings to the school or college where he acquired his elements of the sciences. With the same feeling that Livingstone may recall the old lecture-halls at Glasgow; so do I those of Edinburgh. We may both rejoice that the natural sciences have always had so large a share of the teachings in those Universities. At the same time we cannot forget that we have both been honoured by a degree from the oldest and most classical University of England.

It is, therefore, with every sentiment of gratitude and respect that I propose the toast which has been allotted to me,—"The Universities and Scientific Bodies which have united with the Geographers to honour Livingstone." (*Loud cheers.*)

The BISHOP of ST. DAVID'S said, that nothing but a sense of duty, the duty of submission to the authority of the Chair, could have reconciled him to the seeming presumption of his standing up in that place as a representative of the Universities, and especially in acknowledgment of a toast proposed by one who ranked among the foremost of the princes of modern science. He was conscious that he had no claim to such a character but the obligations under which he lay, in common with multitudes, to one of those learned bodies. He believed, however, he might say of them, that they were doing their duty, and that there never was a time when they had been more alive to the importance of the functions with which they were entrusted, and more earnestly bent on discharging them faithfully. He would add, that they would have missed one of their highest ends if they failed to inspire those who received their training with an intelligent interest in the expedition which was about to leave our shores. (*Cheers.*)

From that expedition, notwithstanding the cautionary hints which had been so prudently thrown out, he augured the happiest results—commercial, scientific, and social. But still, however precious and brilliant those results might be, he was sure that they could not outweigh the worth, or outshine the lustre, of Dr. Livingstone's past achievement, by which he had shown the ascendancy which might be gained over uncivilized tribes by a superior intelligence, animated and guided by the principles of Christian charity. (*Cheers.*)

If anything could heighten their admiration of that great moral triumph, it might be a comparison with an expedition which had been sent out, not many years before, in another part of the same continent. The expedition to which he alluded was

D

sent by the Pasha of Egypt to discover the sources of the Nile. Its history had been related by a Frenchman (M. Thibaut), who accompanied it. It consisted of several barks with troops on board, and was amply supplied with all the resources which the power of the Pasha could furnish. It first passed through the territories of a warlike race, which was treated with prudent respect. Afterwards it came to those of a tribe which had not been reached by any previous voyage of discovery. The natives crowded the banks to gaze on objects which they had never beheld before; the spectacle impressed them not merely with wonder, but with awe; they regarded the strangers as beings of a superior nature; yet the brutal soldiers of the Soudan were permitted, and even instigated, to fire upon these unoffending, almost worshipping, creatures, plundered and burnt their habitations, and carried away their women and children, to be sold as slaves in the market-place of Khartoum, the point from which the expedition started. Could any discovery compensate for the evil which must be caused by such a mode of exploration as this? Must not the people who had been so treated ever after associate the idea of superior civilization with injustice and oppression, robbery and wrong? And must not this contrast heighten their admiration for the traveller who had pursued so directly opposite a course, in which those who came after him could have no higher aim than to tread in his steps, and to approach, at a respectful distance, his illustrious example? (*Cheers.*)

The DUKE of WELLINGTON proposed the health of the Ladies, and especially of Mrs. Livingstone, in a few words complimentary to that lady. (*Drunk with warm cheers.*)

SIR RODERICK MURCHISON.—I now give you the last toast of the evening, and beg you to drink to the good health of the "Proposers of this Festival."

The zealous geographers who sit at the ends of the seven cross tables are the gentlemen who have mainly contributed to make this meeting as harmonious, gratifying, and successful as it has been. (*Cheers.*)

To those good men let us return our sincere acknowledgments, and above all to Dr. Norton Shaw and Mr. Arrowsmith, for the heartiness with which they have gone to work to bring about this farewell festival to Livingstone.

I now therefore call on Dr. Norton Shaw, the untiring promoter of every movement calculated to support geographical science, to answer for this our parting toast. (*Cheers.*)

DR. SHAW, in the name of his brother stewards and himself, having returned thanks for the compliment which had been paid them, the meeting separated.

LONDON: PRINTED BY W. CLOWES AND SONS, STAMFORD STREET, AND CHARING CROSS.

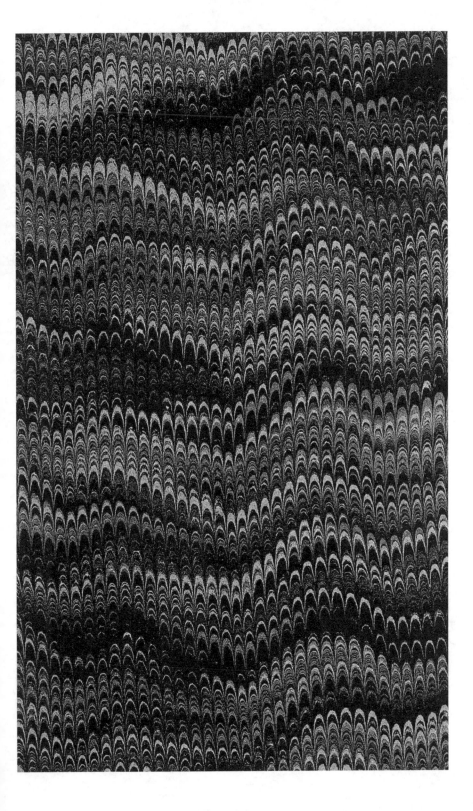

9 781014 600027